PRIMAL SCENES

Primal Scenes

Literature, Philosophy, Psychoanalysis

By NED LUKACHER

Cornell University Press ITHACA AND LONDON

Cornell University Press gratefully acknowledges a grant from the Andrew W. Mellon Foundation that aided in bringing this book to publication.

First published 1986 by Cornell University Press.

International Standard Book Number 0-8014-1886-0
Library of Congress Catalog Card Number 85-25513

Printed in the United States of America
Librarians: Library of Congress cataloging information appears on the last page of the book.

The paper in this book is acid-free and meets the guidelines for permanence and durability of the Committee on Production Guidelines for Book Longevity of the Council on Library Resources.

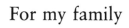
For my family

Et la nature nous dirige, tantôt par l'oubli de l'erreur, tantôt par l'obscurcissement de la vérité.

JOSEPH JOUBERT

Contents

Preface

At the end of "Mnemosyne," Friedrich Hölderlin's last major poem
before his plunge into madness in late 1806, he writes of the destruction of Mnemosyne's city and of the severing of the locks of the goddess herself:

> From her also, when
> God put off his cloak, did the evening afterwards cut
> Locks of hair.
>
> (*Der auch, als*
> *Ablegte den Mantel Gott, das abendliche nachher löste*
> *Die Loken.*)

The evening has disfigured Memory by casting over her a shadow that
will never be lifted. Somehow, she is no longer the same. In the very
last words of the hymn, Hölderlin tells us not to mourn this impair-
ment of Memory: "mourning is in error" (*fehlet die Trauer*). But was
not Hölderlin's madness the expression of his own inability to resist
mourning? Hölderlin's dilemma is the dilemma of the modern world,
and of the postmodern world as well: to recognize that "mourning is in
error" but be nevertheless condemned to mourn; to be unable to
remember the transcendental ground that would once again give
meaning to human language and experience but also unable to stop
mourning the putative loss of an originary memory and presence that
doubtless never existed.

Primal Scenes: Literature, Philosophy, Psychoanalysis is about the severing of the locks of Memory, and about the shadow of mourning and error that characterizes the efforts of modern writers from Hegel to Derrida to think and to write in the wake of Memory's disfiguration. For Hölderlin the loss of the memory of a divine origin marked a crisis that was at once personal and historical. In the period from Hegel to Derrida, we have discovered that the notion of a transcendental ground of memory and presence has been the organizing fiction motivating the history of Western literature and philosophy. *Primal Scenes* is about the recognition implicit in a wide range of modern texts that errancy is, and has always been, the only ground of memory. The locks of memory, it appears, have always already been severed. In the place of the transcendental ground of subjective memory, *Primal Scenes* substitutes a textual memory; in lieu of a human subject, a series of intertextual constructions.

In delineating the notion of textual memory and in making the primal scene the site of its construction, I rely heavily upon the work of Freud and Heidegger, for Freud's notion of the primal scene and Heidegger's of the history of Being are the most profound theoretical efforts in modern thought to account for the lack of what Heidegger calls a *Letzbegrundung,* a final transcendental ground. For Heidegger, the history of metaphysics was the span of two millennia from Plato to Hegel wherein all the fundamental notions of the West—memory, presence, the subject, the realm of Ideas, God, morality, Reason, Progress, and even the idea of civilization itself—"lose their constructive force and become nothing." In the course of his "destruction" of the nihilistic tradition of Western metaphysics, Heidegger also constructs a counterhistory, the history of Being, which is precisely a history of forgetfulness, a history of all those things that thinkers forgot to say but that nevertheless determined their discourse. "The 'doctrine' of a thinker," writes Heidegger, "is that which is left unsaid in what he says."

Likewise, in his notion of the primal scene, Freud developed a theory of the unsaid and a technique for discovering the tropes and figures that determine the shape of a patient's discourse but that the patient himself can never remember. The patient's speech "remembers," while the patient himself remains oblivious and utterly resists all the analyst's efforts to bring the "memory" to consciousness. What, then, is the status of such memory? What is its ground? Its only ground inheres in the act of reading and interpretation, in Heidegger's reading of the history of philosophy and in Freud's reading of his patients' speech. It is against the horizon of this Freudo-Heideggerian critique that I read Hegel's "memory" of Shakespeare, Marx's "memory" of Balzac, Derrida's "memory" of Heidegger, Freud's "memory" of Dickens, and, in Henry James's *The Turn of the Screw,* the governess's "memory" of the events at Bly House.

My concern in the opening chapters of *Primal Scenes* is to demonstrate, across a broad range of texts, how the notions of memory, the event, and the subject have "[lost] their constructive force and become nothing." But having ungrounded these notions, we must still ask, What are the implications of the fictionality of the subject for a theory of history? With the ground beneath the human subject undone, the second movement of *Primal Scenes* poses the question, If it is not the human subject, then what is the subject of history?

In its movement from a Lacanian-Derridean deconstruction of the subject in the first five chapters to an increasingly historicized subject in the last three chapters, *Primal Scenes* attempts to pose some fundamental questions concerning the possibility of a deconstructive theory of history. Beginning with a reading of the analyses of the Wolf-Man by both Freud and Nicolas Abraham, and continuing through readings of Hegel/Shakespeare, Marx/Balzac, and Freud/Dickens, I become increasingly concerned with historical context. The implicit suggestion of the second movement of the book is that the subject of history is not the human subject—whether defined as an individual, a class, or a species—but rather the intertextual process itself. The accumulation of historical detail around an individual subject, which is above all pronounced in my readings of Marx, Balzac, and Dickens, places the relation between subjective and textual memory in even sharper relief; for the more clearly we can see the subject's historical situation, the more fully we can grasp the significance of his alienation from the forces that determine his ability to write and interpret. Beneath subjectivity, and beneath considerations of class and economic structure, I seek to delineate a textual memory that motivates the act of writing in a still more fundamental sense. The primal scene as I conceive it defines a kind of historical "event" that cannot be thought outside the question of intertextuality. In constructing such events, we do not flee from history into formalism. Quite to the contrary, such constructions enable us to grasp something essential in historical experience.

To paraphrase Althusser, *there is no subject to the primal scene; it is the primal scene itself which is a subject insofar as it does not have a subject.* The notion of the primal scene enables us to grasp historical experience at the interface of language and world, at the interface of consciousness and the unconscious. The construction of such primal scenes thus affords us a new strategy for recovering, through intertextual memory, the motive forces of historical change insofar as they enable us to trace the emergence of new discourses, like those of Hegel, Marx, and Freud.

Primal Scenes is also an effort to provide a theoretical basis for a genuinely interdisciplinary mode of interpretation. In the chapters on Hegel/Shakespeare, Marx/Balzac, and Freud/Dickens, it is a literary text that has been forgotten or misconstrued by philosophy or psychoanalysis. Literature is always what philosophy/psychoanalysis forgets in its progress toward the Spirit of Absolute Knowledge. It is not a question of philosophy's falling away from a primordial unity where everything could be held in memory. Forgetting is the essence of philosophy. In his book on Hölderlin, Heidegger writes, "There is only the path of errancy." Since Plato's expulsion of the poets, forgetfulness and errancy with regard to literature have been essential to philosophy. In my last three chapters I construct primal scenes of this essential and constitutive forgetfulness. My effort in every instance is to read the texts of literature/philosophy/psychoanalysis as a single body of knowledge, as a continuous text. It is never a question of "applying" philosophy or psychoanalysis to a literary text but rather of fusing these discourses at the most fundamental level of their historical production.

Between the inability of Freud's patients to remember the primal scene and Heidegger's decision to write B̶e̶i̶n̶g̶ under the mark of forgetfulness, I attempt to refashion the notion of the primal scene into a figure for reading the texts of literature, philosophy, and psychoanalysis. Although it is too early in this epoch of the beginning of the ending of metaphysics to forget the differences between these traditionally distinct discourses, the present book nevertheless attempts to provide reasons for henceforth writing them under the mark of erasure: *Primal Scenes: L̶i̶t̶e̶r̶a̶t̶u̶r̶e̶, P̶h̶i̶l̶o̶s̶o̶p̶h̶y̶, P̶s̶y̶c̶h̶o̶a̶n̶a̶l̶y̶s̶i̶s̶.*

This project was aided at its inception by an Andrew W. Mellon Postdoctoral Fellowship at Duke University and more recently by a Short Research Leave from the University of Illinois Research Board.

This book would not have been completed without the assistance of several friends and colleagues. I thank above all Jonathan Arac, Marie Balmary, Léon Chertok, Jonathan Culler, John Huntington, Frank Immler, Bernhard Kendler, Hal Landers, Jay Levine, Lawrence Poston, François Roustang, Clyde Ryals, Patricia Sterling, Philip Stewart, and the two scholars who read the manuscript for Cornell University Press. I am particularly grateful to my wife, Maryline, for having given *Primal Scenes* its primal reading.

N.L.

Evanston, Illinois

PRIMAL SCENES

Introduction

The call has always taken place; it does not need to be answered because it never really happened; and that's why it's not possible to answer.

MAURICE BLANCHOT, *Celui qui ne m'accompagnait pas*

Language speaks in that, as showing, reaching into all regions of presence, it summons from them whatever is present to appear and to fade.

MARTIN HEIDEGGER, "The Way to Language"

In the case history of the Rat-Man, Freud writes that the narrative construction through which an individual creates its identity involves "a complicated process of remodelling analogous in every way to the process by which a nation constructs legends about its early history."[1] Freud's effort as an analyst is to construct the subtext behind these legends and, in so doing, to bring the patient to recollect these originary scenes. But by the time he gives such constructions the name "primal scenes" (*Urszenen*), in the Wolf-Man case history (1918), he is forced to admit that they cannot be reproduced as recollection. The ground he had hoped to stake out through scenic reconstructions of the setting and chronology of the infantile traumatic event has, as it were, fallen in, collapsed, for without the legitimacy that recollection alone can produce, what is left of the analyst's construction, and what is left of the prospect of a psychoanalytic science?

Freud's answer to these questions reveals the utopian nature of the psychoanalytic project: in the Wolf-Man case history and elsewhere he

---

1. *The Standard Edition of the Complete Psychological Works of Sigmund Freud*, ed. James Strachey et al., 24 vols. (London: Hogarth Press and the Institute of Psycho-Analysis, 1953–74), 10:206, n.1. Subsequent references to this edition are cited in the text as *S.E.* All references to Freud's German text are to *Gesammelte Werke*, 17 vols. (London: Imago, 1940–52).

posits that the patient develops during the transference a "conviction" of the appropriateness of the constructed scene in his or her life story that is in every respect equivalent to the conviction produced through recollection. Freud insists that analysis must be conducted on this ontologically undecidable ground, and that the therapeutic results thus obtained are entirely valid. But it was already difficult for Freud himself to rationalize this latter claim, and as we shall see, the inability to recollect the constructed scene created difficulties for many of his patients.

The crisis in which psychoanalysis finds itself today, especially in the United States, is doubtless related to the difficulty of constructing the sort of scene Freud had in mind. As even Kurt Eissler remarks—and he is certainly one of Freud's staunchest defenders—contemporary analysts do not construct the sort of event Freud meant them to. What they mistakenly call reconstructions are, writes Eissler, "either intellectualizations on the part of . . . the analyst as well as the patient, or else generalizations obtained by way of screen memories. It is not difficult, of course, to demonstrate to a patient that he once harbored aggressive feelings against a beloved father; but a true reconstruction goes beyond the mere unearthing of a hidden impulse and includes those specific details of time, place, environment and inner processes that conjoined to produce a trauma. Yet to take hold of these is a formidable task."[2] Despite Eissler's hopefulness in this article of 1969 that analysis would rise to the challenge, there does not appear to have been much progress in psychoanalytic therapy in the past fifteen years. Analysis is still trying to explain the relation of construction and recollection.

The risk of constructing a primal scene is enormous during an analysis. Ideally a causal network woven by both analyst and patient, the construction of the event can become an uneven exchange, which is to say that it can produce an unresolved and perhaps unresolvable transference. Whether the patient is unable to follow the analyst onto such unfamiliar terrain, or whether the analyst comes to believe too uncritically in the reality of his own constructions, or whether any of a number of alternative scenarios occur, it is clear that the construction

2. Kurt Eissler, "Irreverent Remarks about the Present and the Future of Psychoanalysis," *International Journal of Psycho-Analysis* 50 (1969): 462. This article is intimately related to all the issues that Eissler subsequently confronted in the debacle involving Jeffrey Masson and the Freud Archives. See Janet Malcolm, *In the Freud Archives* (New York: Knopf, 1984), and Jeffrey Masson, *The Assault on Truth: Freud's Suppression of Seduction Theory* (New York: Farrar, Straus, & Giroux, 1984).

of the primal scene is an interpretive exercise that is only with great
difficulty translated into effective therapy.

With regard to the ontological undecidability of the constructed
event, Freudian psychoanalysis is perhaps more closely linked to
Heidegger's philosophy than it is to much of the subsequent history of
analysis. In my critique of the evidential status of the primal scene and
the role of recollection in analysis, I follow closely Lacan's epochal
intertextual reading of Freud and Heidegger. It is Lacan who first
suggested that the difficulties with recollection in psychoanalysis could
be best understood in conjunction with the obstacles Heidegger en-
countered in his abortive project toward a fundamental ontology.

More recently, Jacques Derrida has linked Freud and Heidegger as
the two phantoms who haunt this epoch in the beginning of the end of
metaphysics. The present study argues that the drift that carries Freud
and Heidegger toward a putative overcoming of metaphysics is synonymous with the difficulty of recollection. By insisting on the
therapeutic power of the primal scene, Freud was attempting to reverse
the conventional wisdom that valued the recollected event over the
constructed event. In so doing, Freud opened the way to an interpretive
project that remains contemporary. Like Freud, Heidegger proposes a
notion of recollection that transcends the individual subject, where
Erinnerung is no longer an internalization, no longer a coming into
one's own, or an act of self-possession. Quite to the contrary, it becomes a process of dispossession. Heidegger's expression for this event
is the *Ereignis,* which Derrida characterizes as the uprooting of the
event from ontology: "Finally then, once the question of production,
doing, machination, the question of the event (which is one meaning of
Ereignis) has been uprooted [*arrachée*] from ontology, the proper-ty
[*propriété*] or propriation is named as exactly that which is proper to
nothing and no one."[3] The *Ereignis* is in effect an *Eräugniss,* "epi-

3. Jacques Derrida, *Eperons,* trans. Barbara Harlow (Venice: Corbo e Fiore, 1976),
93. William J. Richardson also speaks to this point in his article "Psychoanalysis and
the Being-Question" in *Interpreting Lacan,* ed. Joseph Smith and William Kerrigan
(New Haven, Conn.: Yale University Press, 1983), 144: "What is at stake is a conception of Being as the process of disclosure that includes an absence intrinsic to its
presencing. This absential component of the presencing process Heidegger expressed in
many ways—for example, as -*lēthē* (-velation) interior to *a-lētheia* (re-velation), as
Verbergung (concealment) interior to *Unverborgenheit* (revealment), as *Enteignis* (non-
appropriation) interior to *Ereignis* (event of appropriation)." Also see Richardson's
classic study, *Heidegger: Through Phenomenology to Thought* (The Hague: Nijhoff,
1963).

phany" or "manifestation" of the *eigen,* the "proper" or "self-same," an event that dispossesses the notion of the event of its self-sameness. What the *Ereignis* unveils behind the "proper-ty or propriation" is, in Heidegger's words, the "unconcealment of concealment because it belongs to the ground-less."[4] The *Ereignis* is an event that discloses its own concealment, manifests its hiddenness. While Freud constructs primal scenes, Heidegger constructs his "history of Being" as the subtext of the history of philosophy; the events recounted are finally as undecidable as Freud's primal scenes. The play of appropriation (*Das Ereignis er-eignet,* "Appropriation propitiates itself") detaches the notion of the event from ontology in much the same way as does the psychoanalytic transference. "Appropriation," writes Heidegger, "makes itself known to humanity at first as a transformation of the essence of truth."[5] Freud's primal scenes and Heidegger's "history of Being" are two of the most significant efforts to mark this decisive transformation.

The primal scene and the history of Being are the sites of a certain literariness in the texts of Freud and Heidegger. At the level of the subtext, literature and philosophy and psychoanalysis come into close conjunction as special kinds of fiction that cannot be placed in simple opposition to the Real. On the one hand, they are constructions that literature has long anticipated; on the other hand, they announce a new notion of "literature" for which we do not have a name. The present study is an attempt to define that notion under the rubric of literature, philosophy, psychoanalysis.

4. Martin Heidegger, "Recollection in Metaphysics," in *The End of Philosophy,* trans. Joan Stambaugh (New York: Harper & Row, 1973), 79.

5. Heidegger, "Recollection in Metaphysics," 82. For Heidegger the primal appropriation is expressed in the phrase *Es gibt Sein,* "There is Being," or literally, "It gives Being," where "It" refers to Time, which in giving Being also takes away presence in a simultaneous double gesture. The history of metaphysics has erred, according to Heidegger, in forgetting the temporality of Being and in posing the Being question without reference to time. But, he goes on to argue, this forgetting was part of the destiny of Being, for it was this concealment of the temporality of Being that preserved and sheltered the Being question throughout the history of metaphysics. It is precisely at the point of its errancy and forgetfulness that Heidegger finds the history of metaphysics most productive: "Errancy is the essential counter-essence to the primordial essence of truth." Errancy opens "the free space for that turning in which insistent ek-sistence adroitly forgets and mistakes itself constantly anew" ("On the Essence of Truth," trans. John Sallis, in *Basic Writings,* ed. David Farrell Krell [New York: Harper & Row, 1977], 136). In the history of Being, as in the psychoanalytic transference, the play of appropriation involves giving and taking, possession and dispossession, truth and error, in an inseparable and incontrovertible union.

Speaking of the "ontological difficulty" of modern literary and philosophical theory, George Steiner remarks that the "operative metaphor" may well be the "unperceived event" that the physicist deduces from the traces in the cloud chamber.[6] These narrative models of thought are relevant to the human and social sciences as well as to the natural sciences. They are attempts to define that for which there are no other methods of establishing evidence. These "metaleptic" narratives operate a double logic in which every cause is always already an effect, every disclosure also a concealment, and every literal truth a figural lie. In making such constructions we neither overcome metaphysics nor forget the question of the origin. Rather we seek to liberate that question from the metaphysical presuppositions that have constrained it.

While the future of psychoanalysis as a therapy is likely to remain in question for some time to come, its theoretical and textual relation to literary and philosophical history should not be regarded as either inconsequential or obvious. The historical destiny of analysis may be something quite different from what analysts imagine; its interpretive rather than its therapeutic ends may finally predominate, for psychoanalysis enables us to illuminate the conjunction between literature and philosophy, between *Denken* and *Dichter*. Psychoanalysis is, I believe, essential to the effort to respond to Heidegger's call for "less philosophy, but more attentiveness in thinking; less literature, but more cultivation of the letter."[7] I use psychoanalysis to delineate a language of dispossession that sustains the language of both literature and philosophy but remains more fundamental than either of them.

Reflecting on Heidegger's statement that "language itself is poetry in the essential sense," Jacques Ehrmann wrote that "poetical language is not another language but rather language itself. More precisely, it is language whose nature (and function) of doubling, of turning back upon itself, is openly exposed."[8] Through the conjunction of psychoanalysis, philosophy, and literature, this dispossessive function of lan-

6. George Steiner, *On Difficulty* (New York: Oxford University Press, 1978), 46.

7. Heidegger, "Letter on Humanism," trans. David Farrell Krell, in *Basic Writings*, 242.

8. Heidegger, "The Origin of the Work of Art," trans. Albert Hofstadter, in *Philosophies of Art and Beauty*, ed. Albert Hofstadter and Richard Kuhns (Chicago: University of Chicago Press, 1976), 696; and Jacques Ehrmann, "La Mort de la littérature," in *Textes* (Paris: L'Herne, 1971), n.p. (All translations not otherwise identified are my own.)

guage, this *retournement,* this *dédoublement,* comes into relief—which
is not to say, however, that the poetic essence of language is thereby
revealed as being other than a fundamental and insurmountable concealment. The opening thus exposed in language is a concealment that
normally remains concealed. The point where language folds back
upon itself reveals most directly the way language conceals its relation
to the Real.

It is with regard to this conjunction of literature/philosophy/psycho-
analysis and the ensuing revelation/concealment that I propose the
notion of the primal scene as a trope for reading and understanding.
For this purpose I do not restrict "primal scene" to the conventional
psychoanalytic understanding of the term: the child's witnessing of a
sexual act that subsequently plays a traumatic role in his or her psycho-
sexual life. In my use of the term it becomes an intertextual event that
displaces the notion of the event from the ground of ontology. It calls
the event's relation to the Real into question in an entirely new way.
Rather than signifying the child's observation of sexual intercourse, the
primal scene comes to signify an ontologically undecidable intertextual
event that is situated in the differential space between historical memory and imaginative construction, between archival verification and interpretive free play. Bringing Freud's notion of the primal scene into
conjunction with Heidegger's "history of Being," I use the expression
"primal scene" to describe the interpretive impasse that arises when a
reader has good reason to believe that the meaning of one text is
historically dependent on the meaning of another text or on a previously unnoticed set of criteria, even though there is no conclusive
evidential or archival means of establishing the case beyond a reasonable doubt. The primal scene is thus the figure of an always divided
interpretive strategy that points toward the Real in the very act of
establishing its inaccessibilty; it becomes the name for the dispossessive
function of language that constitutes the undisclosed essence of
language.

I propose this definition of the primal scene as a step toward solving
the crisis of interpretation that emerges when the question of the origin
becomes at once unavoidable and unanswerable, when the origin must
be remembered but memory fails utterly, when all the evidence points
toward an origin that nevertheless remains unverifiable. The primal
scene is the figure of an interpretive dilemma; it is a constellation of
forgotten intertextual events offered in lieu of a demonstrable, unques-

tionable origin. Thus conceived, the primal scene is a strategic answer to the dilemma of a critical discourse that on the one hand maintains the impossibility of moving beyond interpretation to a discourse of truth but on the other hand has not forgotten that the burden of the truth continues to make itself felt. The primal scene is an effort to answer the unanswerable call of the Real, a call that emerges from the undisclosed essence of language itself.

Freud realized that in *From the History of an Infantile Neurosis* (*Aus der Geschichte einer Infantilen Neurose;* 1918) he had attempted something altogether new, for in this case history of the Wolf-Man he had pursued the implications of his technique of dream interpretation further than before. From a static, motionless, and almost barren dream he had constructed a complex narrative event that he called the "primal scene" (*Urszene*). Although the term appears for the first time in Freud's published work in this case history, it represents the culmination of a project in which he had been engaged since the 1890s. He had constructed early childhood scenes in the course of his analyses with Dora, the Rat-Man, and other patients. Though Freud had difficulty admitting it, the highly problematical nature of these constructed scenes often caused patients to terminate the analysis. That the Wolf-Man persevered helps to explain why in this case Freud was able to articulate the childhood scene in such elaborate detail. Toward the end of the Wolf-Man case history, Freud describes his achievement with characteristic frankness:

> The description of such early phases and of such deep strata of mental life has been a task which has never before been attacked; and it is better to perform that task badly than to take flight before it—a proceeding which would moreover (or so we are told) involve the coward in risks of a certain kind. I prefer, therefore, to put a bold face on it and show that I have not allowed myself to be held back by a sense of my own inferiority. [*S.E.,* 17:104]

From the patient's account of a terrifying dream on the eve of his fourth birthday, Freud deduces a scene which, he argues, occurred when the patient was approximately one and a half years old. Freud had never before pursued the origins of a patient's illness to this early stage; never had dream interpretation led him so far back into the patient's prehistory. At the same time, however, the very remoteness of the scene demands that Freud take a tentative position with respect both to the reality of his construction and the causal instrumentality he attributes to it. The further back into time the origin recedes, the more problematical it becomes. Instead of proclaiming a new clarity, Freud becomes more suspicious of "forming a clear picture of the origin and development of the patient's illness" (S.E., 17:104). In the very act of holding out the promise of an unprecedented revelation, Freud checks himself and reminds his readers that what he has revealed is in fact a more primordial concealment than he has ever imagined before. "We must be content," he writes, "with having clearly recognized the obscurity" (S.E., 17:105).

Psychoanalysis shares with modern philosophy and modern literary theory and criticism not a simple forgetfulness of the question of the origin but a commitment to the task of remembering the primordial forgetfulness that conceals the origin. On the eve of his fourth birthday, the Wolf-Man dreamed that through an opened window he saw a barren tree in winter in which six or seven white wolves were sitting and staring intently at him, obviously about to leap in upon him and devour him. He awoke screaming and remembered throughout his life the terror and the profound impression of reality that the dream created. The first question Freud poses is that of the relation of the dream to reality. The patient presents Freud with both a verbal text and a line drawing of wolves sitting in a tree. The dream was recounted early in the course of a four-year analysis, the remainder of which was largely devoted to determining the relation of the dream to reality. Freud will pose this question in many different ways without reaching a definitive solution. Does the dream point to the historicity of the primal scene, or is it the result of a "primal phantasy"? The dream points toward the origin, but its interpretation cannot reveal the origin.

The Wolf-Man's grandfather had told him a story about a tailor and a tailless wolf, and as a child he also knew other fairy tales involving wolves. While these various sources went into its making, the dream took on a reality for the patient far in excess of that created by the fairy tales. "The dream," writes Freud, "seemed to point to an occurrence the reality of which was very strongly emphasized as being in marked contrast to the unreality [Irrealität] of the fairy tales" (S.E., 17:33). The task of interpretation is that of determining the nature of this "occurrence" (Begebenheit). But this "occurrence" cannot be directly placed in relation to reality. It can only be placed "in contradiction" (*im Gegensatz*) to "unreality." Freud's language is carefully tentative. He wants to know what kind of event the dream "seemed to point to." "The exceptional importance of this case in Freud's work," writes Lacan, "is to show that it is in relation to the real that the level of phantasy functions. The real supports the phantasy, the phantasy protects the real."9 Lacan makes Freud's point very clear. *From the History of an Infantile Neurosis* shows that phantasy "is in relation to the real," but it does not—and it is Freud's point that psychoanalysis cannot—reveal what that relation is. Freud brings his patient, and his readers, to the threshold of an insurmountable concealment.

Freud makes it clear from the outset that the construction of the primal scene is a "supposition": "If it was to be assumed [*anzunehmen*] that behind the content of the dream there lay some such unknown scene—one, that is, which had already been forgotten at the time of the dream—then it must have taken place very early" (*S.E.*, 17:33). The task of analysis is that of remembering that the relation of the object of interpretation to the real has been forgotten. The primal scene is always a scene that is "unknown" (*unbekannte*) and "forgotten" (*vergessene*).

The ontological undecidability that Freud attains in *From the History of an Infantile Neurosis* places his theoretical effort there in close conjunction with the thought of Friedrich Nietzsche, Martin Heidegger, Jacques Lacan, and Jacques Derrida. For in constructing the primal scene, Freud constitutes an "event" that remains outside the grasp of metaphysics. Metaphysics is the science of presence. The Freudian *Begebenheit*, however, can be grasped in the mode of neither presence nor absence. At the same time, the primal scene is the preexistent trace underlying the possibility of the distinction between presence and absence, and between subject and object. It is the enabling mechanism that explains and describes, rather than determining or causing, the structure of the Wolf-Man's experience. The primal scene explains the wolf dream but has not caused it and is not present in it.

In the most dazzling interpretive tour de force of his career, Freud constructs from the dream of the wolves sitting in a tree the primal scene of coitus *a tergo* which he claims the one-and-a-half-year-old Wolf-Man witnessed one summer afternoon at around the hour of five.

9. Jacques Lacan, *The Four Fundamental Concepts of Psycho-Analysis*, trans. Alan Sheridan (New York: Norton, 1981), 41.

Each detail of the dream is translated and elaborated into another narrative frame and into another temporal sequence. The dream narrative points to another narrative. Freud and his patient are certain of one thing, that something happened prior to the wolf dream that explains its intensity and its lasting memory. They cannot agree, however, on precisely what that event was or how it affected the dream. Unlike the philosopher or the literary critic, for whom the ontology of the text's meaning and origin has no immediately perceptible affective content, the psychoanalyst must contend with a patient whose experience of the transference is filled with affect. The text can never remember; it always needs a reader to do the remembering. The analyst, on the other hand, can encounter serious resistance during the transference from patients who either cannot remember or do not otherwise become convinced of the appropriateness of the analyst's constructions. While the analyst may feel free to elude the grasp of metaphysics and to forgo the reality testing that memory affords, the patient is often very reluctant to walk on the Nietzschean tightrope without the security of the metaphysical net of recollection. The Wolf-Man was such a patient, one who was not persuaded by Freud's clear recognition of an intractable obscurity. Unlike his analyst, this patient lingered under the spell of the metaphysics of presence.

In his famous essay "The Function and Field of Speech and Language in Psychoanalysis," Jacques Lacan warns analysts of the dangers of becoming impatient when the analysand seems to be taking an inordinately long time to understand the "truth" of his or her situation. In situating this "truth" outside the field of subjective recollection, Lacan explains, Freud has radically altered the very notion of truth, and in a way that has profound resemblances to Heidegger's project. Lacan takes Freud's conduct during the Wolf-Man analysis as a case in point of what happens when the analyst does not give the patient enough time and becomes too authoritative: "If we then give him the sanction of our authority, we are setting the analysis off on an aberrant path whose results will be impossible to correct. This is precisely what happened in the celebrated case of the Wolf-Man." Lacan's accusation that Freud left the Wolf-Man "in the alienation of his truth" is surely borne out by the patient's subsequent history (which I examine in detail in Chapter 4). Lacan's remarks are so decisive for understanding the terms of my project that it is important to familiarize ourselves at the outset with what he has to say on the subject of the Wolf-Man.

> In the first place, in spite of the whole cluster of proofs demonstrating the historicity of the primal scene, in spite of the conviction that he shows concerning it—remaining imperturbable to the doubts that Freud methodically cast on it in order to test him—the Wolf Man never managed in spite of it all to integrate his recollection of the primal scene into his history.
>
> Secondly, the same patient later demonstrated his alienation in the most categorical way, in a paranoid form.
>
> It is true that here there is at work another factor through which reality intervenes in the analysis—namely, the gift of money whose symbolic value I shall save to treat of elsewhere, but whose import is indicated in what I have already said concerning the link between speech and the constituting gift of primitive exchange. In this case the gift of money is reversed by an initiative of Freud's in which, as much as in his insistence on coming back to the case, we can recognize the unresolved subjectification within him of the problems that this case leaves in suspense. And nobody doubts that this was a factor in the subsequent onset of the psychosis, however, without really being able to say why.[10]

Lacan is suggesting that for both Freud and his patient this case remained in suspense: Freud keeps returning to it in his clinical and theoretical work (Lacan mentions in particular Freud's 1937 essay *Analysis Finite and Infinite*); the Wolf-Man returns to it through symptomatic behavior culminating in the psychotic episode that forced him to return to analysis with Freud's student, Ruth Mack Brunswick. But, Lacan, in speaking as though the case represents an exceptional dilemma, implies that this need not necessarily be the fate of analysis—whereas in fact (though there are certainly exceptional features, like the money Freud gave this patient after World War I), at the most fundamental level this case is a paradigm of the fate of analysis. No other case history and none of the theoretical papers delineate so clearly the problems of generating a dialogic situation that places the "truth" neither in the analyst's authority nor in the patient's subjective recollection. Freud and his patient both find themselves in an impossi-

---

10. Jacques Lacan, *Ecrits: A Selection*, trans. Alan Sheridan (London: Tavistock, 1977), 96–97.

ble dilemma, for they realize at once the necessity and difficulty of generating a notion of recollection that is neither properly subjective nor objective.

Lacan argues that by intervening in the patient's discourse at just the right moment, the analyst can deliver the letter by showing that repetition in the transference presents the repressed material in reverse form. Lacan's discursive *aletheia* lies beyond memory. Unlike Freud in the Wolf-Man case, who erred by making the patient feel that his truth lay with the analyst, Lacan proposes that the analyst perform a "dialectical punctuation" of the patient's speech. It would be a mistake, however, to believe, as the Lacanians appear to, that the problem of conviction has been overcome by Lacan's theoretical displacement of the notion of "true speech" from consciousness to discourse; Lacan simply continued the shift begun by Freud in *Beyond the Pleasure Principle*. But, as we shall see, this putative step beyond conviction is, as Derrida remarks, a *pas au-delà,* a step that leads nowhere. Psychoanalysis, it appears, is repeatedly compelled to proclaim its capacity to go beyond interpretation and beyond conviction. The virtue of Freud is that even though he makes such claims, the honesty with which he presents his case histories invariably undermines the very ground on which these claims rest. With Dora, the Rat-Man, and the Wolf-Man, it is not so much his constructions that are at fault as it is his mode of intervention and the alienation which that mode creates in his patients. It is Freud's timing rather than his technique of construction that brings the analysis to grief. The problem with Lacan, who is so alert to all these problems, is the almost complete absence of clinical material. Lacan's formalism and his avoidance of the potential dangers of narrative case histories diminish the value of his contribution to psychoanalysis. The extensive clinical material in the Lacanian journal *Ornicar?* indicates that his disciples are keenly aware of this problem. While Lacan theorizes brilliantly about the "time for understanding," he did not dare, as Freud did, to elaborate openly on the practical implications of his formal determinations.

Because the transference is a dialectical process, the patient's resistance tends to force the analyst into an authoritarian metaphysical position. Freud succumbs to this fate not only in the Wolf-Man analysis, but, to one degree or another, in each of his well-known case histories. As Lacan suggests, it is all a question of timing or rhythm, of knowing or guessing when the patient is willing to acknowledge that even though the primal or childhood scene cannot be reproduced as recollection, it nevertheless has a "truth" of its own. But if the patient is unwilling to depart from the notion of recollection as self-presence, and if the analyst either mistimes the construction or proposes it with an inappropriate degree of certainty, the analysis is bound to run into difficulties. This problem is an analytic one in the largest sense of the term, for it applies to the "time of understanding" that one allows for any interpretation whatsoever. Psychoanalysis thus presents in very vivid terms the dilemma into which the modern critic is invariably coerced. The task of accounting for a textual event demands that the critic venture, whether intentionally or not, into a zone between the conventional subject-object opposition, a zone where "truth" has become a differential notion that is constituted somewhere between pure construction and historicity.

In *From the History of an Infantile Neurosis,* Freud tackles this problem directly: "So far as my experience hitherto goes, these scenes from infancy are not reproduced during the treatment as recollections, they are the products of construction. Many people will admit that this single admission decides the whole dispute" (*S.E.,* 17:51). Among these "many people" are most of Freud's former patients. The difficulty of soliciting the patient's, or the reader's, "conviction" (*Überzeugung*) outside the confines of recollection constitutes the most profound crisis of modern interpretation.

The crisis Freud confronts as a theorist and as a clinician is one that Nietzsche describes under the rubric of the "calculability of the event."[11] The task of the postmetaphysical analyst is to teach the interlocutor to respond to the incalculability of the event with what Nietzsche calls "the immense, unbounded Yes" (*das ungeheuere, unbegrenzte Ja-sagen*). No less than Freud's, Nietzsche's objective is to make his interlocutor free to live and enjoy, which is Freud's definition of the cure. Like Nietzsche, Freud sees the incalculability of the event as the means, the only means, of achieving that objective. "Joy" in German is of course *Freude.* Whether Freud read Nietzsche is, by the terms of their own logic, immaterial; the question of Freud's reading of Nietzsche is itself an incalculable event. Suffice it to say that Freud knew Nietzsche well enough to know that he had to keep him at a safe

---

11. Friedrich Nietzsche, *The Will to Power,* trans. Walter Kaufmann and R. J. Hollingdale (New York: Random House, 1967), 296.

distance. Derrida cites passages from Nietzsche on the relation of speculation and rhythm that seem to anticipate Freud's notion of the "halt-
ing," "limping" rhythm of psychoanalytic speculation in *Beyond the
Pleasure Principle*.[12] The philosopher and the analyst are destined to
posit their constructions in a tentative mode, never knowing how or
when those constructions will be received. What Lacan calls the "time
for understanding" may indeed extend well into the future. The destination of the "letter" is something that can never be known in advance. The analyst can never know where or when the proposed construction will arrive or, for that matter, whether it will arrive at all.

The haunting possibility that the construction or letter will never
arrive at its destination is a question that Derrida poses to Lacan in
"The Purveyor of Truth."[13] In particular, Derrida questions Lacan's
contention in his famous seminar on "The Purloined Letter" that the
letter always arrives at its destination. I referred above to Lacan's
implication that there is a correct "time for understanding" and that
Freud simply miscalculated it. Derrida is correct, it seems to me, to
question Lacan's rather idealistic belief that forgetfulness can be overcome and that conviction can finally be solicited, regardless of how
much time intervenes between the sending of the letter and its arrival.
It also seems to me, however, that more important than Derrida's
disagreement with Lacan's position is the fact that they are both interested in how the "truth" of the construction relates to the conviction it produces through time. The important point is that only by
virtue of temporal difference does the letter assume its significance,
even if it turns out to be a negative significance. Whether it is a question of the patient's gradual conviction of the appropriateness of the
analyst's construction over the course of an analysis of several months
or several years, or a question of the reception of the ideas of Nietzsche

---

12. Jacques Derrida, *La Carte postale: De Socrate à Freud et au-delà* (Paris: Aubier-
Flammarion, 1980), esp. 433–37. Behind Nietzsche's ideas on the rhythm of speculation may be Hölderlin's ideas of the "caesura," "the alternation of tones" (*der Wechsel
der Töne*), and "the antirhythmic interruption" (*antirhythmische Unterbrechung*)
which for Hölderlin constitutes the "incalculable" element inherent in "rhythm in the
highest sense."

13. Derrida, "Le Facteur de la vérité," in *La Carte postale*, 439–524. See the important discussions of the Lacan-Derrida controversy by Barbara Johnson, "The Frame of
Reference: Poe, Lacan, Derrida," in *The Critical Difference: Essays in the Contemporary Rhetoric of Reading* (Baltimore, Md.: Johns Hopkins University Press, 1980),
110–46; and by Marian Hobson, "Deconstruction, Empiricism, and the Postal Services," *French Studies* 36 (July 1982): 290–314.

or Freud over the course of the twentieth century, what matters is that the sending and the destiny of the letter are always mediated by time, that it is always a relation between at least two discrete temporal frames of reference.

In *The Four Fundamental Concepts of Psycho-Analysis,* Lacan adduces Nietzsche in describing the necessary interval between the sending of the letter and its arrival. Lacan is referring to his own "recollection" of the radicality of the Freudian theory of the unconscious which had been "forgotten" for so long: "There is a danger in public discourse, precisely in so far as it is addressed to those nearest—Nietzsche knew this, a certain type of discourse can be addressed only to those furthest away."[14] Without wanting to reduce Derrida's relation to Lacan on the question of the arrival of the letter to one of simple reflexivity, I believe it is important to note that Lacan too is alert to the danger that the letter encounters in transit. The "danger in public discourse" is, I would agree with Derrida, the danger of any discourse whatsoever. Nietzsche's discourse concerning the "calculability of the event" and Freud's discourse concerning the construction of the primal scene are, for both Lacan and Derrida, exemplary instances of this "certain type of discourse." They are exemplary because their content is precisely at one with their historical destiny: Nietzsche's discourse on the event and Freud's on the primal scene are themselves the kind of event or scene which they describe. They are discourses that have created their own destinations. At the same time, however, they cannot be assimilated by a conventional linear view of causality. The primal scene, argues Freud in the last chapter of the Wolf-Man case history, cannot be assimilated by the scientific notion of causality. He writes that while it is the business of psychoanalysis "to explain the striking symptoms by revealing their genesis, it is not its business to explain but merely to describe the psychical mechanisms and instinctual processes to which one is led by that means" (*S.E.,* 17:105). This distinction between "explanation" (*erklären*) and "description" (*beschreiben*) seems to me to indicate Freud's effort to mediate or mollify the explanatory casual power of the primal scene. The primal scene is that without which the symptoms could not have developed; for all that, it does not explain the causality of the symptoms. Likewise, while the letter creates its destination, it cannot be said directly to cause or determine

14. Lacan, *The Four Fundamental Concepts of Psycho-Analysis,* 23.

it. The discourses of the incalculable event and the primal scene cannot be considered apart from the notion of causality; at the same time, they cannot fully be assimilated by it.

"The supposed instinct for causality," Nietzsche wrote in his notebooks during the 1880s, "is only fear of the unfamiliar, and the attempt to discover something familiar in it—a search, not for causes, but for the familiar."[15] For Nietzsche, the history of metaphysics was an apotropaic attempt to ward off the *Unheimliche*. But we cannot stop thinking about causes; the metaphysical notions of causality and an intending subject will continue to cast their shadows over the discourse of the postmetaphysical analyst. Though Nietzsche entertained the idea of a "positive nihilism"—that is, a complete forgetfulness of the question of the origin and the subject—he found himself, after writing *Thus Spoke Zarathustra,* in the despair of a "negative nihilism" from which he never emerged. Nietzsche's fate is exemplary because of the boldness of his effort to forget the real. Like Nietzsche, Freud tries to think differently about causality. In another notebook entry from the 1880s, Nietzsche outlines two alternative notions of causality that will better help us to situate the relation of the primal scene to causal explanation:

> The explanation of an event can be sought firstly: through mental images of the events that precede it (aims); secondly, through mental images that succeed it (the mathematical-physical explanation).
>
> One should not confuse the two. Thus: the physical explanation, which is a symbolization of the world by means of sensation and thought, can in itself never account for the origin of sensation and thought; rather physics must construe the world of feeling consistently as lacking feeling and aim—right up to the highest human being. And teleology is only a history of purposes and never physical.[16]

Against Nietzsche's interdiction, the primal scene is a carefully staged confusion of these two notions of causality. Freud situates it in the differential space between teleology and the physical explanation. If we regard the wolf dream as the event Freud seeks to describe / explain, it is clear that the primal scene is the set of images that precede the event. At the same time, however, the primal scene is not a teleological notion. The primal scene is a deductive, circumstantial construction that is put

15. Nietzsche, *The Will to Power,* 297.
16. Nietzsche, *The Will to Power* 303–4.

together in the gaps between the mental images or symptoms that succeed the dream and those that precede it. Nietzsche's alternatives cannot in themselves account for the complexity of Freud's notion. Freud relates one set of images to the other, but without either claiming to have accounted "for the origin of sensation and thought" or using those images to construe a world of "feeling and aim." Freud constructs a set of images that precede the event, but he resists giving them a teleological drift.

What enables Freud to circumvent Nietzsche's alternatives is the concept of "deferred action" (*Nachträglichkeit*), which is prominent throughout Freud's work and particularly in *From the History of an Infantile Neurosis*. At its most elementary level, deferred action is a mode of temporal spacing through which the randomness of a later event triggers the memory of an earlier event or image, which might never have come to consciousness had the later event never occurred. The most obvious and immediate effect of deferred action is to undermine and divide the notion of linear causality that works in one temporal direction. Deferred action demands that one recognize that while the earlier event is still to some extent the cause of the later event, the earlier event is nevertheless also the effect of the later event. One is forced to admit a double or "metaleptic" logic in which causes are both the causes of effects and the effects of effects.[17] Rather than offering a simple division between causes and effects, Freud confronts us with causes that are also effects and effects that are also causes. The random seriality of events that precede and follow the wolf dream leads Freud to posit a double logic of causality that repeatedly turns back upon itself.

The patient's wolf phobia and a host of other childhood symptoms that the wolf dream unleashed make the dream the decisive turning point in the etiology of the neurosis. At no point in the argument, however, does Freud posit a teleological or purposive structure. It is in this sense that the primal scene remains a descriptive category. Only through reference to images that precede the event can the "lasting memory" of the dream be explained, but this explanation of mechanisms in no way implies a causal structure. If the Wolf-Man had not experienced a sexual seduction by his sister at the age of three, if he had not been told the tale of the tailless wolf by his grandfather, and so on

17. See Gérard Genette, *Figures III* (Paris: Seuil, 1972), 243–46.

and so forth, the primal scene would never have been activated. "We shall further bear in mind," writes Freud, "that the activation of this scene (I purposely avoid the word 'recollection') had the same effect as though it were a recent experience. The effects of the scene were deferred, but meanwhile it had lost none of its freshness in the interval between the ages of one and a half and four years" (*S.E.*, 17:44). What the primal scene establishes is that at the origin one discovers not a single event that transpires in one temporal sequence but a constellation of events that transpire in several discrete temporal sequences. Everything depends upon the random seriality of the events and upon the specificity of the narrative details that constitute them. For example, in the grandfather's fairy tale, if the tailor had not hidden in a tree and if the wolves had not decided to build a pyramid that would enable some of them to climb into the tree and eat the tailor, the scene of coitus *a tergo* where the one-and-a-half-year-old Wolf-Man sees his father climb upon the back of his mother might never have been called back into consciousness in the form of the dream. The primal scene establishes the originary role of nonoriginary temporal difference. Narrative detail and sequence take on their significance through time. We should not overlook the fact that the primal scene is itself a kind of fairy tale in which the intending subject finds himself caught up in a fateful constellation. If the tailor had not cut off the tail of one of the wolves, they would never have chased him into the tree in the first place. But without the tailor's cutting off of the wolf's tail, the story could not unfold. So too for Freud the primal scene is the event that enables the narrative to unfold.

Freud seems to me to acknowledge the *Unheimliche* with a more resounding "Yes" than even Nietzsche himself. Freud's relentless problematization of the question of the origin is perhaps a more realistic and pragmatic response than Nietzsche's putative forgetting or overcoming. Instead of Nietzsche's "active forgetfulness" of the origin, Freud develops a strategy for speculating on the incalculability of the event. Like Nietzsche, Freud acknowledges the insurmountable unfamiliarity that conceals the origin; unlike Nietzsche, he does not stop there. He wants to go on to construct a narrative about what precedes the event. He wants to overcome metaphysics not by forgetting the origin simply because metaphysics had filled that notion with presence, but by moving back before the origin, back to the point prior to the presencing of the origin. Freud wants to tell a story about what is prior to presence and what has always already been forgotten. Instead of simply celebrating the concealment that forgetfulness brings, he wants to construct a story about what forgetfulness conceals. He does not, however, go so far as to believe that the story has the power to over-come this fundamental forgetfulness. He is always careful to dis-tinguish the therapeutic effect of such constructions from subjective recollection. Freud recognizes that the work of analysis is the transla-tion of one narrative event, like the wolf dream, into another narrative event, like the primal scene. It would be a mistake, however, to equate that work of narrative transposition and transference with the revela-tion of the origin.

In an important article entitled "Fictions of the Wolf-Man: Freud and Narrative Understanding," Peter Brooks discusses Freud's con-struction of the primal scene in terms of narrative theory.[18] Using the now widely known terms from Russian narratological theory, Brooks distinguishes the *fabula* or "story" that is the event of the patient's neurosis from the *sjuzet* or "plot" that is Freud's reworking of it: "The relation between fabula and sjuzet, between event and its significant reworking, is one of suspicion and conjecture, a structure of indeter-minacy which can offer only a framework of narrative possibilities rather than a clearly specifiable plot."[19] Brooks applies the distinction in order to demonstrate how Freud undermines it. Freud, we recall, reminds his readers that it is impossible to provide "a clear picture of the origin and development of the patient's illness." Brooks translates that recognition into the terms of narrative theory. The terms "story" and "plot," or "story" and "discourse," or "*histoire*" and "*récit*," or "*fabula*" and "*sjuzet*" provide guidelines for discussing the difference between two temporal frames of reference. It is a difference, however, that is highly unstable. As we have seen, the wolf dream and the primal scene are in a differential and unstable relation to each other. The wolf dream is the *fabula* or event that the Wolf-Man narrates to Freud; the primal scene is the *sjuzet* or narrative reconstruction that Freud nar-rates to the Wolf-Man. But these terms can be turned around just as

18. Peter Brooks, "Fictions of the Wolf Man: Freud and Narrative Understanding," in *Reading for the Plot: Design and Invention in Narrative* (New York: Knopf, 1984): 264–85. See also Jonathan Culler, "Story and Discourse in the Analysis of Narrative," in *The Pursuit of Signs: Semiotics, Literature, Deconstruction* (Ithaca, N.Y.: Cornell University Press, 1981), 169–87.

19. Brooks, "Fictions of the Wolf Man," 275.

easily as the terms "cause" and "effect": the primal scene is also the *fabula* or event that is reworked in the *sjuzet* or dream. In constituting the primal scene, Freud transforms the very status of the *fabula* or dream from which he had begun. Like cause and effect, *fabula* and *sjuzet* are terms that are at once distinct and indistinguishable. There is a temporal difference between the two narratives, but that difference cannot be used to order the causal relation between them because they are constantly folding back into one another, becoming alternately first and second, second and first, cause and effect, effect and cause.

This book is an effort to place Freud's notion of the primal scene within the context of the critique of the beginning of the end of Western metaphysics, a critique begun by Nietzsche and continued by Heidegger and Derrida. The primal scene is constituted in an unlocatable, undecidable zone of temporal difference, a zone of *différance* which differs from itself, a difference which lacks identity or self-sameness. The primal scene is Freud's category for the originary function of nonoriginary temporal difference. It is a (non-) event whose indeterminant temporality precipitates the temporal ordering of subsequent events.

The kind of reading I am proposing cannot be considered apart from Lacan's effort to link Freud's thought to Heidegger's. In *Lacan and Language: A Reader's Guide to "Ecrits,"* John Muller and William Richardson question the plausibility of this conjunction when they remark that while Freud turns to Empedocles in order to elucidate the "death instinct," Lacan turns to Heidegger, "whose celebrated analysis (1927) of human *Dasein* (i.e., existence, or ek-sistence, in a sense of radical openness to Being) as Being-unto-death follows from a philosophical conception of the human being that is profoundly different from Freud's."[20] Lacan's originality, they maintain, consists in establishing a relation between the operation of the "repetition compulsion" during the transference and the Heideggerian notion of the historicity of the subject and the temporal horizon of death. They question in particular the legitimacy of what they call Lacan's "non-Freudian formula" near the end of "The Function and Field of Speech and Language in Psychoanalysis" linking "the historicizing temporality of the experience

20. John P. Muller and William J. Richardson, *Lacan and Language: A Reader's Guide to "Ecrits"* (New York: International Universities Press, 1982), 91.

of transference" to Heidegger's notion of Being-for-death as "the limit of the historical function of the subject."[21] The "primordial authentic temporality" of Heidegger's Being-for-death establishes the subject's historical finitude. It seems to me, however, that while it was surely Lacan's great achievement to have joined Freud to Heidegger, nothing could be more Freudian than the historicization of the subject through the experience of the limits of recollection during the transference. Muller and Richardson might feel less skeptical about the prospects of Lacan's Freudo-Heideggerian alliance if they considered more closely the history of Freud's experience of his patients' encounters with the "death instinct" at precisely those junctures where the "repetition compulsion" prevents the patient from overcoming the limits of subjective recollection. We must not confuse the "death drive" with the limits of memory but rather see it as what lies beyond the limits of the "reality principle." We should recall that one of Lacan's first papers is entitled "Beyond the 'Reality Principle'" (1936); there he argues that Freud "poses a 'reality principle' whose criticism, according to Freud, constitutes the objective of our research." It is precisely in the patient's nonrecognition, in the compulsive resistance to moving beyond the notion of a subject for whom "reality" inheres only in the self-presence of perception and recollection, that Lacan situates the "death drive." The "death instinct" inheres not in what the patient remembers but in what there is in his or her past that "reveals itself reversed in repetition."[22]

It is just such an instance of the "repetition compulsion" and the "death drive" that Freud experienced during the Wolf-Man analysis. The work of analysis is the joint work of analyst and patient in criticizing the historicity of the analyst's constructions. It is invariably in the course of this process, at the limits of recollection, that instead of "conviction" the analysis produces repetition. The construction of the primal scene and the articulation of temporal difference precipitated a transference neurosis in the Wolf-Man that Freud was unable to cure, that Freud in fact unwittingly exacerbated. No less than Heidegger, Freud brings *Dasein* to its primordial temporal horizon. And no less than Heidegger's, Freud's notion and experience of the transference take him to the point where he is concerned no longer with the an-

21. Lacan, *Ecrits: A Selection*, 103.
22. Jacques Lacan, *Ecrits* (Paris: Seuil, 1966), 92.

thropological, empirical self, no longer with the phenomenological self, but with the structures underlying the possibility of the subject. Psychoanalysis cannot be restricted to an ontical interpretation. No less than Heidegger's analytic of *Dasein,* psychoanalysis is an interrogation of the ontological self.

Lacan's Freudo-Heideggerian alliance has of course not benefited from either Freud's reluctance to link psychoanalysis to philosophy or Heidegger's pregnant silence with respect to psychoanalysis. Toward the end of *From the History of an Infantile Neurosis,* Freud ruefully reminds his readers of the limited implications to be drawn from this case history and warns against "replacing what is left undone by speculation—the latter being put under the patronage of some school or other of philosophy" (*S.E.,* 17:105–6). We can now say of the Wolf-Man case history what Derrida says of *Beyond the Pleasure Principle:* that what Freud has done throughout the analysis is to speculate, that his constructions have always been speculative. Freud's dismissal of philosophy seems as transparent and as ultimately insignificant and unreliable as Heidegger's implicit dismissal of psychoanalysis in the "Letter on Humanism" (1947), where he distinguishes his project from the metaphysical notion of the subject based on the subject's *animalitatas,* or instinctual life. Against these "metaphysical projections," Heidegger proposes that we think of the *humanitas* of the subject in the more specific terms of man's openness to Being: that is, in terms of language. In distinguishing himself from the Sartrean existential project, Heidegger attempts to differentiate *existentia,* or the "lived experience" of the human being in its *animalitatas,* from "ek-sistence," which is "the determination of what man is in the destiny of truth."[23] This "determination" takes place through the "lighting-concealing" which is language. We have seen in *From the History of an Infantile Neurosis* that what Lacan calls "the historicizing temporality of the transference" is precisely the "lighting-concealing" of language, the liminal experience of subjectivity that is at the very basis of Heidegger's thought. Freud's construction of temporal difference is synonymous with Heidegger's notion of the "lighting-concealing" of language.

At the same time, however, we should remember that in the Wolf-Man case history Freud also makes exactly the sort of anthropological, metaphysical turn of thought that Heidegger condemns. He argues that

23. Heidegger, "Letter on Humanism," 204.

the Wolf-Man's repression of the primal scene reveals a phylogenetic mechanism so primitive that it may well mark the point at which the human is linked to the "instinctual [*instinktiv*] world of animal behavior" (*S.E.*, 17:120). Whether one regards this biological speculation as regrettable or laudable, it has no internal or logical bearing upon the language-centered analysis of dreams and of narrative-temporal structures that accounts for the bulk of the case history. As we shall see in Chapter 4, Freud's reduction of the repressive mechanism that conceals the primal scene to the anthropological notion of instinctual behavior is itself a tautological rationalization for his patient's inability to reproduce the scene as recollection. At the end of his most daring theoretical and clinical work, Freud feels compelled to explain the inexplicable forgetfulness that always conceals the origin. But this retreat from the radical ontological undecidability of the primal scene in no way reduces the value of that construction as a challenge to the history of Western metaphysics.

The dream of the white wolves marks the site of the most profound concealment in Freud's psycho-analytic of language. The wolf dream conceals the origin, but it also reveals that the origin presents itself as concealment and forgetfulness. As such, Freud's construction of the primal scene is in close conjunction with Heidegger's notion of the insurmountable forgetfulness or oblivion that conceals the history of Being. Freud's biological reification of the origin is the result of his having forgotten how primal the concealment of the wolf dream is. After having explained that the task of analysis is that of remembering the fundamental nature of forgetting, Freud himself returns to metaphysics by forgetting his own interdiction against forgetting the oblivion of the origin. Freud's achievement in the Wolf-Man case history can be most fully grasped in terms of what Heidegger, in his "Letter of Humanism," calls the "turning" (*Kehre*) from "Being and Time" to "Time and Being," which is how he describes his recognition of the radical temporal concealment that persists in blocking the revelation of the history of Being.[24] *From the History of an Infantile Neurosis* signals Freud's *Kehre*.

For Heidegger, the "turning" is not a departure from the standpoint of *Being and Time* but rather a remembering of the "fundamental experience of the oblivion of Being" from which *Being and Time* itself

---

24. Heidegger, "Letter on Humanism," 208.

emerged. The postwar Heidegger, the Heidegger of the period from the "Letter on Humanism" to *The Question of Being* (1955), turns back upon his project of a "fundamental ontology" and remembers that the forgetfulness of Being is not something that the history of Being can overcome. What Heidegger remembers is that forgetting is part of the history of Being. While the early Heidegger seeks to overcome the forgetfulness that conceals the history of Being within the history of metaphysics, the later Heidegger comes to recognize that the forgetting of Being belongs to the history of Being, that it cannot be overcome with the overcoming of metaphysics.

The thought of Freud and Heidegger comes into its most significant conjunction on the question of the radical irreducibility of nonoriginary temporal difference. Their thought is a continuous "turning" toward the question of the origin. Although it first appears in Freud's published work in 1918, the primal scene is a fundamental category underlying his work from its beginnings. What Freud recognizes in *From the History of an Infantile Neurosis* is that the finitude of temporality demands that the origin be sought not in the past, buried by forgetfulness, but in the future, in the projective repetition of the origin as it is elaborated through the transference. Like the history of Being for Heidegger, the primal scene is for Freud a beginning toward which he is constantly moving. "The primary phenomenon of primordial and authentic temporality," writes Heidegger, "is the future. The priority of the future will vary according to the ways in which the temporalizing of inauthentic temporality itself is modified, but it will still come to the fore even in the derivative kind of 'time.'"[25] The work of temporalization, and of distinguishing authentic from inauthentic temporality, is no longer the work of recollection narrowly conceived. Here Heidegger's constructions in the analytic of *Dasein* and Freud's constructions during the transference both become efforts to extend and project the subject's past into the future, to reconstruct and reenact the forgetfulness of temporal difference, and to bring out what is preserved in the speech of patients and in the history of philosophy by first determining what is repeated in them.

Freud and Heidegger demand that we understand the relation between forgetting and remembering in a new way. The patient has

25. Martin Heidegger, *Being and Time*, trans. John Macquarrie and Edward Robinson (New York: Harper & Row, 1962), 378.

forgotten the primal scene, and the history of metaphysics has forgotten the history of Being. The remembrance of that forgotten history and of that forgotten scene does not occur within the mode of subjective or personal recollection; it occurs as an act of interpretation, as a construction, as reading. Freud and Heidegger force us to confront a process for which there is no model. Much of the difficulty of Lacan's work is attributable to his determination to clarify this different kind of remembering. "Recollection," he writes, "is not Platonic reminiscence—it is not the return of a form, an imprint, an *eidos* of beauty and good, a supreme truth, coming to us from the beyond. It is something that comes to us from the structural necessities, something humble."26 Like Freud and Heidegger, Lacan has very little trouble telling us what recollection is *not* but a great deal of trouble telling us what it *is*. To insist, as he repeatedly does, that recollection is something that "precedes us, at the level of the structure of the signifier," is a constant reminder of how deeply concealed the Freudo-Heideggerian notion of recollection still is. Herein lies the essence of the difficulty of the task of thinking at the beginning of the ending of metaphysics. Lacan's effort to distinguish "the laws of recollection and symbolic recognition" from "the laws of imaginary reminiscence" defines the necessary but perhaps impossible task for thinking.27

Heidegger constructs his primal scene in the history of philosophy in the same differential zone between forgetting and remembering in which Freud and Lacan construct their models of temporal difference. Heidegger's penchant for the expression "*immer schon*" or "always already," which Derrida has made into a household word, indicates the apparent return or repetition of something that has been there all along, but it reveals very little either about how it got there in the first place or about how that return or repetition occurs. Derrida's contribution consists in having revealed that at its most fundamental level the Freudo-Heideggerian notion of recollection is a figure for reading. The primal scene and the history of Being are figures for the "already written," for what has already been inscribed within and between texts. Heidegger rereads the texts of the history of philosophy and rewrites them in the history of Being. Freud rereads the dream and rewrites it as the primal scene. The mystery in which both the history

26. Lacan, *The Four Fundamental Concepts of Psycho-Analysis,* 47.
27. Lacan, *Ecrits: A Selection,* 141.

of Being and the primal scene are shrouded is finally synonymous with
the mystery of reading, the mystery of how we read and understand.

For Freud and Heidegger, recollection is essentially a question of
style. Philosophy, literature, and psychoanalysis come into their most
significant conjunction by virtue of this postmetaphysical attention to
the writtenness of the letter. The differences between *Denken* and
Dichter and between philosophy, literature, and psychoanalysis thus
become infinitely less significant than their common commitment to
the letter.

Freud's construction of the primal scene and Heidegger's of the
history of Being are efforts to define the work of reparation in terms of
the affirmation of the ineluctability of difference and deferral. The
Freud of 1914–18 and the Heidegger of the *Kehre* ask us to let Being
be in the difference between *Denken* and *Dichter*. In my construction
of a certain Freud and a certain Heidegger it is a question not of
retrieving the ur-metaphor at the origin of language but of affirming
that language's irrepressible effect of displacement creates a kind of
"clearing" or "opening" that Freud calls the cure.[28]

28. Medard Boss reports that Heidegger read Freud's metapsychological and clinical
papers in 1958. While Freud's theoretical efforts disgusted Heidegger ("This reading
made him literally feel ill"), the "Papers on Technique" made him "more conciliatory."
See "Martin Heidegger's Zollikon Seminars," trans. Brian Kenny, *Review of Existential
Psychology and Psychiatry* 16 (1978/79): 9.

1 The Primal Scene and the "Ends" of Metaphysics

Rien n'aura lieu exceptée peut-être une constellation.
STÉPHANE MALLARMÉ, "Un Coup de dés"

Mastering the unmasterable is the philosopher's wiliest game.
No speculative trap is made better than the discourse that puts
the unmasterable in the place of mastery. To construct it,
however, one must stage a scene.
JEAN-LUC NANCY, *Le Partage des voix*

In *The Postcard: From Socrates to Freud and Beyond,* Jacques Derrida argues that Freud and Heidegger bring "*la grande époque*" of the history of Western metaphysics to an important juncture.[1] They are the last of the "master thinkers," the last to preside over a tradition that maintained that the scene, the image, or the representation could provide access to the Real. They still believe in ontology, in the capacity of "speech" (*logos*) to grasp "what-is" (*onta*). They still believe that what-is could be represented before a perceiving subject who would experience that representation, that image, that postcard, as a mode of recollection. Freud and Heidegger still think of recollection as a mode of presence. They are still, writes Derrida, "under the same roof" as Plato and Socrates, still under the sway of ontology, still in the same "house of Being." Like Plato and Socrates, Freud and Heidegger still conceive of thinking in terms of *anamnesis*. Unlike Nietzsche, they never learned to forget the "umbrella" of ontology.

Derrida's emphasis is upon those elements of the thought of Freud and Heidegger that link them to the past. My emphasis, however, is

1. Jacques Derrida, *La Carte postale: De Socrate à Freud et au-delà* (Paris: Aubier-Flammarion, 1980).

upon the modernity of their thought, on precisely those elements that anticipate Derrida's work. We should be very clear about the commitment of Freud and Heidegger to the metaphysics of presence before going on, as I shall, to emphasize those elements of their thought that look to the future.

First, however, let us step back and look at the primal scene of the history of philosophy as Derrida has outlined it, for from that perspective we will be able to see more clearly the extent to which Freud and Heidegger still remain under the spell of *la grande époque*.

The famous "atopical" or "placeless" voice with which Socrates communes provides him access to the ghostly world of the logos. Anamnesis describes this process of inner listening. The ghostly "atopicality" of that voice is a mask or concealment behind which, or through which, speaks the voice of the dead. Anamnesis cannot be separated from the mythology of metempsychosis, the transmigration of the soul. The voice of the logos is the echo within the self of an earlier incarnation. Through the logos the origin of the self, the absolutely earliest incarnation, remains present to the self. The dialectical or dialogical structure of anamnesis follows the form of this inner dialogue. Recollection is quite literally the repetition or presencing of the logos. Knowledge and recollection are thus bound to the identity of the subject in its inwardness, and in its ability to bring the logos to presence within itself. Thinking, whether in the mode of logic, ethics, or aesthetics, is a matter of recollection. Anything outside the subject would be secondary and incidental to that which has been interiorized through recollection. Thus Socrates, in the *Phaedrus,* must condemn writing because writing would weaken memory by attenuating one's relation to the atopical voice. One would become, argues Socrates, more and more reliant upon the exteriority of writing, and thus memory would become more and more unreliable.

Freud wants his patients to remember their forgotten pasts, while Heidegger wants to remember what has been forgotten in the history of philosophy. Freud and Heidegger are implicated in the scene of ancestral voices, where the paternal logos can still be heard. In "Plato's Pharmacy," Derrida clearly sets forth the extent to which Plato's doctrine of anamnesis constitutes the paradigmatic primal scene in the history of philosophy. In making the discourse of the truth synonymous with recollection, Plato has also to attempt to differentiate between true memory, or *mnemē,* and artificial memory, or *hypomnesis*

Plato's invention of philosophy relies entirely upon this founding opposition or binarism. The exteriority of writing forever bars it from the self-presence of the logos. Plato invents philosophy by forgetting its writtenness. What Heidegger calls Plato's forgetting of the question of Being becomes for Derrida the forgetting of the question of writing.

In presupposing that living speech and memory are synonymous with the truth, and in presupposing that writing is derivative and therefore harmful to memory, Plato comes to what Derrida calls "something like the major decision of philosophy, the one through which it institutes itself, maintains itself, and contains its adverse deeps."[2] Barbara Johnson's translation of "*son fond advers*" as "its adverse deeps" does not perhaps go far enough in conveying Derrida's suggestion that this epochal decision opens up both the possibility of philosophy and "its opposite extremity." In the primal scene in the history of philosophy, the origin is already divided; the origin has already been marked by the trace of the nonoriginary. This primal scene already contains its "other," "*son fond advers*." Platonism would thus have marked both the instauration of the epoch of logocentrism and its overcoming; it would have breached the trace that opens the possibility of both logocentrism and its opposite. "*Advers*" is not a normal French usage; it is Latin for "opposite." In its nonoriginary dividedness, Platonism constitutes what I call the primal scene of philosophy-literature. Derrida in effect repeats Heidegger's argument that Plato's forgetting of Being belongs to the history of Being by demonstrating that Plato's repression of writing also inscribes the problematic of writing in philosophy's primal scene.[3]

Derrida's technique achieves its analytic and descriptive power because he invariably puts it to work at those junctures in the history of philosophy at which the philosopher must establish a difference, even though that difference cannot be perceived or demonstrated. Everything rides for Plato-Socrates upon this difference between living mem-

2. Jacques Derrida, *Dissemination*, trans. Barbara Johnson (Chicago: University of Chicago Press, 1981), 111.

3. In "Plato's Doctrine of Truth" (trans. John Barlow, in *Philosophy in the Twentieth Century*, ed. William Barrett and Henry Aiken [New York: Random House, 1962], 3:270), Heidegger depicts an ambiguous and divided Plato who on the one hand wants to reveal an unhiddenness beyond the senses, but on the other hand is also deeply concerned with physical seeing. Though Plato comes to a decision, his text remains fissured. Though he decides to place value and meaning in the suprasensuous realm of Ideas, his texts indicate that "the original essence of truth still rests . . . in its hidden beginnings."

ory and artificial memory—yet this distinction can never be verified or located. It is at once absolutely necessary and absolutely impossible to substantiate this difference. The supplemental exteriority of writing must be distinguished from the originary inwardness of speech even though that difference is, as Derrida writes, "barely perceptible." In what Derrida calls "the anamnesic movement of truth," what is repeated through recollection is the *eidos,* which is the visible "idea" or "figure," from *eido,* "to see." The *eidos* is the representation or image that is recollected. For Plato this representation does not simply represent the earlier perceptual event; it presents it insofar as the *eidos* is not simply an image of what-is but *is* what-is. It is the *ontos on;* it is what exists. "Truth unveils the *eidos* or the *ontos on,*" writes Derrida, "that which can be imitated, reproduced, repeated in its identity."[4] The true is "what is represented and present in the representation." To locate what-is in the recollected *eidos,* Plato must exclude the temporal and the immediate. He must exclude writing, sophistics, and *hypomnesis* because they have a material and temporal dimension. Through the logos, anamnesis presents the thing itself in the form of the *eidos.* What-is, for Socrates-Plato, is the image of the voice within.

The Platonic equation of being and truth with the timelessness and immateriality of the recollected *eidos* is purchased at the price of the exclusion and the forgetting of the writing and the signifier that triggered the recollection. Philosophy is born of this distinction between the materiality of the signifier and the ideality of the signified, even though it is a distinction without a difference. The act of privileging the presence of the signified *eidos* over the absent signifier is the founding gesture of Western metaphysics. But it is a foundation without foundation.

In "Plato's Pharmacy," anticipating the terms he explores in *The Postcard,* Derrida describes the difference between writing and anamnesis as "invisible, almost nonexistent," a difference no thicker than a "leaf" or "sheet of paper," a *"feuille."* The paper on which Plato writes Socrates' condemnation of writing is for Derrida an image of the dividedness, the two-sidedness, of the way philosophy has always been written. In this *"feuille"* we have the image that becomes the "postcard." The primal scene is always divided. It always has a recto and a verso, writing and anamnesis, logocentrism and its other: "In being

4. Derrida, *Dissemination,* 111.

inaugurated in this manner, philosophy and dialectics are determined in the act of determining their other."[5]

Philosophy has always had to suppress the dividedness of this primal scene: "Metaphysics has erased within itself the fabulous scene that has produced it, the scene that nevertheless remains active and stirring, inscribed in white ink, an invisible design covered over in the palimpsest."[6] This remark, from Derrida's essay on the relation of philosophy to metaphor entitled "White Mythology," reminds us that this secret forgotten scene at the origin of philosophy is inseparable from the question of metaphor and figural language. The act of privileging the inner over the outer, and of privileging the presence of the logos in speech over the absence of the logos in writing, is the original metaphor. It is the result of the originary transference of the name of one thing to another thing, which is Aristotle's definition of metaphor. The determination of identity, of originality and derivation, the intelligible and the sensible, what-is and what-is-not, is the work of metaphor. The "fabulous scene" of nomination, of defining essences and drawing distinctions, is the founding "philosopheme" that establishes the transference of sense from the realm of sensory perception to that of ideation and intellection. It establishes the locus of truth in the phenomenology of inwardness and interiority. The concept of metaphor ensures the appropriation of the outside by the inside, writing by anamnesis. Though philosophy forgets that this appropriation ever took place, it remains there to be read in the texts of the history of philosophy.

Metaphor—and tropes and figures in general—originated as an aid to memory. Though it emerged in the very absence of living memory, tropology has always been placed in the service of the myth of the logos. The "white mythology" of metaphysics unfolds beneath an invisible sun in a world of pure seeing. This ruse of metaphysical reason and this domination of figural language by the myth of self-presence have been able to persist so long only by virtue of an interdiction against too searching an inquiry into the origin. Metaphysics has concerned itself with presence, not with that which brings to presence. What Derrida calls the "utterly primal scene," the "scene of scenes," has always been under an absolute interdiction: "Visibility should—

5. Derrida, *Dissemination,* 112.
6. Jacques Derrida, *Margins of Philosophy,* trans. Alan Bass (Chicago: University of Chicago Press, 1982), 213.

not be visible. According to an old omnipotent logic that has reigned since Plato, that which enables us to see should remain invisible: black, blinding."[7]

Freud's notion of the primal scene and Heidegger's projective history of Being are the two most decisive efforts in the history of modern thought to overcome that interdiction. Metaphysics is concerned with the appropriation of presence into self-presence. Freud and Heidegger are concerned with that which brings to presence in the first place. The involuntary nature of memory, its independence from intentionality, quite naturally suggests that deep within the self there is another self. Herein lies the basis for the notion of the soul. Nietzsche describes this metaphysical primal scene of memory in the clearest possible terms:

> One must revise one's ideas about memory: here lies the chief tempta-
> tion to assume a "soul," which, outside time, reproduces, recognizes,
> etc. But that which is experienced lives on "in the memory"; I cannot
> help if it "comes back," the will is inactive in this case, as in the coming
> of any thought. Something happens of which I become conscious: now
> something similar comes—who called it? roused it?[8]

But instead of making memory the object of an intensive interrogation, metaphysics has barred any examination into the presupposition that there is a subjectivity deep within the self. It is our narcissism, argues Nietzsche, which has for so long prevented us from calling into question what he calls "the fiction of the subject":

> The subject: this is the term for our belief in a unity underlying all the
> different impulses of the highest feeling of reality: we understand this
> belief as the effect of one cause—we believe so firmly in our belief that
> for its sake we imagine "truth," "reality," "substantiality" in gener-
> al.—"The subject" is the fiction that many similar states in us are the
> effect of one substratum: but it is we who first created the "similarity"

7. Jacques Derrida, "Living On/Border Lines," trans. James Hulbert, in *Deconstruction and Criticism*, ed. Harold Bloom et al. (New York: Seabury Press, 1979), 90–91.

8. Friedrich Nietzsche, *The Will to Power*, trans. Walter Kaufmann and R. J. Hollingdale (New York: Random House, 1967), 274. Elsewhere, Nietzsche writes of the lightning-flash inspiration that characterized his own experience of composition. At such moments memory and imagination become indistinguishable, and the fictionality of the subject is openly exposed: "The involuntariness of image and metaphor is strangest of all; one no longer has any notion of what is an image or a metaphor: everything offers itself as the nearest, most obvious, simplest expression" (*Ecce Homo/On the Genealogy of Morals*, trans. Walter Kaufmann [New York: Vintage Books, 1969], 301).

of these states; our adjusting them and making them similar is the fact, not their similarity (—which ought rather to be denied—).[9]

Tropology has been in the service of this myth of the subject, for it is tropology that creates these illusory similarities. Figures and tropes are the means through which that which comes to presence is appropriated by what Derrida calls "the proximity or properness of subjectivity to and for itself."[10] The originality of Freud and Heidegger is to have questioned the involuntary operation of memory and to have resisted its appropriation by "the fiction of the subject." Unlike Nietzsche, who wants actively to forget the question of the origin and thereby himself becomes opened to Heidegger's charge of metaphysical reductionism, Freud and Heidegger turn to the question of the origin in a new and more critical way.

Derrida is fond of arguing that Heidegger inadvertently naturalizes the fiction of the subject in the very act of criticizing it. In his reading of "The Origin of the Work of Art," for example, Derrida argues that by treating the shoes in Van Gogh's painting as a pair, Heidegger in effect restores them to a human subject. Derrida sees in Heidegger's emphasis on the "reliability" (*Verlässlichkeit*) of the shoes an effort to establish a ground for subjectivity. Like Dupin in "The Purloined Letter," Heidegger wants to restore the shoes to their proper place and to establish a ground (*hupokeimenon*) where there can be no ground. Such a reading ignores, however, Heidegger's effort to transform the shoes and the ground they walk on into the site of the most fundamental concealment. It is a question for Heidegger not of a ground but of the primordial *Riss* or rift where the habitual representations of World give way to the insurmountable concealment of Earth. For Heidegger this division cannot be reduced to a metaphysical notion of ground. Rather than sustaining the fiction of the subject, Heidegger ungrounds it at the most fundamental level.[11]

This critical approach to the question of the ground and the subject does not come to Heidegger or Freud at the very beginning of their careers. It is something that evolves slowly, through hesitations and relapses. The important thing, however, is that it does evolve, and

9. Nietzsche, *The Will to Power*, 269.
10. Derrida, *Margins of Philosophy*, 254.
11. Jacques Derrida, "Restitutions," in *La Vérité en peinture* (Paris: Flammarion, 1978), esp. 396–415.

because it does, our emphasis should be not on the fact that Freud and Heidegger were once "under the same roof" as Plato-Socrates, but on the fact that they were also the first to call the structure of the entire edifice into question.

Freud's discovery of the "talking cure" in the early 1890s begins as the rediscovery of the Platonic doctrine of anamnesis. The Freud of *Studies on Hysteria* believes that recollection is reliable. Only at the conclusion of *Studies on Hysteria* does one glimpse a dawning suspicion that even though he and his patients have assumed that what emerged during their sessions was genuine recollection, something is not altogether right. There is a serious theoretical question at stake here:

> Even when everything is finished and patients have been overborne by the force of logic and have been convinced by the therapeutic effect accompanying the emergence of precisely these ideas—when, I say, the patients themselves accept the fact that they thought this or that, they often add: "But I can't *remember* having thought it." It is easy to come to terms with them by telling them that the thoughts were *unconscious*. But how is this state of affairs to be fitted into our own psychological views? Are we to disregard this withholding of recognition on the part of patients, when, now that the work is finished, there is no longer any motive for their doing so? Or are we to suppose that we are really dealing with thoughts which never came about, which merely had a *possibility* of existing, so that the treatment would be in the accomplishment of a psychical act which did not take place at the time? It is clearly impossible to say anything about this—that is, about the state which the pathogenic material was in before the analysis—until we have arrived at a thorough clarification of our basic psychological views, especially on the nature of consciousness.[12]

This extraordinary passage marks the beginning of Freud's analytic understanding. Through the course of the 1890s he becomes increasingly less reluctant to speculate on the state of the "pathogenic material . . . before the analysis." The discovery of "psychoanalysis" in 1896–97 is synonymous with this new willingness to speculate on thoughts "which merely had a possibility of existing." Here in 1895 he has just begun to question the authenticity of the subject's memories, and he has just begun to suspect that the therapeutic effect of these "recollected ideas" may have nothing to do with their historical reality.

12. Sigmund Freud and Josef Breuer, *Studies on Hysteria,* trans. James Strachey (New York: Avon Books, 1966), 346.

Freud calls his theory of the early and mid-1890s "seduction theory" (*Verführungstheorie*) because he believes in the authenticity of the scenes of seduction that his patients recount to him. By the late 1890s, seduction theory has been replaced by psychoanalysis, and the seduction scene has been replaced by the primal scene. This fulfillment of his promised "thorough clarification of our psychological views" is the result of Freud's relentless problematization of the historicity of the analytic event. The rejection of seduction theory is, it seems to me, the result neither of Freud's unconscious compulsions with respect to his father's alleged sins, as Marie Balmary argues, nor of his unethical zeal for professional advancement, as Jeffrey Masson argues.[13] We can explain this crucial transformation in Freud's thinking by something that is at once much simpler and much more complex than the authors of these provocative new readings of Freud might suspect. What Freud recognized during the year following his father's death in October 1896 was the mediating, concealing power of temporal difference. His own experience of mourning made him aware that the time of the analysis was always inseparable from another temporal frame of reference. His "self-analysis" revealed to him that the operation of unconscious phantasy was such that even though it was "clearly impossible to say anything about . . . the state which the pathogenic material was in before the analysis," analysis would have to take account of that difference regardless of the precision with which it was able to delimit it. It was not the recollections themselves—whose authenticity was rigorously undecidable—but their relation to another event that explained their therapeutic power. It was no longer the content of the recollections, or their historicity, that mattered. The power of analysis to cure inhered in its ability to put temporal difference into play, and to initiate a relation between the work of recollection and construction and another temporal frame of reference whose ontological status would forever be indeterminant.

Freud's self-analysis revealed the resistance that unconscious phantasy poses to the analyst's effort to interpret. His own work of mourning showed him how massively he had underestimated the force and complexity of unconscious phantasy, for during this period he was overwhelmed by dreams and images of a magnitude he had never

13. Marie Balmary, *Psychoanalyzing Psychoanalysis: Freud and the Hidden Fault of the Father*, trans. Ned Lukacher (Baltimore, Md.: Johns Hopkins University Press, 1982); Jeffrey Moussaieff Masson, *The Assault on Truth: Freud's Suppression of Seduction Theory* (New York: Farrar, Straus, & Giroux, 1984).

before experienced. His difficulty in determining the authenticity of his own dreams and memories cast an immense shadow over his previous work. His own work of mourning revealed how primordial was the concealment of the origin by unconscious phantasy. Instead of assuming, as he had, that recollection makes the origin self-present to the subject, he realized that the presence of the origin was itself concealed by irreversible resistances. He discovered how powerful the work of forgetting was. But rather than abandon the search for the origin of the pathogenic event, or the origin of the dream, he devised a structure through which to take account of those resistances. He called this structure the Oedipal complex. In revealing the concealment of the origin, Freud's self-analysis led him to problematize the notions of time, memory, and the nature of the analytic event. Toward the end of *The Interpretation of Dreams,* which marks the culmination of this self-analysis, he writes:

> It is thus a question of relative strength whether our intellectual interest, our capacity for self-discipline, our psychological knowledge and our practice in interpreting dreams enable us to master our internal resistances. It is always possible to go *some* distance: far enough, at all events, to convince ourselves that the dream is a structure with a meaning, and as a rule far enough to get a glimpse of what that meaning is.[14]

Freud's topic in this section is "The Forgetting of Dreams," and he reminds his readers never to forget that dreams can never really be remembered, that "at some point" we lose our way and find ourselves before the mysterious "mycelium" of the mushroomlike "dream-wish." The rejection of seduction theory is not the abandonment of reality for phantasy but rather a recognition that phantasy and reality are, at the most fundamental level, bound together in the "intricate meshwork" that at once reveals and conceals the origin.

In a premourning, preanalytic paper like "The Aetiology of Hysteria" (1896), where Freud insists strongly upon the reality of the "infantile sexual scenes," we can already see the fissures that will break open under the pressure of his self-analysis.

---

14. Sigmund Freud, *The Interpretation of Dreams,* trans. James Strachey (New York: Avon Books, 1965), 563.

> Just as when putting together children's picture-puzzles, we finally after many attempts become absolutely certain which piece belongs to the gap not yet filled—because only that particular piece at the same time completes the picture and can be fitted in such a way as neither to leave a space nor to overlap—so the content of the infantile sexual scenes proves to be an inevitable completion of the associative and logical structure of the neurosis; and only after they have been inserted does its origin become evident—one might say, self-evident.
>
> Without wishing to lay special stress on the fact, I will add that in a number of cases the therapeutic test also speaks for the genuine nature of the infantile scenes.[15]

At this point in his career, Freud claims to be able to offer patients who remember the scenes of their sexual abuse the opportunity to verbalize their memories and thus overcome their symptoms. For patients who cannot remember such scenes, analysis "converts their unconscious memories of infantile scenes into conscious recollections."[16] Although Freud will not recognize it fully for another year, the dilemma concerning the status of these recollections is already evident—"one might say, self-evident." On the one hand he bases the reality of the infantile scenes on the fact that they fit perfectly into the "associative and logical structure"; that is, he bases the reality of the seduction scene on theoretical grounds, thus "seduction theory." On the other hand he feels it is still important to add that "the therapeutic test also speaks for the genuine nature of the infantile scene"; in other words, if the cure is effective, the memory must have been genuine. Freud goes on to say that in some cases the cure does not depend on the analyst's reaching "down as far as the infantile experiences," while in others it does. The pattern is already clear. Every time he seems to have settled the matter of the genuineness of these memories, he reopens the question from yet another point of view. He is eager to establish the efficacy of the cure as a function of the legitimacy of the recollection, but that relation between the historicity of the memory and its therapeutic effect always seems to slip out of reach.

Freud's ambivalence becomes even clearer when we look at the original text. When he says, "Without wishing to lay special stress on the fact" that therapeutic experience confirms the reality of these memo-

15. Sigmund Freud, *Early Psychoanalytic Writings* (New York: Collier Books, 1963), 189. "The Aetiology of Hysteria" is translated by Cecil Baines.

16. Freud, *Early Psychoanalytic Writings*, 195.

ries, the German, translated literally, reads, "without wanting to bring this fact into the foreground" (*ohne diesen in den Vordergrund drängen wollen*). Freud does not say either that the clinical question is not or should not be in the foreground, but only that he does not "wish" to emphasize it. Subsequent history reveals why he is so mysteriously evasive about the verification of the reality of these scenes. He will have to learn to venture beyond the stable ground of anamnesis. He will come to recognize that no test, therapeutic or otherwise, will ever be able to establish in principle the status of a recollection. Furthermore, he will come to recognize that it finally does not matter what the status of the recollection is, that what matters is the role it plays in articulating temporal difference in the narrative work of analysis. The pretense of being able to grasp the real, of being able to test the reality of recollection, of having discovered a veritable science of recollection, is full-blown in 1896. But at the level of style, at the level of syntax, it is already attenuated. Freud is still, as Derrida would say, "under the same roof" with Socrates-Plato, but the foundation has already begun to crumble.

By 1899, in "Screen Memories," Freud's attention is fully on the inseparability of reality and phantasy. His interest is in pointing out the role of unconscious phantasy in falsifying and transforming memory; he questions the reliability of recollection by challenging the coherence of the scene that the patient claims to recollect:

> Above all, there is the following point. In the majority of significant and in other respects unimpeachable childhood scenes the subject sees himself in the recollection as a child, with the knowledge that this child is himself; he sees this child, however, as an observer from outside the scene would see him. . . . Now it is evident that such a picture cannot be an exact repetition of the impression that was originally received. For the subject was then in the middle of the situation and was attending not to himself but to the external world.[17]

Freud puts this insight to most effective use in the paper entitled "A Child Is Being Beaten" (1919). His point is not to discredit the reality of the scene out of hand; his point is the more complex and important realization that the structure of unconscious phantasy provides the only access to the real. Psychoanalysis begins with the recognition that

17. Freud, *Early Psychoanalytic Writings*, 248. "Screen Memories" is translated by James Strachey.

the recollected image is not the repetition of the same, that recollection is not a mode of self-presence. Whether the scene actually happened or not is immaterial, for what analysis has access to is the way unconscious phantasy structures the scene, not its "exact repetition." Freud no longer presupposes that what-is can be represented before a subject. Freud turns from the univocal perspective of the subject *of* the scene to the structure of the subject's displacement *in* the scene.

This important passage in "Screen Memories" continues:

> Whenever in a memory the subject himself appears in this way as an object among other objects, this contrast between the acting and the recollecting ego may be taken as evidence that the original impression has been worked over. It looks as though a memory trace from childhood had here been retrospectively translated into a plastic and visual state at a later date—the date of the memory's "revival." But no reproduction of the original impression has ever entered the subject's consciousness.

After the work of mourning, Freud realizes that temporal spacing and difference have always already been at work in the process of recollection. Recollection does not represent what-is for the simple reason that the scene itself, including the subject's role in it, was never perceived by the subject. Freud's notion here of the "working over" (*Überarbeitung*) or "retrospective translation" (*rückübersetzt*) of the original impression anticipates the notion of "deferred action." Indeed, Freud comes to see that in place of the original impression, one has access only to its nonoriginary revision. Freud is concerned here, as he will be throughout his career, with the question of the reality/unreality of the scene, even though he knows that the question can never be closed. More important, however, his attention has moved to the manner in which the memory has been constructed through time. En route to building what he thought would be a new science of recollection, Freud inadvertently discovered the principle of temporal difference that still places his work at the forefront of modern thought.

"Screen Memories" is a chapter in Freud's self-analysis, for though he never lets on in the essay itself, the "patient" whose memories are the subject of the essay is none other than Freud himself. "I can assure you," Freud tells this imaginary patient, "that people often construct such things unconsciously—almost like works of fiction." From his self-analysis he has learned that the task of analysis is that of convinc-

ing patients to accept the inextricable linkage of childhood memory
and childhood phantasy.

> "But if that is so, there was no childhood memory, but only a
> phantasy projected back into childhood. A feeling tells me, though,
> that the scene is genuine. How is that to be accounted for?"
> There is in general no guarantee of the data produced by our memo-
> ry. But I am ready to agree with you that the scene is genuine.[18]

Freud is willing to acknowledge the genuineness of the scene, even
though his acknowledgement is irrelevant to the course of the analysis.
The analyst's task is to shift the patient's focus from the question of the
scene's reality to the temporal spacing and the structure of the phantasies that provide the only access to the scene. The analyst's willingness to agree with either the patient's resistance against or insistence
upon the scene's reality is part of a general effort to ease the patient
into the difficult task of entertaining the possibility of a cure within the
unstable and undecidable zone of truth/fiction. "You projected the
two phantasies on to one another," Freud tells his imaginary patient,
"and made a childhood memory out of them." He is not saying that
the scene never existed but rather that what is important to analysis is
"the stamp giving the date of manufacture." Through this "*Marke*,"
Freud is able to determine the temporal spacing that characterizes the
scenographic work of unconscious phantasy.

While Freud is led to the discovery of the role of temporal difference
through the patient's forgetfulness of the pathogenic event, Heidegger
is led to this discovery by the history of metaphysics' forgetfulness of
the difference between Being and beings. Like the Freud of seduction
theory, the history of metaphysics forgets the difference between the
subject *of* the scene and the subject *in* the scene. The early Heidegger
seeks to remember this difference between the ontological and the
ontical; for him the task of thinking is that of remembering the "distance" (*Ferne*) and the "throwness" (*Geworfenheit*) that separate the
ontical everydayness of beings from Being itself. In forgetting this distance, the history of metaphysics has forgotten the question of Being.
The later Heidegger, however, renounces this task of remembering and
accepts the impossibility of thinking this difference as such. He turns

18. Freud, *Early Psychoanalytic Writings*, 242.

instead to that which is proximate, nearby—which is to say that he turns to the differential play of language. The concealment of Being comes to presence in the late Heidegger in the "clearing" or "open space" (*Lichtung*) that is language. Derrida maintains that although Heidegger deconstructs "the domination of metaphysics by the *present*, he has done so only in order to lead us to think the presence of the present."[19] What Derrida fails to add is that Heidegger leads us "to think the presence of the present" in terms very different from those of the history of metaphysics. For Heidegger leads us to think of the "clearing" or the "lighting" as a profound concealment of self-veiling. Heidegger does not simply forget the difference between Being and beings in his own turn, which is what Derrida would have us believe. Heidegger does not fill the proximate with presence. What he does is to transform the nearby into a site where the concealment of Being discloses itself as concealment.

The Heidegger of the *Kehre* recognizes that the ontological difference between Being and beings can never be apprehended by language, that language is the site of a difference that blocks all access to ontological difference. From ontological difference as the Being *of* beings, he turns to a more fundamental difference within language itself. Heidegger treats ontological difference as an "ambivalence" (*Zweifalt*) that is "always already pre-given" (*immer schon vorgegeben*).[20] There is, in other words, no way to surmount this ambivalence, no way to resolve it or make it readable. Following the transformation in his thought during the 1930s, which he first announced in the "Letter on Humanism" (1947), Heidegger came to recognize that his own effort to remember the ontological difference that had been forgotten by the history of metaphysics was itself a metaphysical gesture that overlooked the complex resistances inherent in language. He recognized that his effort "to think" ontological difference remained under the sway of metaphysics. The Heidegger who was committed to the project of a fundamental ontology sought to overcome the "onto-theological" interpretation of ontological difference that characterized the history of metaphysics from Plato to Nietzsche. This Heidegger, prior to the *Kehre*, sought to think the question of the relation of beings to

19. Derrida, "The Ends of Man," in *Margins of Philosophy*, 131.
20. Martin Heidegger, *Was Heisst Denken?* (Tübingen: Max Niemayer Verlag, 1954), 174. The *Zweifalt* or *Unterschied* (distinction) marks a persistent concealment within ontological difference itself.

Being in a more fundamental sense, to think of Being not as a kind of superbeing or godhead but as something present in the immanent temporality of *Dasein's* existence.

It is in his 1927 lectures, *The Basic Problems of Phenomenology,* that he announces his overcoming of ontotheology: "The distinction between being and beings exists *pre-ontologically,* without an explicit concept of being, *latent in Dasein's existence.* As such it can become *an explicitly understood difference"* (Heidegger's emphasis).21 Through an analysis of the temporality of *Dasein,* Heidegger hoped to make ontological difference explicit. It is this project that collapsed during the 1930s. In examining *Dasein's* temporality, Heidegger came to discover that the structure of temporality, and therefore the structure of ontological difference as well, was blocked by the complex mediations and deferrals of language. In his effort to render ontological difference explicit, Heidegger discovered that language barred the way. What he thought would be the way to ontological difference turned out to be the way to language, which is the title of his collection *Unterwegs zur Sprache* (1957). In the "Letter on Humanism," Heidegger announced that this "turning" toward the fundamental concealment that is language had always already taken place in his thought, even though it took him until the mid-1940s to recognize it fully. The Heidegger of the *Kehre* accepts the inability of philosophy to pass beyond the *pre-ontological* comprehension of ontological difference, for he regards language as the site of the most fundamental concealment to which philosophy has access. By recognizing that philosophy must bear such constraints, Heidegger transformed the essence of philosophy.22

---

21. Martin Heidegger, *The Basic Problems of Phenomenology,* trans. Albert Hofstadter (Bloomington: Indiana University Press, 1982), 319.

22. Heidegger's confrontation with the poetical texts of Hölderlin is the watershed of the epochal transformation in his thinking that occurred during the 1930s, a decade during which his only publications were the controversial political pamphlets and addresses. Yet he was never more productive, for this is the decade of his lectures on Schelling, Aristotle, Hölderlin, and Nietzsche—lectures that formed the basis for his published work throughout the 1940s and 1950s. With respect to the question of ontological difference, the crucial lectures are surely those on Hölderlin, which Heidegger delivered at Freiburg during the winter semester 1934–35 (they have recently been published as vol. 39 of the Heidegger *Gesamtausgabe* under the title *Hölderlins Hymnen "Germanien" und "Der Rhein"* [Frankfurt am Main: Vittorio Klostermann, 1980]) when, following a decade of lectures on philosophical texts, Heidegger abruptly turned to two hymns by Hölderlin and the question of poetic language. This is also the period of Heidegger's "The Origin of the Work of Art." The sudden turn toward the artwork signals his shift from *Dasein* to Being. After the *Kehre,* Heidegger's focus is no

In the later Heidegger it is a question not of overcoming ontotheology through the comprehension of ontological difference but of recognizing that thinking calls upon us to think preontological difference. In his essay "The Anaximander Fragment" (1946), Heidegger states that although the difference between beings and Being remains forgotten and concealed, we may nevertheless expect that "it has left a trace which remains preserved in the language to which Being comes."[23] Such a trace, which lies beyond presence and absence even as it generates the play between them, would have been incorporated within and sheltered by the texts of the history of philosophy since its beginnings. This *Spur* or trace is synonymous with preontological difference, which Derrida calls "the trace of the trace that has disappeared in the forgetting of the difference between Being and beings." When Derrida responds to this passage from "The Anaximander Fragment" by saying, "There may be a difference still more unthought than the difference between Being and beings," he seems to have forgotten that this is precisely Heidegger's question, the question of preontological difference. The Heideggerian *Spur* already marks the site where Derrida comes to inscribe *différance*. The Heideggerian *Zweifalt* has already breached the path toward the nonoriginary, preontological zone that Derrida calls *différance:* "Beyond Being and beings, this difference, ceaselessly differing from and deferring (itself), would trace (itself) (by itself)—this *différance* would be the first and last trace if one still could speak, here, of origin and end."[24] Heideggerian-Derridean *différance* takes us "a step back" to the nonoriginary, preontological limit function of philosophy that had gone unthought throughout the history of metaphysics. Preontological difference is pregiven in the essence of language, prior to any thought and prior to any subject whatsoever. Heidegger's *Spur* and Derrida's *différance* are names for the nonsubjective, artificial memory of the text. They are the names for the unnameable resistance of language to the

---

longer on the difference *between* Being and beings, but on Being *as* difference, a difference, however, whose identity is blocked by the preontological, irreducibly metaphorical deferrals of language. The *Kehre* is the step back from ontological difference to the preontological metaphoricity of language. The turn to art and language might also have been Heidegger's effort to rethink his position following his brief but inexcusable alliance with the Third Reich in 1933–34.

23. Martin Heidegger, *Early Greek Thinking*, trans. David Farrell Krell and Frank Capuzzi (New York: Harper & Row, 1975), 51.

24. Derrida, *Margins of Philosophy*, 65, 66, 67. *Différance* and *Sein* are metaphors for a nameless, subject-less seriality.

Being question. They are the names for language's capacity to open itself to time, "to give" time to thinking, and for language's concealment-disclosure of its "gift" of time and thought. Derrida's history of writing and Heidegger's history of Being are efforts to account for the radicality of the temporality of language. They are attempts to account for a silent, unidentifiable voice in the text that is always pregiven, prior to the oppositions of identity and difference, subject and object, a mark, a trace, a trait, a *retrait* in the text that veils itself, withdraws into itself, and forgets all about itself.[25]

Consider Heidegger's position in relation to Freud's. Freud discovers that the childhood scene or the dream comes to presence only through the concealment of unconscious phantasy. He does not forget the possibility that the primal scene might have taken place, but he is forced to write it under the mark of erasure. He does not forget the difference between truth and fiction, or reality and phantasy, but he must learn to accept his inability ever to remember, through language, just what that difference is. What is present, what is nearby for Freud, is the structure of unconscious phantasy. But simply because it is nearby, he does not fill the concealing work of phantasy with presence. All that phantasy brings to presence is its own concealment. Freud knows that there is something behind that concealment, and he does not for a moment forget the difference between the phantasy and the thing itself. Likewise, Heidegger learns to accept his inability ever to remember the difference between Being and beings, but he does not, for all that, forget that the difference is still there. He renounces the task of remembering, but that does not change the fact that something has been forgotten. One feels that in order to establish the originality of his own thought, Derrida sometimes finds it convenient to forget that Heideg-

25. Derrida marks his difference from Heidegger in "Différance" (in *Margins of Philosophy*, esp. 23–27), and in "The *Retrait* of Metaphor," *Enclitic* 2.2 (1978): 5–34. Of the many recent discussions of Derrida/Heidegger, the most lucid to date is Rodolphe Gasché, "Joining the Text: From Heidegger to Derrida," in *The Yale Critics: Deconstruction in America*, ed. J. Arac, W. Godzich, and W. Martin (Minneapolis: University of Minnesota Press, 1983), esp. 156–61 and 169–73. Gasché demonstrates the extent to which Heidegger's question of Being and Derrida's question of the Text are "the same." In "Quasi-Metaphoricity and the Question of Being," Gasché argues that "Derrida's exploration of the irreducible metaphoricity of the founding tropes" constitutes a continuation of Heidegger's effort to situate the logos in the "as-structure" of language, in *Hermeneutics and Deconstruction*, ed. H. Silverman and D. Ihde (Albany: State University Press of New York, 1985), 186. The identity of Being *as* difference is concealed/deferred by the metaphorical seriality of the *Als-Struktur* of language. On the threshold between concept and figure, Derrida's "undecidables" speak the voiceless language of Being.

ger does *not* forget the temporal difference inherent in the presence of the present.

"What we need, perhaps, as Nietzsche said, is a change of 'style,'" and Derrida goes on to add, "if there is style, Nietzsche reminded us, it must be plural."[26] We need this plural style in order to be able to account for this radical "otherness" of temporality in language. We would have to write so as to allow this concealed-disclosed voice of temporal difference to be heard, and to be read.

Michel Foucault describes Nietzsche's genealogical project as a history of the errors, reversals, accidents, and miscalculations "that gave birth to those things that continue to exist and have values for us."[27] Foucault's notion of genealogy is not a stylistic model but a model for historical narrative; as a kind of "countermemory," or anti-anamnesis, it is an effort to redefine the relation of historical narrative to the past and the present. Genealogy is thus also a kind of artificial memory that the historian-philosopher deciphers from the archive and, in so doing, transforms the shape of the present by bringing it into conjunction with a past it had forgotten.

Instead of the impossible task of determining the ontological difference between Being and beings, the task of thinking after Nietzsche, Heidegger, Derrida, and Foucault is that of locating and then reinscribing the temporal difference that inheres at the level of both style and narrative. Through a relentless problematization of memory, modern philosophy, literature, and psychoanalysis have shifted their focus from ontological difference to temporal difference. With respect to narrative, the task of interpretation has become that of reconstructing the temporal difference between the *fabula* and the *sjuzet,* which readers have forgotten but the text remembers. With respect to style, the task is to locate the shift in the voice of the text, to determine the tone changes and the rhythmic alternations that separate the voice from itself. This is the focus of the next chapter, where I use Lacan's notion of the "fading of the subject" and Paul de Man's rhetorical figure of "prosopopoeia" to locate the point where temporal difference is registered at the level of style. The task of interpretation is that of constructing primal scenes of other voices and other narratives.

Metaphysics, writes Heidegger in one of his late essays, is "past in

26. Derrida, "The Ends of Man," in *Margins of Philosophy,* 135.
27. Michel Foucault, "Nietzsche, Genealogy, History," in *Language, Counter-Memory, Practice: Selected Essays and Interviews,* ed. Donald Bouchard (Ithaca, N.Y.: Cornell University Press, 1977), 146.

the sense that it has entered its ending. The ending lasts longer than the previous history of metaphysics."[28] The history of Being is the forgotten *fabula* which the *sjuzet* that is the history of metaphysics has forgotten within itself. We have entered the beginning of the ending of the history of metaphysics insofar as we have begun to construct an artificial textual memory through which we are able to retrieve what has been forgotten since the beginning. The beginning of the end occurs across a broad intellectual front. We have paid particular attention to the thought of Freud and Heidegger. I would like to consider briefly some other thinkers, all roughly contemporary with Freud and Heidegger, who have also problematized the notion of the event and the operation of memory. Valéry's *"objet ambigu,"* Proust's *"mémoire involontaire,"* and Benjamin's "dialectical image" are all closely linked to Freud's primal scene. Collectively, they announce the beginning of a twilight epoch which Heidegger believes may last long enough to transform the two thousand years of the ontotheological tradition into a dim and very distant memory.

In an important article on Valéry's *Ëupalinos, or the Architect,* Hans Blumenberg argues that Valéry's *"objet ambigu"* constitutes a challenge to Platonic ontology. In this imaginary dialogue, in which Valéry attempts to rewrite the *Phaedrus,* the young Socrates discovers an ambiguous white object washed up on the beach. What follows is Hans Robert Jauss's summary of Blumenberg's argument, which provides a paradigmatic account of what I have called the primal scene of philosophy-literature. Note particularly the analogies between Blumenberg's argument and Derrida's in "Plato's Pharmacy":

> Finding this object sets off a train of thought in the young Socrates which he cannot bring to a conclusion: "it is an object which cannot be interpreted within a Platonic ontology. Socrates sees this immediately—it is an object which recalls nothing and yet is not amorphous." The question concerning the natural or artificial origin which can always be decided in ancient ontology cannot be answered here. In view of the equivocalness of this object which negates the borderline between art and nature, Socrates must decide whether his attitude toward his find should be one of inquiry or of pleasure, theoretical or aesthetic. The aesthetic attitude "can always . . . content itself with a solution which is not a resolution of what is given but can deliberately ignore

---

28. Martin Heidegger, "Overcoming Metaphysics," in *The End of Philosophy,* trans. Joan Stambaugh (New York: Harper & Row, 1973), 85.

the remaining indeterminacy of other possibilities. The theoretical hypothesis, on the other hand, is burdened with the possibility of other, better solutions none of which can ever definitively exclude the chance that its verification will fail."[29]

"It is an object which recalls nothing and yet is not amorphous." It is just such an object that Freud constructs in the Wolf-Man case history. At the end of the dialogue Socrates throws the amorphous shape back into the sea and thus becomes a philosopher. The Socratic-Platonic doctrine of anamnesis and its ontological imperative demand that this object be rejected just as they demand the rejection of writing. Like Derrida, Valéry has constructed the primal scene of the history of philosophy. Though Derrida has uncovered the scene within Plato's text and Valéry has imagined his own text, they both make the same point concerning the ontologist's forgetfulness and exclusion of what he cannot grasp. Freud and Heidegger reject neither the "*objet ambigu*" nor the theoretical difficulties it entails.

Walter Benjamin's essay "The Image of Proust" is another important document in the modernist deconstruction of the recollected event. Again I will rely on Jauss's summary, for he clearly outlines Benjamin's sense of the radicality of Proust's notion of "*mémoire involontaire.*" For Benjamin, the Proustian image—that is, the Proustian event—constitutes the reversal of Platonic anamnesis. Herein lies the importance of Benjamin's use of the figures of the sock and the tapestry, for Proust empties out the presence of recollection just as the child plays with the rolled and unrolled sock, thus enabling us to look upon the reverse side of the tapestry of memory:

[Proust's] way of writing avoids the "lies of representation" by a specific form of negativity: no element of the objective world or of the factual life story may be described or told in the light of something directly or objectively given. In contrast to the reified milieu of naturalism or the concretized past memoirs, things and events of preexistent reality can enter the world of the novel only in the avowed form of their mediation, just as the remembered world can enter only in the specifically portrayed, temporal process of remembrance, the com-

29. Hans Robert Jauss, *Aesthetic Experience and Literary Hermeneutics,* trans. Michael Shaw (Minneapolis: University of Minnesota Press, 1982), 56–57; Hans Blumenberg, "Sokrates und das 'objet ambigu'—Paul Valérys Auseinandersetzung mit der Tradition der Ontologie des ästhetischen Gegenstandes," in *Epimeleia, Helmut Kuhn zum 65 Geburstag,* ed. F. Wiedmann (Munich: Suhrkamp, 1964), 285–323.

menting reflections only in the imperfect generalization of the remembering self in search of an identity. We thus have the paradox of a way of writing in which, as Benjamin unforgettably formulated it, all action and the identity of the person merely form the "reverse of the continuum of memory" and must be inferred by the reader from the "pattern on the back side of the tapestry."[30]

Recollection in Proust is unable to find what Jauss calls "a transcendent home," though that is what Proust is seeking: transcendence in time itself. Proust's inversion of Platonic anamnesis never succeeds in capturing essences through temporal difference. What Proust does discover is what Benjamin strikingly calls "a world distorted into the state of resemblance." Even though Proust is still motivated by a Platonic search for essences, he succeeds, by virtue of this "distortion," in inverting the Platonic ontology. Proust's concern with involuntary memory places the reader on "the back side of the tapestry," outside the control of the intending subject. In Proust we no longer see the continuous pattern of memory and identity but the irregular pattern of involuntary memory and nonidentity. Proust's radical temporalization of Platonic anamnesis seems to me to bear closely on Nietzsche's notion of "active forgetfulness," for in Proust we also see the paradox of a willful involuntarism.

Benjamin's Proust essay should be placed in conjunction with his work on Baudelaire, who stands at the antipodes of Proust's position. Baudelaire's commitment is solely to voluntary memory. In contrast to Proust, who is concerned with forgetting and temporal difference, Baudelaire, in abject horror of involuntary memory, values recollection only when it can be controlled to produce a feeling of self-presence and atemporal plenitude. Benjamin interprets Baudelaire's neo-Platonic mythology of memory as a dialectical response to radical historical transformations in the nineteenth-century experience of time. While Proust wants to immerse himself in involuntary memory, Baudelaire wants just as desperately to escape from it. Benjamin's "dialectical image" is an effort to account for the relation between memory and historical time. In the notes to his abortive *Passage Work* project, he calls the dialectical image "the primal phenomenon of history."[31]

30. Jauss, *Aesthetic Experience and Literary Hermeneutics*, 90; Walter Benjamin, "The Image of Proust," in *Illuminations*, trans. Harry Zohn (New York: Schocken Books, 1969), 201–16.

31. Walter Benjamin, *Das Passagen-Werk*, ed. Rolf Tiedemann, 2 vols. (Frankfurt: Suhrkamp, 1982), 1:592.

Through the dialectical image, Benjamin projects the radical temporality of the recollected event against the horizon of collective historical experience. The dialectical image is Benjamin's effort at writing a case history of modernity. It is his strategy for reading the archival memory of the collective. Like Proust, Benjamin develops a style that enables him to distort the shape of history into a pattern of resemblance. Like the primal scene, the dialectical image involves the construction of a narrative, which Benjamin sometimes calls a "dialectical fairy tale." Benjamin constructs his *fabula* with a collective Freudo-Marxist therapeutic objective in mind.

The crucial notion for each of these thinkers is recollection. But have they done anything more than merely reverse the Platonic ontology? Baudelaire's mnemotechnics are clearly Platonic, while those of Proust, Valéry, and Benjamin seem to have inverted Platonism rather than overcome it. None of them seems to have renounced the task of determining ontological difference. Like the early Freud and the early Heidegger, they are still "under the same roof" with Socrates-Plato, for whether involuntary or not, subjective recollection is still the chief consideration. It finally makes little difference that for Benjamin it is a question of a collective subject. Adopting a Marxist philosophy of history, Benjamin too invests temporality with the essential attributes of the atemporal. Like Marx, he discovers Platonic essences in the value of the commodity form. Heidegger reminds us that Marx, like Nietzsche and like those thinkers we have mentioned here, has prepared the way for the beginning of the ending:

> Throughout the whole history of thinking, Plato's thinking remains decisive in changing forms. Platonism is metaphysics. Nietzsche characterizes his philosophy as reversed Platonism. With the reversal of metaphysics which has already been accomplished by Karl Marx, the most extreme possibility of philosophy is attained. It has entered its final stage.[32]

"Plato's thinking remains decisive in changing forms." Platonism wears many masks and speaks in many voices, even during the beginning of the end of metaphysics.

32. Martin Heidegger, *On Time and Being*, trans. Joan Stambaugh (New York: Harper & Row, 1977), 57.

2 Prosopopoeia

Ye voices, and ye Shadows
And Images of voice.
WILLIAM WORDSWORTH, "The Power of Sound"

Only a fadograph of a yestern scene.
JAMES JOYCE, *Finnegan's Wake*

Voice and the "Fading of the Subject"

The primal scene is always the primal scene of words. At its most elemental the primal scene becomes the primal *seme*. The primal scene is always constructed from what the analyst-critic hears or reads in the discourse of the patient-text. Interpretation is always a kind of listening or reading that enables one to translate one set of words into another. The voice of the text, like the voice of the patient, is a verbal mask that conceals forgotten words and the forgotten scenes they compose. The analyst must learn to detect modulations and shifts within the patient's speech, to hear the voices of the patient's different selves and the traces of the voices of others. Apropos of Theodor Reik's notion of the analyst's need for a "third ear," Lacan remarks that what we need is not a third ear, "as if two were not enough to be deaf with," but a new way of listening.[1] Like the analyst the reader too must try to determine the gesture that is concealed in the voice of the text.

Let us take as an instance of such an effort at listening a passage from Freud's case history of Dora, where voice, rhythm, intonation, and breathing are explicitly linked to the formulation of the primal scene. Here we see Freud at work as he builds the primal scene out of what Roland Barthes liked to call "the grain of the voice." We may not

1. Jacques Lacan, *The Four Fundamental Concepts of Psycho-Analysis*, trans. Alan Sheridan (New York: Norton, 1981), 258.

often think of Freud as having engaged in the sort of sensuous listening we associate with Barthes. Nevertheless, it is through the voice and the rhythm of breathing that Freud deciphers the primal scene. The key to his deductive construction is the arhythmic, asthmatic breathing that is Dora's most symptomatic trait:

> Dora's symptomatic acts and certain other signs gave me good reasons for supposing [*guten Grund zur Annahme*] that the child, whose bedroom had been next door to her parents', had overheard her father in his wife's room at night and had heard him (for he was always short of breath) breathing hard during their coitus. Children, in such circumstances, divine something sexual in the uncanny sounds that reach their ears [*Die Kinder ahnen in solchen Fällen das Sexuelle in dem unheimlichen Gerausche*]. Indeed, the movements expressive of sexual excitement lie within them ready to hand, as innate pieces of mechanism. I maintained years ago that the dyspnoea and palpitations that occur in hysteria and anxiety-neurosis are only detached fragments of the act of copulation; and in many cases, as in Dora's, I have been able to trace back the symptom of dyspnoea or nervous asthma to the same exciting cause—to the patient's having overheard sexual intercourse taking place between adults.[2]

Dora's famous "catarrh," which Freud interprets as an upward displacement of the classical hysterical symptom of uterine or vaginal paroxysm, along with her other symptoms, such as irregular breathing or her persistent fingering of her handbag, are all unconscious efforts to repeat, to restage, the primal scene of listening. Freud, however, had very little success with Dora, who was so distressed at Freud's constructions that she abruptly broke off the analysis. Freud is surely on the right track here. Dora's illness is doubtless linked to her identification with her father's desire. However, Freud's sexist identification with Herr K. prevented him from fully understanding Dora. As Lacan observes, Freud "is himself still hesitant—a little too early, a little too late. Freud could not yet see . . . that the hysteric's desire . . . is to sustain the desire of the father—and, in the case of Dora, to sustain it by procuring."[3] Procuring Frau K. for her father's impotent pleasure is

2. Sigmund Freud, *Dora: An Analysis of a Case of Hysteria* (New York: Collier, 1976), 98.

3. Lacan, *The Four Fundamental Concepts of Psycho-Analysis*, 38. Also see Lacan's penetrating remarks on Freud's successes and failures in the Dora case in "Intervention in Transference," in Lacan, *Feminine Sexuality,* ed. Juliet Mitchell and Jacqueline Rose (New York: Norton, 1982), 69ff. The disjunction between Freud's art of construction and his handling of the transference is nowhere more acute than in Dora's case.

itself the logical extension of the childhood scene of listening. It is not Freud's interpretation that is errant but rather his miscued effort to engage Dora's conviction. It is not difficult to imagine Dora's stupefaction at the boldness of Freud's constructions. His problem is that of preparing his patients for the unfamiliar and the uncanny. It is an insoluble problem, of course, because the unmasking of the primal scene is something that patients can never be prepared for.

For an elaboration of the analyst-reader's ability to discriminate alternations in the tone or rhythm of the voice of the patient-text, I turn to the work of Barthes, who is surely the preeminent connoisseur-critic of voice in the nineteenth-century and modern text. Barthes often seems much more acutely aware than Freud that the analytic session is itself the primal scene it presumes to reconstruct. It is from Freud that Barthes derives one of his most fundamental themes, which is the conjunction of death and castration in the voice. Like Freud, Barthes is particularly alert to the presence of other voices and other rhythms within the voice. More musically oriented by far than the unmusical Freud, Barthes is particularly attuned to the echo of the past in the present.

One of Barthes' most important works, *S/Z*, is focused almost exclusively on the conjunction of voice, death, and castration. Balzac's *Sarrasine* (1830) provides Barthes with an exemplary transitional text, a text located between the univocal structure of the classical text and the plurivocality of the modern text. For Barthes, the connoisseur of operatic voice and the voice of Schubert's *Lieder,* Balzac's story marks an important moment in the historical transformation of the nature of voice. Zambinella, a castrato in the Cardinal's private opera company, inspires through "her" voice a passion so intense in the sculptor Sarrasine that it literally proves fatal. Voice in *Sarrasine* is no longer, as it is in the classical text, the register of sexual difference and identity. Voice has become a mask from which one can no longer determine the relation between language and subjectivity.

What Barthes has to say about the shift in the nature of voice in the nineteenth century becomes particularly significant in light of the Heideggerian thesis of the beginning of the end of metaphysics. For Barthes, *Sarrasine* occupies the space of the "classical plural," which falls between the classical and the modern. In this space, voice is in an unprecedentedly ambivalent position, for it is at once readable and unreadable, at once a cipher of subjectivity and the mark of the subject's erasure. Balzac's text places us in a position where, just at the moment we believe we can decipher the subject behind the voice, something blocks our way, and the voice once again becomes unreadable. To describe this phenomenon, Barthes borrows Lacan's expression "the fading of the subject" or "the fading of the voice." Like Lacan, Barthes uses the English word *"fading"* in his French text. Lacan, as we will soon see, borrowed the idea of "fading" from Ernest Jones's notion of *"aphanisis."*

In his English translation of *S/Z*, Richard Miller renders the chapter title "Le Fading des voix" as "The Dissolve of Voices." Zambinella's blurring of sexual difference becomes significant for Barthes because it is part of the larger historical problem of the "fading of voice." At the beginning of *Sarrasine* the narrator speaks with an old and wealthy "personage," who, we discover later, is Zambinella. After a lifetime as a brilliant singer and female impersonator, the wizened old castrato has retired to an estate outside Paris. What Barthes wants to know is, "Who is speaking?"

> Here it is impossible to attribute an origin, a point of view to the statement. Now, this impossibility is one of the ways in which the plural nature of a text can be appreciated. The more indeterminate the origin of the statement, the more plural the text. In modern texts, the voices are so treated that any reference is impossible: the discourse, or better, the language, speaks: nothing more. By contrast, in the classic text the majority of the utterances are assigned an origin, we can identify their parentage, who is speaking: either a consciousness (of a character, of the author) or a culture (the anonymous is still an origin, a voice: the voice we find, for example, in the gnomic code); however, it may happen that in the classic text, haunted by the appropriation of speech, the voice gets lost, as though it had leaked out through a hole in the discourse. The best way to conceive the classical plural is to listen to the text as an iridescent exchange carried on by multiple voices, on different wavelengths and subject from time to time to a sudden *"fading,"* leaving a gap which enables the utterance to shift from one point of view to another, without warning: the writing is set up across this tonal instability (which in the modern text becomes atonality), which makes it a glistening texture of ephemeral origin.[4]

As used in French, *"fading"* describes the erasure or effacement of the voice, as in those telephone connections where the other's voice is borne away by waves of static interference. For Barthes as for Lacan,

4. Roland Barthes, *S/Z*, trans. Richard Miller (New York: Hill & Wang, 1974), 41–42.

"fading" describes the negativity inherent in the notion of the subject. For Lacan it is through these gaps in the discourse of the other that the subject emerges in the first place. "The Fading of Voices" is Barthes' version of this primal scene in the history of modern textuality. The task of reading the classical plural and modern text is that of locating these instances of "tonal instability," which Barthes describes as "an iridescent exchange" and "a glistening texture of ephemeral origin" (*une moire brillante d'origines éphémères*). This is a complex notion and a difficult phrase to translate. "*Moire*" is a kind of watered silk that gives a glistening or iridescent effect. Barthes imagines the "fading of voices," the "fading" of the subject, as a disappearance behind the watery luminescence of the *moiré* effect. What appears to be a glittering revelation turns out to be a secret concealment. The *moiré* effect, like writing, is a textual effect, a weaving of voices that discloses and conceals at the same time.

Instead of a subject or an identifiable voice, what Barthes discovers in *Sarrasine* is "*une moire brillante.*" The critic-analyst who knows how to listen can locate just such tone changes, what Barthes calls "*un fading brusque.*" What speaks is not a subject but "the discourse, or better, the language." Barthes is here of course borrowing Heidegger's notion that "*die Sprache spricht.*"

Perhaps Mallarmé is another strand in this fabric. In his essay "The Double Session," Derrida alludes to Mallarmé's wordplay with "*moire,*" "*mémoire,*" and "*grimoire*" (a fortunetelling book).[5] Taking this hint, we might rephrase Barthes' notion of "fading" as follows: instead of *mémoire,* instead of a recollecting subject, we are left with only the *moire,* the glimmering trace of an unrepresentable origin. *Sarrasine* marks the historical point when voice is no longer the expression of the subject who recollects but rather the reminder of the forgetfulness that shrouds the origin. "It is Zambinella's voice that Sarrasine is in love with," writes Barthes, "the voice, the direct product of castration, the complete, connected evidence of deficiency."[6] Balzac's story places the reader in a new relation to voice, for voice has become a mask that conceals not a presence but a "deficiency," *un manque.*

Such an interpretation of voice signals the beginning of the ending of

5. Jacques Derrida, *Dissemination,* trans. Barbara Johnson (Chicago: University of Chicago Press, 1981), 277.
6. Barthes, *S/Z,* 110.

the Platonic notion of voice as presence. Anamnesis enables memory to make voice present to the self in the absence of the voice. In Barthes' reading of Balzac, what voice belongs brings to presence is no longer identity, or the self-presence of the logos; for Barthes, what voice presences is an absence. But it is not a complete absence. It brings to presence neither voice nor the absence of voice. What it brings to presence is static, the ever more distant sound of the drift of voice toward forgetfulness and oblivion. Derrida's parodic characterization of the logocentric Plato who "plugged up his ears the better to hear-himself-speak, the better to see, the better to analyze,"[7] stands at the antipodes of Barthes' remark that in Balzac "the voice gets lost."

"Could one maintain," asks Lacan, "that the voice that guides Socrates is not Socrates himself?"[8] Lacan posed this question of the otherness of Socrates' inner voice in the seminar entitled *The Four Fundamental Concepts of Psycho-Analysis,* which he presented to an audience of nonanalysts at the *Ecole normale supérieure* in 1964. I do not know whether Barthes and Derrida were in attendance, but certainly no idea of Lacan's has proved more decisive to Barthes and Derrida than the one he outlines in this seminar concerning the "fading" of the atopical logos. Sixteen years later, in *The Postcard,* Derrida answers Lacan's question with a resounding "Yes!" The primal scene of *The Postcard* is generated by Derrida's discovery in the Bodleian Library at Oxford of Matthew Paris's engraving in a thirteenth-century fortunetelling book that depicts Plato standing behind the seated Socrates, who is writing at Plato's immediate and urgent dictation. Socrates writes, and the voice he hears, the voice that guides him, is Plato's. Here indeed is a parodic, prophetic image of the overturning of the metaphysical tradition. This image of the unmasking of the atopical logos is, as Derrida remarks, one that not even Nietzsche or Heidegger could have guessed. Like Barthes, Derrida wants to reconstruct the scene that is concealed behind the logocentric myth of identity. Matthew Paris's engraving marks the division that has always been concealed in the primal scene of the history of philosophy. Derrida uses the engraving to create what Barthes calls "tonal instability," for here Derrida causes the atopical voice to fade behind the interference of competing signals.

7. Derrida, *Dissemination*, 170.
8. Lacan, *The Four Fundamental Concepts of Psycho-Analysis*, 258.

In his early collection of aphorisms, *The Book of the Philosopher,* Nietzsche imagines the soliloquy of the last philosopher, whom he calls Oedipus. Nietzsche's Oedipus parodies Plato's Socrates as he announces the fate of the voice of philosophy at the end of the metaphysical tradition. The soliloquy consists of Oedipus's apostrophe to his "beloved voice," which is his own voice, "the last breath of the memory of every human happiness." Oedipus knows that when he dies the logos dies with him. But what Nietzsche depicts is not Oedipus's death but his death-in-life—his capacity, like that of metaphysics, to live on and on: "The last sigh, your sigh, dies with me, this long alas! alas! sighed upon me, the last woe-begotten Oedipus."[9] What the philosopher listens to during the epoch of the beginning of the ending of metaphysics is the interminable "fading" of the voice, the death-in-life of memory and the logos. Writing, Socrates prophesied in the *Phaedrus,* "will produce forgetfulness in the souls of those who have learned it because they will not need to exercise their memories."[10] The weakening of memory and voice makes the ending of metaphysics the epoch of "this long alas!" In the fate of Oedipus, Nietzsche describes the fate of voice in the epoch of its irreversible "fading."

Ernest Jones adopted the word *aphanisis* as a general philosophical term to describe the threat to the subject's desire presented by what Freud called "the castration complex"; it is as much a rebuttal as it is an extension of Freud's notion of castration. Lacan appropriates the concept and makes it one of the cornerstones of his system. For Jones as for Lacan, aphanisis—which derives from the Greek *aphanes* ("invisible")—defines the absolute threat to the subject's desire, the threatened erasure or "disappearance" through which the subject's desire must pass if it is to be sustained. For Lacan it is through the primal gap, or *béance,* created by aphanisis that the subject of desire comes to presence. Lacan appropriates the notion within a Heideggerian frame of reference. Like *Dasein*'s "being-for-death," aphanisis is a primordial process of subjectivization in which the subject is called to presence through a constitutive absence. Aphanisis, writes Lacan, "is to be situated at the level at which the subject manifests himself in this movement of disappearance that I have described as lethal."[11] For Lacan the

---

9. Friedrich Nietzsche, *Le Livre du philsophe/Das Philosophenbuch* (Paris: Aubier-Flammarion, 1969), 100–101.

10. *Phaedrus,* 274e, cited in Derrida, *Dissemination,* 102.

11. Lacan, *The Four Fundamental Concepts of Psycho-Analysis,* 207–8.

"fading of the subject" defines the most primal scene of subjectivization; the subject's relation to language and desire is structured around this primordial gap—the gap that Barthes calls the "hole in the discourse" through which voice can leak out.

In his autobiography, which is his most Proustian book, Barthes writes that proper names, "like voices, like odors, would be the terms of a languor: desire and death: 'the last sigh which remains of things,' says an author of the last century."[12] Barthes does not identify this author, whose words echo those of Nietzsche as well as Proust. In *Roland Barthes par lui-même* and throughout his work, Barthes has generated a series of such terms, the terms of an indefinite living on or a protracted instability, a languorous interval between memory and forgetfulness. For Barthes, the critical and aesthetic faculties are solicited, are called upon, at their most profound level by that which is most ephemeral, that which is destined to death and oblivion but still lingers. "The last sigh which remains of things" is what calls Barthes to thinking. Heidegger might have reminded Barthes that " 'to call' means also, and commonly, to give a name to something."[13] It is the "fading" of the name and of identity that gives the call of "the last sigh" its poignancy.

"Naming," writes Heidegger, "consists by nature in the real calling, in the call to come, in a commending and a command."[14] In the epoch of the beginning of the ending of metaphysics we hear the call, but we can no longer identify the voice; we can no longer trace the name to a single identity. It is the indecipherability of the call that accounts for the languor of the response. As the voice drifts into the distance, we find ourselves unable to take the first step; we find ourselves paralyzed by an unnameable languor. In addition to Barthes, we should mention Samuel Beckett's allusion to the lethargy of Dante's sinners in his Proust essay where he proclaims "the death of the subject," or Maurice Blanchot's similarly tortuous narratives of spiritual paralysis, which Derrida has labeled the rhetoric of the "*pas au-delà*," the non-step into a non-existent "beyond." In "the call to come," Barthes, like Beckett and Blanchot, hears only the tone of exhaustion, fatigue, and despair—only "the fading of the subject."

12. *Roland Barthes by Roland Barthes*, trans. Richard Howard (New York: Hill & Wang, 1976), 51.

13. Martin Heidegger, *What Is Called Thinking?* trans. J. Glenn Gray (New York: Harper & Row, 1968), 119.

14. Heidegger, *What Is Called Thinking?* 120.

Instead of discernible causes or origins, Barthes discovers only the
fetishlike *moiré* effect. Instead of identity and a determinable subject,
he discovers a series of competing tropes and figures. In the early
1870s, Nietzsche remarked that "it is on tropes and not on unconscious connections that our sensory perceptions rest." For Nietzsche,
as for Barthes, the senses are tropes. Prior to any understanding of the
real by the so-called subject, Nietzsche posits a tropology of the senses:
"The primal phenomenon is therefore confusion.—This presupposes
the act of seeing the forms [*setzt voraus das Gestaltensehen*]. The
visual image orders our perception, while rhythm does the same for
our hearing. From the eye we can never reach a representation of time,
and from the ear we can never reach a representation of space. To the
sense of touch corresponds the sensation of causality."[15] What is "in
place," "posited" (*setzt voraus*), before any subject whatsoever
is a tropic inmixing of the senses, a "primal confusion," "*une moiré
brillante.*" For Nietzsche, our representations of reality are simply projections of this tropology of the senses. What we mistake for the
structures of understanding are only projections of specific sensory
functions. The rhythm of the "fading of the voice" in the text returns
us to this "primal confusion," unable to glimpse the shape of time or
hear the rhythm of space.

There is in Barthes' *A Lover's Discourse* a section entitled "Fading,"
which Richard Howard translates as "Fade-out." In this brief four-
page meditation on the memory of ghostly voices "which exist only
after they have disappeared," Barthes knits together a series of allusions to St. John of the Cross, Freud, Proust, and Blanchot. Like St.
John, Barthes is "in mourning for an object which is itself in mourning." Like St. John, he has lost all desire because of the other's abandonment. The other is gone, never to return, and the lover is left alone,
"invaded by the Night."[16] In Proust, Barthes finds one of his constant
themes, that the subject is created in anxiety and is always in mourning
for the lost proximity of the mother. "The fading of the loved object is
the terrifying return of the Wicked Mother," writes Barthes, "the inexplicable retreat of love." "Fading" raises the Fort/Da game in *Beyond
the Pleasure Principle* to the level of an ontological structure. The
presencing power of the mother, who has withdrawn to a ghostly

15. Nietzsche, *Le Livre du philosophe/Das Philosophenbuch,* 135.
16. Roland Barthes, *A Lover's Discourse: Fragments,* trans. Richard Howard (New
York: Hill & Wang, 1981), 113.

distance from which she nevertheless continues to exert a haunting influence, plays for Barthes the role Being plays for Heidegger. The lover is paralyzed, unable to respond to the uncanny sound of her call. "I had to wait for Blanchot," says Barthes, "for someone to tell me about Fatigue."[17]

For Barthes, Being gives itself not through the presence of the voice but through the rhythm of its "fading." We can hear the voice, but can we hear the differential pattern, or rhythm, that underlies the texture of the voice? Barthes' notion of "fading" is an effort to describe the inaudible basis of the audible. Derrida writes that "the difference which establishes phonemes and lets them be heard remains in and of itself inaudible, in every sense of the word."[18] The "fading of the voice" is for Barthes the disclosure of this inaudible concealment.

> What constitutes the voice is what, within it, lacerates me by dint of having to die, as if it were at once and never could be anything but a memory. This phantom being of the voice of what is dying out, it is that sonorous texture which disintegrates and disappears. I never know the loved being's voice except when it is dead, remembered, recalled inside my head, way past the ear; a tenuous yet monumental voice, since it is one of those objects which exist only once they have disappeared.[19]

In his last work, *La Chambre claire,* where he locates this "fading" or disintegration of presence not in voice but in the photographic image, Barthes writes that his objective has always been to supply what he thought was lacking in classical phenomenology, "which never spoke of desire or mourning."[20] The whole of *La Chambre claire* is a meditation on a photograph of his mother, but this particular photograph is never reproduced in the text, for no reproduction could reproduce what is important to Barthes about the image of his mother as a child in the winter garden of her family's home. It is the peculiar rhythm of the image and the peculiar rhythm of the voice that create the "tonal instability," the "fading," of presence. In *La Chambre claire* he calls this destabilizing focal detail the "*punctum,*" the point in the

17. Barthes, *A Lover's Discourse: Fragments,* 116.

18. Jacques Derrida, *Margins of Philosophy,* trans. Alan Bass (Chicago: University of Chicago Press, 1982), 5.

19. Barthes, *A Lover's Discourse: Fragments,* 114.

20. Roland Barthes, *La Chambre claire: Note sur la photographie,* coll. Cahiers du cinéma (Paris: Gallimard/Seuil, 1980), 41.

image where presence seems to leak out, as the voice seemed to leak out through "the hole in the discourse" in *Sarrasine.*

In *Beyond the Pleasure Principle,* Freud describes the tone change that occurs when his grandson, as he attempts to master the anxiety of his mother's absence by restaging it, creates a shift in his voice from "the long-drawn-out 'o-o-o-o'" of the *Fort* (gone), to the short "aah" of the *Da* (there). What Freud calls the game of "disappearance and return" is an effort to master the instability created by the other's absence.[21] It is also an effort to hear the other's voice "way past the ear." It is an effort to hear the inaudible and to represent the unrepresentable. Everything rides upon the differential shift in the rhythm of the voice, and upon the break or perforation of the image. "*Punctum,*" we should recall, is Latin for a "point," or "moment," in time.

Barthes links the "fading of the subject" not to the "the pleasure of the text" but to what he calls, again following Lacan, "bliss" (*jouissance*): "Either relate the text to the 'pleasures' of life . . . and to it join the personal catalogue of our sensualities, or force the text to breach bliss, that immense subjective loss."[22] "What the text says," Barthes goes on, "through the particularity of its name, is the ubiquity of pleasure, the atopia of bliss." Bliss is equivalent to the "fading" and to the "punctum." It is what breaks the stable rhythm of pleasure and the continuity of representation. Bliss is the unrepresentable shift, the atopical, placeless moment of difference that underlies the "sonorous texture" of representation. Pleasure is memory, but bliss is the unstable ground of forgetfulness. *Jouissance* is a way of describing the effect of "the last sigh of things." It is Barthes' way of accounting for the ephemeral essences that underlie his "phenomenology of desire and mourning"—which is also a phenomenology of reading: "Reading and the risks of real life are subject to the same anamnesis": that is, to the same oblivion.

Someplace, in some atopical nonplace "way past the ear," Dora still hears her father's heavy breathing. Her illness is attributable, says Freud, to this unconscious, incorporated, arhythmic instability. It marks the "punctum" through which her subjectivity leaks out. In Barthes' idiom, Dora's hysteria is an uncontrollable "atopia of bliss."

21. Sigmund Freud, *Beyond the Pleasure Principle,* trans. James Strachey (New York: Norton, 1961), 8–9.
22. Roland Barthes, *The Pleasure of the Text,* trans. Richard Miller (New York: Hill & Wang, 1975), 58–59.

Borrowing Lacan's famous homonym, which Barthes has elaborated upon, we can say that Dora's *jouissance* is quite literally the effect of what she heard: "*j'ouis*/I heard," the *passé simple* of "*ouir*/to hear."

Doing analysis, like reading a text, involves pinpointing these inaudible alternations of tone, these shifts from the rhythm of the self to that of the incorporated other. Like Heidegger, Barthes uses the technology of the telephone to describe the fundamental ontology of the voice. For Barthes the "fade-out" of the other's voice over the telephone triggers a primal ontological anxiety. Heidegger describes much the same thing in *Being and Time* when, in response to "the call of conscience," *Dasein* discovers, to its amazement, that no one is on the other end of the line. Like the conscience of the criminal, *Dasein*'s conscience is silent. The telephone rings, but when *Dasein* finally brings itself to answer, there is only an indecipherable noise. The "call" is decisive for *Dasein* because it "gets its ontological understanding of itself in the first instance from those entities which it itself is not but which it encounters 'within' its world, and from Being, which they possess."[23] It is the purpose of the call that it " 'says' nothing which might be talked about, gives no information about events." What *Dasein* instinctively feels in this fearful confrontation with the "fading" of the voice, is guilt and anxiety:

> The call points forward to Dasein's potentiality-for-Being, and it does this as a call which comes from uncanniness. The caller is, to be sure, indefinite; but the "whence" from which it calls does not remain a matter of indifference for the calling. This "whence"—the uncanniness of thrown individualization—gets called too in the calling; that is, it too gets disclosed.[24]

What Heidegger calls "the uncanniness of thrown individualization" (*die Unheimlichkeit der geworfenen Vereinzelung*) constitutes the primordial threat, by virtue of which the subject becomes a subject. *Dasein*'s experience of "thrownness" is its response to the uncanny retreat or fade-out of the voice of the incorporated other. The call punctuates *Dasein* and opens it to "uncanniness." Freud's explorations of the "uncanny" in the experience of hypnosis, suggestion, thought transference, and telepathy, and in the transference generally, should like-

23. Martin Heidegger, *Being and Time*, trans. John Macquarrie and Edward Robinson (New York: Harper & Row, 1962), 85.
24. Heidegger, *Being and Time*, 325.

wise be regarded as extreme or marginal instances of what is a fundamental ontological experience of the subject.

Barthes describes his experience of "fading" on the telephone in
what is, I believe, one of the most brilliant and important passages in
all of his work:

> Freud, apparently, did not like the telephone, however much he may
> have liked listening. Perhaps he felt, perhaps he foresaw that the tele-
> phone is always a cacophony, and that what it transmits is the wrong
> voice, the false communication. . . . No doubt I try to deny separation
> by the telephone—as the child fearing to lose its mother keeps pulling
> on a string; but the telephone wire is not a good transitional object, it is
> not an inert string; it is charged with meaning, which is not that of
> junction but that of distance: the loved, exhausted voice heard over the
> telephone is the fade-out in all its anxiety. First of all, this voice, when
> it reaches me, when it is here, while it (with great difficulty) survives, is
> a voice that I never entirely recognize; as if it emerged from under a
> mask (thus we are told that the masks used in Greek tragedy had a
> magical function: to give the voice a chthonic origin, to distort, to
> alienate the voice, to make it come from somewhere under the earth).
> Then, too, on the telephone the other is always in a situation of depar-
> ture; the other departs twice over, by voice and by silence: whose turn
> is it to speak? We fall silent in unison: crowding of two voids. I'm
> going to leave you, the voice on the telephone says with each second.[25]

"*C'est le fading dans toute son angoisse.*" From the mask of ancient
Greek tragedy to the telephone, Barthes sketches a history of "fading"
that should be read in conjunction with Heidegger's projected history
of Being, for what Barthes suggests is that from Oedipus to Freud there
is another history, one not told in the history of metaphysics. According to Barthes' counterhistory, voice is not an assurance of self-presence. On the contrary, voice has always been a mode of distortion and
concealment, for along with its promise of presence, voice has also
proclaimed, by virtue of its "fading," a haunting message of distance
and absolute separation. For Heidegger, "man is a creature of distance," as he repeatedly reminds us through the use of such words as
werfen/to throw, *entwerfen, überwerfen, vorwerfen.*[26] This is what
Barthes means to suggest by emphasizing "distance" over "junction."

25. Barthes, *A Lover's Discourse: Fragments,* 115.
26. Martin Heidegger, *The Essence of Reasons,* trans. Terrence Malik (Evanston,
Ill.: Northwestern University Press, 1969), 131, 141, n. 43.

From Oedipus to Freud, Barthes seems to say, "the fading of the subject" opens a path to the "other scene" of metaphysics.

Barthes' parenthetical remark concerning the Greek tragic mask links the "fading" of the voice to the problematic of death; more important, perhaps, it suggests that this problematic links Freud to ancient Greek tragedy. Our entire notion of the "Oedipal" is, it seems to me, altered by Barthes' suggestion. The "uncanniness" of the "fading" of the voice is here implicitly linked to the notion of the Oedipal. Barthes enables us to propose a certain conjunction between Heidegger's "call" and Freud's Oedipus complex. The incorporated voice, the mysterious caller who produces anxiety and guilt in *Dasein,* belongs to a conscience that Freud has taught us to regard as Oedipal. Indeed, as Heidegger promised, the "whence" of the call is "disclosed," and it is Freud who discloses it.

In his famous letter to Wilhelm Fliess of October 15, 1897, Freud writes, apropos of *Oedipus Rex,* "Every member of the audience was once a budding Oedipus" (*ein solcher Ödipus*).[27] A little more than two years later, in a reworked version of that letter, he writes "that there must be something which makes a voice within us ready to recognize the compelling force of destiny in the Oedipus" (*Es muss eine Stimme im unserem Innern geben, welche die zwingende Gewalt des Schicksals im Ödipus anzuerkennen bereit ist*).[28] There is a "voice within us" that enables us "to recognize" the "compelling force" of *Oedipus Rex* because this voice has already told us all of this before. Because this voice has already called upon us, and because we have already forgotten it, the repetition of the entire process gives *Oedipus Rex* the appearance of "the compelling force of destiny." Our aesthetic and intellectual response to the tragedy of Oedipus is in effect the unconscious repetition of the primal scene of the call of conscience.

Dasein, writes Heidegger, "is authentically itself in the primordial individualization of the reticent resoluteness which exacts anxiety of itself."[29] It is this primal scene of "*ursprünglichen Vereinzelung*" that accounts for that "something which makes a voice within us ready." Lacan rewrites the Freudian scene of primal anxiety in Heideggerian

---

27. Sigmund Freud, *The Origins of Psychoanalysis: Letters to Wilhelm Fliess,* trans. Erich Mosbacher (New York: Basic Books, 1975), 223.

28. Sigmund Freud, *The Interpretation of Dreams,* trans. James Strachey (New York: Avon, 1971), 296.

29. Heidegger, *Being and Time,* 369.

terms and, once again, in connection with the problematic of aphanisis:

> It is in this point of lack that the desire of the subject is constituted. The subject—by a process that is not without deception, which is not without presenting that fundamental twist by which what the subject rediscovers is not that which animates his movement of rediscovery—comes back, then, to the initial point, which is that of his lack as such, of the lack of his aphanisis.[30]

This "fundamental twist" (*cette torsion fondamentale*) turns the subject, in its anxiety at the gap or "fading" of the other, back into itself, where it discovers not the self-presence it seeks but another, even more alarming lack. *Dasein* thus becomes "authentically itself" (*eigentlich selbst*) by virtue of this "fundamental torsion." Lacan's notion of a constitutive "twisting" or "torsion" recalls Heidegger's notion of the "stamping" or "imprinting" of Being (*Prägung des Seins*). Lacan places this Heideggerian notion of "primordial individualization" within a Freudian, Oedipal context. Both Heidegger and Lacan are predisposed to this technological turn of phrase when it comes to the "imprinting" or forging of subjective identity. We shall see shortly how important the image of "twisting" and "torsion" becomes for Heidegger. Above all, however, what should be noted here is that it is by virtue of the call, and the subsequent "fading" of voice, that this process of subjectivization is put into motion. We might regard this "fundamental torsion" as *Dasein*'s recoil into itself in response to the terrifying drift into the distance of the uncanny voice of otherness.

Jean-Paul Sartre provides us with a very well-known instance of primordial subjectivization in his analysis of Jean Genet's traumatic experience of naming, when at the age of ten Genet was called to consciousness as the result of being called a thief. Sartre discovers the compulsive repetition of this primal scene throughout Genet's oeuvre. In having been named, writes Sartre, he was transformed into a "constituted nature." Sartre's analysis consists in reconstructing Genet's creation of himself in accordance with the image that others forced upon him. This is the primal scene of Genet's theater, where he "makes himself an object for an invisible gaze"[31] and an inaudible voice.

---

30. Lacan, *The Four Fundamental Concepts of Psycho-Analysis*, 219.
31. Jean-Paul Sartre, *Saint Genet: Actor and Martyr*, trans. Bernard Frechtman (New York: New American Library, 1964), 60, 160.

The example of Genet reminds us once again of the theatricality of the Oedipal relation to voice. Heidegger himself makes this point about the theatricality of the subject: "Persona means the actor's mask through which his dramatic tale is sounded. Since man is the percipient who perceives what is, we can think of him as the persona, the mask, of Being."[32] Heidegger also writes of man "as the scene" (*als die Szene*) of Being. The notion of man as the mask or scene of Being is part of Heidegger's refashioning of modern thought in the image of ancient Greece. Like Barthes, Heidegger realizes a new meaning for the "magical function" of the mask. The mask alters the sound of the voice. In covering the voice, the mask distances it and gives it a ghostly resonance. But as Heidegger points out, in concealing the voice, in keeping it hidden, the mask also preserves and protects it. What the mask reveals for Heidegger is the fundamental concealment of Being. In Heidegger the concealment of voice is inseparable from the oblivion of Being.

> In fact, the history of Western thought begins, not by thinking what is most thought-provoking, but by letting it remain forgotten. Western thought thus begins with an omission, perhaps even a failure. So it seems, as long as we regard oblivion only as a deficiency, something negative. Besides, we do not get on the right course here if we pass by an essential distinction. The beginning of Western thought is not the same as its origin. The beginning is, rather, the veil that conceals the origin—indeed an unavoidable veil. If that is the situation, then oblivion shows itself in a different light. The origin keeps itself concealed in the beginning.[33]

The Platonic "beginning" of Western thought is not simply an error that conceals the pre-Socratic "origin," for it is also this mask or veil that preserves and protects the origin. The mask of metaphysics preserves the origin of Western thought, just as the mask of the tragic actor preserves the chthonian origin of the voice of the dead. The history of metaphysics masks the history of Being, just as the persona of human subjectivity masks the question of Being. Heidegger's interest, however, is not in the direct comprehension of either the origin or Being. For him the task of thinking is to return to these fundamental concealments, and "to let Being be" behind the infinite play of masks.

32. Heidegger, *What Is Called Thinking?* 62.
33. Heidegger, *What Is Called Thinking?* 152.

In a provocative characterization of Lacan's work as an analyst, Stuart Schneiderman writes that "Lacan did not teach people how to get along with other people, but rather how to negotiate and to enter into commerce with the dead." A few pages later, Schneiderman cites a passage from *Ecrits* in which Lacan writes of the necessity for the analyst to take up a position "characterized by silence, by coming, one may say, to identify with the position of the silent dead. This does not mean that the analyst cannot talk to his patient, but everything he says will be taken as coming through a filter, as if coming from the dead."[34] Like the tragic actor, the analyst must wear a mask. The efficacy of the cure depends, Lacan seems to suggest, on his ability to entertain this play of masks. The success of the dialogue depends on this fundamental concealment. "The beginning is, rather, the veil that conceals the origin—indeed an unavoidable veil."

Prosopopoeia and the Incorporation of Metaphysics

At the end of his long reading of *Beyond the Pleasure Principle* in *The Postcard,* Jacques Derrida points out that contrary to what is often assumed, Freud does not actually say that the "death drive" (*Todestrieb*) is silent but only that it is "unobtrusive." The "death instincts," writes Freud, "seem to do their work unobtrusively" (*ihre Arbeit unauffällig zu leisten scheinen*).[35] What Freud means by "their work" is the repetition of unpleasurable sensations, which Freud observed in his grandson's Fort/Da game and in the blockage that occurs when the repetition of symptoms thwarts recollection. The problem Freud faces is that of determining precisely what the status of the death drive is. If it works "unobtrusively," then on what basis can he establish this theoretical construction, and more generally, how can observation be distinguished from speculation? Freud's rhetorical ploy is to suggest that everything he has done thus far in his career has been based on observation and that the death drive presents him with a sort of difficulty he has never faced before. As Derrida has no trouble showing, the speculation/observation opposition is Freud's way of deflecting his readers from realizing the obvious, that psychoanalysis has always been speculative. What Derrida calls the "double tonality" of Freud's

34. Stuart Schneiderman, *Jacques Lacan: Death of an Intellectual Hero* (Cambridge, Mass.: Harvard University Press, 1982), 63, 69.

35. Freud, *Beyond the Pleasure Principle,* 57.

writing is attributable to Freud's difficulty in situating his discourse in the differential space between observation and speculation.[36] In the terms of my argument, the difficulty is more directly attributable to the necessity of situating his discourse in the undefinable differential space between recollection and forgetfulness. What he must try to do is to formulate a grammar or a syntax of the death drive, some means of locating that which is never present, of indicating where in the patient's discourse the analyst might deduce that the "unobtrusive" work of the death drive is in progress.

Once again, it is all a question of rhythm and tone. Because Freud's element is the speech of his patients, his accounts of shifts or changes in "cathexis" should be read in terms of the phenomenology of psychoanalytic listening. Freud asks whether the shift from pleasure to unpleasure "indicates a change in the magnitude of the cathexis within *a given unit of time*" (italics in the English but not the German). By reading the expression "a given unit of time" (*Zeitenheit*) in conjunction with the unobtrusiveness of the death drive, Derrida is able to pose a very Heideggerian question about the temporal or rhythmic division that characterizes the work of death: "Something that has to do, not with silence, but with time, with units of time, and therefore with rhythm. . . . Inseparable from the phenomena of 'binding' (of pleasure-unpleasure) and of 'cathexis' (or 'investment'), these units of time cannot help but be metrical or rhythmical values."[37] In the very last paragraph of *Beyond the Pleasure Principle,* Freud speaks of "a peculiar tension which is in its turn either pleasurable or unpleasurable." Following Derrida's suggestion, we might translate that expression, "a peculiar tension" (*einer eigentümlichen Spannung*) as "a specific rhythm," a specific investment in "a unit of time." Is this not Freud's way of talking about the underlying temporality of the pattern of the patient's speech? Lacan remarks that the pathological subject has always taken either too much pleasure or too little pleasure in the primal scene.[38] This "peculiar rhythm" would be Freud's characterization of the temporality of what Heidegger calls the subject's "primordial individualization." The patient who cannot remember is bound by a rhythm and under the spell of either too great or too deficient an investment "in a given unit of time." The task of analysis would be to

36. Jacques Derrida, *La Carte postale: De Socrate à Freud et au-delà* (Paris: Aubier-Flammarion, 1980), 415.
37. Derrida, *La Carte postale,* 435.
38. Lacan, *The Four Fundamental Concepts of Psycho-Analysis,* 69–70.

lift or alternate that captivating rhythm and enable the patient to be free to live and enjoy.

What the patient needs is precisely the "plural style" and the "double tonality" that Derrida discovers in the Freudian text. The patient is cured by recognizing and perhaps even being able to alter the rhythm that has been "stamped" or "imprinted" in him or her. With respect to the question of rhythm, the psychoanalytic cure and the Heideggerian overcoming of metaphysics are in a fundamentally analogous position. Lacan once again makes the link explicit by referring to the subject's "primordial individualization" as a "fundamental torsion."

"Torsion" is the term the late Heidegger uses to describe the effect of his reading upon the history of metaphysics. Though we must not forget that Freud is dealing with patients and Heidegger with texts, what is important for us here is that Freud reads the speech of his patients in much the same way that Heidegger reads the texts of the history of philosophy. In *The Question of Being* (1955), Heidegger made an important decision to change the "overcoming" (*Überwindung*) of metaphysics to the "twisting" or "torsion" (*Verwindung*) of metaphysics. By doing so he hoped to avoid the sort of misunderstanding that had appeared in Ernst Jünger's essay entitled "Over the Line" (*Über die Linie*), written in honor of Heidegger's sixtieth birthday. Jünger read Heidegger's "overcoming of metaphysics" as the "ending of metaphysics." In his response to Jünger five years later, Heidegger wanted to make it clear that it was not a question of "crossing over the line" and leaving metaphysics behind but rather of learning to think "on the line" (also *über die Linie*) that is between metaphysics and its "overcoming," which is the zone where thinking takes place in the epoch of the beginning of the ending of metaphysics. It was to make this perfectly clear that Heidegger proposed the word "*Verwindung*"; instead of "crossing the line," it was a question of "twisting the line," of "wrenching the line" so that concealments long hidden in the history of metaphysics could be revealed. Heidegger proposed that we learn to think *de linea*, "on the line," rather than *trans lineam*, "across the line."[39] The movement from *Überwindung* to *Verwindung* must also

39. Martin Heidegger, *The Question of Being/Zur Seinsfrage*, trans. William Kluback and Jean Wilde (New York: Twayne, 1958). See Philippe Lacoue-Labarthe's discussion of the *Überwindung/Verwindung* question in his essay "L'Obliteration," in *Le Sujet de la philosophie* (Paris: Aubier-Flammarion, 1979), 179 n. 18. I discuss this question in greater detail, and with specific reference to Heidegger's relation to Ernst Jünger, in my essay "The 'Demolition Artist': Nihilism, Textuality, and Transference in the Work of Maurice Blanchot and Ernst Jünger," *Boundary* 2 10 (1982): 251–71.

be considered in light of Heidegger's roughly contemporaneous recognition of the insurmountability of forgetfulness and the persistent concealment of Being. Because the ontological difference between Being and beings can never be recollected, because metaphysics is not properly over, because it has not actually reached its "end," Heidegger now finds that *Verwindung* is a more appropriate term to describe the task of thinking. Derrida has made a point of distinguishing the "end" of metaphysics from the "closure" of metaphysics, and he writes of Heidegger's *Überwindung* of metaphysics as an "eschatological" notion, which, as Derrida notes, is what Heidegger himself calls it.[40] But Derrida does not mention that Heidegger in no way identifies his own project with such a notion. Derrida does not appear to want to acknowledge that Heidegger's discrimination between the *Überwindung* and the *Verwindung* of metaphysics in every respect anticipates Derrida's "own" distinction *"entre la clôture et la fin."* Heidegger's history of Being, his rereading of the history of philosophy, makes precisely the point Derrida makes when he writes that "the ending has always already begun." Derridean closure and Heideggerian "torsion" make the same point about the beginning of a new kind of reading, and a new kind of listening. For both Derrida and Heidegger, the closure or *Verwindung* of metaphysics makes it possible to decipher the "double tonality" of texts, and to hear other voices and other rhythms.

By postulating the death drive, Freud attempts to account for the absolute resistance to recollection that he meets in the transference. Freud has long since acknowledged the concealment of the origin, and the notion of the death drive is his attempt to deal globally with the implications of the domination of repetition over recollection. While one hopes to change the patient's rhythm, it is no longer a question for Freud of overcoming the obstacles to recollection. It is rather a question of learning to live within the limited possibilities afforded by analytic constructions. In Heidegger's idiom, there is no crossing over the line of forgetfulness but rather an effort to learn to accept the fact that analysis is caught in the undecidable zone, caught "on the line," between memory and forgetfulness. By proclaiming that his speculations proceed only in the most hesitant and limping fashion, Freud acknowledges what Heidegger admits to Jünger: that there is no beyond, that there is no way to cross the preontological line, no way to overcome metaphysics once and for all.

40. Jacques Derrida, *D'un ton apocalyptique adopté naguère en philosophie* (Paris: Galilée, 1983), 60–61.

In a note to her translation of some of Heidegger's later essays, Joan Stambaugh suggests that *Verwindung* be translated as "incorporation": "When something is overcome in the sense of being *verwunden*, it is, so to speak, incorporated. For example, when one "overcomes" a state of pain, one does not get rid of the pain. One has ceased to be preoccupied with it and has learned to live with it. Thus, to overcome metaphysics would mean to incorporate metaphysics, perhaps with the hope, but not with the certainty, of elevating it to a new reality."[41] "Overcoming," writes Heidegger, "is worthy of thought only when we think about incorporation."[42] The task of thinking is the task of reading "the primal incorporation of the oblivion of Being." Caught in what Heidegger's *Question of Being* calls "the withdrawing wake" of metaphysics, we discover that through our reading of the tradition we incorporate metaphysics, and that by forgetting Being—just as the history of metaphysics has always forgotten Being—we come to understand more about the history of that forgetting than we would otherwise be able to do. We can read "the primal incorporation of the oblivion of Being" only when we have "ceased to be preoccupied" with metaphysics. Stambaugh's translation of *Verwindung* as "incorporation" reminds us that we uncover the concealments incorporated within the history of philosophy only by incorporating them in our turn.

We can also use *Verwindung* as "incorporation" to link Freud and Heidegger, for in psychoanalytic theory, "incorporation" constitutes the most irreversible psychical defense against recollection. For both Heidegger and Freud, it describes the most profound concealment and forgetting.

The French psychoanalyst Nicolas Abraham is largely responsible for having made "incorporation" an important notion in contemporary psychoanalytic theory.[43] For Abraham, incorporation is a radical defense mechanism that goes into effect when introjection fails. Incorporation is the ego's unconscious defense against something toward which it has such a profoundly divided attitude that it is unable either to introject or reject it; the ego can neither tolerate nor do without the

41. Martin Heidegger, *The End of Philosophy*, trans. Joan Stambaugh (New York: Harper & Row, 1973), 84 n. 1.

42. Heidegger, *The End of Philosophy*, 91.

43. Nicolas Abraham and Maria Torok, *L'Ecorce et le noyau* (Paris: Aubier-Flammarion, 1978), esp. 259–75.

object. As a result, the ego installs the object in a place inside itself that is henceforth split off from the self and forgotten. Incorporation, then, involves a profound split within the ego, which forms what is in effect a secondary unconscious, neither properly inside nor outside the ego, neither properly subjective nor objective. The words or images associated with the object are henceforth buried alive in what Abraham calls a "crypt" inside the ego. The forgetfulness to which the crypt is condemned is absolute and irreversible.

Though Freud does not use the word "incorporation" in this connection, he does theorize about the same process; the basis for all of Abraham's thinking on this question is Freud's notion of *Verwerfung,* or "repudiation," in the Wolf-Man case history (see Chapter 4). Lacan also based his theory of "foreclosure" on *Verwerfung.* Abraham's understanding of incorporation builds on these precedents.

In his essay "Mourning and Melancholia" (1917), which is contemporary with *From the History of an Infantile Neurosis,* Freud describes the process Abraham will call incorporation. The melancholic patient experiences the loss of the loved object so intensely that in order to avoid at all costs the reality of separation, the ego incorporates the lost object and then treats it as part of itself. For Freud, the precipitating cause of the melancholic's disorder is his or her ambivalence toward the lost object. The patient's feeling of guilt at the death of the loved one, as the result perhaps of a deep-seated satisfaction or relief at the other's death, creates an impasse that blocks the normal process of mourning as introjection. Here is Freud's classic formulation of the formation of the split within the ego:

> Thus the shadow of the object fell upon the ego, so that the latter could henceforth be criticized by a special mental faculty like an object, like the forsaken object. In this way the loss of the object became transformed into a loss in the ego, and the conflict between the ego and the loved person transformed into a cleavage between the criticizing faculty of the ego and the ego as altered by the identification.[44]

Such a "cleavage" (*Zweispalt*) marks the site of incorporation. In the notion of the *Zweispalt,* psychoanalytic theory approximates Heidegger's "primal incorporation of the oblivion of Being." Like the melan-

---

44. Sigmund Freud, *General Psychological Theory* (New York: Collier, 1972), 170. "Mourning and Melancholia" is translated by Joan Riviere.

cholic's relation to the lost object, thinking in the epoch of the closure of metaphysics cannot fully overcome the lost metaphysical object. Overcoming ontotheology is not unlike overcoming a death in the family. Metaphysics, like the loved person, can be overcome only by being incorporated. What Freud posits as a marginal and pathological process becomes in Heidegger the fundamental event in the history of philosophy.

Derrida describes the status of thinking during the closure of metaphysics as a kind of "half-mourning" (*demi-deuil*). He is alluding to the nineteenth-century style of dress, particularly the kind of veil designed for the interval between the end of mourning proper and the return to normalcy. The beginning of the ending of metaphysics would thus be in a most precarious "*entre-deux*" between mourning and melancholia. Criticism and theory would thus be, as Derrida says, both "the work *of* mourning and the work *about* mourning, the work of mourning in all its forms: reappropriation, interiorization through introjection or incorporation, or between the two (half-mourning again), idealization, nomination, etc."[45] Half-mourning describes the fate of reading in the epoch of the non-event, of the Mallarméan "constellation," Proustian involuntary memory, or Valéry's ambiguous object. Half-mourning describes the fate of thinking where one is in part outside metaphysics but still under its spell, where one has forgotten metaphysics but still remembers that something has been forgotten.

The veil of half-mourning is a kind of mask, and no less than the tragic mask of the ancient stage, it has a "magical function" linked to the ancestral rituals of death. The Greek *prosōpon* and the Latin *persona* signify an inseparable connection between the theatrical and the chthonian. They signify the inseparable connection between taking on the voice of the other and mourning. In assuming the voice of the dead, the masked actor performs an act of half-mourning, reminding the audience not only that the voice that speaks is already dead but also that it lives on behind the mask. With each utterance the voice announces that it is neither properly dead nor alive but somewhere between the two.

The rhetorical figure of "prosopopoeia" derives from the Greek *prosōpon poiein*, "to confer a mask." Prosopopoeia is the figure of the mask, of the masking of the voice, and of the voice as mask. As such, it

45. Jacques Derrida, "Ja, ou le faux-bond," *Digraphe* 11 (1977): 98.

is a figure for the half-mourning that is the task of thinking during the closure of metaphysics.

In two of his later essays, Paul de Man focuses on the figure of prosopopoeia. In the first, on William Wordsworth's *Essays upon Epitaphs,* de Man describes "the prosopopoeia of voice and name" as "a figure of reading or understanding that occurs, to some degree, in all texts."[46] In the second, on Percy Shelley's last poem, *The Triumph of Life,* in which "Mask after mask fell from the countenance / And form of all," de Man reflects on prosopopoeia as the veritable trope of tropes: "To read is to understand, to question, to know, to forget, to erase, to efface, to repeat—that is to say, the endless prosopopoeia by which the dead are made to have a face and a voice which tells the allegory of their demise and allows us to apostrophize them in our turn."[47] The "endless prosopopoeia" is de Man's marvelous phrase for the fate of reading in the epoch of half-mourning at the beginning of the ending of metaphysics. Through prosopopoeia or the masking of voice, de Man traces in tropological terms what Lacan and Barthes call "the fading of the voice." The falling away of the masks is Shelley's figure for the slipping away of the shadows or simulacra of the self. Shelley explicitly links the "endless prosopopoeia" to the work of death, for they die "soonest from whose forms most shadows past." In Shelley's idiom, the ontotheological tradition is at once a "triumphal pageant" and a "ghastly dance." The procession Shelley depicts will go

---

46. Paul de Man, "Autobiography as De-facement," *MLN* 94 (1979): 926.

47. Paul de Man, "Shelley Disfigured," in *Deconstruction and Criticism,* ed. Harold Bloom et al. (New York: Seabury Press, 1979), 68. Shelley's poetry is cited from *Shelley's Poetry and Prose,* ed. Donald Reiman and Sharon Powers (New York: Norton, 1977). Of the pre-Romantic tradition of the mask, Mikhail Bakhtin writes: "The mask is related to transition, metamorphoses, the violation of boundaries, to mockery and familiar nicknames. It contains the playful element in life; it is based on a peculiar interrelation of reality and image, characteristic of the most ancient rituals and spectacles" (*Rabelais and His World,* trans. Helene Iswolsky [Cambridge, Mass.: MIT Press, 1968], 40). Bakhtin's characterization of the Romantic mask speaks directly to *The Triumph of Life* and to the question of the mask's relation to the closure of Western metaphysics: "The Romantic mask looses entirely its regenerating and renewing element and acquires a somber hue." Concerning Shelley's mask in *The Triumph of Life,* Shelley's editors suggest that Rousseau's elaboration of his amorous crisis in *Julie* is an important element. Shelley doubtless saw in Rousseau's romantic dilemma an image of his own amorous entanglements. And Harold Bloom has made a decisive case for the presence of Wordsworth behind Shelley's Rousseau (*Poetry and Repression* [New Haven, Conn.: Yale University Press, 1976], 107). Wordsworth's loss of poetic voice and Rousseau's affair with Mme. D'Houdetot enabled Shelley to mold his own death mask in *The Triumph of Life.*

on indefinitely, for it is the dance of the death-in-life and the life after
death of metaphysics. What Shelley describes is a cycle of infinite
forgetting and masking. In the poem, Rousseau recounts to the narrator that his visionary experience condemns him to perpetual forgetfulness. Forgetting and death are the motive forces propelling the procession onward.

In *The Triumph of Life* prosopopoeia appears, as it often does, in
conjunction with the related figures of apostrophe and dialogism. For
most of the poem the discourse is accorded to the "grim Feature," the
"strange distortion," that was Rousseau. Prosopopoeia, wrote Pierre
Fontanier in 1830, only eight years after Shelley wrote the poem,
"consists in somehow staging [*mettre en quelque sorte en scène*] those
who are absent, the dead, supernatural beings, or even inanimate
beings."[48] Fontanier's definition reminds us that prosopopoeia stages
what has always been the primal scene of analytic understanding:
namely, the return of the dead and the haunting recollection of forgotten voices and incorporated selves. Prosopopoeia stages the fundamental relation of the subject to voice.

De Man calls prosopopoeia the trope of the "fiction of address."[49]
Prosopopoeia establishes the relation to voice, the "fiction of address,"
as that of an insurmountable concealment, for in establishing the fictionality of every mode of address, prosopopoeia reveals that we never
really know who is talking. Responding to Roland Barthes on the
subject of Poe's story, "The Case of M. Valdemar," Derrida remarked
that the ability to say "I am dead" is the "condition for a true act of
language."[50] The ability of language to signify prior to the possibility
of a referent, which is the point Derrida made to Barthes, is precisely
what prosopopoeia establishes.

Apropos of *The Triumph of Life*, J. Hillis Miller writes that what
compels us to reread the tradition is the search for the "latent ghost
encrypted within any expression of a logocentric system."[51] *The Triumph of Life* is a text of the tradition, but it has also incorporated the
tradition's "other scene," the parasitic disruptions of meaning and

48. Pierre Fontanier, *Les Figures du discours* (Paris: Flammarion, 1977), 404.

49. Paul de Man, "Autobiography as De-facement," 928.

50. Jacques Derrida, in the discussion following Barthes' "To Write: An Intransitive
Verb?" in *The Structuralist Controversy*, ed. Richard Macksey and Eugenio Donato
(Baltimore, Md.: Johns Hopkins University Press, 1975), 156.

51. J. Hillis Miller, "The Critic as Host," in *Deconstruction and Criticism*, 228.

sense that uncannily inhabit the primal scene of Western writing. What de Man calls "the challenge to understanding that always again demands to be read"[52] describes the uncanny call which that spectral voice makes upon us from within the texts of the tradition. It is a voice that is always "fading" into the distance, always borne away by the "ghastly," "triumphal" procession of time and forgetfulness.

Prosopopoeia of the Name

In *The Postcard,* Derrida recounts an incident that turns prosopopoeia into a phenomenological category. Walking in a park in Freiburg-im-Breisgau, Derrida says, he was approached by a man who thought he recognized him but "excused himself at the last moment." "He must suffer as I do," writes Derrida, "from prosopagnosia, a devilish impulse to find resemblances between faces, to recognize them, and then to recognize them no longer."[53] This anecdote introduces Derrida's account of his meeting with the ghost of Heidegger in Freiburg, which I discuss in Chapter 3. Here my interest is in Derrida's elaboration of de Man's "endless prosopopoeia" into the symptomatic, compulsive behavior of "prosopagnosia." Caught up in this *"entraînement diabolique,"* which is as much a "diabolical compulsion" as it is a "devilish impulse," Derrida and all those who suffer from prosopagnosia find themselves invariably falling into error on the very threshold of insight, discovering yet another concealment in the very act of disclosure.

To someone suffering from prosopagnosia—that is, someone who thinks in the epoch of the closure of metaphysics—the determination of identity is no longer possible in terms of a subject. Derrida writes that "the whole history of the postal *tekhnē*"—that is, the history of metaphysics—"tends to rivet destination to identity. To arrive is to reach a subject, to reach an ego."[54] In de Man's "endless prosopopoeia" and in Derrida's "compulsive prosopagnosia," reading no longer involves an event that can be represented before or for a subject. There is no longer one stamp, one voice, or one face but rather a series of postmarks, a legion of voices, an endless pageant of faces. The figure

52. de Man, "Shelley Disfigured," 68.
53. Derrida, *La Carte postale,* 203.
54. Derrida, *La Carte postale,* 207.

of prosopopoeia, in its masking of voice and name, places the univocal proper name under erasure.

For Derrida, the signature is a notion that enables us to overcome the metaphysics of presence inherent in the notion of the proper name. He describes the signature in terms that recall those Barthes and Lacan use to describe "fading" and aphanisis: "The signature has to remain and disappear at the same time, remain in order to disappear, or disappear in order to remain." The signature is the site of a "double demand," a "double blind," which deconstructs the identity inscribed by the proper name. Derrida's effort is to disengage the signature from the proper name. Like the primal scene, the signature is the complex non-event which the notion of the proper name hides and represses. Through a reading of the poet Francis Ponge, who signs not his proper name but a variety of common nouns, Derrida claims that the signature "is no longer linked to a single proper name but to the atheological multiplicity of a new signatura rerum."[55] What is properly Ponge is what is not Ponge at all: "*Et, proprement, le pas de Ponge.*" In signing "*éponge*" (sponge), Ponge suggests the extent to which "the sign sponges the signature." As the proper fades into the common, what seemed to be authentic and originary appears derivative. What seemed to be a face was actually only a mask. What seemed to be disclosure was actually only another mode of concealment. By disengaging the signature from the proper name, Derrida reveals a level of concealment that had remained encrypted within the metaphysical tradition.

"Every philosopher," writes Derrida, "denies the idiom of his name, of his language, of his circumstances, speaking in concepts and generalities that are necessarily improper."[56] Names sometimes have incorporated meanings that can determine our idiom without our ever noticing it. Derrida demonstrates this in many of his books and essays: in "The Parergon" he reads Kant's aesthetic theory in terms of "edges" and "borders" because, among other reasons, *Kante* is a German common noun that means "corner," "margin," "edge"; in *Glas* he reads Hegel in conjunction with the French *aigle* (eagle) and the German *Ekel* (disgust).[57] Decentering the subject is synonymous with displac-

---

55. Jacques Derrida, *Signéponge/Signsponge*, trans. Richard Rand (New York: Columbia University Press, 1984), 56, 60.

56. Derrida, *Signéponge/Signsponge*, 100.

57. Jacques Derrida, "Le Parergon," in *La Vérité en peinture* (Paris: Flammarion, 1978), 21–168; Jacques Derrida, *Glas* (Paris: Galilée, 1974).

ing the proper name into the common nouns that homonymically sound it out. Through the notion of the signature, Derrida is able to breach a textual mode that is common to literature, philosophy, and psychoanalysis. The signature opens the path to incorporated meanings that have long remained forgotten.

In an effort not to deny the idiom of my name, I should add that my own proper name was once translated and dismantled into common nouns in a scene of naming that was as much an unnaming as a renaming. Because it involves Paul de Man, I might call it a "prosopopoeian primal scene," for here a mask was conferred. It happened in 1977 when one of my colleagues introduced me to Paul de Man, in French, a language that still sounded foreign to me then: "*J'aimerais vous présenter M. Lukacher.*" To which de Man responded by turning prosopopoeia into a perfect pun, a perfect French homonym of the French pronunciation of my name: "*Ah! Je vois, M. 'Loup caché.'*" Though I had often heard my name pronounced in French, I had never before had a hint of de Man's pun. In effect, he was naming me "Hidden Wolf," like the white wolves in the Wolf-Man's dream, behind which Freud deciphered the primal scene. What made de Man laugh, what made Philip Stewart laugh, what made me laugh was the echo of Freud and the Wolf-Man and the suggestion that somehow psychoanalytic theory was caught up in this play of the signifier. Somehow we seemed to be laughing at Freud and his ability to name, which de Man had just parodied. The dismantled propriety of my proper name had become a synecdoche for the impropriety of naming in general.

Now, whenever I hear my name in French, particularly in a psychoanalytic milieu, that silent allusion to "*l'homme aux loups*" with his wolves hiding in the tree is always audible. De Man's pun made me realize the extent to which the proper name conceals the subject from him- or herself, made me see that naming is itself one of the most complex and effective technologies of concealment. To name is always to mask, to conceal, and in concealing, to reveal. De Man's pun revealed to me the fundamental unreadability of the subject. The conjunction of the proper name and the signature is always a "hidden place," "*un lieu caché.*"

In *The Postcard,* Derrida poses "a question apropos of the Wolf-Man: Does an 'incorporated' letter ever reach its destination?"[58] An

58. Derrida, *La Carte postale,* 209.

incorporated letter is one that has somehow gotten lost in the postal system, a dead letter of which all memory has been lost. The construction of the primal scene is the only way to remember something of which there is no memory. In constructing primal scenes, one in effect delivers the incorporated letter to what, for lack of a better term, we will call its destination. Like the primal scene and the history of Being, an incorporated letter is what gets lost; its destiny is to get lost, to leak out, to fade away. But without this fundamental and constitutive errancy there would be no language; there would be no World; there would be only Earth.

3 Interdictions

Hard task, vain hope, to analyse the mind
If each most obvious and particular thought,
Not in a mystical and idle sense,
But in the words of Reason deeply weighed,
Hath no beginning. . . .
I cannot say what portion is in truth
The naked recollection of that time,
And what may rather have been called to life
By after-meditation. . . .
Baffled and plagued by a mind that every hour
Turns recreant to her task; takes heart again,
Then feels immediately some hollow thought
Hang like an interdict upon her hopes.

WILLIAM WORDSWORTH, *The Prelude*

*La place de l'inter-dit, qu'est l'intra-dit d'un entre-deux-sujets,
est celle même où se divise la transparence du sujet classique
pour passer aux effets de* fading *qui spécifient le sujet freudien
de son occultation par un signifiant toujours plus pur.*

JACQUES LACAN, "Subversion du sujet et
dialectique du désir"

Forgetting Ontology

"I have forgotten my umbrella," writes Nietzsche in a random entry in his notebooks, which Derrida has taken as his text in *Spurs*. What can be said, asks Derrida, of the subject who remembers the act of forgetting? "The meaning and the signature that appropriates it remain inaccessible."[1] As Derrida reminds us at the end of *Spurs*, Heidegger had also used this citation from Nietzsche, or something roughly equivalent

1. Jacques Derrida, *Eperons: Les Styles de Nietzsche,* trans. Barbara Harlow (Venice: Corbo e Fiori, 1976), 97.

to it, in *The Question of Being:* "figuratively speaking" (*im Bilde zu sagen*), he compares the "forgetting of Being" (*Seinsvergessenheit*) to a philosophy professor who has forgotten his umbrella. Forgetting, Heidegger argues, "belongs to the nature of Being and reigns as the Destiny of its essence."[2] For both Heidegger and Derrida, Nietzsche's forgetting of his umbrella is the primal scene of philosophy in the epoch of the closure of metaphysics, where the philosopher must always remember to forget ontology, to forget that which had previously covered and protected the discourse of philosophy. Derrida wants to remind us of that which we cannot appropriate through meaning and identity, and Heidegger wants to remind us that the forgetting of the Being question is the task of thinking.

The task of psychoanalysis is also to remind the patient that what is most essential has always already been forgotten. Instead of "I have forgotten my umbrella," the analysand must learn to say, "I have forgotten the primal scene." While Heidegger argues that forgetting protects and shelters the Being question, Lacan argues that it is unconscious phantasy that protects the real. Speaking of the Wolf-Man case, Lacan observes: "The exceptional importance of this case in Freud's work is to show that it is in relation to the real that the level of phantasy functions. The real supports the phantasy, the phantasy protects the real."[3] It is unconscious phantasy that forgets the primal scene and, in so doing, "protects the real" in the act of concealing it, just as forgetting protects the question of Being. The Heideggerian echoes of Lacan's account of the task of analysis are very clear in the following passage: "The gap of the unconscious may be said to be pre-ontological. I have stressed that all too often forgotten characteristic—forgotten in a way that is not without significance—of the first emergence of the unconscious, namely, that it does not lend itself to ontology."[4] The unconscious is preontological because "it is neither being, nor non-being, but the unrealized." And it is this fundamental aspect of the unconscious that Lacan rightly believes psychoanalysis tends to forget. What Lacan establishes is a link between the Heideggerian problematic of the "forgetting of Being" and the psychoanalytic theory of unconscious phantasy.

2. Cited in *Eperons*, 111.

3. Jacques Lacan, *The Four Fundamental Concepts of Psycho-Analysis*, trans. Alan Sheridan (New York: Norton, 1981), 41.

4. Lacan, *The Four Fundamental Concepts of Psycho-Analysis*, 29.

In his essay "On Systematically Distorted Communication" (1970), Jürgen Habermas makes an important point about the implications of the notion of the primal scene for the larger question of hermeneutic understanding. He argues that what he calls "scenic understanding" places psychoanalysis beyond "simple hermeneutics" and brings us to "the very structure of communication, hence, the basis of all translation":

> "Scenic understanding" is therefore based on the discovery that the patient behaves in the same way in his symptomatic scenes as he does in certain transference situations; such understanding aims at the reconstruction, confirmed by the patient in an act of self-reflection, of the original scene. . . . Scenic understanding makes it possible to "translate" the meaning of the pathologically frozen communication pattern which had hitherto been unconscious and inaccessible communication.[5]

Scenic understanding joins causal explanatory power to the larger problematic of hermeneutic translation. Habermas is perhaps too sanguine in his estimation that analysis can reveal the "real" origins, and in his implicit suggestion that the patient's "act of self-reflection" confirms the origin through recollection. The drift of Habermas's essay as a whole is far too positivistic in the claims it makes for psychoanalysis. Nevertheless, his point about the hermeneutic implications of the primal scene, if we do not see them as confirming the scene's reality, provides an important link between unconscious phantasy and "the basis of all translation." For Habermas is claiming nothing less than that scenic understanding, which I regard as synonymous with the work of unconscious phantasy, is linked to the most fundamental structure of communication. Scenic understanding takes us beyond "simple hermeneutics" because here we are no longer concerned only with the translation of one language into another but with the most elemental translation from the prelinguistic state to language itself. We need not go as far as Habermas and claim that analysis can reveal the pre- or extralinguistic referent. The point is not that analysis can unveil the real but that scenic construction brings us to the most fundamental concealment. By means of the primal scene and unconscious phantasy,

5. Jürgen Habermas, "On Systematically Distorted Communication," *Inquiry* 13 (1970): 208–9.

psychoanalysis leads us to the insurmountable threshold that Lacan calls the "real."

"From *The Introduction to Metaphysics* onward," writes Derrida, "Heidegger renounces the project of and the word ontology."[6] Heidegger did not publish these 1935 lectures until 1953. The appearance during the 1950s of Heidegger's lectures from the 1930s and early 40s had a tremendous impact on the emergence of the thought of Lacan and Derrida. Heidegger's *Kehre* of the 1930s thus influenced Lacan's own *Kehre* during the early 1950s. With Derrida, Lacan would doubtless have agreed that "one must therefore go by way of the question of being as it is directed by Heidegger and by him alone, at and beyond ontotheology."[7]

In the 1973 "Postface" to his 1964 seminar, Lacan returns to the ontological question that had preoccupied him throughout that seminar: Why should one bother to construct the discourse of analysis if one can never determine its relation to the real? This is a perpetually troubling question for Lacan, and one to which he must repeatedly return, as he does here when he reminds his readers that the circuit of desire with which analysis is concerned has nothing to do with ontology. Though the structure of unconscious phantasy with which analysis is concerned is related to the "real," that relation cannot be determined: "The artifice of the channels through which *jouissance* manages to determine what is read as the world . . . avoids the onto-, everyone take note, onto-, indeed ontotautology."[8] Lacan's "ontotautology" places ontotheology under erasure. We cannot forget that the "real" is what always remains forgotten. Though analysis never forgets that the work of phantasy and desire always leans on the real and protects it, it must never allow the ontological question to be more than (using Derrida's phrase for Heidegger's abandoned ontological project) "a necessary but provisional moment."

In his seminar entitled *Les Ecrits techniques de Freud,* which was presented in 1953—the same year Heidegger published his *Introduction to Metaphysics*—Lacan points out an interesting division in

6. Jacques Derrida, *Of Grammatology,* trans. Gayatri Spivak (Baltimore, Md.: Johns Hopkins University Press, 1976), 22.

7. Derrida, *Of Grammatology,* 23.

8. Jacques Lacan, *Les Quatres Concepts fondamentaux de la psychanalyse* (Paris: Seuil, 1973), 254 (Lacan's "Postface" to the French edition is not included in Sheridan's English translation).

Freud's attitude toward the work of unconscious phantasy. Once again it is the Wolf-Man case history that, for Lacan, signals the turning point in Freud's career. With that analysis, argues Lacan, Freud had clearly established the preeminent role of the work of unconscious phantasy. Phantasy is related to the real, but the nature of that reality no longer has a determining effect on the course of the analysis: "From then on, the event became secondary in order of subjective references. In contrast, the dating of the trauma remained for him a problem that it suited him to preserve, a problem that he preserved, if I can say so, *mordicus*."[9] In other words, Freud continued to insist on dating the traumatic scene even though he conceived of it as an undecidable phanstasmatic event. Even though he realized that dating the primal scene was impossible, he remained determined to do so. It is the division of Freud's attitude toward the ontology of the primal scene that makes *From the History of an Infantile Neurosis* the most extraordinary text in the Freudian canon. By using the word *mordicus*, Lacan means to suggest not simply that Freud held on to the possibility of a psychoanalytic ontology but that in effect he gripped it between his teeth and would not let go; he refused to relinquish the belief that analysis could somehow catch on to the real.

Lacan maintains that there are in effect two Freuds: one who has learned to forget ontology, and another who has bitten too deeply into ontology to let go. To get a better sense of this division, let us consider Freud's most important case prior to that of the Wolf-Man. In the Rat-Man case history, which is entitled *A Case of Obsessional Neurosis* (1909), we are confronted with an acutely paradoxical instance of the effect of Freud's steadfast belief in the reality of the traumatic scene. Lacan does not discuss the Rat-Man case in this connection, but I suspect that he must have been thinking of it when he characterized Freud's attitude toward the dating of the primal scene. If Freud is guilty of having preserved that concern for chronology *mordicus*, "held fast between the teeth," then what might we say of the Rat-Man, whose primal scene, Freud is convinced, is a scene of biting? Indeed, Freud so vehemently insists upon the historical reality of the biting scene that he inadvertently drives the Rat-Man from the analysis.

It is in this case history that Freud argues that the work of unconscious phantasy crases the relation to the real. True to Lacan's observa-

9. Jacques Lacan, *Les Ecrits techniques de Freud* (Paris: Seuil, 1975), 45.

tion about the division in his attitude, on the one hand Freud insists that the patient acknowledge the reality of the traumatic scene; on the other hand he argues that unconscious phantasy has erased the possibility that the reality of the scene can ever be reconstructed. "In constructing phantasies about his childhood," writes Freud, "the individual sexualizes his memories." For Freud, phantasy is sexuality, and sexuality emerges through and is indistinguishable from phantasy. The purpose of unconscious phantasy is "to efface the recollection" of the individual's "auto-erotic activities." Freud compares this process of forgetting the past through the work of phantasy to the way a country forgets its early history behind a fabric of myths and legends. But Freud does not forget that behind all of this there may still linger the trace of the real: the patient "brings commonplace experiences into relation with his sexual activity, and extends his sexual interest to them— though in doing this he is probably following upon the traces [*Spuren*] of a really existing connection."[10] Freud knows perfectly well that this is a theoretical matter and that it is unreasonable and impossible to expect that this hypothetical relation to the real could be confirmed clinically through the patient's recollection. His difficulty is in remembering to forget ontology. In 1909, and even as late as 1917, he finds it difficult to resist the temptation to believe in his own language, to believe in his hypothetical "probably" and those "really existing connections."

The insidious process through which Freud comes to believe in the reality of his own construction explains his emphasis in the Rat-Man analysis upon an account by the patient's mother, that between the ages of three and four the patient was punished for having bitten someone. At just the moment that Freud feels he is pressing close to the real, the patient's recollection fails. As in the Wolf-Man analysis, Freud becomes so encouraged by all the memories he has enabled the patient to reproduce that when he reaches back to the most primordial scene and finds that the patient's memory simply can reach no further, he is invariably at pains to readjust his sights, and thus the stage is set for the termination of the analysis. Freud's greatness as a writer inheres in the honesty with which he relates his own disappointments and anxieties,

---

10. *The Standard Edition of the Complete Psychological Works of Sigmund Freud*, ed. James Strachey et al., 24 vols. (London: Hogarth Press and the Institute of Psycho-Analysis, 1953–74), 10:206–7 n. 1. Subsequent references to this edition are cited in the text as *S.E.*

even if, as in *A Case of Obsessional Neurosis*, he buries the denouement of the analysis in the middle of a very long footnote. Though
Freud staked a great deal on the patient's ability to remember this
scene, the Rat-Man could recall nothing about it and abruptly broke
off the treatment. Freud recognizes that the mother's account need not
have been completely reliable either. Here is his sobering reflection:

> It was impossible to unravel [*abzuspinnen*] this tissue of phantasy
> thread by thread: the therapeutic success of the treatment was here the
> obstacle. The patient recovered, and his ordinary life began to assert its
> claims: there were many tasks before him, which he had neglected far
> too long, and which were incompatible with a continuation of the
> treatment. I am not to be blamed, therefore, for this gap in the analysis.
> The scientific results of psycho-analysis are at present only a by-prod-
> uct of its therapeutic aims, and for that reason it is often just in those
> cases where treatment fails where most discoveries are made. [*S.E.*,
> 10:207 n.1]

"The therapeutic success was here the obstacle" (*Das therapeutische
Erfolg was hier das Hindernis*); because the treatment had proceeded
so well, the patient's interest had returned to those things he had left
behind, and he was thus unable to focus on the course of the analysis.
That this is a very curious kind of "therapeutic success" becomes even
more apparent when Freud equates the scientific results of analysis and
its clinical failures. He seems to be saying that he almost regrets that
the Rat-Man analysis was not a greater failure, for he could then have
learned that much more from it.

Freud makes it very clear, however, that he placed great emphasis on
what he calls the Rat-Man's "childhood scene" (*Kindheitszene*) because he regarded it as a necessary "unconscious supplement" (*un-
bewusste Ergänzung*) which alone could explain how the patient's
relation to his father took its pathological direction. Here Freud assumes the "objective reality" of the reported scene in which the patient
bit his father, primarily because it makes his disappointment at the
patient's inability to recall the scene that much more understandable.
At the same time, the following passage calls into question what Freud
had earlier termed his "therapeutic success":

> I must confess that I had expected it to have a greater effect, for the
> incident had been described to him so often—even by his father him-
> self—that there could be no doubt of its objective reality. But, with

that capacity for being illogical which never fails to bewilder one in such highly intelligent people as obsessional neurotics, he kept urging against the evidential value [*die Beweiskraft*] of the story the fact that he could not remember the scene. And so it was only along the painful road of transference that he was able to reach a conviction [*Über-zeugung*] that his relation to his father really necessitated the postulation of this unconscious supplement. [*S.E.*, 10:208–9; translation modified]

The "supplement" is at once a cause and an effect, at once an origin and an end. "His relation to his father necessitated [*erforderte*]" some kind of "supplement"; whether it is this particular one or not remains to be seen, though this one certainly does appear to be the only piece that could fit the puzzle. Just how "painful" the transference was in this instance, and just how deep the patient's "conviction" was, we have already seen from Freud's footnote. Here in this passage, which is in the body of the text, Freud seems to be suggesting that the analysis was carried through to the end. It is not only the question of "holding fast" to something that Freud and his patient have in common; like his patient, Freud seems prone to forget the facts of the case before him, as well as some of the fundamental guidelines of his own theory. In other words, Freud no less than the Rat-Man appears to be caught up in the complex temporality of the primal scene, for it is because of his failure to maintain the ontological undecidability of the primal scene that the "road of transference" is so painful in this instance.

This case seems to anticipate the Wolf-Man análysis in Freud's attempt to describe from a theoretical perspective why the Rat-Man was unable to recollect the "childhood scene." It is from the same dilemma in the Wolf-Man case history that Freud goes on to theorize about the *Verwerfung* mechanism: on the one hand no one can possibly recollect the primal scene because of the intervening work of unconscious phantasy; on the other hand patients who fail to recollect such scenes, and all of them do, must have undergone some grievously abnormal repressive mechanism. By outlining these mechanisms, Freud is in effect rationalizing his inability to grasp the real through his patients' memories. In the Rat-Man's case, he sees the problem as originating in the patient's "exceptionally strongly developed sadism." The patient's love for his father was born in conjunction with "the sadistic components of the libido." Freud indicates the Platonic provenance of this notion with a footnote to Alcibiades' confession of his occasional hatred for the otherwise beloved Socrates in the *Symposium*. If the sadistic elements are overdeveloped, then they may undergo, writes Freud, "a premature and all too thorough suppression" (*eine vorzeitige und allzu gründliche Unterdrückung*; *S.E.*, 10:240). It is in this space of the "premature and all to thorough" that Freud will situate the notion of *Verwerfung* nine years later. In both instances Freud attempts to marginalize forgetting, and to avoid thinking about the always "premature," or should we say "untimely" (also *vorzeitige*), nature of forgetting. Freud's irrepressible desire to formulate a psychoanalytic ontology forces him from time to time into "ontotautology." Though he admits that he can provide only "a provisional explanation" for the patient's having forgotten the primal scene, it is also clear that Freud himself has momentarily forgotten that psychoanalysis is concerned with the kind of event that always blurs the distinction between remembering and forgetting.

"The Original Phantasy"

In their classic essay, "Fantasy and the Origins of Sexuality," Jean Laplanche and J.-B. Pontalis describe those elements of Freud's theory of unconscious phantasy that Freud himself sometimes forgets:

> The original fantasy is first and foremost fantasy: it lies beyond the history of the subject but nevertheless in history: a kind of language and symbolic sequence, but loaded with elements of imagination; a structure, but activated by certain contingent elements. As such it is characterized by certain traits which make it difficult to assimilate to a purely transcendental schema, even if it provides the possibility of experience.[11]

"Beyond the history of the subject but nevertheless in history." What is the nature of this "structure" that lies between the subjective and the transcendental, and that constitutes both of them without being assimilable to either? Laplanche and Pontalis published this essay in 1964, the year of Lacan's seminar on *The Four Fundamental Concepts of Psycho-Analysis*. With this notion of "the original fantasy," Laplanche and Pontalis situate us, as does Lacan, somewhere beyond epis-

11. Jean Laplanche and J.-B. Pontalis. "Fantasy and the Origins of Sexuality," *International Journal of Psychoanalysis* 49 (1968): 10.

temology but before ontology. In constituting "the possibility of experience" while at the same time being "difficult to assimilate to a purely transcendental schema," the "original fantasy" places us squarely in the zone of the preontological.

In Freud's theory it is through imagination that sexuality emerges. Sexualization is synonymous for Freud with the subject's self-objectification through phantasy. Phantasy is also, as we have seen, synonymous with the work of forgetting. The subject's sexualization is a process through which it remakes its own history; thus, for Freud, phantasy is also linked to the subject's experience of time. It is through phantasy that the subject's primordial experience of time is constituted. Near the end of his essay "Freud and the Scene of Writing," Derrida remarks that "we ought perhaps to read Freud the way Heidegger read Kant: like the cogito, the unconscious is no doubt timeless only from the standpoint of a certain vulgar conception of time."[12] The timelessness of the unconscious is an idea that simply does not stand up in light of Freud's own theory of the imagination. Freud wants to maintain that the unconscious does not have a time sense, yet his theory of phantasy plays a fundamental role in establishing the subject's temporality. As Derrida implies, the truth of the matter is not that the unconscious is timeless but that it involves a different kind of time sense, one that can perhaps be elucidated with reference to Heidegger's reading of Kant.

In *Kant and the Problem of Metaphysics* (1929), Heidegger argues that Kant, through his notion of the "transcendental imagination," anticipated his own notion of "primordial authentic temporality" in *Being and Time*. Heidegger's *Kantbuch* is a text that is fully committed to the project of a fundamental ontology. He enlists Kant as his major precursor in his effort to reveal "the disclosure of the internal possibility of the comprehension of Being." In rediscovering the radical temporality that lay hidden in the forgotten ground of metaphysics, Kant, and Heidegger after him, seeks nothing less than to "wrest from forgetfulness that which it thus apprehends. The basic, fundamental-ontological act of the metaphysics of Dasein is, therefore, a remembering [*Wiedererinnerung*]."[13] This is indeed a "remembering," not only

12. Jacques Derrida, *Writing and Difference*, trans. Alan Bass (Chicago: University of Chicago Press, 1978), 215.
13. Martin Heidegger, *Kant and the Problem of Metaphysics*, trans. James Churchill (Bloomington: Indiana University Press, 1968), 242.

for the history of metaphysics but within the context of Kant's own thought. Heidegger narrates a story in which Kant attempts to conceal and retreat from the radical implications of his theory of the transcendental imagination. Laplanche and Pontalis speak of the difficulty of assimilating imagination to a transcendental schema, and that is precisely the difficulty Heidegger believes Kant had. Through the transcendental imagination, Kant grasped the ground of both sensibility and understanding, sensation and thought. In so doing, he sought the conditions underlying the possibility of our experience of time and space and thus the ground of ontological knowledge. In the first edition of *The Critique of Pure Reason* (1781), Kant argued that through the a priori synthetic unity of the transcendental imagination, we discover "that appearances are not things in themselves but are the mere play of our representations, and in the end reduce to determinations of inner sense." This transcendent function of the imagination is, for Heidegger, a preeminently temporal determination. Though Kant does not proceed in this connection to "an explicit discussion of time," Heidegger believes that what Kant has discovered is the temporal basis of ontological knowledge, which, he argues, "is made up of 'transcendental determinations of time' because transcendence is temporalized in primordial time."[14] What Kant calls the synthetic unity of the transcendental imagination is for Heidegger "nothing other than primordial time. Only because the transcendental imagination is rooted in time can it be the root of transcendence." It is, in other words, through the transcendental imagination that the subject is constituted in time. For it is time that is at the root of our capacity both to feel and to think. The categories of sensory and conceptual experience are rooted in the primordial time-sense of the imagination.

Kant's epochal importance for Heidegger is due to his having remembered what had been forgotten since the beginning of the history of metaphysics: "By virtue of its indissoluble primordial structure, the transcendental imagination opens up the possibility of a laying of the foundation of ontological knowledge and, hence, of metaphysics."[15] But Kant himself, argues Heidegger, could not face the implications of his rediscovery of "the primordial ground of metaphysics." Because

14. Heidegger, *Kant and the Problem of Metaphysics*, 203. The Kant citation is from *The Critique of Pure Reason*, translated from R. Schmidt's collation of editions A and B by Norman Kemp Smith (London, 1929), 132 (A 101).
15. Heidegger, *Kant and the Problem of Metaphysics*, 202.

the "primordial ground" is none other than "primordial time," it is a ground that is no ground at all. Heidegger describes Kant's response to the instability of this primordial ground: "By his radical interrogation, Kant brought the 'possibility' of metaphysics before this abyss. He saw the unknown: he had to draw back. Not only did the imagination fill him with alarm, but in the meantime [between the first and second editions of the first *Critique*] he had also come more and more under the influence of pure reason as such."[16] What happened between 1781 and 1787, the date of the second edition, is that Kant transformed the transcendental imagination into a function of pure reason. Realizing how radically he had broken with the previous history of metaphysics, he sought to reestablish transcendence in the atemporal realm of pure thought: that is, on the stable ground on which the history of metaphysics has always sought to establish the conditions underlying the possibility of experience. Kant's "vigorous language" with respect to the imagination is "thrust aside and transformed" for the "benefit of the understanding." As a result of this egregious misunderstanding of his own insight, Kant ensured that the ground of metaphysics would once again be forgotten. As Heidegger also points out, the subsequent history of German idealism "accentuated" philosophy's blindness to this greatest insight of the Kantian critical spirit.

Freud forgets the primordial time of the unconscious just as Kant forgets the primordial time of the transcendental imagination. "The irreducibility of the 'effect of deferral,'" writes Derrida, "such, no doubt, is Freud's discovery."[17] And with the irreducibility of "deferred action," Freud inadvertently undermines the timelessness of the unconscious. The temporal spacing that characterizes the unconscious is of a different order from that of the conscious experience of time. The primordial time of the unconscious is the time of the "always already but not yet." It is what Heidegger, in his 1927 lectures, calls the time of the "always earlier." The irreducibility of time's deferred effects prevents any notion, be it that of the unconscious or of pure thought, from arresting the drift of what Derrida calls *différance*. Heidegger speaks of Kant's having remembered what had been forgotten since Plato, that "time is earlier than any possible earlier of whatever sort, because it is the basic condition for an earlier as such."[18] What Heidegger says of

16. Heidegger, *Kant and the Problem of Metaphysics*, 173.
17. Derrida, "Freud and the Scene of Writing," in *Writing and Difference*, 203.
18. Martin Heidegger, *The Basic Problems of Phenomenology*, trans. Albert Hofstadter (Bloomington: Indiana University Press, 1982), 325.

Kant might also be said of Freud. For in his discovery of the irreducibility of deferred effect, which is the structure of the "original phantasy," Freud no less than Kant has determined the radical temporality that underlies the possibility of experience.

At the end of *The Basic Problems of Phenomenology*, Heidegger argues that in remembering time as the trace of the "always earlier," which he here calls the "prius," Kant has in a sense fulfilled the terms of the Platonic doctrine of anamnesis. By remembering what Plato himself had forgotten, Kant in effect recollects the forgotten primal scene in the history of philosophy:

> Factically the existent Dasein has forgotten this prius. Accordingly, if being, which has always already been understood "earlier," is to become an express object, then the objectification of this prius, which was forgotten, must have the character of a coming back to what was already once and already earlier understood. Plato, the discoverer of the a priori, also saw this character of the objectification of being when he characterized it as anamnesis, recollection.[19]

Heidegger finds himself in the curious position of describing Kant's discovery of primordial time as though it were the effect of Platonic anamnesis. What forces Heidegger into this position is his recognition that the history of philosophy must in its turn be regarded in terms of the same radical temporality Kant has (re)discovered. The structure of recollection remains Platonic, though what is being recollected—namely, the temporality of being—is not what Plato remembered but what he forgot. Like the patient who has forgotten the primal scene, philosophy always forgets the temporality of being. Moreover, what is remembered, what is objectified, is the "always already" character of philosophical understanding. For if philosophy is to take seriously the radical temporality of the transcendental imagination, it must acknowledge the possibility that all of its discoveries have always already (*immer schon*) been forgotten.

Heidegger, then, must make it clear that he and Kant are returning to, are remembering, a certain Plato, not the "sham-Plato" who dares to speak of recollection as revelation but the Plato who is alert to the persistent undertow of forgetfulness. This is a difficult rhetorical point for Heidegger to make, for he must be careful not to adopt the rhapsodic tone of the "sham-Plato," which can be readily seen in a passage

---

19. Heidegger, *The Basic Problems of Phenomenology*, 326.

like the following from the *Phaedrus:* "Wherefore if a man makes right use of such means of remembrance, and ever approaches to the full vision of the perfect mysteries, he and he alone becomes truly perfect."[20] At the end of *The Basic Problems of Phenomenology,* Heidegger alludes approvingly to this section of the *Phaedrus.* It very much appears that by the end of these lectures Heidegger finds himself coming dangerously close to a kind of abyss. He wants to signal a return to the beginning of the history of philosophy and to make it clear that this return radically transforms the beginning. But by identifying himself with Plato's most ecstatic prose, Heidegger comes dangerously close to linking the project of a fundamental ontology to Plato's putative revelation of the "perfect mysteries." Heidegger's rhetorical dilemma here reveals some of the reasons for the "turning" that his thought will undergo. This kind of dilemma gives credence to his claim in the "Letter on Humanism" that the "turning" was always already in progress.

At the end of his 1927 lectures, Heidegger appears to find the prospect of a science of recollection so tempting that he seems almost about to claim to have established the ground of ontological knowledge. Like Freud when he cannot resist anticipating that the patient will recollect the primal scene, Heidegger at this point seems to have forgotten forgetting. The "turning" is doubtless an effort to protect himself from the threat of such rhetorical excesses.

It is particularly interesting, therefore, that Heidegger should check himself on the very precipice of the mystical by citing the words of Immanuel Kant, the man who checked himself in the second edition of the first *Critique.* We are still, of course, two years before the *Kantbuch.* Heidegger cites a long passage from Kant's late essay, "On a Genteel Tone Recently Sounded in Philosophy" (1796), in which Kant ridicules precisely the sort of Platonic mystical effusion Heidegger had come close to endorsing only a moment before. Using Kant, Heidegger tries to separate himself from the "enthusiast," the "philosopher of feeling," whom Kant ridicules. Of the "sham-Plato," Kant writes that "although he cannot lift the veil of Isis, [he] nevertheless [tries] to make it so thin that one can surmise the Goddess behind it."[21] It appears that Heidegger is using Kant to remind himself and his audience of the veil of forgetting that still conceals Being.

    20. *Phaedrus,* 249d, trans. R. Hackforth, in Plato, *The Collected Dialogues,* ed. Edith Hamilton and Huntington Cairns (New York: Bollingen/Pantheon, 1966), 496.
    21. Cited in Heidegger, *The Basic Problems of Phenomenology,* 326.

Derrida makes Kant's essay the subject of his own recent essay, "On an Apocalyptic Tone Adopted Recently in Philosophy," which is interesting not least of all for its absence of reference to Heidegger. This is particularly curious because, like Heidegger, Derrida turns to Kant in order to address some problems in his own style. Derrida is interested in understanding why his writing should be read as though it were proclaiming the "end" of this or that—of philosophy, metaphysics, literature, or what you will. But in so doing, he conceals—behind the veil, as it were—the Heideggerian primal scene at the end of *Basic Problems*. Derrida defines "the apocalyptic tone" as the "mixing of voices, genres, and codes" and as an "unmasterable polytonality." It is a tone that tells of the approach of the end, and of the difference between closure and end, but also reminds us that "the apocalypse is of long duration" (*l'apocalypse est de longue durée*).22 Like Heidegger's *aletheia*, Derrida's *Apokalupsis* also means "disclosure"; both suggest that there are limits to demystification, that concealment and closure persist within the notion of "disclosure." Like Heidegger's divided tone at the end of *Basic Problems,* Derrida's "apocalyptic tone" remains rigorously preontological, "well hidden under the avowed desire for revelation."23 Because since Plato the end has always already begun, "the apocalyptic tone" is a figure for reading the history of metaphysics. It is a figure for all those voices that have been forgotten in the text, all those voices that have always already spoken but not yet been heard.

Heidegger's Ghost

Even though Heidegger is never mentioned, his presence/absence haunts Derrida's "On an Apocalyptic Tone Adopted Recently in Philosophy." While Derrida does not accept the charges for the prank phone call he receives from someone pretending to be Heidegger, which is an anecdote recounted in *The Postcard*,24 "On an Apocalyp-

---

22. Jacques Derrida, *D'un ton apocalyptique adopté naguère en philosophie* (Paris: Galilée, 1983), 81.

23. Derrida, *D'un ton apocalyptique adopté naguère en philosophie*, 66.

24. Jacques Derrida, *La Carte postale: De Socrate à Freud et au-delà* (Paris: Aubier-Flammarion, 1980), 28. Also see Samuel Weber, "The Debts of Deconstruction and Other, Related Assumptions," in *Taking Chances: Derrida, Psychoanalysis, and Literature,* ed. Joseph H. Smith and William Kerrigan (Baltimore, Md.: Johns Hopkins University Press, 1984), 33–65.

tic Tone" is in every respect a response to Heidegger's call. We might say of Derrida's relation to Heidegger what Heidegger says of Kant's relation to Plato, that he is remembering what his precursor had forgotten; like an analyst, he is remembering the primal scene that his analysand had forgotten.

The ideal denouement to the analyst's construction of the primal scene would be for the patient to say, "It's as though I've known it all along. It's all coming back to me now." Derrida has precisely such an experience in the Bodleian Library at Oxford, where his friends Jonathan Culler and Cynthia Chase "staged" the "spectacle" that was his discovery of a postcard reproduction of Matthew Paris's prophetic drawing of Socrates writing. Derrida launches into a rather parodic stream of consciousness as he wonders why this drawing has such an effect upon him: "All that I don't know and all that I don't want to see also return in the deep waters of my memory, as if I had drawn or engraved the scene, since the first day when, no doubt, in a lycée in Algiers I first heard the names [Socrates and Plato]."[25] Like Heidegger at the end of *Basic Problems*, Derrida finds himself caught in the Platonic scene of anamnesis. Paris's engraving has triggered, however parodically, a kind of involuntary memory. Like Nietzsche or Baudelaire, Derrida thinks wistfully of "making anamnesis impossible," knowing well that anamnesis can never be overcome entirely.[26] Here is an event which like the Wolf-Man's dream, seems "no doubt" to repeat an earlier but forgotten scene. The lycée in Algiers is as close as he can come to reconstructing this scene. The engraving makes Derrida remember something that could explain the effect of this recognition, something that remains lodged between recollection and forgetfulness, a primal scene that seems always already to have occurred without actually having happened yet.

Two years after the scene in the Bodleian Library, Derrida recounts a trip to Freiburg, where Heidegger taught for many years. He introduces this visit with the anecdote about "prosopagnosia" that we discussed in Chapter 2. After the incident of mistaken identity, Derrida introduces the subject of Heidegger by way of the apparently unrelated topic of the "mystery" of laughter, particularly the sort of laughter associated with Jewish jokes: "Apropos of Jewish jokes, you can imag-

25. Derrida, *La Carte postale,* 23.
26. Derrida, *La Carte postale,* 28.

ine to what point I am haunted by Heidegger's phantom in this city. I came for him. I try to reconstitute all his pathways, the places where he spoke (the studium generale for example), to interrogate him, as if he were there."27 The punchline to this Jewish joke comes when Derrida recognizes that, like the man in the park who had mistaken him for someone else, he has mistaken Heidegger for someone else. After having communed with the ghost of Heidegger, Derrida buys two photographic albums, one on Freud and the other on Heidegger. Implying that perhaps this time he is willing to pay the charges for Heidegger's call, Derrida adds that "these books cost me a lot." But it has been worth the expense, for while leafing through the photographs of Heidegger, Derrida makes a surprising discovery: "I burst into laughter on discovering in Martin [Heidegger] the head of an old Jew from Algiers."28 This Jewish joke is yet another instance of prosopagnosia. The ghost with whom he has been talking in the streets and byways of Freiburg is that of Heidegger, but it is also that of someone else, some old Jew from Algiers, whose identity Derrida leaves suggestively open. Could it be the head of his professor at the lycée, the professor who first spoke the names Socrates and Plato? But might we not take this Jewish joke even further and suggest that there is something mysteriously paternal about the head of this old Jew from Algiers? Isn't the joke finally that Heidegger is a kind of father; that in this old photograph of Heidegger, Derrida sees the head of his father? Is not Derrida on the streets of Freiburg very much like Hamlet on the battlements of Elsinore communing with the ghost of his father?

The relation between Derrida and Heidegger is doubtless a filial one. One might see in their relation precisely the sort of "incredible chicanery of filiation and authority" that Derrida sees in Paris's inversion of the roles of Plato and Socrates, where the son dictates to the father the terms of his own legacy.29 If Plato determines just what Socrates will bequeath to him, then we might say that Derrida dictates the terms of his bequest from Heidegger. *From Socrates to Freud and Beyond,* reads the subtitle of *The Postcard.* Heidegger's ghost is situated in this "beyond." The names have changed, but the primal scene remains the same. In the primal scene of literature-philosophy-psychoanalysis, the son always dictates the legacy he will receive. Paris's engraving is the *fabula*

27. Derrida, *La Carte postale,* 203.
28. Derrida, *La Carte postale,* 204.
29. Derrida, *La Carte postale,* 68–69.

that stands behind Plato's oeuvre. It is the scene Plato stages in every dialogue. The father inscribes just what the son says he must. So too Derrida tells Heidegger's ghost just what to say. In the primal scene of his oeuvre, Derrida dictates to Heidegger's ghost what he wants him to leave behind, and the ghost obeys, just as Freud in *Beyond the Pleasure Principle* repeats in his speculative Fort/Da game what his grandson has taught him. Freud's effort to step from the "repetition compulsion" to the "death drive," like Ernest's game with the bobine and thread, is a game without progression or closure. It is the game that thinking and writing have always played, a game of illusory oppositions in which the repetitive "instinct for mastery" (*Bemächtigungstrieb*) is revealed in time, "unobtrusively," as the "death drive." The "step" is revealed as a mode of negation, "*le pas au-delà.*" The "writing" (*Schrift*) takes a "step" (*Schritt*) that leads nowhere. Whatever Derrida claims elsewhere about his putative overcoming of Heidegger, the primal scene of Heidegger's ghost in *The Postcard* tells us otherwise. Derrida cannot stop playing the Fort/Da game with the text of Heidegger. In Derrida's text, Heidegger wears many masks and speaks in many voices.

Bound by this "unobtrusive" rhythm of life/death, caught in the late technology of the "postal principle," the task of thinking and writing is "to work in several rhythms"[30]—that is, to alternate one's tone, to dissolve or "fade" the voice into a weave of voices.

In his *Heraclitus Seminar*, Heidegger remarks of the notion of *rhythmos* that it has nothing to do with flow or current but is instead related to the notions of "imprint" and "confinement"—which is to say that rhythm is the "stamp" or "imprint" of temporality that binds or restricts. Heidegger reminds us that Aeschylus's Prometheus "says of himself, '. . . in this rhythm that I am bound.' He, who is held immobile in the iron chains of his confinement, is 'rhythmed,' that is, joined."[31] Rhythm, for Heidegger, is a kind of "joint" or "fitting." Derrida's stylistic effort is to undo these "fittings" (*Fugen*) and "imprints" (*Gepräge*) by alternating them, by making the text speak in several voices. Though there is no way to ward off the ghost, and no way either to completely remember or completely forget the Heideggerian primal scene, the task is to make the ghost in the text speak in a different tone—indeed, in an "apocalyptic tone."

---

30. Jacques Derrida, "Ja, ou le faux-bond," *Digraphe* 11 (1977): 106.
31. Martin Heidegger and Eugen Fink, *Heraclitus Seminar 1966/67*, trans. Charles H. Seibert (University: University of Alabama Press, 1979), 55.

"Hanging Fire": The Primal Scene of *The Turn of the Screw*

> An obscure revelation of a referentiality that no longer
> refers to anything more than the evidentiality of an event
> that is no longer an event.
>
> JACQUES DERRIDA, "Préjugés"

Of the critics of Henry James's *The Turn of the Screw*, Shoshana Felman writes: "In repeating as they do the primal scene of the text's meaning as division, the critics can by no means master or exhaust the very meaning of that division, but only act the division out, perform it, be part of it."[32] Here indeed is a text whose "polytonality" cannot be mastered. Like the governess herself, the critic is thwarted whenever he or she tries to grasp the real and tries to wrest from the unmasterable tone of *The Turn of the Screw* a determinant or univocal meaning. At every "turn" James invites his readers to make a construction and to attempt a solution. But as Felman's essay "Turning the Screw of Interpretation" definitively establishes, there is simply no way to avoid repeating the text's fundamental division between the uncanny ghostliness of the governess's visions and the hysterical mechanisms that inform them.

The point I would like to make here, however, does not directly concern the difference between the psychic and the sexual. While Felman is quite right to demonstrate how James implicates the reader in every effort by the governess to construct the primal scene, and to demonstrate that the governess's dilemma as analyst is that of every reader, she does not pose the question of the precise nature of the governess's constructions. It is one thing to say that, try as they may, critics can never demystify the governess's mystification and are condemned to repeat it; it is quite another thing to say, as I shall, that James's interest is as much in the specific nature of the governess's process of construction as it is in the indeterminacy of the finished product. What neither Felman nor any other critic of *The Turn of the Screw* has analyzed is the specificity of the governess's visions/hallucinations. Numerous details and many of the most extraordinary scenes in the story have gone unnoticed, or at least unexplained, because the critical focus has been on the governess's state of mind rather than on the particularity of the vision in question.

32. Shoshana Felman, "Turning the Screw of Interpretation," in *Literature and Psychoanalysis: The Question of Reading Otherwise*, ed. Shoshana Felman (Baltimore, Md.: Johns Hopkins University Press, 1980), 113.

I want to make it clear, however, that without Felman's innovative reexamination of the controversy surrounding this text, I would never have been led to the reading that follows. Once again, the Heideggerian principle that errancy is not simply nontruth but rather the primordial "counter-essence" of truth has enabled me to recognize that the governess's errancy preserves traces of the truth of the events at Bly House. The Heideggerian-Derridean position with respect to the truth is not a pluralistic one. Though interpretation is a nonfinite process, this is not to say that all interpretations are equally valid, or that they are indeterminate in quite the same way. Interpretation is open-ended because interpretation is a kind of "remembering," a "remembering" that has been made possible by a particular temporal conjunction. Interpretation is a kind of "remembering" which, in the process of recovering what has been forgotten, keeps itself open to subsequent "memories" in the future. It is this aspect of interpretation that Heidegger suggests by the word *Andenken* or "commemorative thinking," a remembrance that turns forward, toward thinking, *andenken*, in the very act of turning back. From where we are now, a "new" reading of *The Turn of the Screw* is possible—or more precisely, a "commemoration" of what has been forgotten in the text, a "commemoration" of the text's most fundamental level of concealment-disclosure. Without Felman's work, I would not have been able to "remember" what has been "forgotten" by the text and its critics for almost a century.

The critical history of *The Turn of the Screw* reveals that there has been more interest in James's figure of the analyst than in the constructions she makes. Like the critics Freud describes in *From the History of an Infantile Neurosis,* who believe that the fact that the analyst proposes the primal scene and the patient does not remember it decides the whole question, critics of James's text have focused so myopically on either the hysterical projections of the governess or the possibility of psychic phenomena that they never consider the fundamental question posed by Freud's construction of the primal scene: What is the relation of the phantasy to reality? Without forgetting that the real remains out of our grasp, I will attempt here to relate the governess's constructions to the analyst's construction of the primal scene, to determine what primal scene or *fabula* lies behind the *sjuzet* that is her narrative. Her narrative, like the wolf dream, contains within itself a *fabula* that, while not constituting the real, nevertheless brings us closer to it than we could otherwise reach.

The question, therefore, is not whether the governess's visions involve sex or the supernatural but whether they compose an account of the events prior to her arrival at Bly House which, though still concealing the real, at least approximates it. In effect we are shifting what Felman calls "the text's meaning as division" from the *sjuzet* to the *fabula*. Through her visions the governess is trying to remember something that everyone else is trying to forget. But like an intemperate analyst, she comes to believe too vehemently in her own constructions of an event that remains rigorously unknowable. Because of the extent of her mystification, critics have focused solely upon her inability to distinguish reality from phantasy but have forgotten to consider the possibility that those phantasies are nevertheless related to the real. Even Felman, in the course of her otherwise brilliant Lacanian reading of the story, has omitted all reference to the real, which is a profoundly non-Lacanian reading strategy. The concealment of the real and one's inability to grasp it are never for Lacan reasons to forget the real. The critics of *The Turn of the Screw* have forgotten the story's temporality, which is the pathway to the real. Only by reconstructing that temporality will we be able to move beyond mere indeterminacy. Like the ghosts of ontotheology, the ghosts of Peter Quint and Miss Jessel pose the question of the origin through the medium of the question of time. James's "tone" is an achievement that must be placed in conjunction with the Freudo-Heideggerian notion of the temporality of the non-originary "event."

"In so far as the analyst is supposed to know," writes Lacan, "he is also supposed to set out in search of unconscious desire."[33] The governess errs in setting out on this search with perhaps a little too much determination, though we might as easily say too much self-righteousness or prurience: "What it was least possible to get rid of was the cruel idea that, whatever I had seen, Miles and Flora saw more—things more terrible and unguessable and that sprang from dreadful passages of intercourse in the past."[34] While an analyst would be concerned with the neuroses that might have developed in the children as a result of having witnessed the primal scene, the governess is concerned that the spectacle of *coitus flagrante* has placed the children within the diabolical power of the returning spirits of Quint and Jessel. (As we will see, for the governess the primal scene is literally a *flagrant* specta-

33. Lacan, *The Four Fundamental Concepts of Psycho-Analysis*, 235.
34. Henry James, *The Turn of the Screw*, ed. Robert Kimbrough (New York: Norton, 1966), 53. All subsequent page numbers cited in the text refer to this edition.

cle in the etymological sense of the word *flagrante,* "blazing.") Though
these "things" are still "unguessable" at this early point in the text, the
governess will soon be making quite a few guesses, which Freud would
call "suppositions" (*Annahmen*). Like the analyst, the governess cannot expect corroboration except for an occasional slip of the tongue
from Mrs. Grose. Finally, like an analyst who succeeds only in driving
the patient away, the governess will lapse from this salutary skepticism
with regard to the limits of her knowledge into a grotesque certitude
that will no longer admit any interdictions barring the way to the
primal scene.

Suddenly confronted, in broad daylight, with the vision of the ghost
of Miss Jessel at the writing desk—which reminds us that in this story
the primal scene is always one of writing—the governess tries to grasp
the vision in its entirety, to take it all in, only to discover that "even as I
fixed and, for memory, secured it, the awful image passed away" (59).
"Fixing" her gaze and "securing" an image in her memory are emblematic of the governess's behavior. Convinced that the children,
whether unconsciously or not, have been "fixed," or rather fixated,
upon the primal scene, the governess turns all her attention to their
fixation, which in turn becomes her fixation and thus that of the
reader. In the following passage James goes out of his way to fix our
attention on "fixing." Mrs. Grose and the governess are discussing
Miss Jessel:

> Mrs. Grose, at this, fixed her eyes a minute on the ground; then at
> last raising them, "Tell me how you know," she said.
> "Then you admit it's what she was?" I cried.
> "Tell me how you know," my friend simply repeated.
> "Know? By seeing her! By the way she looked."
> "At you, do you mean—so wickedly?"
> "Dear me, no—I could have borne that. She gave me never a glance.
> She only fixed the child."
> Mrs. Grose tried to see it. "Fixed her?"
> "Ah with such awful eyes!" [32]

Mrs. Grose's response to this report of Jessel's "awful eyes" renders
this scene a repetition and displacement of the very scene it describes:
"She stared at mine as if they might really have resembled them." Mrs.
Grose sees in the governess what the governess sees in her vision of
Miss Jessel. She sees the same "fury of intention" and the same desire
"to get hold of" the children. In Jessel's desire to possess the souls of

the children, the governess sees her own desire to seize upon the children's unconscious desire. This is indeed an allegory of the analyst's desire to know. It is the task of the Jamesian "tone" to mark the diacritical point where analysis becomes a kind of possession.

No less than Freud, James too was "fixed," captivated by the voice of the hysterical woman. In a regrettably ignored article, Oscar Cargill suggests that *The Turn of the Screw* is a response to the ideas, if not the text, of Freud's *Studies on Hysteria* and to the mental illness of James's sister, Alice.[35] In "The New York Preface" to the story, James describes his effort as that of catching "those not easily caught . . . the jaded, the disillusioned, the fastidious" (120): that is, those who are not fooled by the supernatural trappings and who recognize that the governess's visions are the result of hysterical repression. Such readers *will* be "caught" if they assume that simply because the governess is phantasizing, her visions have no relation to reality. As Felman demonstrates, nothing could be further from the Jamesian "tone" than a reductive psychoanalytic reading. From his brother William, and from the family's experience with mental disorder, Henry recognized that psychological analysis was situated somewhere between a reductive literality and an ambiguous figurality—which is to say that the Jamesian "tone" is situated somewhere between the philosophical truth and the literary lie. It is situated in the psychoanalytic space that Freud and Lacan carved out between philosophy and literature. Felman, however, allows herself to be "caught" by identifying the Jamesian "tone" with the power of the literary and the figural: "In inviting, in seducing the psychoanalyst, in tempting him into the quicksand of its rhetoric, literature, in truth, only invites him to subvert himself, only lures psychoanalysis into its necessary self-subversion."[36] Felman's "in truth" indicates how securely she has been "fixed" by the Jamesian "tone." Were what Felman says here true, James would be simply a run-of-the-mill modernist. But *The Turn of the Screw* does not stage some putative overcoming of philosophy by literature, any more than it stages the overcoming of literature by analysis. James and Freud and Lacan are more radical than Felman implies, for what they stage is nothing less than the primal scene of philosophy, literature, psychoanalysis. *The*

35. Oscar Cargill, "*The Turn of the Screw* and Alice James," in *The Turn of the Screw*, ed. Kimbrough, 145–65.
36. Felman, "Turning the Screw of Interpretation," 196.

Turn of the Screw subverts those analysts who think of themselves as ontologists. But what Felman forgets is that James's story also subverts those analysts who believe they have overcome ontology thanks to something called "literature." James makes a more profound demand on our notion of reading than Felman or her mentor, Paul de Man, seems willing to admit. The "disillusioned" reader who believes that everything is "literature" believes that everything is demystified insofar as everything is a mystification. Such a reader, standing at the "end" of metaphysics and in possession of "the truth," forgets that fundamental concealments persist. Such a reader believes that we have finished with the ghosts of ontotheology. James recognized, however—and he remains our contemporary because of this recognition—that we have not finished with these ghosts, and that the relation between phantasy and reality, though unreadable, continues to make its uncanny call upon our imaginations. James seems implicitly to have realized that deconstruction is neither an anti-ontology nor a post-ontology but a pre-ontology.

Felman, no less than the governess, renders analysis a kind of possession by privileging the figurality of the "literary." A more attentive reading—one that does not, however, go so far as to be "fastidious"— can still discern the erased trace of the real within the governess's phantasies. The achievement of the Jamesian "tone" is that it grants ontological primacy to neither reality nor language, to neither the literal nor the figural. It "fixes" us in the space where it itself is "fixed," in the space of the preontological, the ghostly space at the beginning of the end of metaphysics.

Miss Jessel is at the heart of the governess's construction of the primal scene. From Mrs. Grose she learns that Miss Jessel became pregnant with Quint's child and was sent home, where she presumably died, as the result of either a miscarriage or an abortion: "She couldn't have stayed. Fancy it here—for a governess! And afterwards I imagined—and I still imagine. And what I imagine is dreadful" (33). These revelations by Mrs. Grose enable the governess to rationalize her strange predisposition to depise her precursor. Her aggressive detestation of a woman she has never met is one of the most disturbing features of her illness. She even speaks, again by way of rationalization, of the ability of women to "read one another." Her propensity to believe the worst of Miss Jessel is in marked contrast to Douglas's

characterization of Jessel in the prologue to the story as "a most respectable person":

> So far had Douglas presented his picture when someone put a ques-
> tion. "And what did the former governess die of? Of so much respecta-
> bility?"
> Our friend's answer was prompt, "That will come out. I don't
> anticipate."
> "Pardon me—I thought that was just what you are doing." [15]

Is Douglas misleading us in the very act of letting us in on the secret? If
he is not, then he is undermining one of the governess's major themes
and in effect suggesting that her bitter recriminations against Miss
Jessel are utterly delusional. Clearly, he is anticipating, despite his
disclaimer. But that still does not make us any more or less certain of
the reliability of his assurances of Jessel's respectability. Here indeed is
an exemplary instance of the Jamesian "tone" at work: it directs us to
a particular problematic at the same time that it calls into question
both its own reliability and the significance of the very thing toward
which it turns our attention. It is precisely by virtue of the hermeneutic
interference it generates that the Jamesian "tone" calls attention to
itself. James questions Miss Jessel's respectability by first establishing
that this is a question that can never be resolved, a question whose
answer will remain concealed, a question that both must be and cannot
be answered.

"Was there a 'secret' at Bly—a mystery of Udolpho or an insane, an
unmentionable relative kept in unsuspected confinement?" (17). The
governess's question poses an interesting critical question about the
relation between the reader of the Gothic novel and the psychoanalyst
who constructs a primal scene. Is it because Ann Radcliffe and Charlotte Brontë construct their romances around a woman's unhappy fate
that the governess's interest is so riveted on Miss Jessel? James certainly does seem to be suggesting something of the kind. The governess's mind is full of Gothic stereotypes. In her visions of Miss Jessel,
James presents a series of vignettes that recall the consummate vil-
lainess of Victorian melodrama, Lydia Gwilt, the antiheroine of Wilkie
Collins' very successful *Armadale* (1866). No less than those of Swinburne or William Morris, Collins' heroines have often grotesquely
fetishized tresses, which are always most striking against a mourning

gown. Behind the governess's vision of her predecessor in the school-room, James's readers would doubtless have thought first of the fiery-haired Miss Gwilt, in mourning, furiously penning her interminable diary.

Unlike James, however, the Gothic tradition from Radcliffe to Collins often seems oblivious to its most glaring contradictions. As always, the effect of stereotype and cliché is to displace attention from contradictions. As readers of *The Mysteries of Udolpho,* for example, we suspect throughout that the heroine is in fact the daughter of an incestuous relation and that all her travails are the effects of an unforgiving God who punishes the children for the sins of the fathers. But Radcliffe hasn't the heart to pursue the question she herself has posed, and we never learn why Emily's father regarded the picture of his sister with such special affection. The Gothic text demands that we construct a primal scene but thwarts our ability to carry through with the effort. Likewise, in *Jane Eyre* we have no idea why Rochester keeps his mad wife in the attic of his main estate rather than on a neighboring estate he also owns. Rochester had claimed that it was unhealthy to live on his second estate but forgets those reservations when, after the fire, he and Jane move there. We are never let into the secret for this particular confinement, just as we never learn how Jane could have heard that mysterious, telepathic voice that marks the climactic point of the novel. The Gothic novel opens the space for the construction of the primal scene and in the same gesture bars access to it.

But in James's story, the governess's madness is, at its most elemental level, a refusal to be barred from learning the "secret": that is, a refusal to forget ontology. It is in order to continue her pursuit of the secret that she produces her visions. Her visions are like analytic constructions, for through each one she is able to sound out Mrs. Grose more fully. The old lady is particularly struck by one detail in the governess's account of her first vision of Jessel's ghost. Through his punctuation of the governess's account, James lets us observe her hesitant, piecemeal method of construction: "In mourning—rather poor, almost shabby. But—yes—with extraordinary beauty." To which Mrs. Grose responds: "The person was in black, you say?" (32). Though this is not at all a verification of her observation, the governess, as in her habit, jumps to conclusions and interprets Mrs. Grose's curiosity about Jessel's mourning dress as an indication that she is really on to something here: "I now recognized to what I had at last,

stroke by stroke, brought the victim of my confidence, for she quite
visibly weighed this."

Who is the "victim" here? Is it really Mrs. Grose? Quite to the
contrary, the governess is victimizing herself. She is the victim of her
own intemperate desire to get to the bottom of it all. Mrs. Grose has no
reason whatsoever to associate Jessel with mourning attire; she is
struck by this detail because it does *not* fit in place. But the governess
sees only what she wants to see, and so she reads the old lady's response as confirmation that she is on the right track. A screenplay
would note that Mrs. Grose poses her question—"The person was in
black, you say?"—with a quizzical tone of surprise. It is precisely this
diacritical mark at the level of tone that the governess is unable to read.
There is indeed a track here, but she errs in thinking that she is on the
right one. The task of reading James is one of remembering that although there is a right track, we are not going to be on it.

The first question, therefore, is why the governess dresses Miss Jessel
in mourning. Is it simply her predilection for the Gothic? In part, yes,
but there is something more at stake here. The governess is so taken
with her apparent success that she employs this detail again in her
highly dramatic vision of Jessel in the schoolroom. The apparition at
the writing desk is "dark as midnight in her black dress, her haggard
beauty and her unutterable woe." As the governess enters the room,
she imagines that the figure at the desk might be a "housemaid" who
"had applied herself to the considerable effort of a letter to her sweetheart." The entire scene is the very epitome of Gothic melodrama: the
vision of a beautiful, distraught ghost of a woman in mourning as she
rises in an eloquently silent gesture of despair. The tone here is also the
epitome of James:

> Then it was—with the very act of its announcing itself—that her iden-
> tity flared up in a change of posture. She rose, not as if she had heard
> me, but with an indescribable melancholy of indifference and detach-
> ment, and, within a dozen feet of me, stood there as my vile predeces-
> sor. Dishonored and tragic, she was all before me; but even as I fixed
> and, for memory, secured it, the awful image passed away. [59]

"With the very act of its announcing itself." What indeed is "announcing itself" in this scene? What does the governess mean by "her identity
flared up"? And why the strange construction, "stood there as my vile
predecessor," rather than the simpler and anticipated "stood there my

vile predecessor"? Every effect of James's carefully crafted tone here
creates an ambivalence between self and other. What is *not* announced
here is the "identity" of the ghost, or even its identity *as* a ghost. What
is announced is the clearly self-reflexive nature of the governess's
imagination.

For whom is Jessel is mourning, and to whom is she writing? If she is
mourning for Quint, then she surely would not be writing to him. The
governess has only recently learned of Quint's death at the time of this
vision, and it is quite natural for her to assume that the lascivious Jessel
is in mourning for her lover; however, such a scenario is contradicted
by the chronology Mrs. Grose sets forth. The question then is, What
kind of events do the visions represent? As far as I can determine, all of
the governess's visions take place in the present. They are not glimpses
into the past but events of a present haunting. Why, then, should Jessel
be in mourning, since Quint is also on the premises? And to whom
could she be writing? One might respond that supernatural visitations
do not have to have a logic and to look for one is misguided. But if that
is the case, why does James take pains to establish a chronology of the
events preceding the governess's arrival at Bly if he does not intend that
chronology to serve as a cipher against which to read the legitimacy of
the governess's visions? Only by taking these details into account can
we reconstruct the temporality of the story.

As we shall see, James's chronology makes it quite clear that Jessel
could never have been in the schoolroom in mourning for Quint. Furthermore, we know that when she has this vision, the governess is
intending to write a letter to the master, in violation of his mysterious
interdiction against such correspondence. This interdiction against
writing, which is indeed the ultimate gesture of an authoritarian metaphysics and which the critics have never explained, looms large in my
reading of the story. What, then, are we to make of the governess's
figure of the "housemaid" about to write a letter to her "sweetheart"?
What is "announcing itself" is the constructive power of the governess's unconscious phantasy. But beyond this obvious point lies the
question of the relation of that phantasy to the actual events concerning the two ill-fated servants. Though her phantasy is merely an image
or a figure of the real, it is only in relation to that unreality that we are
able to deduce a relation to the real. The ghost at the writing desk is a
figure for both Miss Jessel and the governess herself.

The art of James's tone is that it conceals within the governess's self-
mystification an effort to demystify the secret at Bly. James situates us

between the supernatural reading that would insist that this is a psychic phenomenon and the psychological reading that would insist that this is simply a hysterical self-projection. For the governess is really not so mad at all, and the supernatural is really no less uncanny for being a synthesis of the real and the phantasized. We must always remember that James is demystifying not only the supernatural but also our presuppositions about mental disorder. We must always remember to displace both sets of presuppositions when reading *The Turn of the Screw*. Though her phantasy is in error, it forcefully announces the need to construct a more lucid account of the prehistory of this present haunting.

Let us now reconstruct the chronology. The governess arrives in June. Mrs. Grose has had the care of Flora for several months already, and Miles is about to return from school for the summer: hence the pressing need for a new governess. We know from Mrs. Grose that the pregnant Miss Jessel left Bly "at the end of the year," and that by the time she was expected back after the holidays, news came from the master that she had died. This means that she died sometime during the winter. Miss Jessel, already—to Mrs. Grose at any rate—noticeably pregnant, left Bly in December only to die at home some weeks later.

Early in the story, at the point where the governess is questioning the housekeeper about the man she saw on the tower, Mrs. Grose explains that Quint and the master

> "were both here—last year. Then the master went, and Quint was alone."
> I followed, but halting a little. "Alone?"
> "Alone with *us*." Then as from a deeper depth, "In charge," she added. [24]

The italicized *us* and the suggestion of "a deeper depth" imply that this was the period of the primal scene. The children were there, Miss Jessel was there, and Quint was "in charge." Everything is in place, even the chronology, for we are now in the summer, which must have been the time when Jessel became pregnant if her condition was noticeable by December. The master's departure has serious consequences as far as Mrs. Grose is concerned; she is implying that had Quint not been left in charge, the children's otherwise "respectable" governess would never have succumbed, as she did, to a "fellow" whom Mrs. Grose calls "a hound." This is made clear much later in the text when the governess suggests that the master is to blame.

"After all," I said, "it's their uncle's fault. If he left here such people—!"

"He didn't really in the least know them. The fault's mine." She had
turned quite pale. [61]

Here the governess has indeed hit the mark, but this time she doesn't
even recognize it. Clearly, Mrs. Grose agrees with what is for the
governess only an offhand remark. But what is it that makes her turn
"quite pale"? Surely mere negligence on the master's part would not
have been enough. No, James is trying to tell us something more; we
have reached the "deeper depth" that the governess sensed was at
stake. Mrs. Grose knows that it was the master's fault but not because
of his negligence or inattention. She tells the governess that "the master
believed in [Quint] and placed him here because he was supposed not
to be quite in health and the country air so good for him. So he had
everything to say" (27). Reading James closely enough to know how to
read him freely enough reveals that what makes Mrs. Grose turn so
pale is her awareness that the master did know what he was doing
when he left Quint in charge, that he knew Quint well enough to know
what effect the man would have on the otherwise "respectable" Miss
Jessel.

James has set forth not only a chronology of the events of the preceding summer, though one does have to read between the lines to construct it, but also an etiology of the primal scene itself. We know from
the prologue what a playboy the master is and what an effect he has
upon our governess, the narrator. If even Mrs. Grose knew that Quint
was "a hound," then we can be certain that the master recognized
those same instincts in this favored employee, who even has the privilege of wearing the master's clothes (24). We know, even though the
governess never pursues it beyond her passing remark to Mrs. Grose,
that the master is deeply culpable in this scandalous affair. Like the
governess, the critics have been blind to the artful Jamesian tone that
informs Mrs. Grose's speech and gesture. It is for that reason that none
of them has ever remotely guessed why the master absolutely forbids
his servants to write to him. It is the most appallingly obvious thing
that critics always miss. As any reader of Lacan's seminar on Poe's
"Purloined Letter" might have recognized, the master is in the place of
the real. In *The Turn of the Screw* it is not the letter but the absence of
the letter that enables us to trace the path of the signifier to the real.
But like Poe, James can only point to the real without explicating it.

We never know what is in the letter the Minister D—has stolen, and we never know why the master staged the primal scene at Bly. Like a Joycean god, he remains far behind the scenes, paring his fingernails while, unseen, he directs the action. The secret of the primal scene at Bly is finally in his nature, and that nature James keeps securely out of reach.

In sketching the chronology, we have inquired into the etiology of the primal scene. We must still, however, return to the question of mourning and death. We know that Miss Jessel died during the winter, sometime between December and March. Only the master knows the exact date. We know that Quint too died over that same winter. Coming home from the village, no doubt drunk as would befit such a debauchee, he slipped on the ice, hit his head, and died. In other words, Quint and Jessel died at roughly the same time, which means that she could never have been in mourning for him at Bly. Furthermore, she probably would not have mourned his death in any case. Miss Jessel, if I am reading James correctly, is a respectable woman who was seduced and became pregnant with tragic results—the furthest thing from the stormy, romantic heroine the governess makes her out to be. *The Turn of the Screw* is really a pathetic tragedy of a woman caught in the machinations of a decadent patriarchy.

The story is much more sordid and commonplace than the governess would have wanted to admit. She fills every detail with all sorts of Gothic paraphernalia, whereas, like the mystery of the master's interdiction forbidding correspondence, what lies behind the vision in the schoolroom is only a tawdry Victorian tale of the suffering of an innocent woman. The master forbids his servants to write for the very simple reason that he wants nothing more to do with Bly or the children. He has sense enough to recognize the havoc his involvement has brought on and wisely decides to forgo any further involvement in the lives of his servants. He simply wants to cover his tracks and pretend that the whole thing never happened. But something did happen, and Mrs. Grose does not dare let on for fear of losing her job. Only the governess dares to guess at the "unguessable." Her constructions, regardless of the personal investment she has made in them, are always moving toward the rediscovery of that something. And it is only through her constructions that we are able to find our way to the primal scene of the story.

In "The New York Preface" to *The Turn of the Screw*, James describes his achievement in terms of a tone that seems a precursor to

Derrida's "apocalyptic tone": "The study is of a conceived 'tone,' the tone of suspected and felt trouble, of an inordinate and incalculable sore—the tone of tragic, yet of exquisite, mystification" (120). Notice the care with which James calculates the effect of the "incalculable." On the one hand there is the tone of suspicion, the tone that speaks of "an inordinate and incalculable sore"; on the other hand there is a tone of tragic mystification. In other words, the event remains "incalculable" because it can only be approached in terms of a mystified tone. The governess's tragic airs, her lurid Gothic imagination, become for James a synecdoche for the work of unconscious phantasy in general, which is always already at work in the determination of an event. The construction I have made here concerning the master and Quint, and my unraveling of the governess's visions, remain tentative efforts to calculate the "incalculable." Nothing in James's text or letters, or from any other source, will verify them absolutely. What I have constructed is the primal scene of *The Turn of the Screw,* and it is situated, as James made certain it would be, in the zone of *différance,* in that complex temporal space of the always already but not yet. It is an origin that is an effect of its effects. It is not real, but it takes us closer to the real than any other reading has done. Far from extinguishing the "incalculable," the construction of the primal scene opens a new path toward it. In making such a construction we do not dispel the ghosts; to the contrary, we ensure that they live on behind an ineradicable concealment. As the ciphers of an "incalculable sore," the ghosts can never be done away with, for they are the figures of the challenge and necessity of reading. To rest at the level of indeterminacy is to forget that "sore" and to fall victim once again to the ruses of male power.

Like "The Purloined Letter," *The Turn of the Screw* is mediated by a complex narrative frame. The governess writes her manuscript at an unspecified date, and then sends it to Douglas before she dies. Douglas, in turn, reads it at the Christmas gathering and then, before his death, has it sent to his host, who recopies the manuscript and has it published. With each link in the chain of transmission, James is at once establishing the nonoriginary in the place of the origin and focusing our attention on the question of the origin. By presenting his text as a veritable palimpsest of a multiple scene of writing, each layer of which distances us from the voice of the governess, James at once discloses and conceals the question of the origin.

What I want to turn to now is the role that metaphor plays in *The*

Turn of the Screw in revealing and concealing the question of the origin. More particularly, I want to look at the image of fire as a metaphor of the origin. In its self-consuming play of absence and presence, fire perfectly suits the demand that the Jamesian tone makes upon language.

The governess writes of the ghost in the schoolroom that its "identity flared up in a change of posture." At the most expressive moment of its anguish, the ghost appears to burst into flame, to consume itself, and disappear. In a later scene, while on the grounds of the estate with Mrs. Grose, the governess frantically tries to point out to her companion the "hideous" figure of Miss Jessel, who she insists is standing directly in front of them:

> "You don't see her exactly as we see?—you mean to say you don't see now—*now*? She's as big as a blazing fire! Only look, dearest woman, *look*—!" [72]

The old lady responds in a manner that anticipates those critics whose focus is exclusively on the errors of "literature": "It's all a mere mistake and a worry and a joke." This is indeed the response of the "fastidious" reader, the one who reads so closely as to be myopic. Of course, the difference here is that Mrs. Grose, unlike the fastidious reader, knows that there is something behind this sheet of flame, even though she would rather turn her glance away. For the governess, the figure of fire is a most appropriate one to describe the demonic forces she has set out to vanquish. Though she is steadfast in her struggle against evil, she must sometimes remind herself that "it was not my mere infernal imagination" (51). Between her and the secret knowledge that she believes the children possess, there always looms the disfiguring figure of fire. If she could only see through, or beyond it, she would truly grasp the truth. But as soon as it flares up, as if in a moment of apocalyptic revelation, it invariably vanishes into thin air.

Fire in *The Turn of the Screw*, writes Shoshana Felman, "consumes, incinerates at once the content of the story and the inside of the letter, making both indeed impossible to read, unreadable, but unreadable in such a way as to hold all the more 'breathless' the readers' circle round it."[37] Felman is referring to Miles's incineration of the governess's

37. Felman, "Turning the Screw of Interpretation," 148.

prohibited letter to the master, and to the guests gathered round the fireside to hear Douglas read the manuscript. The figure of fire does, as Felman suggests, "eliminate the center," but it does not, for all that, leave us only with emptiness and the loss of the center. It seems to me that on precisely this question we can distinguish the position of Freud, Heidegger, Nietzsche, or Derrida from that of the "Yale School" of deconstruction. In one of his early essays Derrida characterizes Nietzschean affirmation as that which *"determines the noncenter otherwise than as loss of the center."*[38] In other words, even with the loss of the possibility of a determinable origin, there is a kind of gain. Something that is neither presence nor absence persists even in the loss of the origin, and it is to this something that Nietzsche responds with his "immense, unbounded Yes." Felman's notion of unreadability stops short of Derridean *différance*. The figure of fire does not simply destroy the center; it also *"determines the noncenter otherwise than as loss of the center."* At the beginning of her discussion of fire, Felman cites a passage from Lacan that makes the Heideggerian-Derridean point wonderfully clear: "We do not see what is burning, for the flame blinds us to the fact that the fire catches on the real." Everything depends upon our remembering that even though the fire blinds us to the real, we have not forgotten that the real, as the indeterminable noncenter, is there as something other than an absence.

In a footnote to this citation from Lacan, Felman writes of "the crucial importance of fire in Henry James's life, and its recurrent role, both real and symbolic, as a castrating agent." Fire played a tragic role in James's own life and in that of his father. The fact that James's father lost a leg as the result of a fire and that in another incident James himself suffered a permanent back injury forcefully suggests why fire had such an important role to play in manifesting the real as a mode of concealment and withdrawal. In James's texts, fire brings the real to presence only by staging its concealment and withdrawal. James uses fire to blind us to the real, but we should not be blinded to the fact that the real is still there to be blinded to. The French psychoanalyst Jean Laplanche has argued that fire is the paradigmatic figure for the perception of the traumatic event.[39] In James's life and art, this seems indeed to be the case.

38. Derrida, "Structure, Sign, and Play," in *Writing and Difference*, 292.
39. Jean Laplanche, *Problématiques*, 4 vols. (Paris: Presses Universitaires de France, 1980–81), 3:194–96.

There is in the later James a phrase that appears so insistently that one might, at the risk of a slight exaggeration, regard it as a tic, or compulsive element, in the late Jamesian tone. In his texts of the 1890s, above all in *The Turn of the Screw* and *The Wings of the Dove*, James uses the expression "hanging fire" in a variety of permutations and in conjunction with a wide spectrum of character and situation. Regardless of age, social class, or sex, everyone in the latter James seems capable of "hanging fire." Without reservation we can say that this expression is synonymous with the incalculability of the later Jamesian tone. "To hang fire" means "to hesitate," "to remain concealed," "to withdraw, or step back, in the very act of seemingly stepping forward to say something." "To hang fire" is "to keep something hidden in the very act of apparently revealing something." By noting the point at which someone "hangs fire," James locates the point of maximum resistance, the point at which saying something also becomes a way of not saying something else. Felman never mentions the expression and even elides it when it appears in a passage she is citing. Yet she is well aware of the principle that is at stake here: "Mrs. Grose," Felman writes, "in saying less than all, nonetheless says more than she intends to say."[40]

And it is in connection with Mrs. Grose that James repeatedly uses the phrase. The governess remarks of the old lady, "She hung fire, but she overcame her reluctance" (78). In response to her inquiries about the man on the tower, Mrs. Grose "hung fire so long that I was still mystified" (24). "Hanging fire" describes the structure of communication throughout *The Turn of the Screw,* and it is no exaggeration to say that it could easily have been the story's alternate title. "Hanging fire" describes the same "turn" away from determinable meaning which we come to expect at each of the numerous "turns" in the story. "Hanging fire" is synonymous with the hesitation waltz of Jamesian tone.

The expression, from the early history of firearms, describes any discernible delay between the ignition of the powder and the actual firing of the ball. "To hang fire" is thus to be on the threshold between firing and not firing, in the interval between speech and silence. This may well have been a common phrase among the country gentry of James's acquaintance; wherever he learned it, it must have seemed to him made to order to describe the play of concealment and disclosure.

40. Felman, "Turning the Screw of Interpretation," 188.

In Douglas's evasion of his audience's queries in the story's prologue, and especially when his host asks him to begin, we might see an image of James himself. As Douglas turns away from his interlocutors, he turns "round to the fire," which he watches for an instant before facing his audience once again (2). In this alternating rhythm of turning toward and then away from the fire, we enter the primal scene of the Jamesian text.

Heidegger's Heraclitean Fire

In his reading of Heraclitus's fragments on the subject of fire, Heidegger writes that Heraclitus thought of fire "as ever-enduring rising." Fire is the groundless ground of the Heraclitean metaphysic; it is the trace of an always earlier, what "always already rests in itself, before gods and men, what abides in itself and thus preserves all coming."[41] Heidegger renders Heraclitus's Greek in the German "*das Sichentbergen*" (the self-revealing), and he asks us to think of fire otherwise than in terms of cosmology and the philosophy of nature. Heidegger sees in Heraclitean fire something approximating the temporality in which Being gives itself. As such, it is "the bestowal of presencing." It is what "gives measure and takes it away," and what breaches the "opening" to the "logos" and the "world." This is the fire that burns not only before and after the world but also through the world, behind the world, sustaining the world. Like the governess, the philosopher is able to see this invisible fire, to see it flare and flame behind the world it brings to presence.

In their book *The Presocratic Philosophers*, Kirk and Raven remark that for Heraclitus the soul "could be conceived as an adulterated fragment of the surrounding cosmic fire." Macrobius makes the point in *Scipio's Dream*: "Heraclitus said that the soul is a spark of the essential substance of the stars (*scintillam stellaris essentiae*)."[42] Through the notion of the "*aither*," Heraclitus sought to link the "world-fire" to the "soul-fire." Heraclitus's program, argues Heidegger, is to remind those who think truth is hidden "under a hardly

41. Martin Heidegger, *Early Greek Thinking*, trans. David Farrell Krell and Frank Capuzzi (New York: Harper & Row, 1975), 117.
42. G. S. Kirk and J. E. Raven, *The Presocratic Philosophers* (Cambridge: Cambridge University Press, 1975), 207.

penetrable layer of strangeness" that truth is not buried deep but, on the contrary, is ready to hand on the surface of that which comes to presence. For Heraclitus, the world-fire is ready to hand in the soul-fire. But for Heidegger this is not presence as such; it is presence not as self-presence but as concealment, as disappearance.

Like the governess, who seeks truth in "the deeper depth," the philosopher can also be deluded by his reliance on that which can be represented before a subject. Like the governess, the philosopher believes that presence can be secured in the present. But, says Heidegger, such presence is a delusion, for it forgets "the governance of the near," which gives both presence and absence without being reducible to either: "The presencing of the near is too close for our customary mode of representational thought—which exhausts itself in securing what is present—to experience the governance of the near, and without preparation to think it adequately."[43] We must learn to think of the fire not as the hallucinatory coming to presence of the depths of things but as the play of difference in the near-to-hand. We must regard the Heraclitean fire not as burning through the appearance of things in an ecstatic or supernatural vision but as a figure for things as they are in their presentness. Heraclitus opens the clearing for the "*a-lēthia*," the "dis-closure," of Being in the everydayness of things. The clearing is the zone of *différance*. Neither the governess nor the critics of *The Turn of the Screw* think adequately about the play of differences on the surface of the story. They do not see that the letter, as Being, gives itself, through the play of temporal difference, in the space of the always already but not yet.

The Latin *stella*, as in the "*scintillam stellaris essentiae*," indicates a *fixed* star. Its fixity suggests an etymological link to the Greek *stele*, which is a plinth, post, or pillar which commemorates the dead and on which sacrifices are performed. It fixes the limit between the world of the living and the world of the dead. Like the *stele*, the *stella* also fixes the limits of worlds, and it too commemorates the dead. For in the constellations, the stars, and the planets (which are all indicated by the Latin *stella*), the gods and the heroes are monumentalized, commemorated. As Heidegger is fond of pointing out, the Greek root *stele* is also the etymological root of the German *stellen, Stellung, Vorstellung,* and so on—which is to say to the entire problematic of representation in

43. Heidegger, *Early Greek Thinking*, 121.

Western metaphysics.[44] Representation is thus also a kind of com-memoration, and a means of fixing the limits of worlds.

Unlike the Heraclitean notion of the world-fire, however, where what-is is fixed in the flux that is the appearance of things in their presentness, the metaphysical notion of representation is cast in terms of depth and surface, reality and illusion, where what-is is fixed in the image held by the perceiving subject. With Platonism and its legacy, the Heraclitean fire goes under erasure. Metaphysics fixes value and meaning no longer in the coming-to-presence of things but in a mode of ideation and subjective reflection.

Summarizing Heidegger's 1938 lecture, "The Age of the World Picture," Derrida writes: "The Greek world did not have a relation to what-is as to a conceived image or representation. There what-is is presence; and this did not, at first, derive from the fact that man would look at what-is and have what we call a representation (*Vorstellung*) of it as the mode of perception of a subject."[45] But while metaphysics concealed the world-fire, it did not extinguish it; it may in fact have preserved it in the only way it could have been preserved, behind the shadow of representation. At the end of "The Age of the World Picture," Heidegger speaks of a shadow between us and the truth that does not simply conceal the light of the world-fire: "The shadow is a manifest, though impenetrable, testimony to the concealed emitting of light." Under this shadow at the beginning of the end of metaphysics, "we experience the incalculable as that which, withdrawn from representation, is nevertheless manifest in whatever is, pointing to Being, which remains concealed."[46] Like Jamesian tone, the Heideggerian shadow "hangs fire." No less than Heidegger, James remembers the concealment of Being; more important, he recognizes that concealment

44. See Philippe Lacoue-Labarthe's discussion of Heidegger's linkage of *stele* and *stellen* in his essay "Typographies," in S. Agacinski et al., *Mimesis des articulations* (Paris: Aubier-Flammarion, 1975), esp. the section entitled "La Stèle," 190ff. As Lacoue-Labarthe reminds us, Heidegger proceeds as much by "philological *Witz* as by genuine etymology." Derrida elaborates the *stele/stellen* connection into one of the leitmotifs of *La Carte postale* where the "postal effect," which is his euphemism for the history of metaphysics, is defined in terms of "posts," "positions," "theses," and a whole range of predetermined markers and destinations.

45. Jacques Derrida, "Sending: On Representation," trans. Peter Caws, *Social Research*, 49 (1982): 306.

46. Martin Heidegger, "The Age of the World Picture," in *The Question Concerning Technology and Other Essays*, trans. William Lovitt (New York: Harper & Row, 1977), 154.

bears disclosure within itself. Through their notions of "tone" and the "shadow," James and Heidegger inscribe the trace of the incalculable across the primal scene. The trace, writes Derrida, "is as it were pre-ontological":[47] that is, "pointing to Being, which remains concealed."

47. Derrida, "Sending: On Representation," 312.

4 Primal Scenes:
Freud and the Wolf-Man

Mighty is the charm
Of those abstractions to a mind beset
With images, and haunted by itself.

WILLIAM WORDSWORTH, *The Prelude*

"Dreaming Is Another Kind of Remembering"

For a year and a half beginning in September 1974, the Wolf-Man, Sergei Pankejev, granted a series of interviews to Karin Obholzer, an Austrian journalist. Early on, she asked him what he thought of Freud's *From the History of an Infantile Neurosis,* and more particularly, of Freud's construction of the primal scene. He replied:

> In my story, what was explained by dreams? Nothing, as far as I can see. Freud traces everything back to the primal scene which he derives from the dream. But that scene does not occur in the dream. When he interprets the white wolves as nightshirts or something like that, for example, linen sheets or clothes, that's somehow far-fetched, I think. That scene in the dream where the windows open and so on and the wolves are sitting there, and his interpretation, I don't know, those things are miles apart. It's terribly far-fetched.[1]

The fact that "the scene itself does not occur in the dream" has troubled the Wolf-Man since 1918. How, he asks, can Freud's construction be said to have any relevance whatsoever if the patient himself has never, either during the analysis or for decades after, been able to

1. Karin Obholzer, *The Wolf-Man: Conversations with Freud's Patient—Sixty Years Later,* trans. Michael Shaw (New York: Continuum Books, 1982), 35.

remember such a scene? "I have always thought that the memory would come. But it never did."[2] As far as the Wolf-Man is concerned, psychoanalysis stands self-condemned by virtue of its deduction of causes from effects. Instead of Freud's primal scene, the Wolf-Man maintains, it was his seduction by his sister that lay at the origin of his neurosis. In attacking the legitimacy of the primal scene, the Wolf-Man is in effect replaying the history of psychoanalysis, for it is once again a question of the remembered seduction scene vs. the always forgotten primal scene, verification vs. circumstantiality, recollection vs. phantasy. "His seduction by his sister was certainly not a phantasy," writes Freud.[3] The Wolf-Man takes Freud one step further: "Here we have a recollection. It is not a fiction, not an inference, and not a construct."[4] For the Wolf-Man, the seduction scene is the primal scene: "This sister complex is really the thing that ruined my entire life." Because of it, he regarded women of his own social class as inaccessible: "For those women who resemble my sister, I mean as regards social position or education, well, that was a prohibition again, that was incest again." He even suggests that "these psychological illnesses" were the result of heredity. In any case, the Wolf-Man has throughout his life, even down to the amorous complications he is experiencing in his eighties, been driven to women who are socially and intellectually beneath him, for only among such women can he feel desire.

The Wolf-Man is not opposed in principle to the notion of the primal scene, as far as he understands it. It's simply that for him the seduction scene has a far greater explanatory power than Freud's constructed scene. The Wolf-Man's dilemma is emblematic of the division Freud created between his theoretical and clinical work as a result of the primal scene. What the Wolf-Man finds most questionable in psychoanalysis is precisely what Peter Brooks celebrates as Freud's modernist discovery of "another kind of referentiality."[5] While Brooks sees in Freud's subversion of narrative authority a theoretical insight that links Freud's work to that of Mann, Proust, and Faulkner, the Wolf-

2. Obholzer, *The Wolf-Man*, 36.

3. *The Standard Edition of the Complete Psychological Works of Sigmund Freud*, ed. James Strachey et al., 24 vols. (London: Hogarth Press and the Institute of Psycho-Analysis, 1953–74), 17:21. This edition is subsequently cited in the text as *S.E.*

4. Obholzer, *The Wolf-Man*, 37.

5. Peter Brooks, "Fictions of the Wolf Man: Freud and Narrative Understanding," in *Reading for the Plot: Design and Intention in Narrative* (New York: Knopf, 1984), 264–85.

Man treats the loss of the center as a clinical and therapeutic loss as well. He tells Obholzer that Freud assured him the recollection would come: "And that's really how he described it. But no recollection came in my case."[6] Recognizing, no doubt, that the Wolf-Man's complaints call into question this new kind of referentiality, Brooks devotes a footnote to taking Obholzer to task for trying "to discredit psycho-analysis, or at least score points against Freud's claims that his patient was 'cured.' "[7] It seems to me, however, that Obholzer simply provides the Wolf-Man with the opportunity to score his own points. No one can read her conversations with the Wolf-Man and not conclude, as Brooks also has, that this patient remained a compulsive personality. At the same time, one must also acknowledge that, as Brooks remarks, the Wolf-Man "managed to negotiate a reasonably normal existence." Indeed, this is such an ambiguous phrase that it is difficult not to agree with it. But surely psychoanalysts, and those who speak on behalf of analysis, are mistaken if they believe that the Wolf-Man's charges "discredit psychoanalysis." Quite to the contrary, the disclaimers of Freud's most famous patient are the inevitable results of an interpretive method that has itself opened the space where such a dialogue could occur. For even though the Wolf-Man posits his own version of the primal scene, he nevertheless goes on to challenge its authority. He asks whether his seduction must "necessarily have consequences, or is it already a sign of sickness that something like that has conse-quences?" Speaking of another case involving the six-year-old son of a friend of his, he says, "You see, that sort of thing happens, it's no reason for someone to turn into a neurotic."

The Wolf-Man's charges are part of an ongoing interrogation that analysis opens without ever being able to close. Sixty years later, they are still part of the process Brooks sees at work in the analysis itself: "As the analysis of the Wolf Man proceeds, it reveals (as most nar-ratives do) both a drive toward the end and a resistance to ending."[8] The primal scene is the name Freud gives to the construction of that narrative space.

Primal scenes, writes Freud, "are as a rule not reproduced as recol-lections but have to be divined—constructed—gradually and la-

6. Obholzer, The Wolf-Man, 38.
7. Brooks, "Fictions of the Wolf Man," 352 n. 2.
8. Brooks, "Fictions of the Wolf Man," 281.

boriously from an aggregate of indications" (*S.E.,* 17:51). Here we might wish he could have openly acknowledged that with the notion of the primal scene he had formally and finally moved beyond recollection. But Freud was constrained from making such an admission for fear of losing control over the International Psychoanalytic Association. When he writes that "many people will think that this single admission decides the whole dispute," he is thinking of the analysts sympathetic to Jung or Adler who would eagerly exploit such a break from recollection, seeing in it confirmation of Freud's failure as an analyst. Freud alerts us to the larger narrative context in which his narrative of the Wolf-Man is to be read when he comments in a footnote on the first page of the case history that this analysis was written "still freshly under the impression of the twisted reinterpretations of Jung and Adler" (*S.E.,* 17:7). Freud is telling the Wolf-Man's story, but he is also telling a polemical story, which, in contradistinction to the *pars pro toto* approach of Jung and Adler, will provide a "comprehensive solution of all the conundrums." The primal scene has the virtue of being a global solution; it is concerned with much more than the egocentric trends—that is, the subjective recollections—which are all that concern Jung and Adler.

But while the primal scene is Freud's secret weapon in the war for leadership of the IPA, he is careful not to go too far; he must assure analysts that his ostensibly new method is in no way different from an analysis that is confirmed by recollection. Freud needs an interpretive strategy that will decisively distance him from Jung and Adler, yet he does not want to undermine the bases of his own support. These historical exigencies force him into a difficult rhetorical position, and his response to the dilemma may well appear as something of a bluff: "It seems to me absolutely equivalent to a recollection if memories are replaced (as in the present case) by dreams, the analysis of which invariably leads back to the same scene and which reproduce every portion of its content in an inexhaustible variety of new shapes" (*S.E.,* 17:51). This passage is a litany of hyperboles: "absolutely equivalent" (*durchaus gleichwertig*), "invariably leads back to the same scene," "reproduces every portion." Even Strachey seems alert to the hyperbolic tone, for in translating Freud's next sentence, "*Traumen ist ja auch ein Erinnern*"—literally, "Indeed, dreaming is also a remembering"—Strachey writes, "Indeed, dreaming is another kind of remembering."

Freud's point, however, is not simply that dreaming is a kind of remembering that follows the rules of dream formation but that it is "absolutely equivalent." He makes the point so clearly in the next sentence that no translation could hope to lessen its impact:

> It is this recurrence in dreams that I regard as the explanation of the fact that the patients themselves gradually acquire a profound conviction of the reality of these primal scenes, a conviction which is in no respect inferior to one based on recollection.

Of course, we know, and Freud knew, that the conviction of patients with respect to the primal scene was always problematical. The patients to whom he refers here are his own constructions; he is stating a theoretical hope as though it were a clinical fact. More important than such strategic misrepresentations of clinical experience, however, is the fact that Freud no less than the Wolf-Man is driven toward closure. No less than the Wolf-Man, Freud is willing to suppress difference: namely, the difference between what we might call recollected and constructed "conviction." It is precisely this zone of difference that constitutes the specificity of analysis, even though it is also this difference that Freud and the Wolf-Man, for their very different reasons, try to forget in their respective efforts to establish their own subjective authority.

While the Wolf-Man wants to retain the authority of his own subjectivity, Freud wants to construct a narrative that demonstrates, through its hermeneutic power, the authority of his leadership. In that footnote on the first page of the Wolf-Man case history, he explains that the work "supplements" (*ergänzt*) *On the History of the Psychoanalytic Movement* (1914), which he had finished writing just as he began *From the History of an Infantile Neurosis*. In a very real sense, the whole of the Wolf-Man case history is a supplement to the vitriolic last chapter of the previous work, in which Freud makes it very clear that this book was a pretext for the condemnation of Jung and Adler with which it concludes. *From the History of an Infantile Neurosis* is, in other words, a protracted effort to bring the confrontation with Jung and Adler to a kind of closure. But what prevents both Freud and his patient from reaching the closure they seek is the irreducible nature of what Freud in *The Project for a Scientific Psychology* (1895) called "*Bahnung*," "breaching" or "facilitation," which in the Wolf-Man case he calls "deferred action." No demand for closure, regardless of the personal or collective forces that inform it, can overcome the radical problematization of the origin and the bases of explanation that Freud has put into effect through his notion of the differential pathway, the temporal spacing, that always characterizes the joint work of memory and unconscious phantasy. Nothing can halt the process of deferral in which the notion of the origin and the etiology of the event are caught. There will always be the need for yet another supplement, yet another version of the originary function of the nonoriginary. There will always be the need for yet another version of the primal scene. "I therefore proceed," writes Freud in one of the notes he added to the Wolf-Man case in 1918, "by way of supplement and rectification.—There remains the possibility of taking yet another view of the primal scene underlying the dream" (*S.E.*, 17:57). Neither Freud nor his patient can arrest the play of difference in which they are both seized.

Analysis *a Tergo*

Freud's effort to erase the difference between the conviction produced by recollection and that produced through the construction of the primal scene is a necessary defense against those who would claim that without recollection only the most ephemeral kind of conviction could be produced. He poses the argument for the opposition when he writes that "the sense of conviction felt by the person analysed may be the result of suggestion, which is always having new parts assigned to it in the play of forces involved in analytic treatment" (*S.E.*, 17:52). This is the most damning charge against which Freud must defend himself. It is in order to separate himself from what he here calls this "old-fashioned" method of suggestion and hypnosis that Freud invented psychoanalysis in general and its specific motive force, the primal scene, whose construction, he assures his readers, takes place "independently of the physician's incentive."

The Wolf-Man makes a closely related observation to Karin Obholzer when he argues that the primal scene was Freud's effort to base analysis on "something more rational" than the analyst's hypnotic, suggestive influence over the patient. "The rational," he says, "is the explanation by these constructs."9 Interestingly, the Wolf-Man makes the comment in direct connection with Freud's construction of

9. Obholzer, *The Wolf-Man*, 38.

his primal scene. His point is that though Freud thought these constructions a more rational basis than the analyst's suggestion, the fact remains that they are themselves the instruments of suggestion. Though hypnosis and the transference are supposedly distinct, insofar as in the transference one is supposed to "adopt a more critical attitude," the fact remains that "basically the two things are similar, of course"; "When I do what transference shows me, it is really like being hypnotized by someone. That's the influence. I can remember Freud saying, 'Hypnosis, what do you mean, hypnosis, everything we do is hypnosis too.'"

Freud would have agreed heartily with François Roustang's contention that while analysis is always already hypnosis, it is also something more: "Analysis departs from earlier methods through the progressive extension of the course of the treatment and through the addition of numerous detours."[10] It is never a question of overcoming once and for all the corporeal-affective substratum of suggestive or hypnotic influence but rather of working through it, of mediating it through a series of interpretive strategies. In the second chapter of his book, *Psychoanalysis Never Lets Go,* Roustang traces Freud's often contradictory statements with respect to the role of suggestion or hypnosis in analysis. As Roustang makes abundantly clear, it is a question neither of apologizing for Freud's inconsistencies nor of demonstrating that they undermine the efficacy of his entire system. Roustang dares to make the point that Freud could not make openly, and which perhaps can never be made openly in certain analytic circles, that "everything we do is hypnosis,"—which is not to say, however, that we do not do something else as well. Though everything is hypnosis, hypnosis is far from being everything.

The Wolf-Man simply wants to discredit the logical foundation of analysis by linking the construction of the primal scene to the hypnotic session. We cannot explain this away by attributing his charges to Obholzer's prodding. The Wolf-Man is Freud's most famous patient not despite these allegations but because of them. Indeed, how much more eloquent could any tribute be when after sixty years he is still carefully probing these questions and weighing the elements all over again? Perhaps one might counter that analysis is its own treadmill, and that in the best analysis the patient's neurosis is simply exchanged

10. François Roustang, *Psychoanalysis Never Lets Go,* trans. Ned Lukacher (Baltimore, Md.: Johns Hopkins University Press, 1983), 87.

for a transference neurosis. Such a statement may be alarmingly close to the mark; however, the point remains, as Roustang reminds us, that analysis can work only for those whose need is desperate. For such patients, for whom analysis is something of a last hope, exchanging their neurosis for a transference neurosis may not be a simple exchange at all but a means of survival. In this sense as well, the Wolf-Man is deservedly Freud's most famous patient.

Freud was not the first therapist the Wolf-Man consulted. His experience prior to coming to Vienna in 1910 offers a veritable catalogue of therapeutic techniques. The Wolf-Man had confronted the questions of hypnosis and suggestion before ever meeting Freud. In his *Memoirs,* which he wrote in 1970–71 at the age of eighty-three, the Wolf-Man gives an account of the therapy he received in St. Petersburg in 1908 when, after his sister's suicide, he suffered acute depression and withdrew from the university there. Under his father's direction, he sought help from the city's leading neurological expert. In the *Memoirs* he refers to him only as Professor B., but to Obholzer he identifies him as Dr. W. M. Bechterev, a leading Russian psychiatrist and author of the book *Suggestion and Its Role in Society* (1898). At the time the Wolf-Man sought Bechterev's help, the doctor was trying to establish a neurological institute in St. Petersburg. By a strange coincidence, the Wolf-Man's wealthy father was at that moment in the process of establishing a neurological institute in Odessa in honor of his late daughter, whose acute schizophrenia had been evident for many years.

During their first session, the Wolf-Man alleges, Bechterev used hypnotic suggestion to persuade his patient to talk his father into funding the institute in St. Petersburg rather than the one in Odessa. Without assuming anything about the accuracy of this anecdote, there can be no doubt, particularly in the context of his estimate of therapists generally, that the Wolf-Man's parody of Bechterev is also a parody of the special interests that can motivate any analyst.

> As a consequence of the confusion of my treatment with the question of the Neurological Institute, the first hypnotic session was also the last. For I had to expect that Professor B. would question me at the next session about my intervention with my parents, and what could I have answered. My father had, by the way, no great liking for hypnosis, because he saw the danger of the patient's becoming excessively dependent on the doctor. I shared this opinion.[11]

11. *The Wolf-Man by the Wolf-Man,* ed. Muriel Gardiner (New York: Basic Books, 1971), 45.

Thus began his pilgrimage through the psychiatric wards of Europe, in the course of which he was admitted to Dr. Kraeplin's sanatorium in Bavaria, where he fell in love with a nurse named Therese; with Freud's permission, he married her in 1914. He also tells us in his *Memoirs* that no other therapist but Freud would permit him to see Therese again, and for that reason alone he entered into analysis with Freud! It was only after several years that the Wolf-Man discovered that analysis entailed some of the same risks he had feared under hypnotic treatment. Returning to Vienna in 1919 after a period of desperate existence in Odessa, where he and Therese spent the war years, the Wolf-Man went back into therapy with Freud in order to deal with (as Freud puts it) "a piece of the transference which had not hitherto been overcome" (*S.E.*, 17:122). The patient, Freud remarks, "had been seized with a longing to tear himself free from my influence."

The irony, of course, is that in spite of fleeing Bechterev the Wolf-Man would never really escape the power of the physician's suggestion; as the years passed, he found it impossible to detach himself from the psychoanalytic milieu. The depth of his transference neurosis became most obvious during his analysis with Ruth Mack Brunswick, which began in 1926 following the onset of paranoid psychosis. The Wolf-Man's transference neurosis was never "successfully dealt with," whatever Freud claimed. This patient seems to have been permanently caught somewhere between hypnosis and analysis.

The Wolf-Man relates a story that Freud told him about the origin of the "psychoanalytic situation," which suggests that analysis itself might also be caught in the undecidable space of its own prehistory. Freud's story takes us back to the ostensible beginning, to the point where the specificity of analysis was first defined:

> This "situation," as is well known, is that of the patient lying on the couch with the analyst sitting near the couch in a position where he cannot be seen by the analysand. Freud told me that he had originally sat at the opposite end of the couch, so that the analyst and analysand could look at each other. One female patient, exploiting this situation, made all possible—or rather all impossible—attempts to seduce him. To rule out anything similar, once and for all, Freud moved from his earlier position to the opposite end of the couch.[12]

In Freud's published account of this incident in *An Autobiographical Study* (1925), he reveals what the Wolf-Man does not, that the new

12. *The Wolf-Man by the Wolf-Man*, 142.

analytic scenography was linked to and synonymous with the rejection of hypnosis:

> One of my most acquiescent patients, with whom hypnotism had enabled me to bring about the most marvellous results, and who I was engaged in relieving of her suffering by tracing back her attacks of pain to their origins, as she woke up [on] one occasion, threw her arms round my neck. The unexpected entrance of a servant relieved us from a painful discussion, but from that time onwards there was a tacit understanding between us that the hypnotic treatment should be discontinued. I was modest enough not to attribute the event to my own irresistible attraction, and I felt that I had now grasped the nature of the mysterious element that was at work behind hypnotism. In order to exclude it, or at all events to isolate it, it was necessary to abandon hypnotism. . . . So I abandoned hypnosis, only retaining my practice of requiring the patient to lie upon the sofa while I sat behind him, seeing him, but not seen myself.[13]

The scenography of this event is more than a little reminiscent of the primal scene. Here it is not the child but the servant who accidentally glimpses the amorous couple. When Freud takes up his position behind the couch, he too becomes like the spectator in the primal scene, seeing but unseen.

Of course, Freud is unable to "rule out anything similar, once and for all." Shifting his position vis-à-vis the couch does not put hypnosis behind him, and he knows this perfectly well. What he *has* been able to do is to sublimate and conceal the old hypnotic relation within the new "psychoanalytic situation." Perhaps most alarming in this passage is Freud's claim to have "now grasped the nature of the mysterious element that was at work behind hypnotism": that is, apparently, to have fathomed the *"mystischen Elements"* by recognizing that they were synonymous with the sexual or erotic instincts. It is at such points that Lacan has taught us to recognize Freud's self-mystification and to remember what Freud has forgotten, that affect works through and within language and that the object of analysis is therefore the logic of the signifier. Had Freud acknowledged that the mysterious force of suggestion worked through the rhythms of language, he would have been deprived of any means with which to defend against it. He must sexualize the hypnotic relation in order to be able "to exclude it, or at

---

13. Sigmund Freud, *An Autobiographical Study*, trans. James Strachey (New York: Norton, 1963), 49–51.

all events to isolate it." The very ambiguity of this phrase suggests how very difficult it is "to exclude" the hypnotic relation.

At the center of this primal scene in the history of psychoanalysis, not a word is spoken. And the reason for that is that language cannot, and must not, be allowed into the scene. Was it actually the servant's entrance that spared Freud from a "painful discussion," or was it simply not knowing what to say? Once again, Strachey's translation moderates the force of Freud's German. "*Einer peinlichen Auseinandersetzung*" is perhaps closer to "an embarrassing confrontation" than it is to "a painful discussion." In lieu of this "*Auseinandersetzung*," Freud and his patient reach a "tacit understanding," a silent reconciliation rather than a verbal confrontation.

Samuel Weber, who has much to say on Freud's use of the term *Auseinandersetzung,* describes it as the dynamic through which "Freud's concepts articulate and disarticulate themselves."[14] What Weber calls the "movement of conflictual decomposition and recomposition," in which the confrontation between two terms generates a third term that "inexorably replaces and displaces the other two," can be seen at work in Freud's account of the origin of the "psychoanalytic situation." In setting psychoanalysis apart from hypnosis and suggestion, Freud inadvertently created a differential space that is neither one nor the other, neither the independence of the patient that Freud seeks in analysis nor the extreme dominance of the analyst that he sees in hypnosis. It is the achievement of his discourse that it became seized in the irreducible drift of the nonoriginary, caught in the interminability of an incalculable transference neurosis.

Die Fragestellung

In the opening paragraph of his 1964 lecture "The End of Philosophy and the Task of Thinking," Heidegger describes his effort since 1930 as an "attempt to shape the question of being and time in a more primal way."[15] "To shape the question" translates "*die Fragestellung*," which is more precisely a "setting forth" or "placing of the question." We might even risk "timing the question," since both

14. Samuel Weber, *The Legend of Freud* (Minneapolis: University of Minnesota Press, 1982), 34.
15. Martin Heidegger, *Of Time and Being,* trans. Joan Stambaugh (New York: Harper & Row, 1977), 55.

Heidegger and Freud would agree that it is all very much a matter of timing. Both Freud and Heidegger try to pose the question in the most "primal way." Concerning the undecidability of the reality/phantasy of the primal scene, Freud writes, "I must confess, however, that I regard it as greatly to the credit of psychoanalysis that it should even have reached the stage of *raising* such questions as these" (*S.E.*, 17:96). There are no italics in the German, which reads, literally translated, "that it should have reached such formulations" (*dass sie zu solchen Fragestellungen gekommen ist*). What Freud is reluctant to recognize here is that in his search for the even more primordial question, the analyst inevitably not only "stages the question" but also writes the patient's script as well. The analyst finds it difficult to stage such questions in an absolutely neutral way.

"I regard it as a methodological error," writes Freud, "to seize on a phylogenetic explanation before the ontogenetic possibilities have been exhausted" (*S.E.*, 17:97). After all the analyst's efforts to bring the patient to recollect his past have failed, the task of analysis becomes that of "filling in the gaps in individual truth with prehistoric truth." In so doing, he argues, analysis retraces the pathways through which the child constructs its identity. The child, like the patient, "replaces experiences in its own life with the experiences of its ancestors" (*setzt die Erfahrung der Vorahnen an die Stelle der eigenen Erfahrung ein*). But Freud seems unwilling to acknowledge that once the transferential *Fragestellung* is underway, there is no means of bringing it to a close. This "putting in the place of" (*setzt . . . an der Stelle*) is ideally the joint work of analyst and analysand. The problem can be that in reaching this "stage" in the construction of the question, the analyst may find himself performing alone.

In his 1915–17 lectures at the University of Vienna, Freud's emphasis in speaking of primal phantasies is on the question of credulity. When he delivered these lectures, *From the History of an Infantile Neurosis* had not yet been published, but the manuscript had been nearly complete since late 1914. Though the Wolf-Man is not mentioned by name in the lectures, there is little doubt that Freud is thinking of him when he warns his analysts in training to avoid the risk of the patient's "accusing us of being mistaken and laughing at us for our apparent credulity."[16] They must let the patient know from the outset

16. Sigmund Freud, *Introductory Lectures on Psychoanalysis*, trans. James Strachey (New York: Norton, 1977), 368.

that phantasies have a psychical as well as a material dimension, and that it is with the psychical that the analyst is chiefly concerned. Here, then, is the lesson Freud has learned from the four-year analysis he has just completed. We would have preferred that he situate himself between the psychical and the material, and Freud himself seems to have some difficulty in accepting his own advice. "It will be a long time," he remarks, "before [the patient] can take in our proposal that we should equate phantasy and reality and not bother to begin with whether the childhood experiences under consideration are the one or the other." A subsequent reference to phantasies of "intercourse from behind, *more ferarum* (in the manner of animals)," demonstrates that Freud is addressing just those strategies from the Wolf-Man analysis that he feels could be improved.

But when and how does one raise the question of the reality/phantasy of the event? Freud obviously wishes he had posed it earlier to the Wolf-Man; presumably, there would then have been fewer misunderstandings between them. The question Freud does not want to dwell upon is how long it will take for the patient to be ready to join the analyst on that rather forbidding stage of the reality/phantasy question. "It will be a long time," and we know from the Wolf-Man just how long that can be. In the twenty-third lecture, Freud seems to be stepping back from the chances he had taken in *From the History of an Infantile Neurosis*. Instead of molding the phantasy/reality question in an ever more "primal way," he wants to postpone it indefinitely. There is a tone of disappointment and cynicism here, as though Freud were telling analysts not to bother trying to raise such important questions, since it will take so long for patients to be able to understand what they're talking about. It is as if Freud had been surprised by the Wolf-Man's resistance to his construction of the primal scene, as if he had begun to sense a new level of resistance that could never be overcome. Perhaps the war or, a few months later, the death of his daughter Sophie (whose son appears as the inventor of the Fort/Da game in *Beyond the Pleasure Principle*) explains Freud's intimation that there is an absolute resistance. Nevertheless, his interest in the death drive and the repetition compulsion, though bearing the mark of recent events, is the inevitable result of a process on which he had embarked in the 1890s. Freud has begun to theorize openly about something that he had succeeded in suppressing or rationalizing since the 1890s: he had tried for years to forget that patients could never remember the primal scene. But even after being forced to recognize that fact in the Wolf-Man case, he would attempt during the 1920s to cover his tracks, to insist that such resistance was the exception rather than the rule.

Verwerfung

"It was not a single sexual current that started from the primal scene," writes Freud of the Wolf-Man, "his sexual life was positively splintered up by it" (*eine Aufsplitterung der Libido,* "a splintering of the libido"; *S.E.,* 17:43–44). Freud makes this remark early in the case history, and so we assume that he is describing an event that happened in one time and place. By the time we have finished *From the History of an Infantile Neurosis,* we recognize that this splintering is a very complex sort of event. What Freud seems to be saying is that at some point in the Wolf-Man's childhood something happened that predisposed him to multiple sexual identifications. More particularly, the primal scene of coitus *a tergo,* which is Freud's figure for what Heidegger would call the "trace of an always earlier," is an effort to explain why the Wolf-Man took both his mother and his father as sexual models. The primal scene is the template of the splintering that determines the shape of his sexual life, enabling him to identify with his mother's passivity as well as his father's aggressivity. Whether the source of this figure of coitus *a tergo* was an actual event that the Wolf-Man witnessed, or a phantasy, or an event involving animals, its explanatory power inheres for Freud in its inclusion of the whole range of sexual identifications. This figure has the effect of situating the Wolf-Man in the space of sexual undecidability.

Although the patient admitted the reality of castration and sexual difference, Freud maintains, he nevertheless identified with the model of feminine sexual pleasure. The Wolf-Man's homosexual identification with the woman by way of an anal complex led him into what Freud calls a "logical contradiction." Freud is most struck by the fact that the Wolf-Man's bisexual currents both remained active. Freud praised above all the Wolf-Man's relationship with Therese and called it his "breakthrough to the woman," which is to say his movement toward a stable heterosexual identification.

The repressive mechanism that Freud calls "*Verwerfung,*" or "repudiation" (translated by Lacan as "foreclosure"), comes into effect to bar access to the memory of the scene in which the splintering occurred. Because the splintering is a very peculiar sort of event, it requires a correspondingly peculiar mechanism of repression. What is required in order to keep this contradiction from consciousness, Freud suggests, is an "extraordinarily powerful force" that differs decisively from and goes further than repression (*Verdrängung*), for "it also excludes [the contradiction] from being worked over later in consciousness" (*von späterer bewusster Verarbeitung auszuschliessen; S.E.,* 17:79). In other words, what it represses stays repressed. "A repression," Freud concludes, "is completely different from an exclusion" (*Eine Verdrängung ist etwas anderes als eine Verwerfung*).

Freud appears to be explaining a particularly primitive mode of repression, rather as if he were a psychical anthropologist. What he is doing in fact is rationalizing his patient's inability to recollect the primal scene. We must remember also that Freud himself sought during the period 1914–18 to repudiate and exclude Jung and Adler. His claim at the end of the Wolf-Man case history to have discovered something new about the life of the instincts seems a necessary show of bravura, especially given the polemical context. We might also consider that Lacan himself was "repudiated" and "rejected" by the French Psychoanalytic Society. His celebration of the mechanism of the most radical break with reality, which he called *forclusion,* came at just the moment in his career when he too had been cast out, forgotten.

Lacan's understanding of "foreclosure" cannot, however, be equated with *Verwerfung.* Because Freud was not terribly rigorous about his terminology, it is very difficult to come to a precise understanding of the differences between *Verwerfung, Unterdrückung,* and *Verleugnung.* As Laplanche and Pontalis point out, there is more than a little confusion "as to what it is that is repudiated (*verworfen*) or disavowed (*verleugnet*) when the child rejects castration."[17] The question is how much of reality is repudiated? Daniel Paul Schreber's break with reality was certainly of a very different order from that of the Wolf-Man. The discrimination of psychotic mechanisms is something of a minor genre in psychoanalytic writing, largely, no doubt, because it is essentially a theological debate. Lacan's "foreclosure," which opened the floodgates, is a composite drawn from across the spectrum of Freud's theory

17. Jean Laplanche and J.-B. Pontalis, *The Language of Psychoanalysis,* trans. Donald Nicholson-Smith (New York: Norton, 1973), 167.

of psychosis. Lacan does not, however, place this notion in conjunction with that of memory. For what is truly radical and specific to the mechanism of *Verwerfung* in *From the History of an Infantile Neurosis* is that, unlike other modes of repression, it creates a gap at the very origin of memory.

Fetishists disavow the woman's castration and attempt, through their symptoms, to recover the lost maternal phallus. The Wolf-Man, Freud explains, did nothing of the sort. He neither rejected nor accepted castration, and at the same time he both rejected and accepted castration. Unlike the fetishist who rejects the reality of castration, the Wolf-Man, as a result of the primal scene, simply refused to deal with the question at all. His anal identification with the woman's pleasure made him in a sense impervious to the castration threat, for he had devised a strategy through which he maintained his identification with the woman even though she was castrated:

> He rejected [*verwarf*] castration, and held to his notion of intercourse by the anus. When I speak of his having rejected it, the first meaning of the phrase is that he would have nothing to do with it, in the sense of having repressed it [*im Sinne der Verdrängung*]. This really involved no judgement upon the question of its existence, but it was the same as if it did not exist. [*S.E.*, 17:84]

When Freud goes on to say in the same paragraph, as though in passing, that such rejections were "characteristic" of the Wolf-Man, and when he says that it is *Verwerfung* that "makes it so difficult to give a clear account of his mental processes or to feel one's way into them," it becomes unpleasantly clear that *Verwerfung* is Freud's explanation of the patient's failure of memory. In other words, Freud himself seems to be caught in a kind of Lacanian "foreclosure," in which "what has been foreclosed from the Symbolic reappears in the Real."[18] Had Freud been free to acknowledge the universality of such failures of memory, and had he been able to reflect on its implications, he would not have had to abolish the difference between recollected and constructed conviction, and therefore it would not have returned as a delusional projection in the real in the form of the *Verwerfung* mechanism. Here the delusional element of Freud's theoretical practice, to which he often draws attention, stands in bold relief. Borrowing the

18. Jacques Lacan, *Ecrits* (Paris: Seuil, 1966), 388.

words of his famous remark in the Schreber case history, there is indeed more delusion in Freud's theory of the instincts than he appears willing to admit.

Like the governess in *The Turn of the Screw,* Freud begins to believe in the mechanism he has just invented. His desire to discover the origins of the other's unconscious desire becomes itself a compulsion. In his quest for the origin he often seems as driven by instinct as his patient. For example, in order to set the stage for the perfectly formed "logical contradiction" that will trigger the repetition of the *Verwerfung* mechanism, Freud is "driven to assume" (*Wir haben ja annehmen mussen*) that the Wolf-Man had a dream in which he somehow "understood that women are castrated" (*S.E.,* 17:79). In other words, the demands on his theory are such that Freud is "driven to assume" that the Wolf-Man experienced a moment of understanding in a dream. This enables Freud to articulate the intricate operation of the *Verwerfung* mechanism:

> First he resisted and then he yielded; but the second reaction did not do away with the first [*hatte die anders nicht aufgehoben*]. In the end there were to be found in him two contrary currents side by side, of which one abominated the idea of castration, while the other was prepared to accept it and console itself with femininity as a compensation [*der Weiblichkeit als Ersatz*]. But beyond any doubt a third current, the oldest and deepest, which had simply repudiated castration [*die Kastration einfach verworfen hatte*], where the question of the reality of castration was not even raised [*das Urteil über ihre Realität noch nicht in Frage kam*], was still capable of coming into operation. [*S.E.,* 17:84]

The Wolf-Man reports in his *Memoirs* that Freud once called him a "dialectician."[19] He seems, however, more like a failed dialectician, for instead of performing the synthesis that should bring the castration complex to a close, he steps back into a predialectical state of indifferentiation. The Wolf-Man is suffering, in effect, a failed *Aufhebung:* instead of a synthesis, what he achieves is an *a*dialectical stage prior to difference.

You will not find the full translation of the foregoing passage in the *Standard Edition.* For reasons unknown to me, in Strachey's translation the last sentence is substantially cut by collapsing the "which" and "where" clauses into one: "which did not as yet even raise the question

19. *The Wolf-Man by the Wolf-Man,* 144.

of the reality of castration." What is foreclosed from the *Standard Edition* is nothing less than the clause where *Verwerfung* itself is explained! Strachey seems to be thinking of the passage where Freud expresses his delight at being able to "reach the stage of *raising* such questions." And indeed, it is precisely the Wolf-Man's inability to raise (*aufheben*) the question of castration that is being described here. *Verwerfung* is thus, for the Wolf-Man as well as for Freud, a mechanism to explain one's inability to raise a question—which is to say, one's inability to articulate difference. The question of castration is of course the question of phenomenality, the reality/phantasy question. Because the patient cannot deal adequately with the question during analysis, Freud concludes that it must be because he had been unable to deal with it since it emerged in its most primal form in the course of the castration complex. Freud then attributes his failure to raise the question in a productive fashion to the most primitive stage in the patient's psychical evolution. The simple fact is of course that both parties are responsible for the necessarily imperfect *Fragestellung* that is achieved in every analysis. Freud's gambit in articulating the theory of *Verwerfung* depends upon an implicit assumption of full recollection and self-presence. What Freud seems unwilling to admit in this particular case is that the conviction generated by the analyst's *Fragestellung* will always fall short of such an ideal. Strachey's mistranslation should remind us that the *Fragestellung* is always a question of translation, and thus always a question of reading, in the largest sense of the word.

Of the Wolf-Man, Freud writes that between the ages of one and a half and four, between the primal scene and the seduction scene, "some sort of hardly definable knowledge, something, as it were, preparatory to an understanding, was at work in the child" (*S.E.*, 17:120). Freud concludes that we have no way of thinking about this gray area, this "preparation to understanding" (*Vorarbeitung zum Verständnis*), other than in terms of the "instinctive knowledge of animals." This brings him to his dramatic summary of the implications of his findings in the Wolf-Man case. He has just devoted a considerable portion of the last three chapters of the case history to explaining why the Wolf-Man presents such a marginal and exceptional repressive mechanism. How much more effective, then, is Freud's rhetorical strategy here where he considers, however fleetingly, the possibility that what he has revealed in the Wolf-Man may well be true for everyone: "This instinctive factor would then be the nucleus [*die Kern*] of the uncon-

scious, a primitive kind of mental activity, which would later be de-
throned and overlaid by human reason, when that faculty came to be
acquired, but which in some people, *perhaps in every one,* would retain
the power of drawing down to it the higher mental processes" (*S.E.,*
17:120; my emphasis). Freud's "perhaps in every one" (*vielleicht bei
allen*) is one of what Nietzsche calls those "dangerous perhapses"
(*gefährlichen Vielleicht*),[20] for it calls into question the horizon against
which Freud measures the efficacy of analysis. With this "perhaps,"
Freud casts a shadow over his entire argument and, in so doing, becomes one of the "new species of philosophers" that Nietzsche prophesied, "philosophers of the dangerous 'perhaps.'"

Freud speaks of "this instinctive factor" as "a third current, the
oldest and deepest." It is this current that has the power to draw
"down to it the higher mental processes." Two years later, in *Beyond
the Pleasure Principle,* Freud calls this deepest current the "death
drive," and the *Todestrieb* marks not the "third current" but the
"third step." In this later text he also openly links the operation of the
death drive to the patient's difficulty with recollection. But even there
Freud shifts his ground to biology and the theory of the instincts when
discussing the inner workings of the death drive, instead of pursuing
the question—as one would expect after the first two chapters of
Beyond—in terms of the transference and the differential play of construction and conviction. Of Freud's displacement of the question of
the death drive, François Roustang writes: "It must not be revealed,
because it would be much too dangerous to recognize it at work in the
mainspring of analysis, namely, the transference."[21] In reading *Beyond*
and the other works of the 1920s—particularly *Inhibitions, Symptoms, Anxiety* (1926)—it is important to remember, as Lacan phrases
it, that "it is to the difficulties of recollection that we must always
return if we want to know where psychoanalysis came from."[22]

In *Beyond,* Freud describes the first two steps in his theory of the
instincts as the discovery of first the sexual instincts and then the ego
instincts. Freud insists that these first two steps were based purely on
"observation." To maintain, however, as he is about to do, that it is
the most elemental instincts that block the way to the cure, is for Freud

20. Friedrich Nietzsche, *Beyond Good and Evil,* trans. Walter Kaufmann (New
York: Vintage Books, 1966), 10–11.
21. Roustang, *Psychoanalysis Never Lets Go,* 82.
22. Jacques Lacan, *Les Psychoses,* ed. Jacques-Alain Miller (Paris: Seuil, 1981), 119.

a very risky kind of undertaking, one that leaves the ground of observation for that of "speculation." But of course, as Derrida remarks, from its beginnings the theory of the instincts was "always already speculative."[23] The status of speculation is like that of the analyst's constructions in general. Freud wants to suggest that speculation somehow stands outside analysis, whereas in fact everything that analysis has discovered has been discovered through the medium of construction. In other words, what Freud is constructing in *Beyond* is the primal scene he constructed in *From the History of an Infantile Neurosis,* only in this case he is addressing not the history of the individual but the history of the species.

Freud discovers the deepest current, the death drive, already at work in the primal scene in the history of the instincts, where "from the very first" (*vom allen Anfang*) the sexual instincts "were associated with" the death instincts.[24] So the apparent step ahead is really a step back. Freud is in effect rediscovering the dividedness of the origin. He had believed that the life or sexual instincts were primordial and that the death or ego instincts were derivative. But then why, he asked, do patients continue to repeat unpleasurable events and remain unable to enter into the spirit of the analyst's constructions? For all its evasions, *Beyond* reveals, even as it conceals, a disturbing disjunction between language and recollection, one that would profoundly undermine the efficacy of analysis. If the death instincts were primordial, always already in conjunction with the life instincts, then analysis, through the instrument of language, could never probe further than the differential play between them; thus it could never achieve through construction—which is to say, through speculation—the sort of conviction obtained through recollection. The death instincts would always block the way to the necessary conviction. To recognize the implications of the theory of the death drive explicitly in terms of the transference would endanger the future of analysis, which is no doubt part of the reason why analysts have always been so suspicious of *Beyond*.

They have not been nearly so suspicious of *Inhibitions, Symptoms, and Anxiety* (1926), perhaps because here Freud managed to bury the most troubling questions in the "Addenda." He no longer speaks of

23. Jacques Derrida, *La Carte postale: De Socrate à Freud et au-delà* (Paris: Aubier-Flammarion, 1980), 407.

24. Sigmund Freud, *Beyond the Pleasure Principle,* trans. James Strachey (New York: Norton, 1961), 46.

either *Verwerfung* or the *Todestrieb* as the defensive mechanism that presents the most serious resistance to analysis but rather of a process of "isolation" (*Isolierung*), in which memories are blocked more effectively than through repression:

> Our attention has, moreover, been drawn to a process of "isolation" (whose technique cannot as yet be elucidated) which finds its direct symptomatic manifestation, and to a procedure, that may be called magical, of "undoing" what has been done—a procedure about whose defensive purpose there can be no doubt, but which has no longer any resemblance to the process of "repression."[25]

This "magical" technique of "undoing" (*Ungeschehenmachens*) blocks the patient's efforts at recollection. The memories in question are not simply repressed but "isolated" in some completely irrecoverable way. Far from the "perhaps in every one" at the end of the Wolf-Man case history, Freud is here ensuring that this notion of "isolation" is itself isolated in the text of *Inhibitions, Symptoms, and Anxiety*. Furthermore, Freud makes no effort to link this notion to that of "primal repression" (*Urverdrängung*), which earlier, and in the main body of the text, he likewise marginalized. Freud is reluctant to examine any question that might pose in advance a theoretical obstacle to the therapeutic overcoming of repetition through the recollection of the past. In a sense, this book provides a wonderful reassurance to analysts, for Freud is saying in effect that the discovery of the death drive is indeed irrelevant to the work of analysis. They can forget all of that now; it was only speculation anyway.

Nicolas Abraham's Wolf-Man

Nicolas Abraham took very seriously Freud's notions of *Verwerfung* and isolation. In his posthumous masterpiece, *Cryptonomie: Le Verbier de l'homme aux loups,* prepared with the assistance of Maria Torok, Abraham reinterprets the primal scene in terms of the "primal words" (*les mots originaires*). He wanted to know precisely where and how these memories were isolated. Abraham's solution to the topo-

25. Sigmund Freud, *Inhibitions, Symptoms, and Anxiety*, trans. Alix Strachey, ed. James Strachey (New York: Norton, n.d.), 90.

graphical dilemma Freud had gotten himself into, "a process of 'isola-tion' (whose technique cannot as yet be elucidated)," was to locate the space of incorporation within the Wolf-Man's language. Where Freud speaks of *Verwerfung*, Abraham speaks of incorporation; where Freud says the Wolf-Man's libido was "splintered," Abraham speaks of the "shattered symbol" (*le symbole éclaté*) and the formation of the "crypt." Abraham locates these fault lines and fissures (*fêlures*) not in terms of a psychical topography but in linguistic terms. By isolating certain word chains, certain hidden associations that inhere in the relation of the Wolf-Man's German (the language he speaks to Freud) and native Russian, Abraham constructs his version of the primal scene, which he calls—perhaps thinking of the "magic theater" in Hesse's *Steppenwolf*—the Wolf-Man's "phantasmatic theater."[26]

"Anasemia" is the name Abraham gives the principle that guides him through his transliteral reading of the Wolf-Man's German. He reconstructs the magical, secret enclosures in this patient's speech through a continuous translation into the Russian. "A psychoanalytic theory can be recognized as such," writes Abraham, "precisely to the extent that it works with anasemes." In practice this means that Abra-ham systematically deciphers the Russian homonyms that are con-cealed behind and in effect support the patient's German. The "ana-seme" is the unspoken word or sound that is always somehow adjacent to the spoken word, that is always "over," "under," or "beside" the patient's speech.

More particularly, Abraham argues that there are three fundamental anasemic constructions that support the incorporated primal scene within the Wolf-Man's language. Adjacent to the famous "white wolves," or *weisse Wölfe,* Abraham discerns the Russian *Goulfik,* which is pronounced exactly like *Wölfe* and which means the fly or zipper on a pair of pants. In Russian "to dream" is *vidiet son,* which leads Abraham to the Russian homonym *vidietz,* which means "wit-ness." Thus far the Wolf-Man's dream about an opened window through which he sees the white wolves becomes, in his "phantasmatic theater," something like witnessing an event that involves an opened fly. The third term in Abraham's equation is the word *tieret,* which in Russian means to "rub." Abraham hears the echo of this word at

26. Nicolas Abraham and Maria Torok, *Cryptonomie: Le Verbier de l'homme aux loups* (Paris: Aubier-Flammarion, 1976), 236.

several points in the Wolf-Man's discourse. In his *Memoirs,* for example, the Wolf-Man writes that after his sister's suicide he went into the
wilderness around the *Tierek* river in the Caucasus Mountains. In the
name of the Wolf-Man's wife, *Therese,* Abraham hears the Russian
tieretsia, "to rub oneself." Most important, he hears it behind the
entire *a tergo* motif. Reinforcing the *a tergo* position is the motif of
"rubbing." Abraham's anasemia pursues in earnest the Lacanian principle that desire is a metonymy; for the Wolf-Man's desire, the secret
scene of his desire, is inscribed through a bilingual homonymic chain,
where the adjacency of the various sound shapes counts for everything.
And so, writes Abraham, "These three words, *vidietz:* 'witness';
goulfik: 'zipper'; and *tieret:* 'to rub,' appear to constitute the three
invisible but solid pillars that the Wolf-Man has built from his impossible desire to occupy each of the three positions in the observed scene,
his truly 'primal scene.'"27

Abraham constructs a primal scene that is located between Freud's
scene of parental copulation and the patient's seduction scene with his
sister. In this "truly" primal scene the Wolf-Man sees his father's
seduction of his sister. The three positions he tries to occupy are those
of himself as witness, and of his father and sister. While the fundamental Freudian dynamic stays in place, Abraham has succeeded in refining
it in several respects. Moreover, Abraham's notion incorporates a seduction scene within a primal scene: what the Wolf-Man witnesses is
the other's seduction. In such a reading, one detail in particular from
Freud's case history takes on a new significance. Staying with his sister
at a German sanatorium, the Wolf-Man saw his father give her some
money: "In imagination he had always had suspicions of his father's
relations with his sister; and at this his jealousy awoke. He rushed at
his sister as soon as they were alone, and demanded a share of the
money with so much vehemence and such reproaches that his sister, in
tears, threw him the whole lot" (*S.E.,* 17:83). Abraham's construction
of the primal scene, in addition to the way it calls into question the very
difference between the primal scene and the seduction scene, is to a
certain extent corroborated by the Wolf-Man's own reflections on the
case. Above all, Abraham's construction meets all the requirements
Freud had set for himself.

In his introduction to *Cryptonomie,* Derrida summarizes Abraham's

27. Abraham and Torok, *Cryptonomie,* 157.

narrative revision of the Freudian primal scene. For both Freud and Abraham the crucial issue remains the Wolf-Man's divided and contradictory patterns of identification. Less important than the scene itself is the nature of the double-bind that it precipitates:

> The Wolf-Man's crypt does not shelter his own lost and incorporated object, as would that of a melancholic, but the illegitimate object of another, of his sister, the sister seduced by the father. Like the guardian of a cemetery who, even though he does not own the tombs, is at least officially in charge of them, the Wolf-Man is also only an assistant, delegated (by procuration) to the role of guardian. At least this is the case with respect to seduction. Hysterical insofar as he is disappointed not to have been seduced by the father, he keeps the secret, he does not denounce it, he does not divulge it in these extraordinary scenes of "witnessing" only so that he will be able to "supplant" his sister. The words he will use will enable him, from one angle or another, to denounce *and* to remain silent in order to enjoy.[28]

It is in the incorporated crypt that the Wolf-Man jealously guards the secret words which, as Freud remarks, "magically" have the power to call forth the primal scene. These magical words are Abraham's answer to Freud's query concerning the "technique" of "isolation." Abraham calls his construction a "transphenomenal event," which is in effect the analyst's interpretation of the "angularity" of the words in the Wolf-Man's "*verbier*." Rather than precluding the historical truth, the constructions of Freud and Abraham keep the space of the historical opened. As for Freud, the analyst's construction of the "transphenomenal event" seeks to open rather than close the analysis. The Wolf-Man becomes ill because the maintenance of the crypt is exhausting, paralyzing work and, above all, because playing on both sides at once, on both scenes—concealing and revealing the primal scene—eventually takes its toll.

In his book *The Assault on Truth*, Jeffrey Masson provides information which may soon open the way to another construction. Masson claims to have seen some unpublished notes by Ruth Mack Brunswick, who, at Freud's request, analyzed the Wolf-Man following a psychotic seizure in 1926. During this analysis the Wolf-Man told her that, in Masson's words, "as a child he had been anally seduced by a member of his family—and that Freud did not know this." Masson's conclu-

---

28. Jacques Derrida, Introduction to *Cryptonomie*, 52–53.

sion, as the subtitle of his book, *Freud's Suppression of the Seduction Theory,* indicates, is that Freud did not know because he did not want to know, and that Mack did not report this information to Freud "because she sensed this."[29] Masson's rush to judgment betrays a certain lack of concern for the context of the Wolf-Man's statement. He might have stopped to consider that the Wolf-Man's analysis with Dr. Mack was characterized by an insistent effort to play Freud off against his student. One need only read her significantly titled *A Supplement to Freud's "History of an Infantile Neurosis"* (1928) to see that the Wolf-Man played the master-disciple game for all it was worth.

This is not to say that we are to throw the Wolf-Man's remark out of court, however. First, we must know more about these notes in order to determine whether Mack Brunswick withheld publication because she suspected that the Wolf-Man's remark was spurious. When I read Masson's account, I immediately thought of the Wolf-Man's uncle, a mysterious character in Freud's case history, of whom we know only that he died insane. But even if the Wolf-Man's anality is indeed traceable to such an event, it still would not go to the heart of Freud's project. Masson's naive view of the historical truth does not admit the role of unconscious phantasy in the etiology of the neuroses. In his either/or reduction of the relation of seduction theory to psychoanalysis and of the subjective recollection of real seduction vs. the analytic construction of the primal scene, Masson disregards the fact that Freudian analysis is situated in the differential play between the terms of this binarism. Masson still longs for a simple, remembered origin.

Such nostalgia for the originary provides an interesting contrast to Abraham's reading of the Wolf-Man's analysis with Dr. Mack. For Abraham, it is a classic example of the way the analytic session itself incorporates and repeats the primal scene; in this case, Freud, Mack, and the Wolf-Man play the roles of father, sister, brother. For Abraham, everything in the Wolf-Man's experience is double and divided. It is never a question for him of a simple origin but of a "transphenomenal event." The father's seduction of the sister is such an event. Abraham's technique is to deduce an underlying structure that is never present as such. The Wolf-Man's fury, for example, at the sight

29. Jeffrey Moussaieff Masson, *The Assault on Truth: Freud's Suppression of Seduction Theory* (New York: Farrar, Straus, & Giroux, 1984), xix.

of his sister accepting money from their father takes on its full significance for Abraham in the context of the Mack analysis, in which the Wolf-Man's finances and their link to the seduction scene become focal points. Abraham seeks not historical referents but patterns of repetition.

Abraham describes the "other scene" of the Mack analysis from the perspective of the Wolf-Man's crypt—that is, from the viewpoint of the brother jealous of his father's love of the sister, who seems to say: "You will never be as intimate as I am with the father. It is me he loves and if you accuse me of having seduced you it is because I too have been seduced by the father's love. He owes me money for the pleasure I gave him in order to satisfy his love. I suffer from having been loved too much."[30] Indeed, Abraham's construction seems to anticipate, and can certainly accommodate, a broad variety of incidents, from the primal scene to homosexual rape. More important for Abraham's purposes is the fact that the conjunction Freud/Mack/Wolf-Man brought the sexual jealousy and the cash nexus of the conjunction father/sister/brother unexpectedly close to the surface. But even though Mack Brunswick was able, in Abraham's words, "to deconstitute the image of Freud the seducer," the primal scene, whatever it might really have been, remains in the crypt, unalterably "outside the circuit of speech." In a chapter entitled "Dramaturgy of the Unconscious," Abraham makes a seemingly definitive case concerning the underlying principles of the Wolf-Man's obsession with psychoanalysis. Rather than blaming Freud for sending the Wolf-Man to see Dr. Mack, which would be to take the attitude of the patient himself, Abraham makes us wonder whether it was not the best thing Freud could have done for his favorite patient.

In her account of the analysis, Mack Brunswick sees in one of the Wolf-Man's dreams a restaging of the seduction scene with his sister. The Wolf-Man dreamed that when Dr. Mack entered her office she was dressed like a man and that instead of taking her normal position behind the couch she sat on his lap.[31] For Mack Brunswick, this dream is a major step in overcoming the threatening paternal image of the analyst and, in fact, marks the beginning of a "normal transference."

30. Abraham and Torok, *Cryptonomie*, 101.
31. Ruth Mack Brunswick, "Supplement to Freud's 'History of an Infantile Neurosis,'" in *The Wolf-Man by the Wolf-Man*, 294.

For Abraham, the dream is important because even in its apparent disclosure it constitutes a profound concealment: what it finally does is reinforce the lie that the Wolf-Man has been telling himself for all these years, that " 'Anna is sitting not in my father's lap but in mine. I am at fault. Dr. Mack is sitting on my lap, not on Freud's. I alone am the guilty one.' "[32] He had no suspicion of the debt his family owed him for his silence, no suspicion of what Freud owed him for his theory, but only an unbearably guilty consciousness of his debt to Freud.

In his conversations with Obholzer, the Wolf-Man remarks that he spent a great deal of money during his analysis and complains, after all these years, of Freud's high prices. The Wolf-Man's financial problems began with the Bolsheviks' seizure of his family's estates. On his return to Vienna he had a very meager capital and a few family jewels. Mack Brunswick is the authority on this phase of the Wolf-Man's history. In 1919, she writes, Freud "collected a sum of money for this former patient, who had served the theoretical ends of analysis so well, and repeated this collection for six years."[33] We also know from Mack Brunswick how fearful the Wolf-Man was of losing Freud's support and how jealously he treasured it. After 1922 particularly, when he acquired some family heirlooms through a delicate negotiation, he was acutely fearful that Freud would discover this little cache of jewels and withdraw his aid. "In his fear of losing Freud's help," Mack Brunswick continues, "it evidently did not occur to him that Freud would never have considered permitting the patient to use his little capital."

The Wolf-Man's thoughts in the years between the end of his second analysis with Freud and the start of his analysis with Mack turned incessantly on the questions of debt and guilt. It was during this period that he "began concealing financial facts from his wife, and in the period of inflation, he who had always been cautious, speculated and lost considerable amounts of money." No doubt he gambled in an effort to be free of Freud's help, to release himself from his bad conscience. His thoughts turned on the question of Freud's death and on the possibility that he might inherit. Freud was seriously ill during this period and underwent the first of several operations on the oral cancer that would eventually kill him. Just prior to his dream of Dr. Mack in male attire, the Wolf-Man had seen the emaciated Freud following this

32. Abraham and Torok, Cryptonomie, 220.
33. Mack Brunswick, "Supplement," 266.

operation, and Mack describes his response: "As he went away, he wondered whether Freud would die, and if so, what his own fate would be. He hoped for a small legacy, but feared it might amount to less than the collected sums of several years. Thus it would be more profitable for him if Freud recovered."[34] These speculations are indeed abysmal. The Wolf-Man wants to end the vicious circle, but he finds himself paralyzed because on the one hand he knows that Freud, the father-seducer, is in his debt, while on the other hand he remains convinced of his own guilt. His paranoia denounces the father-seducer, the analyst, while on the scene of the transphenomenal event he alone is the guilty one.

Dr. Mack's appearance in male attire is the last sequence of a dream in which the Wolf-Man's anxiety of indebtedness is vividly dramatized. The dream begins with the Wolf-Man confronted by another doctor, who hands him a bill that he is unable to pay, though the doctor insists that he can afford it. As the Wolf-Man tries to leave the office, the doctor attempts to force upon him some useless gifts, which the patient refuses: "But at the door the doctor presses on him some colored postcards, which he has not the courage to refuse." It is then that Dr. Mack enters and sits on the Wolf-Man's lap. Why does the Wolf-Man "not dare refuse" these "colored postcards" (*färbige Postkarten . . . die zurückweisen ich nicht getraue*)? Here is Mack Brunswick's interpretation:

> Certainly these are symbols of the gifts of Freud, now grown valueless to the patient. The meaning is clear: no gift is now sufficient to compensate the patient for the passivity involved in its acceptance. Thus at last gifts, which at the time of the patient's fourth birthday on Christmas Day, had precipitated the wolf-dream and, indeed, the entire infantile neurosis, and had played a leading role in all his later life and analytic treatment, were now robbed of their libidinal value.[35]

Mack Brunswick links the presents that hung on the Christmas tree, and were transformed into the six or seven wolves hiding in a tree, to Freud's gifts. The patient dare not denounce these gifts, just as he dared not denounce his father and sister's secret or, for that matter, any of a series of secrets one might construct here.

Abraham's constructions consistently relate the details of the Mack

34. Mack Brunswick, "Supplement," 286.
35. Mack Brunswick, "Supplement," 293.

analysis to the revised version of the primal scene. The triangularity of
the Wolf-Man's analysis with Mack enabled him to grasp (as he had
not with Freud) the need, in Abraham's words, "to deconstitute the
image of Freud the seducer"—which is to say, the father as seducer.
Even so, he still was unable to refuse the "postcards," those postcards
illustrating the primal scene, postcards that are in fact the analyst's
constructions, which the Wolf-Man has never been able either to accept or reject. The merit of the Mack analysis was to have revealed the
paralytic dilemma into which the Wolf-Man had been coerced by his
divided attitude to the scenes depicted on those postcards. But even
though the Mack analysis brought the terms of the primal scene into
relief through repetition, it failed to enable the Wolf-Man to move
beyond his insistence on recollection and the seduction scene with his
sister. Mack brought him as close perhaps as anyone could to the most
fundamental level of concealment. He had explained to Freud that he
found it impossible to mourn for his sister when she committed suicide
in 1905; with Dr. Mack he came to understand how profound his
sister complex was. Writing his *Memoirs* in 1970, he included a chapter entitled "Unconscious Mourning: 1905–1908" that relates the
events between his sister's death and his psychiatric pilgrimage through
Europe. Freud was surely right to assume that another event had pre-
ceded the wolf dream and the seduction scene, and Abraham is surely
correct to suppose that this prior scene also involves the sister. The
Wolf-Man himself remained unable to grasp that entire problematic
and maintained that he could not credit the explanatory power of a
prior scene without being able to recollect it himself. But because the
terms of his analysis had become caught up with his "unconscious
dramaturgy," the Wolf-Man's rejection of his analyst's gifts or constructions enabled him at least partly to overcome the unconscious
power of a forgotten scene. As Mack puts it, they "were now robbed of
their libidinal value." Even though the Wolf-Man would not acknowledge a primal scene, analysis nevertheless helped him to move somewhat outside the orbit of a particularly compulsive rhythm. It put an
end to the anxiety of indebtedness. No longer would the son feel as
though he owed a debt; no longer would he bear the burden of passivity. Though he would not denounce the father or any other symbolic
father figure, he was at least released from the power of the primal
words that told of the buried secret. The crypt remained locked and
secure, but henceforth he would not have to tend to it so assiduously.

Freud's Phantasmatic Theater

In his reading of *Beyond the Pleasure Principle,* Derrida comes up against a fundamental concealment of the difference between cognition and performance. What are we to make of texts that are themselves "part of the objects they depict,"

> when they themselves are an example of what they are speaking or writing about? What one gets is certainly not a self-reflexive transparency, quite the contrary. An accounting is no longer possible, nor is a summation; the edges of the whole are neither closed nor opened. Their trait is divided, and the connections can no longer be undone. There one finds perhaps the ultimate resistance to a solution.[36]

No less than *Beyond the Pleasure Principle,* the Wolf-Man dossier—particularly the Wolf-Man/Mack/Freud relationship—is a text whose edges "are neither closed nor opened." Here indeed is a case of what Derrida calls "the double chiasmatic invagination of the edges," where cognition and performance have become impossible to distinguish. Such an analysis truly becomes the space of incorporation, a zone of *différance* where oppositions are folded into one another, where every outside is also an inside. At such points we are brought up against the most fundamental concealment, against the encrypted, encysted spaces that seem able interminably to resist a solution. At such points the experience of the transference and the act of reading and interpretation come into an important but perhaps unanalyzable conjunction. For like the transference, reading is what Derrida, speaking of *Beyond the Pleasure Principle,* calls a "calculation without foundation," an "endless speculation . . . without capital of its own." No less than the transference, a certain kind of reading repeats the text without either fully opening or closing its edges.

The French psychoanalyst Wladimir Granoff has opened the question of Freud's exceptional relationship with the Wolf-Man.[37] Why, asks Granoff, did Freud take such an interest in the Wolf-Man, first as a patient and then as a ward? The Wolf-Man, who was Freud's only Russian patient, came from Odessa, which is the one city in Russia with which Freud's own father and mother were associated. In particu-

---

36. Derrida, *La Carte postale,* 417.
37. Wladimir Granoff, *La Pensée et le féminin* (Paris: Minuit, 1976), 346–48.

lar, Granoff notes Freud's involvement in the Wolf-Man's marriage. When the Wolf-Man introduced Therese to Freud in 1914, Freud remarked that she "looked like a czarina," and so, the Wolf-Man continues, "my intention to marry Therese now met with his full approval."[38] He adds that Freud regarded "the breakthrough to the woman" as his patient's "greatest achievement." A specific feature of Therese's appearance seems to have captured the Wolf-Man's imagination; he alludes to it twice in his *Memoirs* and includes a photograph of Therese in which it is prominent—the same photograph Granoff in turn uses on the cover of his book. "Her blue-black hair," writes the Wolf-Man, "was parted in the middle."[39] His fascination with this "part" or *Scheitel* seems to echo the *Aufsplitterung* motif that Freud had noted. Granoff takes this one step further by suggesting that Freud may have seen in Therese either his own first love from Freiberg—a certain Gisela Fluss—or his mother, Amalie Freud. According to Ernest Jones, Freud "attributed his infatuation to Gisela's black hair and eyes," and Granoff points out that in an 1876 family portrait, among the women only Amalie wore her hair with a part down the middle. To this list of circumstantial details, let me add that when the Wolf-Man rejoined his wife after a brief separation near the end of World War I, he was shocked to discover "that Therese, who had left Odessa with beautiful black hair, had turned snow-white."[40] Returning to Vienna in 1918, the couple must have indeed reminded Freud of his own parents and his own past.

Without wanting to take Granoff's suggestions too far, I believe his constructions do have the virtue of adding yet another dimension to our understanding of the complex filiations that defined Freud's relationship with the Wolf-Man. In this case the father-son relation may have incorporated the terms of its own reversal: that is, Freud and the Wolf-Man as alternately father and son in relation to each other. In their Nietzschean game of debt and guilt (*Schulden*), Freud and his patient may have each played out the terms of their respective primal scenes, and in each case the son would have written the terms of his own legacy; in other words, the son who pays off his debt to the father could also be the father who places his son in his debt. Whatever the underlying reasons for Freud's extraordinary interest in the Wolf-Man,

38. *The Wolf-Man by the Wolf-Man*, 90.
39. *The Wolf-Man by the Wolf-Man*, 49.
40. *The Wolf-Man by the Wolf-Man*, 110.

they led him to the very limits of his experience as an analyst and a theorist. While Abraham reminds us that Freud was for the Wolf-Man a kind of father-seducer, Granoff reminds us that the Wolf-Man and Therese were for Freud the figures of Jakob and Amalie Freud.

In 1920, following his second analysis with Freud, the Wolf-Man wanted to return to Russia in order to reclaim some of his confiscated property. Mack Brunswick reports that the Wolf-Man told her it was Freud who persuaded him to stay in Vienna. She marks her consternation and her refusal to accept her patient's story with a significant parenthesis: "and by his persuasion (*sic!*) kept the patient in Vienna."[41] Mack Brunswick finds it inconceivable that Freud could have exerted such an influence. But is it really so difficult to believe?

Therese, like the Wolf-Man's sister Anna, took her own life: when Hitler marched into Vienna on March 31, 1938, she put her head in the oven. To Karin Obholzer the Wolf-Man revealed that after their return to Vienna, even though he still loved Therese, he had sought sexual satisfaction from other women. Furthermore, he told Obholzer, Therese identified strongly with Anna, but that had nothing to do with her suicide. Hitler, he insisted, "had something to do with her suicide."[42] Nevertheless, Therese had somehow been caught up in the Wolf-Man's sister complex—in ways that no doubt remained hidden to the Wolf-Man himself.

After her death the Wolf-Man went to London. Freud arrived not long after. Although he considered visiting Freud in London, he did not. Instead, he returned to Vienna, where he spent the duration of the war. He no longer needed the analytic world, which had transplanted itself to London. Analysis had done all it could for him. It had taught him how to keep the crypt intact and to survive.

41. Mack Brunswick, "Supplement," 282.
42. Obholzer, *The Wolf-Man*, 104.

5 From Imitation to Dissemination: Mallarmé's "Hamletism"

There's no fixed connection with the Castle, no central exchange that transmits our calls further.

FRANZ KAFKA, *The Castle*

There could be nothing more striking than this shock, this uneasiness which the silence of art inspires in the lover of the spoken word.

MAURICE BLANCHOT, "The Beast of Lascaux"

In the early 1920s, the French poet Max Jacob complained that French literature for the preceding sixty years had been dominated by what he calls "Hamletism," which, he insisted, should "no longer be taken as a model."[1] Jacob defines Hamletism as "the essence of subjectivism" and blames it for having created an atmosphere of "false profundity" in French letters. Believing that this hypersubjectivism has been brought to an end by the tragedy of World War I, which has "de-hamletized avant-garde literature," he writes "L'Hamletisme" to announce the end of an epoch and to warn writers not to repeat the errors of the past.

The immediate occasion for this polemic is Jacob's irritation at a sentence that one of his friends annoyingly repeats: "I believe there are also spiders' webs in the absolute" (*Je crois qu'il y a aussi des toiles d'araignées dans l'absolu*). Even without recognizing Mallarmé as the

---

1. Max Jacob, "L'Hamletisme," in *Art poétique* (Paris: Emile-Paul Frères, n.d.), 38–42.

source of this sentence, one could easily guess it from Jacob's having dated the epoch of Hamletism from the 1860s, which is when Mallarmé began publishing. Jacob's friend Marcel (probably Marcel Schwob) keeps Hamletism alive by citing his version of a line from "Frisson d'hiver" (1864), which is one of Mallarmé's most widely known prose poems, in England as well as in France, thanks to George Moore's translation of it in his memoir of the epoch in question, *Confessions of a Young Man*. Jacob's friend has lighted upon what is a compelling refrain not only in "Frisson d'hiver" but in Mallarmé's work in general. The image of "the spiders' webs high up in the casement windows" is typical of his fascination with arachnian imagery of webs and weaving. Marcel's refrain combines the spiders' webs from "Frisson d'hiver" with the emphasis on the absolute of Mallarmé's *Igitur,* which was written between 1867 and 1870 and published posthumously in 1900. In a sense, then, Jacob is justified in regarding this refrain as emblematic of an epoch in which Mallarmé's influence was pervasive.

What Jacob finds so objectionable about Mallarmé and his influence is his incessant ontological posturing. In the terms of my argument, Jacob would regard Mallarmé as the epitome of an anti-Platonic metaphysic wherein the absolute has been equated with nothingness yet remains knowable for the Mallarméan subject. Mallarmé's inverted Platonism would nonetheless remain bound to a Platonic ontology wherein what-is, even if what-is is nothingness, can be grasped within the depths of subjectivity. Writing at the beginning of the end of metaphysics, Jacob accuses Mallarmé of having staged the final apotheosis of the Platonic mystification of the subject in the history of French literature.

Jacob's attitude vividly points out the difficulty of writing the history of the overcoming of metaphysics and, more particularly, of determining the role of what is called "literature" in that history. For Jacob, Mallarmé represents a regressive element that has held French literature back and bound it to an inappropriate and outdated subjectivism. I begin with Jacob's "L'Hamletisme" because it provides such a perfect foil for Jacques Derrida's contradictory argument in "The Double Session," which presents Mallarmé as the figure in French literature who has decisively altered the relation of literature to the truth and who, furthermore, has managed to avoid the traps of both Platonism and its negation. Focusing on a late prose piece by Mallarmé entitled

"Mimique" (1886), Derrida maintains that "between Plato and Mallarmé . . . a whole history has taken place."[2] While Jacob's Mallarmé remains bound to a subjective notion of the truth, Derrida's Mallarmé has discovered an alternative to the binarism of Western metaphysics. In this brief chapter I am going to use the terms of Derrida's argument to conduct a rereading of "Frisson d'hiver," which Derrida does not mention, and in so doing expose the bias of Jacob's position by pointing out how his presuppositions prevented him from reading Mallarmé on Mallarmé's own terms.

Derrida does not provide even a hint of what this "history" between Plato and Mallarmé might look like. He does not, in other words, suggest the point at which the beginning of the end of metaphysics might have begun; he tells us only that by the time of Mallarmé, the beginning had begun in earnest. Jacob, like almost everyone else who has thought about literary history, provides us with neat and convenient beginnings and ends. But Derrida is concerned with the kind of event that is not constituted in one time and one place. The problem of articulating the history of literature's relation to the truth is the problem of the "between." It is the problem of articulating an event that is at once the cause and the effect of another event, an event that is always dislocated and displaced by another event. Jacob's account, for example, points out the significance of Mallarmé's relation to the text of *Hamlet,* which Jacob seems to regard as a purely regressive relation. But need we restrict ourselves to such a one-directional notion of influence? If Mallarmé is under the influence of a Hamletian cult of the subject, then might it not also be the case that *Hamlet* itself is changed by this relation? In the next chapter, I will argue that the beginning of the end has already begun in *Hamlet,* and that the subsequent histories of both literature and philosophy bear the decisive imprint of that text. By treating Mallarmé's radical critique of the notion of representation in this chapter, I will posit in advance an alternative to the Hegelian reading of *Hamlet.*

Max Jacob interprets "Frisson d'hiver" against the horizon of the numerous French adaptations of *Hamlet* during the decadence, and perhaps that is why for him Mallarmé's text becomes indistinguishable from the parodic Hamletism of a Laforgue or a Villiers de l'Isle-

2. Jacques Derrida, "The Double Session," in *Dissemination,* trans. Barbara Johnson (Chicago: University of Chicago Press, 1981), 183.

Adam.[3] Writing of Mallarmé's Pierrot, whose mimed performance of the murder of his wife is the subject of "Mimique," Derrida remarks, "Pierrot is brother to all the Hamlets haunting the Mallarméan text."[4] But against the tendency to read Mallarmé's fascination with Hamlet, as other critics have, in conjunction with what Derrida calls his "supposed Hegelianism" and thereby to reduce his text to "a brilliant literary idealism," Derrida argues that Mallarmé's Hamletism is something that cannot be recuperated by any idealism, by any dialectic, or by any ontology. Mallarmé does not simply proclaim the ascendancy of literature over philosophy but rather redefines the most fundamental assumptions of these discourses. The play that Mallarmé's nephew Paul Marguerite stages in his mime of "Pierrot, Murderer of His Wife" cannot be accounted for by either a subjectivist or an objectivist notion of mimesis. In miming Pierrot's murder of his wife by tickling her to death, the mime presents an event that has no actuality in the world— an event, as Derrida observes, that does not have "to conform, with an eye toward verisimilitude, to some real or external model, to some *nature*, in the most belated sense of the word." But neither is this an event of which we can have any *ideal* notion, no "representation of the thing through thought."[5] Instead of following a preestablished model of the event, the mime creates through his performance what Derrida calls "reality-effects." Mallarmé's Hamletism—that is, Mallarmé's mimicry or mimesis of *Hamlet*—is not at all the essentializing subjectivism Jacob makes it out to be.

Mallarmé does not do away with the notion of mimesis. What he does, says Derrida, is to disengage it from "its Platonic or metaphysical interpretation, which implies that somewhere the being of something that *is*, is being imitated."[6] Mallarmé's Hamletian view of the mimetic event can be recuperated neither by something that *is* nor by the nothingness of something that *is not*. It is between being and nothingness, between the Platonic cave where delusory figures and shadows flicker on the wall and the world illuminated by the sunlight of the Idea, the truth, the *eidos*, the logos, the absolute spirit. Mallarmé situates the

3. See Peter Brooks, "The Rest Is Silence: Hamlet as Decadent," in *Jules Laforgue: Essays on a Poet's Life and Work,* ed. Warren Ramsay (Carbondale: Southern Illinois University Press, 1969), 93–110.
4. Derrida, *Dissemination*, 195.
5. Derrida, *Dissemination*, 194.
6. Derrida, *Dissemination*, 206.

event in the preontological space of undecidability between the cave and the sun, between the figural lie of literature and the literal truth of philosophy; in lieu of the platonic cave (*antre*) comes the Mallarméan "between" (*entre*).

While Jacob's reading of Mallarmé remains bound to a reductive notion of mimesis and Hamletism, Derrida's reading follows the intricate weave of the Mallarméan text into the primal scene of literature-philosophy. It is in the irreducible folds of this "hymenal" space where Pierrot and his wife stage their tragicomic "hymenal rites" (that is, the murder that takes place on their wedding night); it is in this space of "the in-between-ness of the hymen" that we can situate the spider webs of "Frisson d'hiver." As Derrida points out, the hymen is a veil, a fold, a fabric, a weave; the word derives from *huphos,* which means "textile, spider web, net, the text of a work."[7] Like the dumb show, or Elizabethan mime, that introduces "The Mousetrap" in *Hamlet,* the preontological trace of the hymen at once reveals and conceals the imitated event by situating it, by weaving it, between the outside and the inside, "between desire and fulfillment, between perpetration and its recollection." It is in this space, in this interval—and Derrida reminds us that *antre* (cave) comes from the Sanskrit *antara,* which signifies "interval"—that the primal scene of literature-philosophy at the beginning of the end of metaphysics is invariably situated. While Jacob claims that he and those who share his views have performed what he calls "the undressing of Hamlet," Mallarmé seems to have already "undressed" the presuppositions that underlie Jacob's argument. In "Frisson d'hiver" the undecidable space of the hymen is rendered as the space of the "casement windows," in whose recesses the spiders weave their uncanny webs.

We can suggest further that, in light of Mallarmé's Hamletism, Hamlet may be said to have already "undressed" Jacob. From Plato to Shakespeare, then, a "whole history" would have taken place—would have taken place, that is, as long as one knew how to read it. With respect to the problematic of mimesis, one could say that Mallarmé delivers the text of *Hamlet,* that he makes it readable, or even that he enables us to grasp the nature of its unreadability. But one can go still further and say that what Mallarmé has revealed is nothing less than "an internal division within *mimesis,*"[8] an internal division within

7. Derrida, *Dissemination,* 213.
8. Derrida, *Dissemination,* 191.

Plato's theory of mimesis. One might say that "from Plato to Plato a whole history has taken place." Perhaps, as Derrida remarks, one mode of mimesis is always being displaced by another, "as though it were destined to mime or mask *itself*," and perhaps the "history of literature" is synonymous with that shuttling back and forth from one mode of mimesis to another. "Mimique" would contain the history of that division and therefore the history of literature. It would contain that history without being contained by it. It would contain the ensemble of theories of mimesis that literature has always purported to be about without any longer being committed to any one of them. Through this "double inscription," this "double science," "Mimique" would stage the primal scene of philosophy-literature, where the essence of mimesis would have always already been divided or, in keeping with the metaphorics of the hymen, "spilled," disseminated. But again, this does not imply a simple loss of the center but rather, as Mallarmé writes at the conclusion of "Mimique," "the condition and delight of reading": that is, the affirmation of the noncenter. Dissemination, writes Derrida, "*affirms* the always already divided generation of meaning."[9]

"Frisson d'hiver" (Winter Shiver) recounts a conversation between a man and a woman on a winter's evening. Their conversation turns to the subjects of time, desire, and death. Punctuating the five brief paragraphs of the poem are four parenthetical expressions that function as a refrain reflecting the growing anxiety and isolation of the speaker's private thoughts. In the first paragraph the speaker wonders aloud about the old Saxon clock in their apartment and thinks how many years have passed since it was brought from Saxony. In the second paragraph he considers his wife's antique Venetian mirror:

And your Venetian looking-glass, deep as a cold fountain, in a shore of tarnished wyverns, what is mirrored in it? Ah! I am sure that more than one woman has bathed in this water the sin of her beauty; and perhaps I should see a naked ghost if I looked long enough.

"Naughty man, you do say wicked things."

(I see spiders' webs at the top of the big casements.)[10]

9. Derrida, *Dissemination*, 268.

10. Stéphane Mallarmé, *Oeuvres complètes*, ed. Henri Mondor and G. Jean-Aubry (Paris: Gallimard, Pléiade, 1945), 270.

In the next sequence the speaker catalogs the curious decor of their apartment and considers once again the effects of time. At this point, the spiders' webs begin to "quiver." He then reflects upon his wife's penchant for the phrase "the grace of withered things" (*la grâce des choses fanées*). In the final sequence, she is reading an eighteenth-century German almanac. The speaker asks her to close the book, which tells only of dead things long past. He wants to turn the anxious drift of their conversation in a more amorous direction, but his companion's mind is already too distracted to think of love. His desire thwarted, the man's gaze returns to the spider webs, still "shivering at the top of the big casements."

Let us return to the image of the antique Venetian mirror: "in a shore of tarnished wyverns, what is mirrored in it?" (*en un rivage de guivres dédorées, qui s'y est miré*). A "*guivre*" or "wyvern" is a heraldic serpent, which means that this mirror is indeed an ornate space of representation, a mirror framed by the tarnished figures of serpents. The mirror is like a river, the river of time, and along its banks are the phantasmagoric serpents of myth. Mimesis is, in part, precisely the sort of conjuration trick the speaker refers to when he expresses the hope of seeing the "naked ghost" of a woman who has been dead for centuries. Like the governess in *The Turn of the Screw*, the speaker of "Frisson d'hiver" wants to glimpse a primal scene—in this case, the primal sin of female vanity. But this desire, like all other desires in this poem, is thwarted. The speaker is left before a surface that gives back only his own reflection.

The German almanac his wife is reading is more than a century old, "and the kings it announces are all dead." At the top of the casement windows the spider webs are "shivering," and no doubt the spiders, who are never mentioned, have long since abandoned them. This poem is situated in a funereal space of melancholy and mourning. It is also the space of a haunting, for the speaker is haunted by his "naked ghost," his "dead kings," and his shivering spider webs. He lives in what Mallarmé in "Mimique" calls "the false appearance of the present." He is suspended between the present and the future by the unbearable burden of a past that he cannot remember. He suffers from a belatedness he cannot dispel, like a patient who is compelled to repeat what he cannot recollect.

The speaker of "Frisson d'hiver" is under the deathly spell of the compulsion to repeat, which is an effect that is inscribed most notably in the incantatory refrain of the "spiders' webs high up in the large casement windows" (*toiles d'araignées au haut des grandes croisées*). Instead of being able to remember the ghosts of the past, the speaker can see no further than the ghostly shroud of the spiders' webs. The refrain itself seems to reinforce the spell of a repetitive rhythm that moves from "*araignées*" to "*croisées*," and from "*tremblent*" to "*grelottent*" (shivering). Mallarmé's suspicion of mimesis is intensified and displaced into the even more fundamental question of rhythm. As Derrida says, rhythm for Mallarmé is the essence of the literary, which he wants to escape—as he had escaped mimesis—without doing away with it altogether:

> The crisis of verse (of "rhythm," as Mallarmé also puts it) thus involves all of literature. The crisis of a *rythmos* broken by Being . . . is "fundamental." It solicits the very bases of literature, depriving it, in its exercise, of any foundation outside itself. Literature is at once reassured and threatened by the fact of depending only on itself, standing in the air, all alone, aside from Being: "and, if you will, alone, excepting everything."[11]

"Frisson d'hiver" stages this exquisitely anxious crisis of the literary, this shiver which is at once pain and pleasure. "Winter is for prose," writes Mallarmé. "With the splendor of autumn, verse ceases. . . . Silence, sole luxury after rhymes . . ." Here at the corporeal-affective base of mimesis, the task of writing for Mallarmé is to stage the overcoming of rhythm, to generate rhythms that cancel themselves. To be "rhythmed," as Heidegger remarked, is to be bound or "confined." In his own version of the Fort/Da game, Mallarmé binds himself only in order to make the breaking of his bindings that much sweeter.

In "Le Phénomène futur" (The Coming Phenomenon; 1864), Mallarmé writes of poets (like himself) "haunted by Rhythm and forgetting they exist in an age that outlives beauty" (*hantés du Rythme et dans l'oubli d'exister à une époque qui survit à la beauté*).[12] In the beginning of the ending of metaphysics, Mallarmé sees his task as that of disengaging the fundamental Platonic notion, which is the link between rhythm, harmony, and the truth. In this epoch of crisis, as he sees it, we have forgotten the unifying rhythm, but we have not forgot-

11. Derrida, *Dissemination*, 279–80.
12. Mallarmé, *Oeuvres complètes*, 272.

ten that we have forgotten something. With Mallarmé we leave the Platonic notion of harmony and measure in an effort to experience the noncenter as something other than a loss of center. There is no more question of escaping rhythm than there is of escaping mimesis. *It is rather a question of escaping the interpretation in which that notion had been bound or confined.* In this autumnal space, in what Heidegger in *Zur Seinsfrage* calls "the withdrawing wake" of Being, rhythm still casts its aural shadow over the present forgetfulness.

Barbara Johnson writes that what haunts Mallarmé's prose poems is poetry itself: "At the interior of the explicitly phantomatic space of the Mallarméan prose poem, verse appears visibly, as a ghost, a revenant."[13] Johnson also cites a letter of 1864 in which Mallarmé describes the process of writing a prose poem during which he rejected a thousand "beautiful verses that haunted my mind." A poet haunted by Rhythm seeks always to break the rhythm, to change tone, to shift from the familiar to the unfamiliar. The "double scene" of the Mallarméan prose poem includes both the solicitation of rhythm's spell and the dissonant overcoming or erasure of a phantom that can be parodied but not utterly demystified.

"Frisson d'hiver" is the title Mallarmé gave this prose poem in 1875; its original title was "Causerie d'hiver" (Winter Gossip). He made only one other change in the text. In the second and fourth refrains, he shifted the location of the spiders' webs from *en haut* ("high up," or "way up") in the casement windows to *au haut*—"at the top," "at the very top" of the "*grandes croisées.*" Like Freud's grandson, Mallarmé seems to be playing "Here/Gone" with these spiders' webs. Even the tone change from *en haut* to *au haut* is reminiscent of Ernst Freud's "a-a-a-o-o-o." In the place of the rhythmic refrain of *en haut* with its soft, melodic line, Mallarmé inserts the anxiously dissonant, almost arhythmic *au haut*. Pronounced like "oh-oh," *au haut* is pure repetition, a quiet cry of anxiety, like a *Fort* without the *Da*.

Writing in 1896 on the subject of the ballet, Mallarmé cites another writer's account of the "spell of the dance, where the body [of the dancer] appears as the rhythm on which everything depends but which remains hidden."[14] The dancer's movements reveal, in the mode of concealment, the rhythm that secretly sustains the whole. The dance

13. Barbara Johnson, *Défigurations du langage poétique* (Paris: Flammarion, 1979), 173.
14. Mallarmé, *Oeuvres complètes,* 311.

becomes a figure of the process in which rhythm is revealed through its concealment. This divided interval, this hymen, this veil, this *"eventail"* between the concealment of rhythm and the disclosure of its conceal- ment, constitutes the haunting primal scene of the Mallarméan text. Like the ballet, the prose poem is the clearing in which this concealment is disclosed. The casement windows, *"les grandes croisées,"* are the privileged site of such a clearing.

The *"croisée"* is an opening that is neither inside nor outside but on both sides at once. It is an incorporated space where the outside has been incorporated by the inside, the boundary space where outside and inside are interwoven. This encrypted space is the site of the unper- ceived event, the space of the unheard rhythm, the space opened by the withdrawal of the question of Being, by the silent retreat of the spiders' webs into the distance. Mallarmé's critique of the metaphysical notions of rhythm and representation stands in the incorporated space at the beginning of the end of metaphysics; it stands between the death of literature and philosophy and the birth of literature-philosophy.

6 Shakespeare in the Ear of Hegel

The completion of metaphysics begins with Hegel's metaphysics of absolute knowledge as the Spirit of will.

MARTIN HEIDEGGER, "Overcoming Metaphysics"

What are you building?—
I want to dig a subterranean passage.

FRANZ KAFKA, "The Pit of Babel"

Music i'the air, under the earth.
It signs not well, does it not?

WILLIAM SHAKESPEARE, *Antony and Cleopatra*

Prologue: The "Will to Style"

"To define style," writes Fredric Jameson, "as language which deliberately calls attention to itself, and 'foregrounds' itself as a key element in the work, is to reassert, as over against stylistics, the profoundly historical nature of the phenomenon."[1] Jameson has always been particularly attentive to the question of style. In his first book, *Sartre: The Origins of a Style,* he writes of the "constant presence [in Sartre] of a single, special style of doing things and a will power moving through all of them in the same characteristic direction."[2] Twenty years later, in *The Political Unconscious,* Jameson is still concerned with this notion, which in his discussion of Conrad he now calls the "will to

1. Fredric Jameson, *Marxism and Form* (Princeton, N.J.: Princeton University Press, 1971), 335.
2. Fredric Jameson, *Sartre: The Origins of a Style* (New Haven, Conn.: Yale University Press, 1961), 203.

style."[3] Even more recently, in an essay entitled "Postmodernism, or the Cultural Logic of Late Capitalism," he argues that the postmodern decentering of the subject, its dislocation from any sense of an individual identity, brings with it the "end of style": "For with the collapse of the high-modernist ideology of style—what is as unique and unmistakable as your own fingerprints, as incomparable as your own body (the very source for an early Roland Barthes, of stylistic invention and innovation)—the producers of culture have nowhere to turn but to the past: the imitation of dead styles, speech through all the masks and voices stored up in the imaginary museum of a now global culture." In this "as yet untheorized original space of some new 'world system' of multinational or late capitalism,"[4] the will to power as style has been overcome by the leveling power of capital. Computerized information storage and retrieval now constitute a collective memory that has radically altered the role of individual memory, to which style is intimately linked. Time, which was the dominant category in the modernist epoch, has now, argues Jameson, been replaced by the leveling horizontality of space. Style, which is inseparable from time and memory, has been overwhelmed by capital's recreation of a new kind of "constant presence." In short, the electronic archive has made style obsolete.

The notion of the "end of style" cannot of course be separated from the notion of the overcoming of metaphysics. Jameson's thinking poses several questions, such as that of the relation of language to capital and of the commodification of language in the wake of the massive recapitalization that has taken place over the last thirty years. In the words of Jean-François Lyotard, whose ideas have been important to Jameson, "The effects of the penetration of capitalism into language have only just begun."[5] Instead of the individual "will to style," Jameson and Lyotard would agree that capital itself has usurped the prerogatives of the erstwhile "human" desire for infinite extension. Capital itself would thus be the locus of the will to power and thus also the agent of the overcoming of metaphysics.

What kind of an event is this transformation from modernism to

---

3. Fredric Jameson, *The Political Unconscious* (Ithaca, N.Y.: Cornell University Press, 1981), 225.

4. Fredric Jameson, "Postmodernism, or the Cultural Logic of Late Capitalism," *New Left Review* 146 (1984): 65, 88.

5. Jean-François Lyotard, *Tombeau de l'intellectuel* (Paris: Galilée, 1984), 82–83.

postmodernism? In this chapter I am going to analyze a moment in the prehistory of that transformation. In the thinking of Freud and Heidegger we have traced in miniature the story of the overcoming of style, for we have seen how they came to recognize the fundamental concealment in language that blocks all efforts to use language to conceive of the relation between language and the world. The overcoming of metaphysics and logocentrism is, at its most elemental, the recognition that language cannot account for its own effects; it is the recognition that the will to power has moved outside of language, and that perhaps it has always been outside of language. In Heidegger's idiom, we might describe the transformation as the recognition that language is neither *for* man nor *of* man; rather, man is the guardian of language, whose true subject remains concealed. Psychoanalysis and Marxism, along with the other strategies of poststructuralism, are efforts to generate terms through which to discuss the radical otherness of the subject of language. "Capital," the "unconscious," "*différance,*" and the rest are terms through which we attempt to describe man's dispossession of language.

The work of Hegel stands as the apotheosis or culmination of philosophy's effort to account, through language, for the effects of language. My focus is on a moment in Hegel's style when the language of philosophy is called into question by the language of literature that it attempts to appropriate. It is at the very moment when Hegel wants to express his own style, when he wants to impress his own character into the text of philosophy by citing the text of Shakespeare, that the spirit of the will working through both philosophy and literature becomes radically inaccessible and unreadable. It is at the point where Hegel attempts to incorporate Shakespeare into the text of philosophy that the subject of language—that is, the locus of the will to power, the spirit of absolute knowledge—becomes radically other. In this conjunction between Shakespeare and Hegel, we will discover a moment in the prehistory of the postmodernist overcoming of the "will to style."

Jameson's focus on the question of style and on the historical transformation it has undergone in the late modernist epoch provides, I believe, a basis on which to begin to think about relating Marx's history of capital to Heidegger's history of Being. Jameson indicates the outlines of such a conjunction when he remarks of Heidegger's "The

Origin of the Work of Art" that it "is organized around the idea that the work of art emerges within the gap between Earth and World, or what I would prefer to translate as the meaningless materiality of the body and nature and the meaning-endowment of history and of the social."[6] It is in the Heideggerian *Riss* or rift between Earth and World that Marx would locate the work of capital. Language, capital, and the will to power are all means of describing how a world comes into being and how man appropriates the earth and makes it his own. But within that history of appropriation there is another history, a history of expropriation and dispossession that can be determined at the levels of both social and cultural history. It is in terms of the metaphorics of the movement through the "meaningless materiality" of the earth into the "meaning-endowment" of the world that the conjunction between Shakespeare and Hegel is inscribed, for what Hegel cites is Hamlet's enigmatic apostrophe to the ghost of his father as the "old mole." "Shakespeare in the Ear of Hegel" is an effort to determine exactly what might be burrowing its way from Shakespeare to Hegel as well as within the texts of Hegel and Shakespeare themselves.

Jameson's notion of the transformation from modernism to post-modernism brings us once again to the question of the nature of the event: how is it constituted, and where does it begin? For my purposes, the importance of Jameson's project consists in his having defined the Marxian-Althusserian notion of the event and its causality in terms that enable us to relate it to the thinking of Freud and Heidegger. From Althusser, Jameson derives the notion of "structural causality," which is to say that the cause of the event has no identity in itself and can only be determined as an immanent structure that inheres within its own effects. In short, Althusser uproots the event from ontology. As in Freud's primal scene and Heidegger's "beginning that veils the origin," in Althusser there is no origin as such but rather an ensemble of beginnings, a causal network that remains immanent in its effects. All of these thinkers propose a metaleptic logic of causality and the event. By virtue of this conjunction, Marxism, psychoanalysis, and the Heideggerian-Derridean project discover a unity that is perhaps more important than their many differences. Jameson calls his structuralist-Marxist version of the primal scene the "subtext," where, as in the

6. Jameson, "Postmodernism," 59.

formation of the symptom, the precipitating causes are inscribed in the very act of their erasure:

> The literary or cultural object, as though for the first time, brings into being that very situation to which it is also, at one and the same time, a reaction. It articulates its own situation and textualizes it, thereby encouraging and perpetuating the illusion that the situation itself did not exist before it, that there is nothing but a text, that there never was any extra- or con-textual reality before the text itself generated it in the form of a mirage.[7]

Like Freud/Heidegger/Lacan, Althusser/Jameson never forgets that the text has always already forgotten the Real, and that the task of thinking is a certain kind of "remembering."

Jameson's readings of Conrad, Balzac, Gissing, and others proceed through a synchronic analysis of style and narrative in order to deduce the subtextual historical mode of production. The political unconscious that one deduces from the text can never be more than an approximation of the Real: that is, a construction situated at the juncture between phantasy and reality. In its phantasized resolution of conflicts that remain unresolved in the social field, the text projects what Jameson calls a "utopian solution." In this respect Conrad is exemplary: "Seen as ideology and utopia all at once, Conrad's stylistic practice can be grasped as a symbolic act which, seizing on the Real in all its reified resistance, at one and the same time projects a unique sensorium of its own, a libidinal resonance no doubt historically determinate, yet whose ultimate ambiguity lies in its attempt to stand beyond history."[8] Style is the site of the dialectical interplay between ideology and utopia, where the historically determinate structures of reification come into relief against the horizon of a phantasized utopian resolution. In its effort to overcome history, style enables us to glimpse the shape of the Real.

It is difficult if not impossible to imagine how Jameson could have gone about the act of interpretation without recourse to the question of style. Were style to be erased utterly, without leaving a trace, interpretation itself would no longer be the critic's prerogative. To go beyond style is to go beyond interpretation. I suggest, therefore, that

---

7. Jameson, *The Political Unconscious*, 82.
8. Jameson, *The Political Unconscious*, 237.

we regard the overcoming of style as something like an apocalyptic horizon, something like the end of history itself, something like the closure of the narrative of human experience. The overcoming of style is an event that has never occurred but whose possibility defines the very nature of style. Style is defined in the continuum between the possibility of an absolutely private language and that of an end of style. Jameson's contribution is to have recognized that the question of history cannot be separated from the question of style.

From Jameson's consideration of style and history I would like to turn to Heidegger's linkage of these same questions in his reading of Nietzsche. For Heidegger's Nietzsche, philosophy realizes its will to power through the question of style. Philosophy has heretofore failed to realize its will to power because it has failed to pose the question of style; that is, it has failed to pose the question of its own language. For Nietzsche, the nihilism of Western metaphysics is inseparable from its failure to pose the question of the immediacy and specificity of its own language. Against Hegel's prophecy of philosophy's overcoming of art and religion, Nietzsche posits the will to power as art and the overcoming of philosophy by art. Nietzsche is reacting above all, argues Heidegger, to the excessive romantic style that begins with Hegel and reaches its apotheosis with Wagner, whose career marks the artist's ultimate betrayal of his art in the interests of a mystico-philosophical truth. For Nietzsche, writes Heidegger, Hegel "marks the end of the classical style," and with Wagner we reach the "complete dissolution of style."[9] For Nietzsche, there is no returning to the classical, rigorous style of the eighteenth century, and the romantic style, initiated by Hegel and consummated by Wagner, constitutes only the latest and most virulent form of nihilism. Nietzsche's solution to this dilemma is "the grand style," which embodies the rigor of the classical style without its humanizing presuppositions. "Nietzsche is the first," writes Heidegger, "to release the 'classical' from the misinterpretations of classicism and humanism."[10]

Here is Heidegger's account of the Nietzschean "grand style":

The grand style is the highest feeling of power. Romantic art, springing from dissatisfaction and deficiency, is a wanting-to-be-away-from-

9. Martin Heidegger, *Nietzsche*, vol. 1, *The Will to Power as Art*, trans. David Farrell Krell (New York: Harper & Row, 1979), 135.
10. Heidegger, *Nietzsche*, 1:127.

oneself. But according to its proper essence, willing is to-want-oneself. Of course, "oneself" is never meant as what is at hand, existing just as it is; "oneself" means what first of all wants to become what it is. Willing proper does not go away from itself but goes way beyond itself; in such surpassing itself the will captures the one who wills, absorbing and transforming him into and along with itself.[11]

The grand style goes beyond merely aesthetic or psychological considerations. What Nietzsche tries to write is a style that, instead of rapturously carrying one away from oneself into a world of abstractions, utterly transforms the self by undoing the very oppositions (classic/romantic, active/passive) that define the notion of style. The grand style does not enable the self simply to escape itself but rather to find itself "way beyond itself." While both the classical and romantic styles leave the self fundamentally unchanged, the grand style changes the very nature of the historical self. The grand style tries not to escape history but to transform it.

The grand style is a style that completely transforms the subject's will to power. Indeed, the will to power is overcome by the "will to style," which opens language to desire and to history in an unprecedented way. The grand style, as the purest expression of the "will to style," would constitute the concealed, dispossessive element within the will to power.

Heidegger's characterization of Nietzsche's style, when considered in these terms, is very similar to Stanley Cavell's account of Wittgenstein's style, which he describes as a relentless probing into "what conviction, whether by proof or evidence or authority, would consist in."[12] In other words, Wittgenstein's style is a calculated effort to explore the relation of language to the will to power, to probe the way language generates conviction and thus transforms our notion of the world. To write such a style is to live dangerously; it is to set out to examine the relation between language and power, without any assurances that language can ever hope to account for that relation. Such a style calls into question the very nature of conviction and thus, as Cavell explains, lends itself to and in fact actively solicits misreadings, because it is precisely by virtue of such misreadings that it can work its transformative will: "Such writing has its risks: not merely the familiar ones of

11. Heidegger, *Nietzsche*, 1:136.
12. Stanley Cavell, "The Availability of Wittgenstein's Later Philosophy," in *Wittgenstein: The Philosophical Investigations: A Collection of Critical Essays*, ed. George Pitcher (New York: Doubleday, 1969), 184.

inconsistency, unclarity, empirical falsehood, unwarranted generalization, but also of personal confusion, with its attendant dishonesties, and of the tyranny which subjects the world to [one's] personal problems. In asking for more than belief it invites discipleship, which runs its own risks of dishonesty and hostility." In this respect Cavell compares Wittgenstein's style to Freud's: "Like Freud's therapy, it wishes to prevent understanding which is unaccompanied by inner change."

Heidegger says precisely the same thing of Nietzsche's style. Like the Freudian transference and the Wittgensteinian language game, the grand style involves the ensemble of one's experience, which is doubtless why Heidegger maintains that "the grand style can be created only by means of a grand politics, and the latter has the most intrinsic law of its will in the grand style."[13] In questioning and transforming our notions of the event, of causality, of the world and our own convictions, the grand style—as Heidegger remarks—absorbs the self "into and along with itself."

It is in this sense that Derrida understands the question of style in *Eperons,* and it is this understanding of style that he uses to define the notion of the Heideggerian *Ereignis* or event of appropriation. Derrida uses Nietzsche's notion of style to locate the dispossession or expropriation within the event of appropriation. As style comes to define the ensemble of one's experience, the experience of being taken up and transformed by style becomes the experience of Being itself. In what is in effect a preface to Heidegger's *Nietzsche,* Derrida demonstrates the extent to which Heidegger's own thought has been absorbed and transformed by Nietzsche's style even as Heidegger tries to distance himself from Nietzsche's project.

Truth is like a woman, remarks Nietzsche, insofar as it never lets itself be seen or grasped in its essence. Hence Derrida's coupling of "*la forme du style et le non-lieu de la femme*": "Perhaps truth's abyss as non-truth, propriation as appropriation/a-propriation, the declaration become parodic dissimulation, perhaps this is what Nietzsche is calling the form of style and the non-place of woman."[14] Style, like a woman, lets the truth be seen only insofar as it conceals it or takes it away. Thus the relation between style, woman, and the "gift of Being." In the Heideggerian formula *Es gibt Sein* ("There is Being," or literally, "It

13. Heidegger, *Nietzsche,* 1:158–59.

14. Jacques Derrida, *Eperons,* trans. Barbara Harlow (Venice: Corbo e Fiore, 1976), 93.

gives Being"), the "*Es*" (It) is "time." For Nietzsche, however, "It" is a woman. The "gift" that woman gives is no gift at all but rather a poison, and not only because, in Derrida's homonymic translation, the German *Gift* means "poison." "The gift," writes Derrida, "the essential predicate of woman, which appeared in the undecidable oscillation of to give oneself/to give oneself for, give/take, let take/appropriate, has the value or the cost of a poison." For what it gives is a concealment, which enables it to take in the sense of "to take in." Like the *pharmakon,* the gift of Being, the gift of woman is a poison as well as a remedy. Style, as woman, as Being, transforms us dangerously indeed, for while it can appear to give so much, to enable us to reexamine the grounds of our conviction, it also can take away. That is, in appropriating the grand style we find ourselves expropriated, dispossessed of ourselves; what had seemed our own has become radically improper, radically other. It is for this reason that the etymology of the word "style" is important for Derrida: style is always a *stilus,* a *spur,* something that protrudes and inscribes, "a long object, an oblong object, a word, which perforates even as it parries."[15] Like Nietzsche's umbrella, style in this sense of dispossession and expropriation is what we tend to forget. Recollection is a figure for learning to read the style of the history of metaphysics. The task of reading the grand style is that of locating these protruding, perforating words and of determining how they work their will upon us.

In the lectures entitled *Hegel's Concept of Experience,* which Heidegger delivered in 1942–43 when he was bringing his Nietzsche lectures to a close, the question of style defines what is most essential to Hegel's project. For the Hegel of the *Phenomenology of Spirit,* writes Heidegger, "experience is the movement of the dialogue between natural and absolute knowledge."[16] The *Ereignis* or *parousia* of the absolute cannot be separated from the question of style, since style is the means through which the function of Hegel as the author of his text is appropriated into "the reality of consciousness itself." It is only by following Hegel's sublation of his author function that we, like Hegel, are led into true experience, into "the true occurrence of the *parousia* of the Absolute," into consciousness's "appropriation [*Aneigung*] of its

15. Derrida, *Eperons,* 35.

16. Martin Heidegger, *Hegel's Concept of Experience* (New York: Harper & Row, 1970), 148.

own abode." Heidegger's text is organized as a series of readings of selected sections of the Preface to the *Phenomenology of Spirit,* each of which is reproduced prior to Heidegger's commentary. Heidegger's objective is to outline in brief how Hegel's text permits the release within natural consciousness of the absolute knowledge that is already within it. Hegel's text performs—instead of simply describing—this transition from the phenomenology of experience to the phenomenology of the Absolute, and it does so through a "departure from ordinary representations," which "marks the style of the sections and determines their sequence."[17] Heidegger does not delineate in detail the specific features of Hegel's style that contribute to this transition from the preontological to the ontology of absolute knowledge. The road or way (*Weg*) leading from ordinary representations to the *parousia* or coming to presence of absolute knowledge is, Heidegger notes, marked by certain keywords—like "being," "beings," and "consciousness"—which he goes on to relate to their Greek and Latin antecedents. The path to the *parousia* is marked by what in *Being and Time* Heidegger calls "primal words," which we will consider momentarily. Though Heidegger does not explain how Hegel's "inversion" of consciousness leads to these primal words, he does reveal that Hegel's putative overcoming of representation cannot be separated from the question of style. Heidegger's thesis is that the *parousia* of the Absolute is synonymous with the transformative effect of Hegel's style on the reader. When at the end of the *Lectures on the History of Philosophy* Hegel turns to the image of the "old mole," it is in order to describe the moment at which the deferrals of representation are finally overcome, the moment at which natural consciousness has finally broken through to the sunlight of absolute knowledge. The path to the *Ereignis* is a question of style, a style in which certain keywords lead the reader away from ordinary representations, through the language of philosophy, and into the realm of the Absolute. On the path to absolute knowledge the "will to style" seeks its own overcoming.

Heidegger's project comes very close to Freud's in its isolation of certain keywords. The transformative effect of "the phenomenology of the Absolute" is closely related to the therapeutic effect of the psychoanalytic transference. While Heidegger reads the history of philosophy as the history of the translation of such keywords as *parousia, prae-*

17. Heidegger, *Hegel's Concept of Experience,* 152.

sens, essentia, Freud likewise focuses not on the connectives or syntactic elements of the style of his patients but on the spacing of certain repeated words. Style for both Freud and Heidegger is a question of the configuration into which certain words fall. While Heidegger's technique is to trace words from the German to their Greek and Latin etymological and philosophical origins, Freud is concerned with the patterns of repetition defined by certain symptomatic words. Metaphysics, like the unconscious, is structured like a language. More precisely, metaphysics and the unconscious are structured like a paratactic language. François Roustang has demonstrated that what enables Freud to fit the style of his theory into his clinical practice, to translate theory into therapy, is *parataxis.* Because parataxis relates to the nonsyntactic elements of style—that is, those whose spacing is not defined by connectives, conjunctions, or prepositions—it has less difficulty than syntax in, as Roustang writes, "presenting the simultaneity of unconscious processes in succession": "The analyst who really listens is not interested in syntax, in the way the words are linked together in order to produce meaning, but in the words themselves, in their respective positions—the proximity, the distance, the intervals which constitute the fundamental relations that syntax most often veils."[18]

Parataxis involves a certain overcoming of grammar. In suggesting that we will believe in God as long as we believe in grammar, Nietzsche seems implicitly to privilege parataxis as the style of the overcoming of metaphysics. We might think of the grand style as marking such a shift toward a paratactic style. Psychoanalysis and philosophy are both concerned with the search for privileged vocabularies: that is, with the search for a paratactic style that engages and transforms the reader. Roustang has, I believe, come upon the fundamental principle underlying the stylistic experiments of Nietzsche, Freud, and Heidegger when he writes, "The temporalization of unconscious simultaneity can be accomplished only through parataxis." The paratactic or grand style is a minimal style whose rigor inheres in its capacity to put into relief, to bring to consciousness, elements of style that are ordinarily buried by syntax. Rather than overcoming representation and the preontological, rather than reaching the atemporality of the unconscious or the phenomenology of the absolute, what philosophy and psychoanalysis

18. François Roustang, *Psychoanalysis Never Lets Go,* trans. Ned Lukacher (Baltimore, Md.: Johns Hopkins University Press, 1983), 21–22.

achieve is the suspension of the syntactical. Moreover, it is by virtue of their meticulous desublimation of the paratactical that philosophy and psychoanalysis are able to produce the transformative effects of the grand style.

Heidegger discusses parataxis in his reading of Parmenides in *What Is Called Thinking?* which Roustang mentions. Though he does not use the term in his lectures on Hölderlin, what Heidegger calls Hölderlin's "primordial speech" (*Ursprache*) nevertheless has clear affinities with parataxis.[19] Neither Heidegger nor Freud, however, attempts to formulate a theory of parataxis with respect to either the history of philosophy or the treatment of neuroses. We must turn to Erich Auerbach's *Mimesis* for the most serious treatment in modern literary or philosophical theory of the question of paratactic style.

Jameson has remarked of *Mimesis* that Auerbach's "series of synchronic moments is intersected, albeit very imperfectly, by the structural opposition between paratactic and syntactic styles which inaugurates his work and whose historical status is never fully articulated."[20] Auerbach's opening move in *Mimesis,* his contrast between the Hellenic style of the *Odyssey* and the Hebraic style of the Bible, is a contrast between parataxis and syntax. When the old housekeeper Euryclea recognizes the disguised Odysseus by the scar on his thigh, Homer—who is Auerbach's consummate paratactic stylist—presents the incident of the boar hunt, in which Odysseus had received the scar years earlier, literally side by side with the events that are unfolding in the present time of the narrative. There is no syntactical subordination marking the temporal difference between the time of the narration and the time of the interpolated story. It would have been perfectly easy, argues Auerbach, for Homer to present the boar hunt as a recollection that is triggered in Odysseus's mind when he sees that Euryclea has recognized him, "but any such subjectivistic-perspectivistic procedure,

19. See Martin Heidegger, *What Is Called Thinking?* trans. J. Glenn Gray (New York: Harper & Row, 1968), 182ff.; Martin Heidegger, *Erläuterungen zu Hölderlins Dichtung* (Frankfurt: Klostermann, 1951). It was Theodor W. Adorno who first noted these affinities; see his "Parataxis: Zur Späten Lyrik Hölderlins," in *Noten zur Literatur*, ed. Rolf Tiedemann, vol. 11 of Adorno's *Gesammelte Schriften* (Frankfurt: Suhrkamp, 1974), 447–91.

20. Fredric Jameson, "Marxism and Historicism," *New Literary History* 11 (1979): 59. To be precise, Auerbach opposes parataxis to hypotaxis; in the former there is no syntactic relation between propositions, while the latter entails syntactic subordination between propositions. Following Jameson and Roustang, I use "syntax" to indicate the hypotactic subordination of propositions.

creating a foreground and background, resulting in the present lying
open to the depths of the past, is entirely foreign to the Homeric style;
the Homeric style knows only a foreground, only a uniformly illuminated, uniformly objective present."[21]

Against the Homeric parataxis, Auerbach places the syntactic constructions of the Bible, where the contrast between darkness and light,
foreground and background, depth and surface, is fundamental and
pervasive. Having announced that the history of style is defined by the
intersections of these alternatives, Auerbach fails to follow up on his
own suggestion. As Jameson indicates, it is only sporadically that Auerbach returns to this ostensibly overarching principle. It figures prominently, however, in his account of medieval Latin and vernacular literature, where he relates paratactic constructions to the scriptural
accounts of the "hiddenness of God and finally his parousia, his incarnation in the common form of ordinary life." The thesis of *Mimesis*
concerns the relation between style and reality, and the ways in which
style can either restrict or expand the extent to which reality can be
represented. The advantage of parataxis is that it enables the artist to
integrate everything into the present. The story that Auerbach seems to
be trying to tell concerns the failure of medieval literature—largely
because of the hierarchical structure of Christian dogma—to realize
the great potential of paratactic style, which, instead of being used to
expand the range of reality open to artistic representation, was used to
close it off, to move it into the background while the images of the
divine life were foregrounded. Of the *Chanson de Roland*, Auerbach
writes, "It would seem that the series of similar events and the resump-
tion of previous statements are phenomena related in character to the
parataxis of sentence structure." As in Roustang's reading of parataxis
in *The Interpretation of Dreams*, Auerbach notes the constant return
to the beginning in medieval parataxis. Events "are placed side by side
paratactically" but not after the Homeric style, for these events are
isolated, fixed into a frame, "interpreted figurally in isolation from
their historic context."[22] With the rise of figural interpretation, the
paratactic styles of antiquity become subordinated to Christian teaching, and instead of foregrounding the presentness of historical experi-

21. Erich Auerbach, *Mimesis: The Representation of Reality in Western Literature*,
trans. Willard Trask (Princeton, N.J.: Princeton University Press, 1968), 7.
22. Auerbach, *Mimesis*, 119, 105, 116.

ence, as the ancients had done, the Christian tradition places parataxis in the service of the increasing rigidity of the figural mode. This failure to exploit the possibilities of parataxis seems to Auerbach one of the great missed opportunities in the history of Western literature.

Auerbach's thinking has deep and obvious similarities with the thinking of Nietzsche and Heidegger. His valuation of the Homeric style is at one with Heidegger's claim that in the ancient Greek world, Being was present in the nearby and the ready-to-hand. Here too is the archetype of the classical style to which Nietzsche wants to return. Auerbach's last chapter, which includes his reading of Virginia Woolf's *To the Lighthouse,* also strikes a Heideggerian tone. Though parataxis is never mentioned in connection with modern literature, it is precisely what is in question in Auerbach's analysis of the fragmentation of both time and the continuum of events. What is important to Auerbach in *To the Lighthouse* is the "sharp contrast" between subjective and objective time, what we might call the time of the *fabula* and the time of the *sjuzet.* In the modernist "stream of consciousness" we are once again concerned with the paratactic placement of events side by side, free of the syntactic links of the realist tradition. But what is being emptied out here, just as in medieval literature, is the presentness of the present. In modern literature, instead of an emphasis on the divine life and its figural forms, "the stress is placed entirely on what the occasion releases, things which are not seen directly but by reflection, which are not tied to the present of the framing occurrence which releases them."[23] The modernist epiphany replaces the medieval parousia. In Auerbach's history of style, parataxis, which affords the opportunity of bringing the present to presence, is invariably appropriated in post-Homeric literature by a variety of other interests, ideological and cultural as well as psychological. *Mimesis* establishes that throughout the history of Western literature parataxis is the element of style that enables us to define the meaning of presence.

Parataxis is a figure for reading as well as for writing, a mode of interpretation as well as a method of composition. Regarding the need for philosophy to isolate certain key words, and the need to "avoid uninhibited word-mysticism," Heidegger declares that "the ultimate business of philosophy is to preserve the *force of the most elemental words* in which Dasein expresses itself, and to keep the common un-

---

23. Auerbach, *Mimesis,* 538, 541.

derstanding from levelling them off to that unintelligibility which functions in turn as a source of pseudo-problems."[24] When philosophy listens closely, what it discovers is that *Dasein* speaks paratactically. Derrida's primal words—such as "supplement," "pharmakon," "parergon"—play this etymological game and at the same time effectively block the path to any originary meaning. Derrida's "undecidables" continue Heidegger's effort to locate the beginning that veils the origin, to pinpoint the unveiling that reveals the veil.

Theodor Adorno argues, in *The Jargon of Authenticity,* that Heidegger's primal words are in effect a kind of bondage or radical unfreedom, and he sees in Heidegger's word-forms and sound-shapes the emergence of a new Platonism and a new "language mythology." Of Heidegger and the vogue he has created, Adorno writes that "primalness now has the same place in the philosophical atlas in which nature was once registered."[25] One cannot ignore the fact that the Heideggerian word hoard remains too close to the mystagogic effusions of the religion of the *Volk* not to be compromised by it. The paratactic regression to primal words historically entails its own political agenda. Heidegger's dilemma reminds us how dangerous the proximity of style and politics can be. Nevertheless, Adorno's Heidegger remains a caricature. If prior to the *Kehre* Heidegger makes excessive claims for philosophy, it is also true that after the *Kehre* even his metaphorics of presence, of listening, of proximity are checked by a metaphorics of concealment and limitation. Derrida's eagerness in some of his earlier essays, above all in "Ousia and Gramme," to distance himself from Heidegger by insisting on his own rejection of any notion of originary presence, even a concealed one, belies how strong this threat remains. By attempting to distinguish his notion of infinite deferral from Heidegger's notion of a fundamental concealment, Derrida succeeds only in revealing how close his project is to Heidegger's, for what indeed is the difference for reading and interpretation between remembering the concealment of the origin, as Heidegger does, and remembering nothing at all, as Derrida claims? The simple fact is that in both cases we are left with the awareness that thinking is always a mode of blocked or inadequate recollection. If, to use Heidegger's

24. Martin Heidegger, *Being and Time,* trans. Edward Robinson and John Macquarrie (New York: Harper & Row, 1962), 262.
25. Theodor Adorno, *The Jargon of Authenticity,* trans. Kurt Tarnowski and Frederic Will (Evanston, Ill.: Northwestern University Press, 1971), 42–43, 98.

idiom, thinking (*Denken*) is a kind of commemoration (*Andenken*), we must always remember in our turn that *Andenken* is a very special kind of recollection indeed.

Philippe Lacoue-Labarthe writes of Heidegger's "overvalorization of the philosophical" that it is the "mark of Heidegger's belonging to the philosophical (to the metaphysical), and the first political determination of his philosophy."[26] By appropriating too much for philosophy, by claiming too much of the truth, Heidegger sets the stage for the appropriation of philosophy by politics. "Heidegger always submits," writes Lacoue-Labarthe, to the "belonging-together of the philosophical and the political." For the prewar Heidegger, "the polis is thought [of] as 'the foundation and the place' of Dasein, the very Da of Dasein." To lay anew the foundations of metaphysics was synonymous with laying anew the foundations of the state: hence the Rectoral Address at Freiburg in 1933, after which Heidegger's parataxis was appropriated by the syntax of the Third Reich. The destiny of Being became indistinguishable from the destiny of Germany. Lacoue-Labarthe reminds us that Heidegger's style cannot be separated from the larger problem of his national identification; furthermore, that style itself is the means whereby the project for a fundamental ontology becomes in effect a "fundamental mimetology."[27] The *Seinsfrage* is thus overwhelmed by the demands of the national will to self-affirmation. Heidegger's collaboration, however limited and fleeting, clearly indicates that philosophy's "will to style" can be expressive of another will, one much stronger than the will of philosophy itself. That the will to put the elemental words in the history of philosophy into relief should have been appropriated by another will does not, however, condemn the project out of hand. Heidegger's fate is a warning to philosophy that its efforts to read closely have implications beyond the academy. Derrida's unrelenting skepticism with respect to the keywords and paleonyms he isolates in his readings is a necessary defense against the "overvalorization of the philosophical." Derrida has learned from Heidegger's example that even though the proximity of a grand style and a grand politics is unavoidable, one may nevertheless guard against its dangers.

26. Philippe Lacoue-Labarthe, "Transcendence Ends in Politics," trans. Peter Caws *Social Research* 49 (1982): 431.
27. Lacoue-Labarthe, "Transcendence Ends in Politics," 439.

"To Tympanize Philosophy"

> A Spirit aërial
> Informs the cell of Hearing, dark and blind;
> Intricate labyrinth, more dread for thought
> To enter than oracular cave.
>   WILLIAM WORDSWORTH,
>   "The Power of Sound"

"To have the ear of philosophy," "to tympanize philosophy," is to situate oneself where one can overhear philosophy's conversation with itself, to situate oneself within the ear of philosophy.[28] In "Tympanum," Derrida inscribes his text as a running commentary or companion text to a meditation on voice from Michel Leiris' *Biffures*, in which Leiris, in a quasi-Heideggerian etymology, links the goddess Persephone to the *perce-oreille* or earwig: that is, Persephone as *percéphoné*. While Derrida wants us to listen to philosophy as it listens to the sound of its own voice, Leiris takes us on an imaginary journey into "a subterranean kingdom," into a "deep country of hearing, described in terms of geology more than in those of any other natural science, not only by virtue of the cartilaginous cavern that constitutes its organ, but also by virtue of the relationship that unites it to grottoes, chasms, to all the pockets hollowed out of the terrestrial crust whose emptiness makes them into resonating drums for the slightest sounds." Philosophy tries to recuperate it all, to hear everything, to hear itself fully, without loss, without censorship.

There is something that it cannot hear, however, something that gets lost in what Geoffrey Hartman calls "the ineluctable ear, its ghostly, cavernous, echoic depth."[29] While Leiris takes us into "the matrix in which the voice is formed," Derrida disrupts the proximity of voice to Being by locating that which expropriates the voice, thus making it improper to itself: "The logic of the event is examined from the vantage of the structures of expropriation called *timbre* (*tympanum*), *style*, and signature. Timbre, style, and signature are the same obliterating division of the proper. They make every event possible, necessary, and

28. See Lucette Finas's interview with Derrida, "Avoir l'oreille de la philosophie," in *Ecarts: Quatre Essais à propos de Jacques Derrida*, ed. Lucette Finas et al. (Paris: Fayard, 1973), 303–16; and Jacques Derrida, "Tympanum," in *Margins of Philosophy*, trans. Alan Bass (Chicago: University of Chicago Press, 1982), ix–xxix.
29. Geoffrey Hartman, *Saving the Text* (Baltimore, Md.: Johns Hopkins University Press, 1981), 123.

unfindable."[30] Style is what philosophy can't hear, what defers voice from reference, and what renders the identity of sense into the drift of difference. In Derrida's idiom, every percussion is already a *re*percussion, every effort to bring to presence is already marked as a representation of presence. To tympanize philosophy is to locate what separates it from phonic presence, what refers it back to other traces. To tympanize philosophy is to use style to perforate or pierce the illusion of phonic presence. It is to position oneself at the subterranean level of the text, at the very limits of the audible. It is at this level that we will attempt to locate ourselves in the text of Hegel.

One might think of a bad style as the result of an inability to listen to oneself. In this respect Hegel's account (in his letter to Schelling of May 1, 1807) of finishing the *Phenomenology of Spirit* with the roar of the cannons in his ears, as Napoleon laid siege to Jena, appears very much like an excuse for what has often been called the most notoriously bad style in the history of philosophy. Hegel's contemporaries recognized his contributions to the short-lived *Critical Journal:* as the philosopher Jacobi remarked, "It is the bad style that makes me certain it is he." Friedrich Schlegel complained to his brother of "Hegelisms."[31] The litany of charges against Hegel's style would make an interesting study in itself. Writing to Voss, the translator of Homer, Hegel remarked that he wanted "to teach philosophy to speak German." There are many who wish he had never made the effort.

At the end of the introduction to his lectures on the fine arts, which he first delivered in the early 1820s, Hegel provides some indication of how he may have ideally conceived of his own style. In recounting the historical transition from what he calls "the poetry of the imagination to the prose of thought," his concern is above all with the role of sound. With the end of romantic art, which occurred during the early modern period, sometime between Shakespeare and Goethe, poetry

30. Derrida, "Tympanum," xix.
31. Cited in H. S. Harris, *Hegel's Development: Night Thoughts (Jena 1801–1806)* (Oxford: Clarendon Press, 1983), xxiv. For a typical later view of Hegel's style, see William James's essay "Hegel and His Method," in which he complains of Hegel's "abominable habits of speech" and his "passion for the slipshod in the way of sentences, his unprincipled playing fast and loose with terms; his dreadful vocabulary," and "his whole deliberately adopted policy of ambiguity and vagueness." James concludes, "It is surely the grand style, if there be such a thing as a grand style in philosophy" (*A Pluralistic Universe* [1909], reprinted in William James, *Essays in Radical Empiricism and A Pluralistic Universe*, ed. Ralph Barton Perry [New York: Dutton, 1971], 163, 171).

loses "the feeling of sonority" and sound becomes "a *sign*, by itself void of significance, a sign of the idea which has become concrete in itself, and not merely of indefinite feeling and its nuances and gradations." At this point poetry passes into the language of the spirit; the sounds of poetry are henceforth used to compose the words of another language: "Sound in this way becomes a *word* as a voice inherently articulated, the meaning of which is to indicate ideas and thoughts." Voice is now, strictly speaking, a medium in which the self has been transcended. Voice has become the pathway of the absolute spirit. The "sensuous element" of sound "is here cut free from the content of consciousness, while spirit determines this content on its own account and in itself and makes it into ideas." Spirit, in other words, appropriates the *phonē* for itself. The sound of the poetic text is now an empty shell, a body from which spirit has ascended into the realm of ideas: "To express these it uses sound indeed, but only as a sign in itself without value or content. The sound, therefore, may just as well be a mere letter, since the audible, like the visible, has sunk into being a mere indication of spirit." It is in this context, I believe, that we should understand Heidegger's notion of the role of style in Hegel as leading us from ordinary representations to the phenomenology of the absolute. In his own style Hegel attempts to recapitulate the historical transition that has led the poetry of the imagination to the prose of thought. The dialogue between natural and absolute knowledge cannot be separated from this crucial stylistic transition in which poetry frees itself of sensuous feeling and "launches out exclusively in the inner space and the inner time of ideas and feelings." It marks the point where representation (*Vorstellung*) is overcome, where the "picture thought" of art and religion is transcended by the imageless thought of philosophy. This is not, however, the death of art but rather the crossing over of the spirit of art from the arts to philosophy: "[Art] passes over from the poetry of the imagination to the prose of thought."[32]

"When philosophy paints its grey on grey," writes Hegel in the preface to the *Philosophy of Right* (1820), "then has a shape of life

---

32. G. W. F. Hegel, *Aesthetics: Lectures on the Fine Arts*, trans. T. M. Knox, 2 vols. (Oxford: Clarendon Press, 1975), 1:88–89. My thinking throughout this part of my argument has been formed by Jacques Derrida, "The Pit and the Pyramid: Introduction to Hegel's Semiology," in *Margins of Philosophy*, 69–108; and Paul de Man, "Sign and Symbol in Hegel's *Aesthetics*," *Critical Inquiry* 8 (1982): 761–76.

grown old."[33] Though philosophy cannot rejuvenate these shapes, Hegel continues, it can understand them. Like the owl of Minerva, philosophy takes flight "only with the falling of the dusk." As the arts set forever behind the horizon of history, philosophy's night thoughts seek a self-canceling style, a style that tries to erase itself. In this dark night of the spirit, philosophy uses style to stage the Christlike resurrection of the spirit from the crypt of the letter. Style, writes Hegel in the *Aesthetics,* is the "inherently necessary mode of representation," which is dictated not only by the demands of a specific art but also by the artist's "subjective activity." An original style for Hegel is not simply an idiosyncratic mannerism but rather a crossover between a subjective activity and an objective medium, where "the most personal inner life of the artist" becomes synonymous with "the nature of the object, so that the specific character of the artist's work appears only as the special character of the thing itself."[34] For Hegel, the most desirable style is that which seeks to overcome itself, to burst through and consume itself. In its overcoming of its own content, the style of philosophy becomes the paradigmatic *Aufhebung.*

In the Preface to the *Phenomenology of Spirit,* the emergence of natural consciousness into the life of the spirit is figured in the act of bursting through a crumbling crust into the sunlight: "The gradual crumbling that left unaltered the face of the whole is cut short by a sunburst which, in the flash, illuminates the features of a new world."[35] Philosophy cannot do without figures even in staging, as Hegel does here, the overcoming of "*figurative representation.*" Spirit "must travel a long way and work its passage" through the cavernous underworld of sound before it breaks through into the silent world that is properly its own. The passage is not, however, one in which "the sensuous mode of apprehension" is simply purged away but rather one in which "determinate thoughts" are freed "from their fixity so as to give actuality to the universal, and impart to it spiritual life."[36] One passes beyond the sensuous element of sound only by moving through it.

33. G. W. F. Hegel, *Philosophy of Right,* trans. T. M. Knox (New York: Oxford University Press, 1967), 13.

34. Hegel, *Aesthetics,* 1:294.

35. G. W. F. Hegel, *Phenomenology of Spirit,* trans. A. V. Miller (New York: Oxford University Press, 1977), 7.

36. Hegel, *Phenomenology of Spirit,* 18, 15, 19–20.

The subtitle of the first volume of H. S. Harris's *Hegel's Development* is *Toward the Sunlight,* a phrase Hegel derived from a passage in T. G. von Hippel's *Lebenslaufe* (1781): "Strive toward the sun, my friends, that the salvation of the human race may soon come to fruition."[37] The task of philosophy is to leave the dark night in which it finds itself after the departure of sense and to discover the sunlight of the spirit. Style is a crucial element in constructing this invisible world of the spirit beneath an invisible sun. The claims of reason become synonymous for Hegel with the claims of style. The figure of the sunburst is so pervasive in Hegel that it should be regarded as the very figure of the autodestruction of the Hegelian style.

It is at the end of his *Lectures on the History of Philosophy,* also from the 1820s, that Hegel alludes twice to *Hamlet* in order to figure forth philosophy's attainment of preeminence over all other discursive modes. Shakespeare's enigmatic "old mole" is Hegel's figure for the overcoming of figure itself, for the end of deferrals, for the end of representation:

> It goes ever on and on, because spirit is progress alone. Spirit often seems to have forgotten and lost itself, but inwardly opposed to itself, it is inwardly working ever forward as Hamlet says of the ghost of his father, "Well done, old mole"—until grown strong in itself it bursts asunder the crust of earth which divided it from its sun, its Notion, so that the earth crumbles away.[38]

The owl of the *Philosophy of Right* and the eagle of *Reason in History,* who strikes down art and religion in his flight toward the sun of the spirit,[39] have here given way to the "old mole," who instead of winging his way through the night air burrows his way through the ground

---

37. H. S. Harris, *Hegel's Development: Toward the Sunlight, 1770–1801* (Oxford: Clarendon Press, 1972), 184. Von Hippel was one of Laurence Sterne's German followers. The citation is from Hegel's letter to Schelling of April 16, 1795. Also see the discussion of Hegel's imagery in Robert Solomon's *In the Spirit of Hegel* (New York: Oxford University Press, 1983), 45.

38. G. W. F. Hegel, *Lectures on the History of Philosophy,* trans. E. S. Haldane and Frances H. Simpson, 3 vols. (New York: Humanities Press, 1974), 3:546–47 (translation modified). My German text of the *Vorlesungen über die Geschichte der Philosophie* is vol. 20 of the *Theorie Werkausgabe* edition of Hegel (Frankfurt: Suhrkamp, 1971). The textual problems of these lectures are notorious. A definitive edition is planned by the Hamburg publisher, Felix Meiner.

39. G. W. F. Hegel, *Reason in History,* trans. R. S. Hartman (New York: Bobbs-Merrill, 1953), 21.

of sound and sense. Hegel's *"Brav gearbeitet, wackerer Maulwurf"* (Well done, old mole), which has become a veritable Hegelian signature, is not exactly what Shakespeare wrote. It is important to note that it is not actually a quotation but a revision, a rewriting of Shakespeare.

At the end of Act One, Hamlet returns to Horatio and the sentinels on the battlements after his interview with his father's ghost. As he asks them to swear an oath of silence never to speak of what they have just seen, the Ghost, having secretly returned beneath the battlements, echoes the words of the oath-taking ceremony. It is as though Hamlet is hearing his own echo, as though he is hearing himself speak, hearing himself as though he were an other. Standing on the battlements with the Ghost invisibly beneath, Hamlet's companions, as well as the audience, find themselves in effect within Hamlet's inner ear, hearing what would normally remain inaudible. In the "echoic depth" of this famous "cellarage" scene, it is indeed saying, hearing, and listening that are in question rather than doing or being, as Hegel would like to believe.

> *Ghost.* Swear by this sword. [They swear.]
> *Hamlet.* Well said, old mole. Canst work in th'earth so fast?
> A worthy pioner! Once more remove, good friends.
> *Horatio.* O day and night, but this is wondrous strange!
> [1.5.169–72][40]

Were Hegel to write, "Well said, old mole," the rhetorical power of his discourse would be utterly lost. At the epochal moment when the spirit breaks through the crust of earth, Hegel must make Hamlet say, "Well done, old mole." As we shall see, it is precisely the difference between saying and doing that is in question in this truly "wondrous" passage.

Hegel's second allusion to *Hamlet* comes at the very end of the *Lectures on the History of Philosophy*, where he remarks that the historian of philosophy must "listen" to the spirit as it performs "its *unconscious* work, in the course of which it appears to itself as something different, and not spirit." The historian's task is to chronicle the upward movement that brings it to the state of being a "self-present

---

40. All line citations are from the Arden edition of *Hamlet*, ed. Harold Jenkins (New York: Methuen, 1982). References to other Shakespearean plays rely on *The Complete Works*, ed. Alfred Harbage et al. (Harmondsworth: Pelican, 1969).

spirit" (*demselben gegenwärtigen Geiste*). The history of philosophy is
literally a kind of listening to the "individual pulses which beat in [the
spirit's] life." The history of philosophy is in effect the sound made by
the spirit as it burrows its way through the language of philosophy:
"To its urgency—when the mole within burrows onward—we have to
listen and to make it a reality."[41] Hegel's first allusion to the "old
mole" concerned its breakthrough into the sunlight; the second concerns the sense of hearing. It is as though Hegel were describing the
experience of listening to the sound of his own voice as he reads aloud
to himself the language of the history of philosophy. It is as though in
the act of reading he hears something calling: "It is my desire that this
history of philosophy should contain for you a summons to grasp the
spirit of the time, which is present in us by nature." He wants others to
hear what he has heard. The sound of burrowing acts as "a summons"
(*eine Aufforderung*) that calls upon us "to grasp" the spirit within
ourselves and "consciously bring it to light" (*mit Bewusstein an den
Tag zu bringen*). Here Hegel has mixed his metaphors, for he is asking
us to bring a sound to light—yet this crossover of sight and sound is no
accident. Indeed, it is the key to Hegel's teaching, for it is precisely the
movement of sense toward the absolute that the mole is intended to
signify. It is in order to figure this movement of sense toward ideation
that Hegel has turned to Shakespeare, for the passage from sense to the
idea is synonymous with the passage from literature to philosophy.

Hegel's dialogue with Shakespeare unfolds throughout the course of
his career. From his schoolmaster the eight-year-old Hegel received a
set of Shakespeare's works in 1778. The upstart from Swabia who
wrote such awful German heard the woodnotes wild of that "upstart
crow" from Stratford early on. Hegel discusses *Hamlet* and other plays
by Shakespeare in the *Phenomenology of Spirit* as well as in the *Aesthetics*. Perhaps the most important influence on his understanding of
Hamlet in particular was Goethe's *Wilhelm Meister's Apprenticeship*
(1796). A glance at Goethe's novel will help us to get a sense of why
Hegel should turn at important moments in his own work to such a
complex and difficult Shakespearean figure as the "old mole."

Goethe plots a conjunction between the life of his hero and the
character of Hamlet. One of the climactic scenes occurs when Wilhelm,
who is part of a troupe of players, is confronted by the reality of his

41. Hegel, *Lectures on the History of Philosophy*, 3:552–53. Translation modified.

own experience and of his own relationship to his father during a performance of *Hamlet* in which he plays the leading role. The climax occurs during the cellarage scene (1.5), which, writes Goethe, creates "a profound impression" on the troupe and the audience as well as on Wilhelm himself. During the Ghost's return beneath the battlements, little flames pierce through the floor of the stage to heighten the effect. While the "old mole" is busily occupied "underground," Wilhelm is seized with "powerful and conflicting impulses."[42] Hamlet's paralysis becomes Wilhelm's. For Goethe, *Hamlet* has a negative exemplary value insofar as it dramatizes the fate of a character upon whom too awesome a task has been imposed.

It is in the *Aesthetics* that Hegel confronts and disagrees with Goethe's interpretation of the play: Hamlet's indecision does not indicate that he has been overwhelmed by the Ghost's call to revenge; his character was already predisposed to melancholy and death before hearing anything about Claudius's crime and before ever having been called to revenge. Hegel's dispute with Goethe is about nothing less than the nature of Hamlet's will. While Goethe argues that Hamlet's will is overwhelmed by the Ghost's imperative, Hegel maintains that it remains constant throughout the play. The flaws in Hamlet's character are, in Hegel's opinion, independent of the revenge plot: "Death lay from the beginning in the background of Hamlet's mind"; "he is a lost man, almost consumed already by inner disgust before death comes to him from outside."[43]

Hegel's impatience with Goethe's emphasis on indecision becomes apparent in the following passage:

> But Shakespeare excels, precisely, owing to the decisiveness and tautness of his characters, even in the purely formal greatness and firmness of evil. Hamlet indeed is indecisive in himself, yet he was not doubtful

42. Johann Wolfgang von Goethe, *Wilhelm Meister's Apprenticeship*, trans. Thomas Carlyle (New York: Collier, 1968), 302. Thirteen years after the publication of *Wilhelm Meister's Apprenticeship*, Goethe is still listening to the burrowing of the "old mole" in *Elective Affinities* (1809). The excavations and the laying of new foundations on Eduard's estate symbolize the disruption of the ground of his marriage to Charlotte, which leads to the emergence of primordial chthonian powers that reassert their preeminence in the modern world. One evening after the workmen have stopped, Eduard listens to the silence: "It was so still that in the ground beneath him he could hear the burrowing of busy animals, to whom night and day are alike" (*Elective Affinities*, trans. Elizabeth Mayer and Louise Bogan [Chicago: Henry Regnery, 1966], 104–5).

43. Hegel, *Aesthetics*, 2:1231–32.

about *what* he was to do, but only *how*. Yet nowadays they make even Shakespeare's characters ghostly, and suppose that we must find interesting, precisely on their own account, nullity and indecision in changing and hesitating, and trash of this sort. But the Ideal consists in this, that the Idea is actual and to this actuality man belongs as subject and therefore as a firm unity in himself.[44]

It should be clear now that by using the "old mole" as a figure for philosophy's attainment of absolute knowledge, Hegel is issuing yet another counterblast to Goethe's reading of the play. The importance of Hegel's own reading cannot be overestimated, for he grasps something that Goethe and most critics and readers have failed to understand, that Hamlet's will is flawed by forces that remain outside the main action of the revenge plot. Later in this chapter I will pursue Hegel's insight into the preexistent origins of Hamlet's indecision, and we will see that Hegel's suggestion enables us to understand the relation between the "old mole" and Hamlet's character in terms that Hegel himself only remotely anticipated.

Like Goethe and Hegel, Coleridge also recognized that the cellarage scene is crucial to understanding the nature of Hamlet's will. "Now comes the difficult task," writes Coleridge when he comes to the problem of interpreting Hamlet's behavior after his interview with the Ghost.[45] I should remind the reader that the scene falls into three parts: in lines 1–90, Hamlet speaks with the Ghost; lines 91–112 are Hamlet's soliloquy; lines 113–98 present the cellarage incident. The entire scene is organized around the question of what it means to take a vow or swear an oath: that is, around the binding power of language. "I am bound to hear," Hamlet tells the Ghost, who responds, "So art thou to revenge when thou shalt hear" (1.5.6–7). At the end of his soliloquy, Hamlet says, "Now to my word. / It is 'Adieu, adieu, remember me.' / I have sworn it" (1.5.110–12). Then comes the oath-taking ceremony in which the Ghost takes part. Taking an oath involves a very special use of language, one in which saying becomes synonymous with doing. Without this conjunction of saying and doing, an oath loses its validity. Hamlet's indecision would suggest that something in his character prevents this conjunction from taking effect,

44. Hegel, *Aesthetics*, 1:244.
45. Samuel Taylor Coleridge, *Shakespearean Criticism*, ed. T. M. Raysor, 2 vols. (London: J. M. Dent, 1960), 1:36.

and Coleridge locates this disjunction at the moment when Hamlet begins his soliloquy following his interview with the Ghost:

> I remember nothing equal to this burst unless it be the first speech of Prometheus, after the exit of Vulcan and the two Afrites, in Aeschylus. But Shakespeare alone could have produced the vow of Hamlet to make his memory blank of all maxims and generalized truths that "observation had copied there," followed by the immediate noting down the generalized fact, "That one may smile, and smile, and be a villain."[46]

Having just vowed to himself to "wipe away all trivial fond records" (99), and having declared that writing is unnecessary because it will be impossible to forget what the Ghost has just told him, Hamlet nevertheless proceeds to jot in his notebook a reminder of Claudius's villainy. In this highly stylized gesture, Shakespeare reveals at a stroke the deep division in Hamlet's resolve. The division becomes even more sharply marked when Hamlet rejoins Horatio and the sentinels.

In the majority of the productions of *Hamlet* I have seen, 1.5 suffers as much as if not more than any other scene in the play. Not understanding its significance, most directors rush their actors through it, leaving the audience as confused and mystified as the players. Confusion is indeed Shakespeare's objective in this scene, but his more important objective is to articulate Hamlet's vacillation at this early stage in the play. The scene must be drawn out and developed in order to set forth the sorts of contrasts Coleridge has alerted us to.

Hamlet cannot decide, on rejoining Horatio, whether to tell him what he has heard from the Ghost. When Horatio and Marcellus agree not to say a word, Hamlet begins to make a disclosure, then checks himself just in time. The break between his next two lines must be carefully articulated, or the effect is lost:

> There is never a villain dwelling in all Denmark
> But he's an arrant knave.
>
> > [1.5.129–30]

Hamlet then becomes extremely disoriented and is about to dismiss the men for fear he will tell them more than he really wants to. When Horatio remarks, "These are but wild and whirling words, my lord"

---

46. Coleridge, *Shakespearean Criticism*, 1:23.

(139), Hamlet seems to collect himself, apologizes for his confusion, and then, having just taken an oath himself, decides to administer one to his men.

"The great object of [Hamlet's] life," writes Coleridge, "is defeated by continually resolving to do, yet doing nothing but resolve."[47] This is nowhere more evident than in the oath-taking scene when Hamlet asks his men to swear not one but three oaths: "Never to speak of this that you have seen" (161); "Never to speak of this that you have heard" (168); not to expose the "antic disposition" that he promises to put on (188). Such threefold oaths, writes Harold Jenkins, editor of the Arden *Hamlet*, "had a particularly binding force (sometimes explained by the invocation of the Trinity), and this one will have still further solemnity from seeming to be sworn at the behest not of Hamlet only but of a supernatural agent also."[48] Jenkins may well be right, but this seems to me the sort of recondite scholarly explanation that could easily be improved upon by a simple attentiveness to the dynamic of the play itself. Hamlet is simply overdoing it; he is trying to compensate for the uncertainty of his own resolve with an excessive and perhaps arcane oath-taking ceremony. His hysterical levity during this ostensibly solemn occasion underlines his fundamental lack of resolve. Coleridge goes to the heart of the matter when he remarks that Hamlet's "quick relapse into the satirical and ironical vein" during the cellarage scene establishes the characteristic way in which his "instant and over violent resolve . . . wastes in the efforts of resolving the energies of action." All of these conflicting forces come together in the image of the "old mole," which marks the apogee of Hamlet's desperate gaiety. Here is Coleridge's altogether extraordinary analysis:

> The familiarity, comparative at least, of a brooding mind with shadows is something. Still more the necessary alternation when one muscle long strained is relaxed; the antagonist comes into action of itself. Terror [is] closely connected with the ludicrous; the latter [is] the common mode by which the mind tries to emancipate itself from terror. The laugh is rendered by nature itself the language of extremes, even as tears are. Add too, Hamlet's wildness is but *half-false*. O that

47. Coleridge, *Shakespearean Criticism*, 2:155.
48. *Hamlet*, ed. Harold Jenkins, 459. This was first pointed out by A. C. Bradley in *Shakespearean Tragedy* (London: Macmillan, 1905).

subtle trick to pretend the *acting* only when we are very near *being* what we act.[49]

With each repetition of the oaths, with each of the Ghost's uncanny echoes, Hamlet's language becomes more extreme. The radical tone change or shift in style that culminates in his addressing the Ghost as "truepenny," "old mole," and "worthy pioner," reveals, as Coleridge suggests, something about Hamlet's *being*. The low or colloquial style perforates and calls into question all that has gone before. Noting how foreign these rank colloquialisms are to Hamlet's "tone and attitude earlier in the scene," Stephen Booth remarks that the end of 1.5 "jars with the expectations aroused by the manner in which he and the play have been treating the ghost." "For a moment," Booth continues, "the play seems to be the work of a madman."[50] Hamlet's tone in the cellarage scene is calculated to point to this preexistent conflict in his being as well as to undermine the binding power of the oath he had just sworn.

In appropriating the image of the "old mole" into the text of philosophy, Hegel has wandered onto very unstable ground, for if any image resists interpretation, this is the one. Like Coleridge, Hegel realizes that the "old mole" is a figure of Hamlet's inner state, and that by the sheer extravagance of the image Shakespeare is pointing to something deeper in Hamlet's character than even the awesomeness of the moment could account for. Hegel writes that the Ghost is "an objective form of Hamlet's inner presentiment,"[51] which is to say that the "old mole" is a figure of the flaw in Hamlet's own character. In Hegel's dialectical scheme the tragedy unfolds as objective events draw out the "old mole" that has long been concealed within the subject himself. But how can Hegel be certain that what is emerging from the depths of subjectivity is the absolute spirit? Unlike Coleridge, Hegel does not

49. Coleridge, *Shakespearean Criticism*, 1:36. At one point in his argument, Coleridge translates this division in Hamlet's character into dramaturgical terms and suggests that Shakespeare divides the stage into two parts during 1.4, where Horatio and the sentinels act "as a support, a stimulation *a tergo*, while the *front* of the mind, the whole consciousness of the speaker, is filled by the solemn apparition" (*Shakespearean Criticism*, 1:23).

50. Stephen Booth, "On the Value of Hamlet," in *Literary Criticism: Idea and Act*, ed. W. K. Wimsatt (Berkeley: University of California Press, 1974), 300.

51. Hegel, *Aesthetics*, 1:231.

appear to be aware of the stylistic and tonal ambivalence of the image of the mole. In opposing Goethe, Hegel seems to have lighted upon an image that is more disturbing in its implications than he may have suspected. The fact remains that Hegel is the only reader of the play to have recognized that *Hamlet* is indeed about the emergence of the "old mole." In reconstructing the metaphoric and historical network from which the "old mole" emerged, we will discover something about the nature of the absolute spirit that Hegel did not foresee, even though he points the way to its discovery.

"Examples Gross as Earth"

"Everything in the hero's sphere," writes Nietzsche, "turns to tragedy."[52] For Nietzsche, the philosopher-hero's fearless search for knowledge always ends in tragedy; so searching an inquiry into the bases of knowledge and society invariably triggers destruction. Herein lies the meaning of Nietzsche's promise of a "grand politics," for having disrupted all the old power structures, having revealed that they are all built on lies, Nietzsche promises "a war of the spirits" (*Geisterkrieg*) in which the "concept of politics" will be "totally consumed": "There will be wars the like of which have never been seen on earth. It is only with me that the earth knows a grand politics."[53] The philosopher-hero is not indecisive. The apocalyptic tone of the "*grosse Politik*" is a tone of profound and unwavering certainty. For Nietzsche, Hamlet is the very type of the philosopher-hero. Like Hegel, Nietzsche knows that Hamlet's fundamental problem has nothing to do with indecision: "Is Hamlet understood? Not doubt, *certainty* is what drives one insane.—But one must be profound, an abyss, a philosopher to feel that way.—We are all *afraid* of the truth."[54]

What, however, is Hamlet so certain of? By following Hegel's advice, by *listening* to the "old mole," we will discover that the Ghost, rather than inspiring doubt and indecision, confirms something that Hamlet felt even before his appearance. We will discover also that, like

52. Friedrich Nietzsche, *Beyond Good and Evil*, trans. Walter Kaufmann (New York: Vintage Books, 1966), 90 (translation modified).

53. Friedrich Nietzsche, *Ecce Homo*, trans. Walter Kaufmann (New York: Vintage Books, 1969), 327 (translation modified).

54. Nietzsche, *Ecce Homo*, 246.

Nietzsche, Hamlet's abyssal experience of the truth is synonymous with the question of feminine desire. No less than for Nietzsche or Freud, the great question for Hamlet is, "What does a woman want?"

James Joyce makes the most famous case for the link between *Hamlet* and a grand politics when, in his lecture on *Hamlet* in *Ulysses,* Stephen Dedalus reflects upon the violence of the play:

> —A deathsman of the soul Robert Greene called him, Stephen said. Not for nothing was he a butcher's son wielding the sledded poleaxe and spitting in his palm. Nine lives are taken for his father's one, Our Father who are in purgatory. Khaki Hamlets don't hesitate to shoot. The bloodbolted shambles in act five is a forecast of the concentration camp sung by Mr. Swinburne.

Taking quite literally Nicholas Rowe's apocryphal story of Shakespeare playing the role of the Ghost in the first production of the play, Stephen argues that the Ghost is indeed a projection of Shakespeare himself. In Stephen's biographical reading of the play, Shakespeare's bitterness at having been sexually betrayed by his wife, in conjunction with the death of his son Hamnet in 1596, which condemned the male line of the Shakespeares to extinction, unleashed in the bard an unprecedented taste for violence and revenge. Sexual loathing and mourning, argues Stephen, are responsible for the violence of Hamlet's will to power. While it is true that Stephen's lecture must be read in terms of his relationship to Bloom, as well as in terms of Joyce's concern with fathering his own identity, the lecture nevertheless links the emergence of the "old mole" to the question of nihilism in a way that is more analytically sound than the vast majority of *Hamlet* critics seem ever to have guessed. Like Hegel, Joyce recognizes that the play is about the emergence of the "old mole" but unlike Hegel, Joyce believes that the absolute spirit of the will that it brings in its wake is a spectacle worthy of horror rather than celebration: "That mole is the last to go."[55]

We saw in Chapter 5 that the French poet Max Jacob linked Hamletism not only to a spirit of hypersubjectivism but also to a certain apocalyptic tendency in Western history that had expressed itself, at the time of Jacob's writing, in the cataclysm of World War I. With the end of that war, Jacob hoped he had seen the last of Hamletism in French literature.

55. James Joyce, *Ulysses* (New York: Random House, 1961), 187, 194.

Closely linked to the attitudes of Joyce and Jacob on *Hamlet* is that of T. S. Eliot in his famous essay "Hamlet and His Problems" (1920). The most curious thing about that essay is Eliot's reluctance to name just what it is he finds so reprehensible in *Hamlet*. But then again, that's precisely Eliot's point, that something "inexpressibly horrible" haunts Shakespeare's text, something so horrible that Shakespeare himself "cannot objectify it, and it therefore remains to poison life and obstruct action." The "problem which proved too much for [Shakespeare]" proves too much for Eliot as well. In view of Hegel's reading of the play, Eliot's concern with Shakespeare's inability to bring "it" "into the sunlight" refers to none other than the "old mole": "*Hamlet,* like the sonnets, is full of some stuff that the writer could not drag to light, contemplate, or manipulate into art. And when we search for this feeling, we find it, as in the sonnets, very difficult to localize."[56] For Eliot, this "stuff" seems to have very little to do with the course of world history and a great deal to do with sexual loathing. From his own intuitive sense of the play, however, Eliot seems to approximate Hegel's position that something of rather crucial significance is making its way to the surface in *Hamlet.* While Hegel celebrates it and sees it as the will to power of the absolute spirit, and while Joyce prophetically sees it as the prefiguration of the Nazi holocaust ("the concentration camp sung by Mr. Swinburne"), Eliot simply finds it repugnant and unspeakable.

The great critics of *Hamlet,* such as Hegel, Nietzsche, Joyce, Goethe, Coleridge, and Eliot, despite all their differences, agree on the fact that *Hamlet* signals a qualitative transformation in the nature of the human spirit. I find the universalism of Hegel and Nietzsche most attractive and compelling because they celebrate Shakespeare's discovery in *Hamlet* of an entirely new world of previously buried forces and motivations. Through the metaphorics of the "old mole," Shakespeare marked a pathway into the underlying principles of our *humanitas,*

---

56. T. S. Eliot, *The Sacred Wood* (New York: Barnes & Noble, 1966), 102, 100. Eliot's terms echo, perhaps consciously, Jules Laforgue's remark apropos of his own hypersubjective Hamlet, "*il faut s'objectiver*" (*Hamlet et quelques poésies* [Paris: Stock, 1924], 30). Eliot also complains of the scenes in Act One involving Polonius and Laertes, and Polonius and Reynaldo. But far from being "unexplained," as Eliot believes, these scenes are both elaborations of the theme of the fault. In the first, Polonius warns his son against the faults of youth; in the second he sends his servant to France to discover what improprieties his son has been up to. Once the centrality of the "old mole" is understood, the unity of Act One becomes obvious.

whether in the form of the Hegelian *Geist* or the Freudian unconscious. If that understanding of man's nature in the here and now, that revelation of the specificity of human nature, horrifies some of us, and if that new-found power of language to probe into the deepest recesses of our nature has led historically to a generalized desublimation and has therefore contributed to the primitive and violent direction in which twentieth-century history is certainly tending, it is nevertheless blindness and madness to put all of this at Shakespeare's door. Shakespeare did not build Axel's castle; he has simply been appropriated into it by an increasingly nihilistic culture. Hamletism as a byword for any of a variety of human excesses and transgressions seems to me a grotesque parody of literary and cultural history. Indeed, it is flattering for an artist to think that a work of literature, even so magnificent a work as *Hamlet,* could have had the sort of historical instrumentality that Jacob, Joyce, and Eliot cautiously hint at. In Shakespeare's discovery of the dark side of human desire, Hegel saw the illumination of the absolute spirit. While the course of human history since Hegel makes it impossible for us to share his almost rhapsodic enthusiasm, we must also be careful to guard against the anachronistic misreading of *Hamlet* that characterizes the modernist period. We must not forget that the "old mole" is still burrowing and that any judgment on our part as to its ultimate destiny would be both premature and foolhardy.

Let us begin, then, as Eliot would say, "to localize" the "old mole's" pathway in *Hamlet.* The central passage that defines the initial horizon against which the cellarage scene must be read comes early in the fourth scene of Act One, in Hamlet's speech to Horatio as the two of them, on the battlements overlooking the nightly revels of Claudius's courtiers, reflect upon the corruption of life at Elsinore. This passage has never to my knowledge been linked to the image of the "old mole," though several critics have come close to recognizing its significance. Hamlet begins by ridiculing the drunken debauchery of the Danish court but then launches into a larger attack on the weakness of human nature in general. He has not yet seen the Ghost and has no evidence of Claudius's crime. Most students of the play know the speech in 1.4.17–38 only from the scholarly vantage point of Shakespeare's incorporation there of Thomas Nashe's diatribe against drunkenness in *Pierce Penniless.* Its significance, however, goes far beyond its sources. Once we grasp the synchronic importance of the passage within the context of the play itself, we will be able to return to the question of

Shakespeare's relation to Nashe and elucidate it in a completely new way. Several critics, as I said, have noted how this speech seems to anticipate the subsequent direction of the play. They have seen in Hamlet's reflection on "some vicious mole of nature" (1.4.24) a foreshadowing of Hamlet's tortuous obsession with the themes of corruption and decay following the revelation of Claudius's crime. Mark Rose remarks of the speech that Hamlet has "vague premonitions about the curse of his nativity"; John Dover Wilson writes of 1.4.17–38 that it is "the most striking instance of Shakespeare's cunning in preparing the minds of the audience for effects he will introduce later"; finally, Wolfgang Clemen comes closest to fathoming its importance when he asks, "Why does Hamlet speak in such detail of these matters here? For at this point in the play he has as yet heard nothing of his uncle's murderous deed. And still he touches in this speech upon that *leitmotif* of the whole play."[57] Even so, as Dover Wilson remarked over thirty years ago, its "relevance . . . to the theme of *Hamlet* as a whole has been somewhat neglected." Obviously, this passage works entirely in favor of Hegel's argument that Hamlet's will is flawed by something that finally has nothing to do with Claudius or the murder of old Hamlet.

Historical and textual problems in part explain why so crucial a passage should have suffered such critical neglect. To begin with, 1.4.17–38 appears in neither the First Quarto nor in the First Folio, and there has been a long-standing scholarly debate on the reasons why this speech appears only in the Second Quarto. Dover Wilson argues that because Hamlet insults the drunkenness of the Danish people, the passage may have been omitted in performance after 1603, when James I and his queen, Anne of Denmark, came to the throne.[58] The Second Quarto of 1604–5 would thus present us with the uncensored version of the play as it was performed prior to James's accession. Harold Jenkins believes that the omission of the speech in the First Folio was the result of simple dramatic expediency, especially since it also omits Horatio's closely related meditation on ill omens and

57. Mark Rose, *Shakespearean Design* (Cambridge, Mass.: Harvard University Press, 1972), 106; John Dover Wilson, *What Happens in Hamlet* (Cambridge: Cambridge University Press, 1951), 206; Wolfgang Clemen, *The Development of Shakespeare's Imagery* (London: Methuen, 1977), 115.

58. John Dover Wilson, *The Manuscript of Shakespeare's Hamlet and the Problems of Its Transmission*, 2 vols. (Cambridge: Cambridge University Press, 1963), 1:25–26.

portents in 1.1.115–28.[59] In such a long and difficult play, it is indeed conceivable that a director who fails to grasp the importance of the speech should choose to omit it; in modern performances it is still often omitted, which doubtless helps to explain why so much *Hamlet* criticism is misguided. If this was also the case during James's reign, however, then we must insist that it could only have happened after Shakespeare's involvement with the King's Men had substantially diminished. It is impossible for me to imagine that Shakespeare could ever have countenanced the omission, for reasons of either censorship or expediency, of one of the most decisive passages in the entire play. Dover Wilson's argument that Shakespeare was probably not involved with the production of *Hamlet* lends credence to this position.[60] It would also suggest that Hemmings and Condell, in assembling the First Folio, had been out of touch with Shakespeare for a very long time indeed. It is one of literary history's greater ironies that one of the most important passages in one of Shakespeare's greatest plays should have been from its inception a problematic element in both the performance and the text.

Here, then, is the speech in question:

> So, oft it chances in particular men
> That for some vicious mole of nature in them,
> As in their birth, wherein they are not guilty
> (Since nature cannot choose his origin),
> By their o'ergrowth of some complexion,
> Oft breaking down the pales and forts of reason,
> Or by some habit, that too much o'erleavens
> The form of plausive manners—that these men,
> Carrying, I say, the stamp of one defect,
> Being Nature's livery or Fortune's star,
> His virtues else, be they as pure as grace,
> As infinite as man may undergo,
> Shall in the general censure take corruption
> From that particular fault. The dram of evil
> Doth all the noble substance often dout
> To his own scandal.
>
> [1.4.23–38]

---

59. *Hamlet*, ed. Harold Jenkins, 209.
60. Dover Wilson, *The Manuscript of Shakespeare's Hamlet*, 1:172–73. This would mean of course that Shakespeare never played the part of the Ghost.

Not least among the difficulties of this passage is the fact that its first
sentence is fourteen lines long (23–36: "So . . . fault") and the syntax
so complex that the meaning of the speech must almost literally burrow its way through the sentence. In the kind of production I imagine
Shakespeare envisioned, this speech would be so patiently and clearly
articulated that its echo a few lines later in the "old mole" in 1.5 would
be unmistakable to the audience. Everything in the passage follows
from the "vicious mole." On first reading one might think that here
"mole" means "fault" or "flaw" or, as Hamlet says, "the stamp of one
defect." This meaning of the word has a different etymology from that
which means a burrowing animal. I am not suggesting that Shakespeare knew that "mole" as "blemish" comes from the Old English
mál and that "mole" as mammal comes from the Middle English
molle. What I am suggesting is that here in the first appearance of the
word, Shakespeare is already playing on both meanings of the term.
The sense of a blemish on one's "complexion" (27) is of course the
primary sense, but the notion of the mole "breaking down the pales
and forts of reason" (28) follows immediately after. The blemish is an
internal one, and what Hamlet is describing is its awful progress toward the surface. This "mole" is always already a "mole." Though
Hamlet is uncertain whether it comes from nature or nurture, he is
certain that it can corrupt the individual's whole identity. And though
he begins by talking about mankind in general, it soon becomes obvious that he is talking about himself. There is no question here of a
literal and a figurative sense of "mole," for Shakespeare has undermined such a distinction from the start. When Hamlet calls his father's
ghost "old mole," he knows, as Hegel recognized, that he is talking to
himself. The "mole" is always already the figure of a figure. We might
recall here what Hegel said of the spirit's "*unconscious* work," that
first it appears not as spirit at all but as something radically other.
Shakespeare reveals through his play on the word "mole" that the
"unconscious work" of the spirit is synonymous with the work of
language. Like Hegel, Shakespeare demands that we listen very closely
to the "mole."

We might wonder, however, if Hegel could have guessed just how
radically other the spirit's first incarnation is in *Hamlet*. In order to
reconstruct the referent of Hamlet's speech in 1.4, we must turn to
1.2—the first scene in which Hamlet appears—after Claudius up-
braids him for mourning excessively for his father's death. It is in this

scene that Hamlet makes his Hegelian claim for the existence of an unfathomable, unrepresentable subjectivity. Here Hamlet claims that behind his "inky cloak" (1.2.77) he conceals within himself that which "passes show," that which none of the "forms, modes, shapes of grief" could ever hope to "denote . . . truly" (82–85). Claudius and his court, along with the audience, assume that Hamlet's problem is excessive mourning, that what Claudius calls "a fault to heaven. / A fault against the dead, a fault to nature" (101–2) is attributable to the depth of Hamlet's sorrow over his father's death. Hamlet's first soliloquy makes it unmistakably clear, however, that what "passes show" in the depths of his inwardness is precisely the opposite of excessive mourning. As Jacques Lacan argues in his essay "Desire and the Interpretation of Desire in *Hamlet*," the problem of "central importance" in the play is that of "insufficient mourning." *Hamlet*, writes Lacan, "is a tragedy of the underworld,"[61] an underworld of sexual loathing and Oedipal guilt.

Lacan's argument is a brilliant revision of Freud's famous interpretation of the play. For what Lacan does is to direct our attention away from the revenge plot and toward the question of Hamlet's response to his mother's desire. Unlike Freud, who argues that Hamlet is not psychopathic "but only *becomes* psychopathic in the course of the action of the play,"[62] Lacan rightly maintains that it is the revelation of the nature of Gertrude's desire from the beginning of the play, and indeed even before the beginning, that has predisposed Hamlet to madness. The brilliance of Lacan's reading lies in its understanding that Gertrude's desire for Claudius—not the revenge plot—is the dominant factor in Hamlet's psyche.

Lacan plays in relation to Freud the same role Hegel plays in relation to Goethe. Freud believes that the coming to consciousness of the normally repressed structure of Oedipal desire is attributable to the extraordinary pressures under which Hamlet is placed by the Ghost's call to revenge. Hamlet is thus, argues Freud, forced to commit in

61. Jacques Lacan, "Desire and the Interpretation of Desire in *Hamlet*," in *Literature and Psychoanalysis*, ed. Shoshana Felman (Baltimore, Md.: Johns Hopkins University Press, 1982), 39.

62. Sigmund Freud, "Psychopathic Characters on the Stage," in *The Standard Edition of the Complete Psychological Works of Sigmund Freud*, ed. James Strachey et al., 24 vols. (London: Hogarth Press and the Institute of Psycho-Analysis, 1953–74), 7:309. This paper from 1905–6 offers a more complete version of Freud's ideas on *Hamlet* than his discussion in Ch. 5 of *The Interpretation of Dreams*.

reality precisely that which must be repressed in one's phantasies in order for one's sexual and psychical life to develop normally. For Freud, the "old mole" is the parricidal aspect of the Oedipal complex, which is "repressed in all of us, and the repression of which is part and parcel of the foundation of our personal evolution. It is this repression which is shaken up by the situation in the play." By "the situation," Freud means the Ghost's appearance and the revelation of Claudius's crime. But as we have seen, the "mole" is already beginning to burrow before any of that has happened. Lacan recognizes that what shakes up that repression and that what disrupts the normal process of mourning is a displacement of what he calls Hamlet's position in relation to the phallus: that is, his position in relation to his mother's desire. It is in this context that the "old mole" takes on its truly Shakespearean significance.

When Hamlet speaks in his first soliloquy of "this too too sullied flesh" (1.2.129), it is of his relationship to Gertrude that he is thinking. It is her failure to observe the normal conventions of mourning that disrupts his own experience of mourning and that poisons it with the despair of sexual loathing and contempt. In his recent book *The Renaissance Hamlet,* Roland Mushat Frye outlines the context of sixteenth-century mourning practices and concludes that "when judged in sixteenth-century terms, Gertrude's behavior is utterly scandalous. Widows were held to even more rigorous and prolonged mourning than were widowers."[63] It is the break with this blatantly patriarchal convention, prior to the opening of the play, that explains Hamlet's psychopathic predisposition. It is this unanticipated excess of feminine desire that precipitates the emergence of the "old mole." Here we can see how radically other the first emergence of the spirit is in *Hamlet,* for what is emerging from the depths of subjectivity is nothing other than the unrestrained expression of feminine desire.

This is precisely what Lacan means when he argues that Hamlet's position with respect to the phallus is "entirely out of place in terms of its position in the Oedipus complex." For Lacan, feminine desire is synonymous with the desire for the phallus. "There must be something very strong," writes Lacan of Gertrude and Claudius, "that attaches her to her partner. And doesn't it seem that that is the point around

63. Roland Mushat Frye, *The Renaissance Hamlet: Issues and Responses in 1600* (Princeton, N.J.: Princeton University Press, 1984), 84.

which Hamlet's action turns and lingers?" Lacan has succeeded in localizing the "old mole" in terms of the play's psychological dynamic. Instead of being veiled, as it is supposed to be, the phallus in *Hamlet* has become all too real. Hamlet cannot kill Claudius because of his "narcissistic connection" to him. It is not the Ghost but the emergence and open expression of Gertrude's desire that makes Hamlet aware of this repressed Oedipal desire in himself for his mother. It is the de-sublimation of feminine desire that triggers in Hamlet a strange sense of his own feelings of sexual rivalry and longing for the mother, which would otherwise never have come to the surface. It is only against the backdrop of the intemperance of her desire and the violation of the mourning customs that the Ghost's imperative to revenge can be as-sessed. Had Gertrude's desire not been so openly displayed, and had the rites of mourning been observed, Hamlet would doubtless have had no difficulty at all in fulfilling the Ghost's command. It is Gertrude's desire that is burrowing toward the surface, bringing with it Hamlet's own repressed desires. "The thing is strange and obvious," writes Lacan, "recorded in all sorts of little riddles in Hamlet's style."[64] The "old mole" is clearly the site where the question of what a woman wants and the question of style become synonymous.

The "old mole" marks the point where Gertrude's desire intersects that of her son. But in saying this, have we done anything more than localize for the first time what remains an essentially conventional psychoanalytic reading along the lines of Ernest Jones's *Hamlet and Oedipus?* There can be no denial that Hamlet's initial response to the spectacle of feminine desire is misogyny and an impulse to matricide. The many deaths that atone for old Hamlet's death are, as Lacan writes, "offered in expiation of that primordial offense." But Hamlet comes to recognize in himself something infinitely more complex than "the soul of Nero" (3.2.385). Hamlet's uniqueness inheres in the fact that he is not simply horrified by the realization that feminine desire is not synonymous with maternal desire; it is his transcendence of the Oedipal structure of desire rather than his exemplary entrapment with-in it that constitutes Shakespeare's greatest achievement in the play. What separates Hamlet from Orestes is the fact that the "old mole" of feminine desire burrows beyond the depths of Oedipal revenge and toward a new abstract subjectivity; for Hamlet is the first character in

64. Lacan, "Desire and the Interpretation of Desire in *Hamlet*," 50–51.

Western literature to be able to reflect upon the nature of his subjectivity, to look at it as though from outside himself and reflect not simply on the content of that subjectivity but on its capacity for self-reflection. Shakespeare goes beyond the Oedipal structure of revenge tragedy to ponder the relation between feminine desire and abstract subjectivity, for it is precisely in the discursive space that has been opened by the feminine that Hamlet is able to represent himself to himself in an entirely new way. It is from this space, which Hamlet regards as the site of his maternal genealogy—a genealogy that has left in him the trace (the "old mole") of a too uncontrollable desire—that there springs a discursive practice new to Western civilization. If on the one hand Shakespeare, like Freud, is compelled to reduce this phenomenon to a biological curse, on the other hand the text reveals that the space of the feminine is the site of an epochal rift whose subject is not biological but linguistic. It is in this space that Shakespeare will come to challenge and transform the notion of representation itself.

Though Freud's reading is clearly inadequate, it has the virtue of having been the first to recognize the role of repression in the play, even if it did mistake the nature and the dramatic articulation of that repression. Though Freud was somewhat presumptuous in claiming to have been the first "to unearth" the mystery of *Hamlet,* he was also wise enough to insist on the unnameable nature of the impulses at work in the play: "It appears as a necessary precondition of this form of art that the impulse that is struggling into consciousness, however clearly it is recognizable, is never given a name; so that in the spectator too the process is carried through with his attention averted, and he is in the grip of his emotions instead of taking stock of what is happening."[65] We can say that Freud himself was somewhat diverted by his own theory from fully taking into account exactly "what is happening." We saw earlier how much difficulty Eliot had in naming just what kind of desire was at stake in *Hamlet.* Freud and Eliot are, it seems to me, pointing to something very important about *Hamlet:* that the play itself seems to repress or bury precisely that which is necessary to its interpretation. The very dynamic of the play is, in other words, caught in the structure of repression it sets out to analyze. It is as though Shakespeare were determined to listen to the mole and equally

---

65. Freud, "Psychopathic Characters on the Stage," 309.

determined to bury the mole so deeply within the language and the structure of the play as to make it inaccessible.

This is another way of saying that without Hegel it would be difficult to find one's way into the deep structure of the play. And even with Hegel's extraordinary contribution, it is still necessary to assemble a wide range of critics from Coleridge to Lacan in order remotely to begin to make sense of "what is happening" in *Hamlet*. It would appear that the historical desublimation of desire that *Hamlet* seems to chronicle could have become the subject of artistic representation only at the price of a countervailing sublimation of language itself. This brings us back once again to the relation between style and feminine desire, for style is at once the element that reveals and conceals the emergence of previously sublimated desire. The allegory of desire has been so successfully buried at the level of style that actors, directors, audiences, and critics have for centuries been prevented from "naming" exactly what that desire is. But Shakespeare did name it—nor should we be fooled into thinking that the "old mole" is the only name he gave it. "We pray you throw to earth / This unprevailing woe" (1.2.106–7), Claudius says to Hamlet. The "old mole" is only the point of entry into a subterranean metaphoric network in which Shakespeare at once inscribes and buries the name of this most disruptive of desires.

In the introduction to the *Aesthetics,* Hegel discusses the relation between the experience of mourning and the effect of the artwork. Though he does not mention *Hamlet* in this connection, his remarks are plainly relevant to his reading of the play. For Hegel, the philosopher is always in mourning for the artwork. Writing in the epoch of the death of art, the philosopher nevertheless cannot do without the artwork. Throughout his career, art was for Hegel an essential pathway toward the absolute. The philosopher experiences the artwork as a kind of death, as "a deficiency and a negation *in* the subjective which it struggles to negate again." For Hegel the work of art is synonymous with the work of mourning. Art is experienced as a loss, as negation, which is a feeling that must in turn be negated: "To go through this process of opposition, contradiction, and the resolution of the contradiction, is the higher privilege of living beings."[66]

66. Hegel, *Aesthetics,* 1:97.

We can understand what I have called the countervailing sublimation of language in *Hamlet* in terms of this second phase of the double negation. The double negation is Shakespeare's effort to "throw to earth / This unprevailing woe" that he had somehow managed to uncover. "Foul deeds will rise," says Hamlet when Horatio tells him of the Ghost's appearance, "Though all the earth o'erwhelm them to men's eyes" (1.2.257–58). But as the revenge plot rises to the surface, the theme of feminine desire is gradually resublimated. Hegel's notion of the double negation provides us with a context in which to understand Shakespeare's dialectic of naming and unnaming in *Hamlet*. Sexual loathing remains a prominent feature in Hamlet's character throughout the play, but its causal role in the etiology of Hamlet's neurosis is concealed behind the revenge plot, which is presented as though it were the motive force of the tragedy rather than as the catalyst or precipitating agent that it is. Sexual loathing appears as the effect of the revenge plot and thus its true instrumentality is, as I remarked, resublimated. All of which transpires under the rubric of insufficient mourning and within the dialectic of the double negation.

Herein lies the significance of all the images of earth, the underworld, mining, burying, and the like, which pervade the play, as even the most cursory glance will indicate. The "old mole" is the point of entry into a vast network of subterranean imagery. From the "worthy pioner" of 1.5 to the gravedigger in 5.1 is finally a very short step indeed. One is always either burying or unburying things in *Hamlet*. From that "fellow in the cellarage" (1.5.158) to Hamlet and Laertes struggling in Ophelia's grave, it is more than obvious that *Hamlet*, in the words of Lacan, is a "tragedy of the underworld." For every inch the mole burrows forward, there is a corresponding spade full of dirt to check his progress. In a rare moment of lucidity in his otherwise dissembling conversation with Ophelia, Hamlet wonders, "What should such fellows as I do crawling between heaven and earth?" (3.1.128). The language of Hamlet reduces all the players to a molelike existence.

In 3.4, following the performance of "The Murder of Gonzago," Hamlet pursues Gertrude to her bedchamber, where he castigates her lack of conscience and her unbridled lust in terms that recall his speech to Horatio in 1.4. We tend to think of the play-within-the-play as a means of testing the "conscience of the King" (2.2.601), but it is also an effective way of revealing the lack of conscience of the Queen. Despite Hamlet's protestations that "The Murder of Gonzago" is intended solely for Claudius, its dramatic import is to bring his sexual loathing with regard to his mother to a climax. It is consistent with my thesis and demonstrable in the play itself that Hamlet's fundamental objective in producing the play-within-the-play is to bring Gertrude to a cathartic recognition of her lust. The effect on Claudius is precisely what Sidney prescribed in *An Apology for Poetry*. With Claudius, the cathartic effect is fully achieved. But in my Hegelian reading, killing Claudius was never Hamlet's real objective. The underworld of Hamlet's desire is occupied solely with thoughts of Gertrude. "You go not till I set you up a glass," he tells her, "Where you may see the inmost part of you" (3.4. 18–19). Indeed, the representation of the woman's desire has been Hamlet's true objective since the beginning. While Claudius could see his "inmost part" reflected in "The Murder of Gonzago," Gertrude saw nothing of herself in the Player Queen's easy virtue. But now, as Hamlet holds up to Gertrude the figurative glass of his discourse, she begins to see:

> Thou turn'st my eyes into my very soul,
> And there I see such black and grained spots
> As will not leave their tinct.
>
> [3.4.88–90]

It is these spots, these vicious moles of nature, that Hamlet had been hiding all along behind his "inky cloak." They are blemishes not on Gertrude's skin but deep underneath, or, in Hamlet's idiom, underground:

> It will but skin and film the ulcerous place
> Whiles rank corruption, mining all within,
> Infects unseen.
>
> [3.4.149–51]

This is where the "worthy pioner" does his work. The true underworld in *Hamlet* is the underworld of feminine desire. Murdering Polonius behind the arras and speaking with the Ghost who remains invisible to Gertrude are of little matter to Hamlet compared with his excitement at having apparently broken through at last to his mother's conscience. Once again the dramaturgy of the scene seems to substantiate such a reading. Seizing the moment, Hamlet attempts to persuade her not to return to Claudius's bed. It is in this speech that he reverts to the language of 1.4. Once again we are concerned with "the frock or livery" of habit—but with a difference: while Hamlet was convinced in 1.4 of the incorrigibility of feminine desire, he is now more hopeful:

> For use can almost change the stamp of nature,
> And either lodge the devil or throw him out
> With wondrous potency.
>
> [3.4.170–72]

Earlier the corruption seemed irreversible; now Hamlet "almost" feels there is hope. If only Gertrude would stop sleeping with Claudius, her wayward desire would begin to mend accordingly.

Hamlet's exuberance at having broken through to this underworld of feminine desire carries over to his speech at the end of the scene where he uses the figure of tunneling and mining to forewarn the audience what he will do to Claudius's spies, Rosencrantz and Guildenstern:

> For 'tis the sport to have the enginer
> Hoist with his own petard, and it shall go hard
> But I will delve one yard below their mines
> And blow them at the moon.
>
> [3.4.308–10]

Hamlet will burrow deeper than these scheming "enginers," set his charges, and blow them off the earth. Having blasted out the infestation of feminine desire, Hamlet, himself a "worthy pioner," is ready to deal with Claudius and his minions.

Such enthusiasm is, however, very short-lived. Just before Claudius conspires to send him to England, Hamlet achieves the veritable apogee of his resolve to kill Claudius. Still exuberant at his relative success with Gertrude, he sees the armies of Norway and Poland as they prepare to do battle over a worthless scrap of land. The structure of the scene (4.4) is very much like that of the scene in which the First Player recites Pyrrhus's murder of Priam (2.2). In both cases Hamlet contrasts his own inaction in the face of a real grievance with the action of others in the face of an unreal grievance. But in 2.2, at a point when Hamlet is deep in the throes of his sex loathing, he resolves only to stage the play-within-the-play; in 4.4, when "Examples gross as earth exhort [him]" (4.4.36), he proclaims, "from this time forth / My thoughts be bloody or be nothing worth" (65–66). But his resolve is cut short, when he returns to Denmark, by the spectacle of Ophelia's funeral. The shock of her death, the spectacle of Laertes' grief, and their confrontation before the funeral procession push Hamlet over the brink into madness and passive despair.

Hamlet's resolve reaches its apogee in 3.4 when he succeeds in purging Gertrude of the "dram of evil," and thus also in purging himself of whatever he bears of her taint. In the first half of the play Hamlet is concerned more with Gertrude's catharsis than with Claudius's guilt. But what prevents Hamlet from turning to revenge after 3.4? Is it his despair at Ophelia's death or his intellectual aversion to revenge?

Though Shakespeare's emphasis is on Gertrude's transgressions, there are also traces in the play of old Hamlet's sinful nature. Hamlet's loathing of Gertrude's passionate nature antedates the opening of the play. He has, however, only the noblest memories of his father. But how are we to reconcile those memories with the fact that the Ghost startles "like a guilty thing" (1.1.149) when Horatio addresses him? And why have critics never been able to explain why old Hamlet is condemned to an unspeakable penance in purgatory? Could it be that Hamlet fears that it is his father's "Foul deeds" that "will rise"?

The fact that Shakespeare does not elaborate on these putative faults of the father suggests that they may well be traces of the Ur-*Hamlet*. Had Thomas Kyd written the Ur-*Hamlet*, it would be easy to imagine a plot in which the son knows that his father was a murderer. The Ur-*Hamlet*'s delay would then be the expression of his paralyzing inablilty to forget the vicious circle of revenge in which he is caught. René Girard believes that this is still to some extent true of Shakespeare's Hamlet, to whom Claudius looks "like one more link in an already long chain, and his own revenge will look like still another perfect link, perfectly identical to all the other links."[67]

While Kyd may have pointed to old Hamlet's treachery in the duel with old Fortinbras, Shakespeare does not give us the clues from which to reconstruct the father's crime. Instead, he turns to the question of the feminine, that is, to the question of style. I am going to read "The Murder of Gonzago," which is Hamlet's stylistic means of staging the

67. René Girard, "Hamlet's Dull Revenge," *Stanford Literature Review* (Fall 1984): 174. Girard wants critics to stop regarding Hamlet's reluctance to kill Claudius as a kind of pathology; for Shakespeare's purpose is to reveal that "the sanctity of revenge provides a perfect vehicle for all the masks of modern *ressentiment*" (198).

catharsis of the King and Queen, as the consummate expression of
Shakespeare's "will to style," for it is there that he elaborates the
abyssal seriality of the revenge plot into a critique of artistic
representation.

Murdering Mimesis: The Primal Scene in *Hamlet*

Several elements of my reading of *Hamlet* echo Hegel's reading of
Sophocles' *Antigone* in the *Phenomenology of Spirit,* above all the
association of woman with the rites of mourning, and with the darkness and mystery of the chthonian world in general.[68] Hegel never
links the *Antigone* to *Hamlet,* but let us consider for a moment what
the terms of such a relation might be. What is striking first of all is the
importance of mourning. There is an interesting and almost uncanny
chiasmus between the two plays in this respect. For while Antigone
suffers a tragic fate because she follows the prescribed rites of mourning so rigorously, Gertrude unleashes the forces of tragedy by failing
utterly to follow the appropriate conventions. The historical importance of the *Antigone* for Hegel is that it marks the transition from a
tribal society based on the communal laws of the family to a class
society based on the laws of the state. Antigone is for Hegel the essence
of the "ethical life" or *Sittlichkeit,* and as the embodiment of purely
intuitive ethical knowledge, she represents a stage in the evolution of
the absolute spirit. In the primitive epoch whose ending she dramatizes, the absolute spirit is synonymous with the spirit of the feminine.
With the coming of the state power as manifested by Creon, the absolute spirit takes on a decidedly masculine aspect. In Hegel's thinking,
we are not quite at the point of Goethe's "Eternal Feminine" but rather
in a system where the world spirit alternately takes on feminine and
masculine aspects. There is an "Eternal Feminine" for Hegel, but it
does not continuously dominate the course of world history. Given
these terms, it is entirely plausible that had Hegel read *Hamlet* as
closely as we have, he might well have regarded the crucial role of
feminine desire in effecting the progression of the absolute spirit as
signaling a resurgence, after almost two millennia, of the spirit of the
feminine. Just as Antigone's tragedy is a necessary historical stage in

68. *Phenomenology of Spirit,* 267ff.

the upward spiral of the spirit, so too Hamlet's tragedy would mark an epochal historical transformation, but this time one in which the power of the state would take on a new character by virtue of an unprecedented subjectivism. *Hamlet* would thus signal a certain *Aufhebung* of the chthonian underworld of feminine desire within a new epoch of limitless subjective energy. To be sure, the sanctity of Antigone's sisterly devotion to her brother's burial rites makes Gertrude's violation of her duties, in conjunction with the excess of her desire, appear almost a parody of the chthonian essence of the feminine. But it is the sharply chiasmatic relation between the two texts that would doubtless appeal to Hegel most. It is entirely appropriate that at this stage of the evolution of the absolute spirit, the instrumentality of feminine desire should appear under the sign of negativity. In both the *Antigone* and *Hamlet,* feminine desire supplies the motive force that enables the spirit to progress.

In his 1805 lectures, *The Philosophy of Spirit,* Hegel describes the operation of "Practical Reason" as a collaboration of male and female forces, and compares them to the relation between Oedipus and the Sphinx. H. S. Harris conveniently summarizes Hegel's argument:

> The intelligence is the feminine power, dwelling in the Earth, but knowing what happens in the daylight, and manipulating the male strength of the manifest forces of Nature, so that in spite of its womanly weakness those forces may produce the result that it predicts, although that result is quite the opposite of what the manifest forces produce spontaneously or by their own will.[69]

We could readily elaborate this account into a summary of the plot of *Hamlet.* Spirit's self-realization as pure subjectivity is possible only by virtue of the subterranean mysteries of feminine power. What *Hamlet* demonstrates above all is that the absolute spirit as will can only define itself in relation to feminine desire. The will appears in the unlikely form of unchecked female passion before passing into and thus creating the space of abstract subjectivity. We can see now that such a notion is as Shakespearean as it is Hegelian.

"'Sblood," Hamlet exclaims to Rosencrantz, "there is something in this more than natural, if only philosophy could find it out" (2.2.364). In *Hamlet,* Shakespeare had intuited much that philosophy and psy-

---

69. Harris, *Hegel's Development: Night Thoughts,* 480.

choanalysis would take centuries longer to discover. The "old mole" of Oedipal desire breaches the pathway to the absolute spirit. In so doing it reaches the threshold of representability. Because of Gertrude's passion, Hamlet feels within himself the emergence of incomprehensible desires that lead him in turn to an entirely new level of self-knowledge. Desire and the desire to know are inwoven in *Hamlet* to the point of being indistinguishable. In seeking to understand the hidden motivations of Claudius and Gertrude, Hamlet is invariably also seeking to understand his own motivations. The problem Hamlet faces, however, is that at this profound level of the human psyche, representation itself is no longer adequate. The problem Hamlet faces is that of representing what has never been represented before. In his conversation with the First Player, he advises, "Suit the action to the word, the word to the action, with this special observance, that you o'erstep not the modesty of nature" (3.2.16–19). The duty of the artist "is to hold as 'twere the mirror up to nature," but one must not do so immodestly. Herein lies for Hamlet the difference between good and bad imitation. The problem is that his knowledge has utterly transformed his notion of nature: his knowledge has taken on so terribly immodest a character that the very difference between good and bad imitation is overthrown. The "old mole," "the stamp of nature," and the "black and grained spots" are highly figurative representations for that which remains unrepresentable. As I observed earlier, Shakespeare wants to reveal the unrepresentable nature of desire and to conceal it at the same time. The play seems to conspire against itself by repressing the revelation of precisely the unrepresentable aspect of nature that it calls forth. These unrepresentable desires are indeed "more than natural"—both in the sense of being unnatural according to a certain view of nature, and at the very foundation of nature according to another view. Like the Freudian *Unheimliche,* the "old mole" has a strangely familiar unfamiliarity.

"The Murder of Gonzago" is Hamlet's most concerted effort to hold the mirror up to nature. Contrary to current critical opinion, it is also, as we have seen, as much an effort to represent the unrepresentability of feminine desire as it is an effort to strike Claudius "to the soul" and make him proclaim his "malefactions" (2.2.587–88). And dramatically, its most powerful effect is not Claudius's overheard confession in the chapel but Hamlet's scathing attack upon Gertrude in her bedchamber. In "The Murder of Gonzago," Shakespeare is doing much more than filling the Sidneyan prescription. What he performs there is nothing less than a thoroughgoing deconstruction of the notion of imitation. "The Murder of Gonzago" brings us up against the structural limits of representation. No less than Mallarmé's "Mimique"— which is Derrida's text in "The Double Session"—"The Murder of Gonzago" undermines the hierarchy between copy and model, between an original and its representation. With the desublimation of feminine desire, the very notion of representation is called into question. It is in "The Murder of Gonzago" that we can see the emergence of a new and abyssal form of subjectivity.

The manner of Claudius's crime is so strikingly original that, except for the Ghost, it is the most memorable thing in the play. The introduction of poison through the ear is so theatrically satisfying that its actual plausibility becomes entirely irrelevant. It is part of a large network of ear-related imagery that pervades the play, often in conjunction with the subterranean imagery of the "old mole." Speech in Hamlet is a kind of ear-piercing dagger: "These words like daggers enter in my ears" (3.4.95), says Gertrude to Hamlet's merciless assault. The theatrical prerogative itself is "to amaze indeed / The very faculties of eyes and ears" (2.2.5), to "cleave the general ear" (2.2.557), or, in the case of bad imitation, "to split the ears of the groundlings" (3.2.10). The cumulative effect of all this is to call into question the relation between literal and figurative ear-poisoning. For if indeed there is no such thing as actual ear-poisoning—that is, if Shakespeare had no historical referent in mind, and we will consider this question in a moment—then Claudius's crime would be the figure of a figure, a literalizing figure of the insidious effects of speech.

Nicolas Abraham makes this argument in his otherwise highly fanciful reconstruction of the primal scene in *Hamlet*.[70] Abraham argues that the manner of Claudius's crime reveals symbolically that Claudius

---

70. Nicolas Abraham, "*Le Fantôme d'Hamlet ou le VIe acte, précédé par l'entr'acte de la 'verité'*," in *L'Ecorce et le noyau* (Paris: Aubier-Flammarion, 1978), 447–74. André Green elaborates and refines Abraham's thesis in *Hamlet et Hamlet: Une Interprétation psychanalytique de la répresentation* (Paris: Balland, 1982). He too wants to reconstruct "the latent text" that reveals the father's "anterior crime" (82). Green effectively focuses attention on the connection between the dissimulations of woman and the theater. For a less ambitious attempt to invent the play's primal scene, see Otto Rank's "The 'Play-Within-A-Play' in 'Hamlet,'" trans. Paul Lewison *Journal of the Otto Rank Association* 6.2. (December 1971): 5–21; Rank argues that in staging "The Murder of Gonzago" Hamlet is trying to recreate his infantile glimpses of his parents' coitus.

poisoned his brother with words, and more particularly, words that revealed to old Hamlet that he, Claudius, knew of his brother's treachery in poisoning old Fortinbras. Crucial to Abraham's slightly misguided interpretation is the "vial" (1.4.62) in which the poison is contained and which for Abraham becomes a kind of *viol*, or rape. Abraham manufactures old Hamlet's treachery in the death of old Fortinbras, about which the play says absolutely nothing, and furthermore makes Polonius his accomplice, citing Ophelia's familiarity with various plants as evidence that she knew her father was a poisoner. Abraham's reading of the play, and the supplemental sixth act that he appends, are no less amusing for being utterly preposterous; in fact, they provide an interesting example of the confrontation between French rationalism and the English imagination. Whether Polonius helped old Hamlet poison his sword in the duel with old Fortinbras (whom the play does tell us he slew) and whether Polonius later aided Claudius in poisoning his brother are irrelevancies in comparison with the issues the play itself raises.

What Abraham does grasp, however, is the important link between words and wounding and poisoning. This is where the play's primal scene lies, not in some deluded reconstruction of events that took place thirty years before. To Laertes' inappropriately ornate rhetoric in expressing his grief at his sister's demise, Hamlet replies:

> What is he whose grief
> Bears such emphasis, whose phrase of sorrow
> Conjures the wand'ring stars and makes them stand
> Like wonder-wounded hearers?
>
> [5.1.248–51]

The capacity of words to wound and the failure, as in this case, to suit the word to the action, are notions that are explored throughout the play.[71] Shakespeare's interest in these questions is not specific to *Hamlet,* although it is in *Hamlet* that they receive his most searching analysis. In *Othello,* in an aside to the audience before continuing his "ear-piercing" torture of Othello, Iago remarks, "Dangerous conceits are in their nature poisons" (3.3.326). And "I never yet did hear," says

---

71. See Geoffrey Hartman's remarks on what he calls "word-wounding" in *Saving the Text,* esp. ch. 5, "Words and Wounds," 118ff.

Brabantino of his daughter's tragic passion, "That the bruised heart was piercèd through the ear" (1.3.218–19). *Hamlet* reveals that this is precisely how the heart is bruised.

"The Murder of Gonzago" presents the act of ear-poisoning not once but twice, first in the dumb show and then in the play itself. Situated precisely at the center of *Hamlet,* the play-within-the-play in effect constitutes the inner ear of the play. Through it, Shakespeare is able to tympanize the philosophical presuppositions underlying literary representation. Harold Jenkins convincingly argues that the ear-poisoning was Shakespeare's innovation, his original contribution to the now lost Ur-*Hamlet.* In order to revive such a well-known play, it was doubtless necessary for Shakespeare to introduce some new elements that would captivate an audience already familiar with the basic outlines of the plot. Jenkins concludes of the ear-poisoning: "As a relic unlikely to survive rehandling it points rather to Shakespeare than his predecessor as the innovator."[72] Shakespeare probably based Claudius's crime on reports of the murder of the Duke of Urbino in 1538. Despite Hamlet's assurance to Claudius that the play is "extant, and written in very choice Italian" (3.2.256), it appears that the only basis Shakespeare had was the report of an exotic assassination of an Italian duke by his barber. The manner of the crime is in effect Shakespeare's own signature in the play, the inimitable mark of his originality. With the ear-poisoning, Shakespeare signs his text twice, once as the author on the title page and again, in a kind of antonomasia, by dismantling his proper name into the common nouns that compose it: ShakespEARE.

Though he never commented on the subject of the ear-poisoning, we can well imagine that Hegel would have found Shakespeare's concern with ears extremely interesting. It is in the ear, we recall, that the transit from literature to philosophy and from music to thought takes place. Moreover, a passage in the *Aesthetics* suggests that it would not be at all fatuous to regard Hegel as the veritable philosopher of the ear: he explains that the ear's privileged access to the soul depends first upon its power to negate space and then to negate itself. In other words, the ear is for Hegel the model case of the double negation we discussed earlier. Sound, he writes, "is an externality which in its coming-to-be is annihilated again by its very existence, and it vanishes

72. *Hamlet,* ed. Harold Jenkins, 102.

of itself." This "double negation of externality" enables music to pass into the experience of abstract subjectivity and to become "a mode of expression adequate to the inner life." The internal "resounding" that is created by sound and music mark "the depth of a person's inner life as such." What Shakespeare's metaphorics of the ear in *Hamlet* call into question is precisely what Hegel calls "the essence of that formal freedom of the inner life," which is synonymous for Hegel with the power of "recollection," with one's ability to appropriate or internalize oneself for oneself, and which he writes as *Er-innerung*.[73]

Shakespeare, like Webster and Mallarmé, reminds us that evading the space of representation is the special prerogative of the criminal. Webster's Flamineo anticipates Mallarmé's Pierrot, even to the point of his punning homonym, "Machivillian."

> O the rare tricks of a Machivillian!
> He doth not come like a gross plodding slave
> And buffet you to death. No, my quaint knave,
> He tickles you to death; makes you die laughing.[74]

The originality of the crime is invariably judged by its capacity to erase its traces, and the ear-poisoning is just such a crime. Claudius is so masterful a "Machivillian" that the absence of traces enables him to report that his brother was stung by a serpent, which leads Shakespeare to the sort of "quibble" that Dr. Johnson found so vexing:

> so the whole ear of Denmark
> Is by a forged process of my death
> Rankly abus'd.
>
> [1.5.36–38]

Shakespeare simply can't let go of his metaphor. The important point here is that in abusing or poisoning the ear, one is somehow able to

---

73. Hegel, *Aesthetics*, 2:890–91, 897.
74. John Webster, *The White Devil*, 5.3.195–98, in *Three Plays*, ed. David Gunby (New York: Viking/Penguin, 1972). Webster is as fond as Shakespeare of the image of the mole. Bosola in *The Duchess of Malfi* is Webster's version of a proletarian Hamlet, a low-life villain, a spy and informer, whose coming to consciousness is one the play's major focuses. Antonio calls him a mole at one point: "This mole does undermine me" (2.3.12). Shakespeare also uses the image of the mole in plays other than *Hamlet*; the most famous is surely in *The Tempest* when Caliban refers to Prospero as "the blind mole" (4.1.194), which seems particularly fitting in view of Prospero's vow to bury his staff "certain fathoms in the earth" (5.1.55).

evade or disrupt the space of representation. "The Murder of Gonzago" poisons or disrupts the space of representation just as surely as Claudius poisons his brother. And though Shakespeare, like Claudius, does not leave a trace behind, we will nevertheless be able to reconstruct the scene of the crime.

Let us begin with the dumb show. In his use of this convention Webster demonstrates how deeply influenced he was by Shakespeare. The effect of the dumb show in *The White Devil* and *The Duchess of Malfi*, as in *Hamlet*, is to emphasize how very stylized and artificial the space of theatrical representation actually is. The dumb show is a dream space, an effort to temporalize the unconscious and to speak in a silent language. This space of the pantomime is also, however, the space of transgression, the privileged space of the criminal. In *The White Devil*, a conjuror's trick enables us to observe Flamineo's crime. In the madhouse dumb show in *The Duchess of Malfi*, we reach, as Brecht recognized, an early modern surrealism, a theater of violence. The horrifying charade perpetrated upon the unsuspecting Duchess is the acme at once of violence and artifice. What is being violated above all is the integrity of theatrical space. The violence of the depicted action reinforces the violence directed against the presupposition that the theater could ever be the site of good imitation, that it could ever hold the mirror up to nature. The dumb show is a stylistic device that perforates the illusion of theater as the space of good imitation. In the work of Webster and Middleton, the greatest artists in the so-called "school of Shakespeare," the most archaic theatrical elements—and the dumb show is the most archaic of them all—become the objects of the most intensely stylized treatment. In a purely dialectical historical moment, the most archaic element becomes the site of the most modern and highly stylized aesthetic investment. As Adorno and Benjamin would say, that which is most modern in subjective and aesthetic experience is experienced as prehistory and archaism.

After Hamlet has complained to the players that "inexplicable dumb-shows and noise" (3.2.12) are for the popular rather than the court theater, we are a little surprised to find one of these vulgarities staged at the opening of his production. Why does Shakespeare introduce this antique convention? It was outmoded even to Ophelia, who asks Hamlet what it means, although she concludes rightly that it "imports the argument of the play" (3.2.136). We see the Player King "upon a bank of flowers"; a man enters and "pours poison in the sleeper's ears." After this silent, ghostly mime, the play begins. At the point where the Player King goes to sleep in the garden, Claudius asks Hamlet if he has "heard the argument? Is there no offense in't?" To which Hamlet replies, "No, no, they do but jest—poison in jest" (3.2.230). But why would Claudius wait until well into the performance to object if he had seen the dumb show, where the argument is very clearly announced? While the others might have had difficulty understanding it, surely Claudius would have known what the argument imported. A few moments later, as Lucianus pours poison into his uncle's ear, Claudius and his entourage leave in an uproar.

Critical controversy has surrounded the question of Claudius's whereabouts during the dumb show.[75] Harold Jenkins remarks that a director would be foolish to focus on Claudius's inattention during the mime for fear of creating an inattentive audience. But Jenkins surely overestimates the dangers of such a focus, or rather he underestimates the intelligence of the audience, who already know the manner of Claudius's crime and can easily watch Claudius and the dumb show at the same time.

The important point, which the critics have never quite understood, is that the purpose of the dumb show is to introduce an element of ambiguity with respect to the source of Claudius's murder method. The question of Claudius's whereabouts and the instrumentality of the dumb show are inseparably related. It will not do to explain the introduction of the dumb show as Shakespeare's parody of the conventions of public theater and their inappropriateness at a court performance; that's just the beginning of his purpose, for he goes on to call into question the appropriateness and the origin of the manner of Claudius's crime itself. A good production, like a good reading, should exploit the undecidability that Shakespeare has built into the scene. It is the ambiguity of Claudius's position and attitude during the pantomime and the play and the fact that we are watching Hamlet watching Claudius, as well as watching the performance itself, that make "The Murder of Gonzago" the focal point of a new abstract subjectivism. The dumb show, that most archaic element, is the key to setting off this complex structural effect. A good director will play on the interaction of the subscenes

---

75. See the summary of the scholarship in *Hamlet*, ed. Harold Jenkins, 501–5. Briefly, critics believe either that Claudius simply did not see the dumb show or that he saw it but did not perceive immediately the connection with his own crime.

within the scene without ever revealing exactly what Claudius is doing during the dumb show. The director has no right to resolve this ambiguity, because Shakespeare himself leaves it unresolved. Everything in the scene should move toward the fundamental question of the origin of Claudius's crime, to which the question of his guilt is only an ancillary or superficial adjunct. It is not the language but the structure of the scene, and the all-important element of dramaturgy, that move us far beyond the problem of Claudius's guilt. Without the dumb show and the uncertainty of Claudius's attitude toward it, the scene presents a relatively simple and straightforward mise-en-abyme.

But herein lies the inimitable Shakespearean twist to the dumb show convention, that it calls into question the imitativeness of Claudius's crime without allowing us to discover precisely what the ground of the imitative process is. Silently, Shakespeare focuses our attention on the imitative structure of the crime without providing an answer as to what the model of the imitation could possibly be. Whose idea was it? Did Claudius think of it on his own? Had he seen "The Murder of Gonzago" or a similar play before? Nicolas Abraham's frivolous notion that Polonius is behind everything is an effort, however fanciful, to answer the question Shakespeare poses regarding the primal scene of the crime. *It is a question, however, that can never and should never be answered.* For Shakespeare's genius consists precisely in concealing the origin in the very act of posing the question of the origin. To pretend to be able to answer it is as misguided as previous criticism of the play has been in failing even to pose the question. The mystery of Claudius's whereabouts during the dumb show is the silent and almost undetectable trace that allows us to reconstruct Shakespeare's deconstruction of theatrical representation.

In a play as long and as complex as *Hamlet,* Shakespeare could surely have told us if he wanted to just where Claudius was at that critical moment. By not telling us, he leaves open the possibility that Claudius may have seen the play before, that his crime is the copy of a copy, that the murder of old Hamlet is the *re*-presentation of a theatrical representation. The text nowhere openly suggests this, and there is not a word to this effect in Claudius's soliloquy in the chapel afterward. By the same token, however, the text nowhere precludes this possibility. Indeed, the effect of "The Murder of Gonzago" is to set off a series of displacements that cannot be arrested. There is Claudius's relation to the dumb show; there is the question of the relation of the dumb show to "The Murder of Gonzago"; and there is the question of the relation of "The Murder of Gonzago" to *Hamlet* itself.

The historicists who believe they have fathomed the mystery of Shakespeare's imagination will protest that such a reading is anachronistic, that Shakespeare could never have had a notion of so vertiginous a mode of representation. What they mean to say of course is that because they could have no such notion, then neither could Shakespeare. But we need not implicate Shakespeare's imagination or intentionality in this matter at all. The simple fact is that the text of *Hamlet* warrants such a speculation. While the question of Claudius's familiarity with "The Murder of Gonzago," or with a similar account of such a crime from some other source, can never be answered, the logic, the language, and the structure of *Hamlet* demand that the question be posed. In such a highly critical and self-reflective play, is it conceivable that Shakespeare never posed to himself the question of what an extraordinary coincidence it is that an "extant" play should depict precisely the crime that his villain has committed? And having posed this question, is it conceivable that he should suspect that no one should ever pose it again? Did he imagine that he would get away with the crime? Did he think he could murder mimesis and get away with it? We can say of *Hamlet* what Derrida says of Mallarmé's "Mimique," that it "describes a scene of writing within a scene of writing and so on without end, through a structural necessity that is marked in the text."[76] The principle of reference remains, but the referents have been suspended. We can no longer determine which is the copy and which the model; we can no longer tell the derivation from the original. Through "The Murder of Gonzago" and its dumb show, Shakespeare has poisoned the notion of representation.

It should be clear that this is not simply a *mise-en-abyme,* where all of the infinite copies refer back to one original model. Speaking specifically of "The Murder of Gonzago," Thomas De Quincey called this sort of *mise-en-abyme* effect an "*introvolution*" or "retrocession," and he argued that it serves to heighten the reality of the principal drama.[77] And this is indeed the effect it has on an uncritical spectator or reader, who is persuaded that nothing could be more commonplace than ear-

76. Jacques Derrida, *Dissemination*, trans. Barbara Johnson (Chicago: University of Chicago Press, 1981), 223.

77. Thomas De Quincey, "The Theory of Greek Tragedy," in *Collected Works*, ed. David Masson, 14 vols. (Edinburgh: A. and C. Black, 1889–90), 10:344–45.

poisoning. The play-within-the-play has the effect of naturalizing the almost surrealistic unreality of the event. But such a response is a superficial one, which, though necessary in creating the desired dramatic effect, must nevertheless be elaborated and worked through in the course of repeated readings and performances. When that is done, the effect is precisely opposite to what De Quincey describes, for no longer is the reality of the originary event reinforced; rather it is relegated to the status of a figure of a figure, and so on.

In the ear-poisoning, Shakespeare had come as close to the perfect crime as it is possible to do. His disciples were left to such artificial devices as poisoned paintings or poisoned skulls. As Jenkins has remarked, ear-poisoning is so stylized that it has an in-built protection against imitation. With beautifully Shakespearean symmetry, it is precisely the element of style that undermines the very notion of imitation that is protected from imitation in its turn. Shakespeare boldly announces his dismantling of the machinery of imitation in "The Murder of Gonzago" when the Player King proclaims that "our devices still are overthrown" (3.2.207). As Alvin Kernan remarks, this speech places us "somewhere near the absolute center of playing—an actor in a play playing an actor king talking about life as a series of changing roles."[78] The key term here is "series," for it is this dismantling of the hierarchy implicit in the logic of representation that is achieved in "The Murder of Gonzago." The effect of the play-within-the-play and the dumb show is to inscribe the trace of *différance*, the trace of the always earlier, of the always preexistent text. There is no way to arrest the drift of *différance*, no way out of the trap, no way to close the abyss. To return to our terms earlier in this chapter, there is no longer a syntactic, hierarchical organization of the elements in the series but rather an infinite paratactic seriality. It is at the archaic center of the text that Shakespeare poses the question of style most dramatically. In this sense also we can understand Hamlet's subtitle for "The Murder of Gonzago": "The Mousetrap—marry, how tropically" (3.2.232). Shakespeare's archaic paratactic style burrows beneath the ground of representation, turning the trope into a trap.

We mentioned earlier that Hamlet's diatribe against the drunkenness of the Danes was inspired by Thomas Nashe's *Pierce Penniless* (1592).

78. Alvin Kernan, *The Playwright as Magician: Shakespeare's Image of the Poet in the English Public Theater* (New Haven, Conn.: Yale University Press, 1979), 100.

We can also assume that Shakespeare knew Nashe's preface to Robert Greene's *Menaphon* (1589).[79] The preface contains the famous reference to the Ur-*Hamlet*. More important, especially in view of Shakespeare's assault on representation, it is here that Nashe discusses the distinction between good and bad imitation, which, he argues, depends upon a particular faculty of invention that he calls the "extemporal vein." Without the "extemporal vein," imitation is reduced to mere lifeless "translation." For Nashe, good imitation is closer to what we would call interpretation. It is in any case at the opposite extreme of a "trivial . . . translation" of a prior text. Nashe wants to "persuade" men who possess too much learning "to physic their faculties of seeing and hearing" and put their "apish devices" behind them. It is at this point that Nashe turns to the Ur-*Hamlet,* which he regards as the most egregious contemporary instance of "trivial translation." Such bad imitators of Seneca, writes Nashe, have "no more learning in their skulls than will serve to take up a commodity"; they "will afford you whole *Hamlets*, I should say handfuls of Tragical speeches." Such poor work as this, Nashe concludes, "at length must needs die to our stage." In flying in the face of Nashe's advice by reviving *Hamlet,* Shakespeare also revived all of Nashe's questions. It may even have been partly in response to Nashe that Shakespeare selected the most resistant material from which to refashion the notions of representation and dramatic form. He transmuted what had been a mere commodity, "whole *Hamlets*" (as in "whole hams") into the space in which a new abstract subjectivity could unfold itself.

Robert Greene's famous attack on Shakespeare as the "upstart crow" appeared in 1592 (three years after *Menaphon*) in his *Groatsworth of Wit.* Nashe had said of bad imitators that they "swarm like Crows to a dead carcass." In the *Groatsworth of Wit,* Shakespeare becomes one of those crows. Shakespeare plays for Greene the role the Ur-*Hamlet* played for Nashe (*Hamlet* was still eight years in the future). Not only does Greene ridicule Shakespeare's bombastic blank verse; he also ridicules the playwright himself for daring to think of himself as a poet or a genius. Shakespeare, writes Greene, "is in his own conceit the only

79. Thomas Nashe, "Preface to R. Greene's 'Menaphon,'" in *Works*, ed. R. B. McKerrow, 4 vols. (Oxford: Basil Blackwell, 1958), 3:311–25. All references are to the text of this edition, though I have modernized the spelling.

Shake-scene in a country."[80] Greene must have enforced upon Shake-speare a deep sense of his affiliation with the sellers of "whole *Hamlets.*" And Shakespeare would certainly not have been impartial to Greene's antonomasia of his name. The Scene-shaker would in *Hamlet* become the Ear-shaker, the Ear-piercer, the Earth-shaker—indeed, the "old mole."

Doubtless he found even more interesting a line in Greene's *Pandosto:* "One mole staineth a whole face: and what is once spotted with infamy can hardly be worn out with time."[81] We can perhaps glimpse here the extent to which some of the violence of *Hamlet* may be attributable to a certain aesthetic, intellectual revenge in Shakespeare's response to his critics. It is not unlikely that Greene, in calling Shake-speare "an upstart crow," was inspired by Nashe. But Shakespeare transformed their rank abuse of his ear into something they could never have dreamed of.

In a section of *Pierce Penniless* called "The Nature of an Upstart," Nashe ridicules those who affect "the livery of wit" and falsely add an Italianate touch to their speech. The very model of such an aberration is a certain "Monsieur Mingo de Mousetrap," the epitome of the hypocritical and pretentious upstart.[82] In this primal scene in the battle of the Elizabethan wits, there can be no doubt who finally built the better mousetrap.

---

80. Cited in Samuel Schoenbaum, *William Shakespeare: A Compact Documentary Life* (New York: Oxford University Press, 1980), 151.

81. Cited in *Hamlet*, ed. Harold Jenkins, 448.

82. Nashe, *Pierce Penniless*, in *Works* 1:170.

7 Phantom Politics: Marx's Reading of Balzac

> With the reversal of metaphysics which has already been ac-
> complished by Karl Marx, the most extreme possibility of
> philosophy is attained.
>
> MARTIN HEIDEGGER, "The End of Philosophy and
> the Task of Thinking"

> What has hitherto been called metaphysics cannot satisfy any
> critical mind, but to forgo it entirely is impossible.
>
> IMMANUEL KANT, *Prolegomena to Any Future
> Metaphysics*

Most modern readers know the "old mole" not from Hegel's *Lectures
on the History of Philosophy* but from Marx's *The Eighteenth Brumaire of Louis Bonaparte,* where Marx is concerned not with the
future of philosophy but with the future of the revolutionary class.
Marx's "old mole" has been forced to forgo the sunlight of the revolution and to return underground. For Marx it is not a question of the
ascendancy of the absolute spirit but of the disappointments and reversals that the proletariat suffered in the period of political reaction
following the uprisings of 1848. My fundamental concern in this chapter is with Marx's response to the reactionary climate of 1848–52.
Though this remains a relatively unknown period in Marx's career, we
will see that it is a decisive one, for it was during this period that Marx
was forced to rethink his notions of production, ideology, and historical change. We can glimpse an undecided Marx, committed neither to
a human subject of history nor to a purely structural principle of
economic necessity. It is at this time that Marx resists the drift toward
a social ontology more strongly than at any other time in his career.
Framed on one side by his pre-1848 focus on the enabling role of

human agency and on the other by the economic determinism of the *Grundrisse*, the Marx of the early 1850s does not fit into any conveniently available categories.

My argument is that under the revisionary pressure of the moment, Marx found himself unconsciously depicting the historical-political present in terms of a Balzac novel from the 1840s. Since this intertextual primal scene involves works by both Marx and Balzac that have received little or no serious critical attention, this chapter is in part an effort to redirect attention to these works. But much more important than the question of their canonical status is the nature of the intertextual relation that emerges between these texts. Balzac's novel in effect plays the role of an "old mole" burrowing its way into Marx's text. Here as elsewhere in my use of the term, the primal scene cannot be reduced to either a historical event or a text; rather it is securely lodged in the preontological undecidability between them. It is a question not of Marx's failure to see the post-1848 milieu for what it was, but rather of the fact that he saw most deeply into it when he "thought" in terms of Balzac's fictional constructions. I am not suggesting that Marx's unconscious memory of Balzac's novel blocked access to the real. Quite to the contrary (and this is central to my notion of the primal scene), it is *as a result* of this unconscious memory that Marx was able to approximate the real as closely as he did. History becomes accessible and assimilable to Marx not despite but *through* this memory of Balzac. Rather than barring access to history, the intertext is the medium through which history gives itself to thought.

Paraphrasing Marx's well-known remark that "men make their own history, but not the way they want to," we might say that in 1848–52 Marx found neither history nor his own texts conforming to the intentions of either a collective or a human agency. In the attempt to present an intersubjective theory of history, Marx inadvertently produced an intertextual theory of history. What emerges in the Marxian text, in lieu of the elusive historical event, is the primal scene of literature-philosophy.

Marx experienced the period 1848–52 as a time of pathos and anxiety. Having lost his grasp on the subject of history, he found himself without a ground for a theory of history. In *The Eighteenth Brumaire*, he recognized that Louis Bonaparte's success was largely attributable to the rhetoric of politics: that is, to the images and the ideological mystique of Napoleonism, which continued to hold at bay precisely the class that should have risen to explode that mystique once and for all. This image sphere is part of the larger ensemble of cultural production, whose instrumentality in effecting social change Marx had underestimated prior to 1848. Marx's unconscious elaboration of a Balzacian rhetoric that likewise was deeply linked to the Napoleonic mystique indicates that the cultural artifact was no longer incidental but fundamental to his mode of textual production. Moreover, the emergence of the "literary" in Marx is a direct response to what is at once a subjective crisis and a crisis in the very notion of the historical subject.

I begin this chapter with a prologue concerning *Oedipus the King* in order to suggest, in a poetic or tonal way, that in the Marxian crisis of the subject we can see something that always haunted the Western tradition. I am suggesting that the "Oedipal" is synonymous with the crisis of the subject, and that traces of such a crisis mark all the great texts of the tradition. Like Heidegger, Marx teaches us how to unveil the fundamental concealments that have shrouded what, following Heidegger's history of Being, we might call the Marxian history of Politics. As a result of Marx's revisionary moment, we can see that the crisis of the subject has always already been a political crisis, even in Sophocles.

Prologue: *Oedipus Politicus*

> Everything was long seen, by the young and ardent among us, in inseparable connection with politics and practical life. We have pretty well exhausted the benefits of seeing things in this connection, we have got all that can be got by so seeing them.
>
> MATTHEW ARNOLD, "The Function of Criticism at the Present Time"

Were it not for the servant who publicly announced to the Thebans that Laius was slain by not one but many murderers, *Oedipus the King* would be shorter by perhaps half of its fifteen hundred lines. The servant's eyewitness account of the murder of Laius and his entourage at Phocis provides the crucial element resonsible for the play's dramatic suspense. For as long as Oedipus believes that there were several murderers, he has no reason to assume his own involvement. Not until he hears a description of his predecessor (ll. 740–45) does Oedipus begin to suspect that the man he slew was Laius.[1] This startling recollection displaces all memory of the servant's story. Oedipus sends a messenger into the country to bring this servant to Thebes, so that he can interrogate him about his story. But when he arrives, Oedipus is so preoccupied with the circumstances of his own birth that he does not even question the servant about the crime at Phocis. It is as though Oedipus were no longer interested in holding on to the one bit of hope he has left. At one point the Chorus tells Oedipus, "Until you see this man face to face and hear his story, hope" (l. 835). Sophocles might have added here what Walter Benjamin remarked of the star-crossed lovers in Goethe's *Elective Affinities:* "Only for the hopeless are we given hope."

It would clearly undermine Oedipus's stature as a tragic hero were he still, at the end of the play, to appear to be hoping for a way out. It would likewise demean Oedipus's stature were Sophocles to appear to be hammering down the nails on Oedipus's coffin by having the servant not only reveal the circumstances of his birth and abandonment but also confirm that he was indeed a parricide. The economy of dramatic form demands that the one element that could definitively prove Oedipus's guilt *not* be presented. The tragic effect of *Oedipus the King* cannot be separated from Oedipus's inability at the play's climactic moment to pose to the servant precisely the question that he, along with all of Thebes, the Chorus, and the audience, have been anxiously waiting to ask throughout the play. Regardless of this signal omission in the case against Oedipus, there is absolutely no doubt that he is the guilty one. The question is not whether Oedipus is guilty but rather why Sophocles has chosen to establish his guilt in this particular way. Why does Sophocles introduce this apparently immaterial complication? Why pose the question of the indispensability of the servant's eyewitness account only to forget it at the very moment when the answer is so near at hand? The servant is the key here, and in

---

1. Sophocles, *Oedipus the King*, trans. David Grene, in *Three Tragedies* (Chicago: University of Chicago Press, 1954). All references in the text are to line numbers in this edition. See also Sandor Goodhart's "Oedipus and Laius's Many Murderers," *Diacritics* 8 (Spring 1978): 55–71; and Jonathan Culler's remarks in *The Pursuit of Signs* (Ithaca, N.Y.: Cornell University Press, 1981), 173–75.

reconstructing his role in the play we will reconstruct what is in effect a play-within-the-play in *Oedipus the King,* which in turn will lead us to the question of Oedipus's politics.

When Jocasta first tells Oedipus that Laius "was killed by foreign highway robbers," she adds, "so goes the story" (ll. 715–16). The significance of this apparent euphemism becomes clear only later. In his highly informative reading of the play, Charles Segal translates this line to read, "Robbers killed him, as is the rumor *(phatis)*." *Phatis,* Segal points out, means both "rumor" and "prophecy."[2] It is on precisely the question of the undecidability of the servant's utterance that this initial account already focuses our attention. Is this simply servant's gossip, or is this the truth of Phoebus Apollo?

Creon adds that the servant "fled in terror" from the scene of the crime, and that when he finally returned to Thebes he was clear about "one thing only," that the murder was the result of "no man's single power" (l. 123). Again Sophocles' phrasing is cautiously ambivalent, suggesting as it does that in retrospect—from our perspective at the end of the play—Oedipus's acts are indeed never truly his own, that they are also the work of the gods, that everything Oedipus does is always already an expression of Apollo's curse.

Hugh Lloyd-Jones observes that Sophocles' audience in the Theater of Dionysus at Athens would have been very familiar with Apollo's curse on the house of Labdacus, Laius's father, not only because it was so well-known a myth but also because it figures prominently in Aeschylus's *Seven against Thebes:* "May not a family curse inherited from the past have more importance for the plot of *Oedipus Rex* than most scholars have allowed?"[3] The curse defines nothing less than the context of the entire play. It is the implicit horizon against which everything in the play must be read. More recently, Marie Balmary has carefully reconstructed Sophocles' use of verbal echoes to inscribe the curse of Apollo as a repetition of the faults of the father in the suffering of the son, from Labdacus to Laius, and from Laius to Oedipus.[4] While the reasons for Apollo's hatred of the Labdacidae lie buried in the

2. Charles Segal, *Tragedy and Civilization: An Interpretation of Sophocles* (Cambridge, Mass.: Harvard University Press, 1981), 237.

3. Hugh Lloyd-Jones, *The Justice of Zeus* (Berkeley: University of California Press, 1971), 119, 111.

4. Marie Balmary, *Psychoanalyzing Psychoanalysis: Freud and the Hidden Fault of the Father,* trans. Ned Lukacher (Baltimore, Md.: Johns Hopkins University Press, 1982), ch. 1. The curse is a figure for the abyssal origin of tragic victimage.

abyss of history, the curse itself will continue to be reinscribed in the offspring until the line is exhausted. As the Chorus reminds Antigone, "Perhaps you are paying for your father's pain."[5] With Antigone's tragedy the last of the Labdacidae has been laid low; the old order has finally been extirpated.

This curse permeates *Oedipus the King*. Everyone in Thebes knows about it, including the servant who survived the massacre at Phocis. This servant is, as Charles Segal reminds us, a house servant, an *"oikeus"* (l. 756). This is significant in terms of Sophocles' opposition between the household or *oikos* and the savage world of uncultivated nature. It is this same servant who, at Laius's command, abandoned the mutilated body of the infant Oedipus to the wilds of Cithaeron. We must ask how the curse is related to the opposition between the natural and the social world. In his reading of the *Antigone*, Segal focuses on the opposition between the chthonian law of the family and the ouranian law of the state.[6] Sophocles' Oedipus cycle, which originally included the now lost *Laius*, is structured around this opposition between nature or *physis* and law or *nomos*. In the *Antigone*, Tiresias accuses Creon of having "confused the upper and lower worlds" (l. 1068). In so doing, Creon becomes Apollo's instrument in his revenge against the Labdacidae. Laius precipitates the tragedy in *Oedipus the King* when he tries to secure the *oikos* from the effects of the curse. In order to avoid the prophecy of parricide, he commands his house servant to place Oedipus in the wilderness. He must do this because he has violated Apollo's prohibition against fathering a child. But the curse cannot be circumvented, and the house servant, as a synecdoche of the social world, becomes the very instrument through which the curse surmounts all the obstacles that Laius has placed in its way. Here we approach the question of Sophocles' conservatism, for he seems clearly to suggest that the epochal transformation of human law, whose emergence and development is chronicled in the Oedipus cycle, is throughout vulnerable to the edicts of fate and the gods. The tragic necessities which this transformation entails are the effects of a divine intervention that operates according to its own principles and thus remains oblivious to the course of human history; it intersects the

---

5. Sophocles, *Antigone*, l. 855, trans. Elizabeth Wyckoff, in *Three Tragedies*. Line numbers in the text refer to this edition.
6. Segal, *Tragedy and Civilization*, 152ff.

course of human history without actually being part of it. In the *Oedipus*, Sophocles is concerned not with justifying the ways of the gods but with the tragic response of an individual caught within a fateful mechanism that neither he nor anyone else can ever hope to comprehend; not primarily with the victimizing mechanisms of destiny but with Oedipus's heroic human acceptance of the justice of an incomprehensible fate. It is against this horizon that the role of Laius's servant assumes its significance.

We get our deepest insight into the servant's character from Jocasta as she explains to Oedipus the servant's decision to quit his service in the palace.

> *Oedipus.*   Is he at home now?
> *Jocasta.*   No, when he came home again
>   and saw you king and Laius was dead,
>   he came to me and touched my hand and begged
>   that I should send him to the fields to be
>   my shepherd and so he might see the city
>   as far off as he might. So I
>   sent him away. He was an honest man,
>   as slaves go, and was worthy of far more
>   than what he asked of me.
> *Oedipus.*   O, how I wish that he would come back quickly.
>   [ll. 758–76]

This account of the servant's touching Jocasta's hand is one of the most exquisite marks of Sophocles' artistry. Indeed, in that touch the servant speaks volumes, though as always Jocasta fails to understand. We understand, however, why he wants to flee so far from Thebes, why he is willing to settle for so much less than he is worth, and why such a valuable house servant should be content to become an obscure shepherd. This servant, like everyone in Thebes, knows of the curse; furthermore, he has been privy to Laius's schemes. In the gesture of the touch we realize that when he saw Oedipus on the throne, the servant recognized what was happening; even before Tiresias, he knew that the curse had been fulfilled, and he wanted only to be as far from the palace as possible. So worthy and honest a servant could not fail to anticipate that he would eventually be summoned to tell his story again. And in being summoned he would thus run the risk of being recognized by Oedipus and perhaps of being slain himself. The story he recounted to the Thebans was perhaps itself already an evasion of the truth, though there is nothing in the text to suggest this. His account of the murder was in any case ambivalent enough to suggest either that he knew the fulfillment of the curse had already begun in this god-inspired crime or simply that in his panic he actually believed he saw several murderers. That this servant is not only honest but wise, as we learn indirectly from Jocasta, further complicates our ability to reduce the ambivalence of his story. But regardless of that ambivalence, it is certain that he recognized the new king as either one of the murderers or the murderer himself. His decision to flee was clearly an effort to protect himself from the disastrous revelations that he knew were imminent and in which he was deeply implicated. He flees the palace as he fled the crossroads at Phocis, "in terror," which he reveals by touching Jocasta's hand as he begs to be sent "as far off as he might."

Oedipus of course never becomes aware of any of this. The servant's story is like an interpolated play-within-the-play that the audience is left to reconstruct but that remains unseen by the players themselves. When Oedipus questions this servant-turned-shepherd, his concern is only with the circumstances of his birth. By making it possible for Oedipus to continue to hope, and then by having him neglect that possibility, Sophocles underlines the heroism of Oedipus's character. By virtue of the ambivalence of the servant's story, Sophocles makes it possible for Oedipus to postpone the tragic revelations that await, gives him the chance to divert attention from the overwhelming circumstantial logic that has emerged from all the other evidence. "Be sure, at least," Jocasta says in an effort to encourage Oedipus, "that this was / how he told the story. He cannot / unsay it now, for everyone in the city heard it—not I alone" (ll. 849–52). The key to the play's tragic effect and to Sophocles' conservatism as well inheres in Oedipus's refusal to play politics, in his refusal to equivocate, in his refusal to postpone the inevitable. The servant's story provides him with all the ammunition he needs to play politics. From that one piece of outstanding evidence he could weave any of a number of stories to preserve his power and maintain his innocence. He could continue to accuse Creon of conspiring against him. He could refuse his *moira* or portion of fate (l. 1458) in several ways, in each case the servant's story would be the linchpin. But Oedipus refuses to hold on for the sake of his own power or for the sake of his safety; he is willing to experience that "fearful hearing" (l. 1169) to which the servant's story could have enabled him to deafen himself.

Jean Anouilh makes this point in his *Antigone* when he has Creon say: "And if tomorrow a lowly servant came down out of the mountains to tell me that he is not certain of my birthright, I would simply ask him to go back where he came from."[7] Creon is precisely what Oedipus is not—a politician. Oedipus's rejection of politics is synonymous with his acceptance of his destiny as *pharmakos*. By accepting his fate as a phantom politician, Oedipus becomes a victim who tragically recognizes the irrepressible and unreadable necessity of the structures of victimage.

Nietzsche wrote of Oedipus in *The Birth of Tragedy* that the "Dionysian wisdom" he achieves can be achieved only through such "an unnatural abomination" as murdering his father and marrying his mother: "that he who by means of his knowledge plunges nature into the abyss of destruction must suffer the dissolution of nature in his own person."[8] Here in the early 1870s we can already anticipate the "grand politics" of the tragic philosopher-hero of the 1880s. In this sense we can say that Sophocles' Oedipus renounces politics on behalf of a "grand politics." The cataclysm to which Oedipus says "Yes" will destroy him, and it will lead to the destruction of an entire society, for his sons will enter into a civil war with Creon that will ravage Thebes for a generation. But in the final analysis, this process of destruction is the only way toward the new order. To prolong the old order would have been even worse. This is the process outlined in *Oedipus at Colonnus* and the *Antigone*. By refusing to play politics in the narrow sense of gaining temporary personal political power, Oedipus enables the historical process to continue to unfold. In the *Antigone* even Creon, the consummate politician, is destroyed in the very essence of his being by the role into which destiny has forced him. His family is consumed along with that of Oedipus in the cataclysm of a truly "grand politics."

Though Oedipus refuses to play politics after the fashion of a Creon, his "forgetfulness" when it comes to his father's house servant is nevertheless a kind of transpolitical gesture. Jean-François Lyotard argues that Oedipus is simply " 'hung up' on Apollo's text" and thus fails to vary the story so as to preserve himself. Lyotard would have Oedipus

---

7. Jean Anouilh, *Antigone* (Paris: La Table Ronde, 1946), 74.
8. Friedrich Nietzsche, *The Birth of Tragedy*, trans. Walter Kaufmann (New York: Vintage Books, 1967), 69.

play politics with the servant's story, à la Creon; he even remarks that the Greeks must have found Oedipus's dilemma a source of comedy rather than tragedy since "it is always possible to tell things differently."[9] Sophocles does make it possible to do just that, but it is Sophocles' chief point that by *not* telling things differently, Oedipus achieves a much higher kind of politics. Had the servant's testimony with respect to the Phocal crime never been in question, we could say, with Lyotard, that Oedipus's tragedy is somehow comic insofar as he believes that he is being punished by the gods when in fact it is his own insatiable curiosity and impatience that have brought him to grief. The old servant's gesture of touching Jocasta's hand makes it clear, however, that some deeper current is at stake here. Oedipus's higher politics, which I shall call his phantom politics, inhere in the refusal, at the level of the unconscious, to tell things differently and in the decision to stop talking and thus begin that "fearful hearing."

Thus conceived, *Oedipus the King* provides us with the model of the experience of a certain political impasse that I want to explore in the texts of Marx and Balzac. More particularly, the failure of the Revolution of 1848 brings Marx to the recognition that, for the present, politics is not a viable alternative. It signals the beginning of a "fearful hearing" for Marx, when he learns to listen closely so that he will be able to play politics later, after the decade-long political reaction to 1848 has spent its fury. The text that Marx finds himself repeating during this political impasse takes the form not of a divine curse but of a Balzac novel that seems uncannily to sketch out, years in advance, the precise terms in which historical destiny will, at least temporarily, exclude Marx and the Communist movement from politics. This moment of paralysis will entail a certain conservatism on Marx's part, a certain wisdom that enables one to know when to start listening.

Finally, the problem of Sophocles' politics deserves a brief if tentative remark. The anthropologist Sir James Frazer wrote that "the marriage of Oedipus with the widowed queen, his mother, fits in very well with the rule which has prevailed in some countries that a valid title to the throne is conferred by marriage with the late king's widow."[10] In most countries, of course, this custom did not prevail. That *Oedipus*

9. Jean-François Lyotard, "The Insistence of Pragmatics," trans. Robert Brinkley, *Mississippi Review* 31 (1983): 89–90.
10. Sir James Frazer, *The Dying God*, pt. 3 of *The Golden Bough* (London: Macmillan, 1919), 193.

the King is somehow related to the epochal transition from a matrilinear to a patrilinear genealogy of power has long been a provocative hypothesis. Hegel's reading of the *Antigone* is implicated here as
well. Like her father, Antigone refuses to play politics; she refuses to
abandon the elemental chthonian world of *Sittlichkeit* as did her ill-
fated brother, Polyneices. She proclaims at one point to Creon, "When
was it shame to serve the children of my mother's womb?" (l. 511).
Her solicitude about the fate of her brother's corpse, like Oedipus's
concern for the welfare of the Thebans, bears the traces of a deep
identification with the *nomous chthomos* or chthonian law of the
family rather than with the abstract notion of the power of the state,
which is clearly in the ascendant. It does appear that Sophocles is
concerned with the shift away from woman and the family and toward
the notion of male-centered state power. Whether or not this can be
related to a historical phenomenon is something that no one has yet
been able to determine with certainty. We can, however, explore the
ideological interspace between the Sophoclean text and the historical
reality. From an ideological perspective, by marrying his mother,
Oedipus would appear to have irreversibly damaged or contaminated
the notion of a matrilinear genealogy. The ideological function of the
myth would seem to be that of pointing out the most terrible potential
danger that such a genealogical structure would hold in store. The
complex mechanism of the curse would thus have been necessary in
order to make a very simple ideological point: that as long as a title to
the throne can be granted through marriage to a widowed queen, there
is the possibility of the sort of tragedy *Oedipus the King* depicts.

George Devereux, who is both an anthropologist and a psychoanalyst, argues that the Oedipus cycle indicates "that the old [chthoni-
an, matrilinear] system was reluctant to relinquish its hold on the
imagination of the people." The *Oedipus* is thus for Devereux a "cau-
tionary legend or conservative political manifesto" in which Sophocles
reminded his contemporaries how high a price their ancestors paid for
their historical development.[11] It was only by learning the hard way, in
other words, that they came to be what they were. I repeat: these are
only speculations, but they seem to me to be very valuable ones, for they
remind us that the Oedipus cycle probably had a very profound ideologi-

11. George Devereux, "Sociopolitical Functions of the Oedipus Myth in Early
Greece," *Psychoanalytic Quarterly* 32 (1963): 208, 215.

cal function. If that is the case, then the servant's story was a decisive element in the ancient Greek experience of the play. Through that story Sophocles might have been telling his contemporaries that tragedy is synonymous with a certain rejection of politics and, more terrifyingly, that such a rejection of politics, however horrible its consequences, is sometimes not only necessary but even desirable.

Marx in Mourning

During the 1850s Marx was in mourning not for the death of an individual but for the death, at least in the foreseeable future, of the idea of the revolution. His exile and the political reaction to the Revolution of 1848 kept him in political mourning for over a decade. It would not be until 1864 and with the formation of the First International Workingmen's Association that Marx would reemerge into the political daylight. The reading I offer of Marx's writings during the 1850s is an exemplary instance of the widespread retreat from politics after 1848. As Jean-Paul Sartre has remarked, "The treason of the petty bourgeoisie in 1848 discredited *politics* in the eyes of the exploited—all politics was bourgeois, even when practiced by politicians who claimed to be socialists."[12] Louis Bonaparte's successful co-optation of those elements of French society that should have opposed him forced Marx to reevaluate the terms of a radical politics. In the succeeding decade Marx learned to listen to the "old mole" of the revolution that had been forced even deeper underground by a series of conditions to which Marx had not been sufficiently attentive during the revolutionary heyday of the 1840s.

With the failure of 1848, Marx was exiled first from Germany and then from France. After several years during which he enjoyed a truly Continental reputation as an editor and an agitator, he arrived in London in August 1849 at the age of thirty-one, suddenly isolated and powerless. All of his ideas would have to be reexamined, a process that eventually led to his massive researches in economic theory in the British Museum. As he wrote in a famous moment of Hegelian revisionism in *The Eighteenth Brumaire of Louis Bonaparte* (1852), the "old mole" of the revolution had gone underground "on its journey

12. Jean-Paul Sartre, *Critique of Dialectical Reason*, trans. Allan Sheridan-Smith (London: NLB, 1976), 756.

through purgatory."[13] Eventually the time would come for it to break through into the sunlight, but for now there was only darkness. Disillusioned with the possibility of political revolution in a climate of unprecedented bourgeois consolidation and reaction, Marx turned toward the idea of the "permanent revolution," the thoroughgoing subterranean process that somehow continues onward even in the face of apparent defeat. But all of that, as Marx knew very well, was, for the moment, only so much facile rhetoric. Before he could even begin to think about the strategies for revolution, he had first to try to account for the political conditions of the period 1848–52. The "old mole" had first to understand how it had come to be where it was before it burrowed any further.

Reflecting in 1859 on his activities of the previous decade, Marx describes his nonpolitical years in purgatory:

> After I had been driven out of Prussia in the spring of 1849 and out of France in the late summer of the same year, I went to London, where following the dissolution of the [Communist] League (1852) and the departure of most of my friends from London, I have been living without joining any associations whether public or secret, and indeed without society of any sort. I do, however, from time to time, give free lectures on political economy to a select group of workers.[14]

This was also the period of an unanticipated expansion and strengthening of capitalism: "In fact it was precisely during the reactionary period from 1849 to 1859 that industry and trade on the Continent, and along with them the material foundations for the political domination of the bourgeoisie, developed to an extent unheard of previously."[15] Faced with such obstacles, Marx's main concern was to restrain the political hotheads in the Communist movement from foolish efforts that would only further jeopardize the long-term goals of the revolution. During the 1850s Marx was utterly astonished, and I use that word quite deliberately, both by the course of European political and economic history and by the counterproductive madness of some members of the ill-fated Communist League. While he used the

13. Karl Marx, *The Eighteenth Brumaire of Louis Bonaparte,* reprinted in *Surveys from Exile,* ed. David Fernbach (New York: Vintage Books, 1974), 236.
14. Karl Marx, *Herr Vogt,* in Marx/Engels, *Collected Works,* 20 vols. (New York: International Publishers, 1975–), 17:264.
15. Marx, *Herr Vogt,* Marx/Engels, *Collected Works,* 17:93.

time for reflection and research, they played into the hands of the enemy.

My interest is in the early years of Marx's English exile, the period leading up to the dissolution of the Communist League in the spectacular Cologne Communist trial of October 1852. From 1849 to 1852, Marx spent much of his time trying to convince his fellow members of the League, both in London and Cologne, that it was not the time to play politics. In the words of the editors of their *Collected Works,* Marx and Engels, faced with a rising tide of post-1848 reaction, "attached great importance to exposing these circles, whose adventurist, conspiratorial and pseudo-revolutionary activities were accompanied by internal strife and squabbles, provided opportunities for police provocations, and diverted attention of the proletarian and democratic forces from the truly revolutionary tasks."[16] For Marx, these men were as dangerous to the revolution as the Franco-German police, who dogged his steps even in London. This was not the time for engineering political schemes, much less for conspiracy and revolt. Propaganda, not sabotage, was Marx's limited objective during this period. And the main objective of his propaganda was to reeducate the radical members of his own Communist cell. The dissolution of the Communist League in the Cologne trial was the disastrous result of the unwitting collaboration of the Prussian and Bonapartist secret police with those members of the League who were most antipathetic to Marx. It was their open revolt against his leadership that led to their manipulation by the Prussians. We will want to focus, therefore, on Marx's *Revelations Concerning the Communist Trial in Cologne* (1852), which, though relatively unknown even among Marxists, is as important a source for understanding Marx in the post-1848 period as the better known *Eighteenth Brumaire of Louis Bonaparte* and *The Class Struggle in France, 1848–1850.*

In his accounts of the failure of the Revolution in France, Marx repeatedly emphasizes the extent to which the identification of the peasant class and the petty bourgeoisie with the imperialistic ideals of Bonapartism prevented them from acting in their own best interest. Hence, when Napoleon's nephew, Louis Bonaparte, seized power in the *coup d'état* of December 2, 1851, he met with no resistance. He was simply consolidating the forces of reaction that had been building

16. Marx/Engels, *Collected Works* 11:656 n. 155.

since the Revolution had failed in 1848. Marx's strategy is to point out
how the potentially revolutionary forces of the present are restrained
by the spectral grasp of the Napoleonic past.

Marx had always had a healthy respect for the forces of the past, but
after 1848 he recognized in an entirely new way the extent to which the
ideological forces of the past can operate even in the face of the most
compelling economic and political exigencies of the present. In the
1840s, Marx believed that France was less compelled by the forces of
the past than Germany. After 1848 he had to reevaluate that assess-
ment. His 1843 essay on Hegel's *Philosophy of Right* puts into play
some of the terms that will figure prominently in *The Eighteenth Brumaire*. It almost seems that as early as 1843, Marx is already anticipating the failure of 1848: "The struggle against the German political
present is the struggle against the past of modern nations, which continues to be harassed by reminiscences of this past. It is instructive for
them to see the *ancien régime,* which in their countries has experienced
its *tragedy,* play its *comic* role as a German phantom [*als deutschen
Revenant*]."17 The failure of the Revolution of 1848 in Germany was
therefore much less of a surprise to Marx than its failure in France,
where the German comedy became, following Bonaparte's coup, a
French farce. After 1851, Marx recognized that France no less than
Germany was "harassed by reminiscences" of its past. During the
1850s Marx saw Franco-German history in the ensemble as haunted
by the specter of Bonapartism. Just as Napoleon I sought to control
German economic and political development, his nephew continued to
play havoc with Germany by encouraging and manipulating the forces
of reaction from afar.

As Marx analyzes the forces that led to the demise of the Communist
League, as he considers the machinations of the Prussian police, he is
invariably led back to the specter of Bonapartism and the mythology of
the imperialistic state ideology. He recognizes that it is the constant
vigil of the Napoleonic eagle that keeps the "old mole" underground.
Bonapartism is the political expression of the economic relations of
production and exchange that Marx in *The Communist Manifesto*
(1848) describes in the figure of the "sorcerer, who is no longer able to
control the powers of the nether world whom he has called up by his

17. Karl Marx, *Early Writings,* ed. Quintin Hoare (New York: Vintage Books,
1975), 247.

spells."[18] Marx was forced to admit after 1848 that the conjuror would be able to maintain his spell for just a little longer.

There is another important element here; it has to do with the relation between this political impasse and what Jerrold Siegel has called Marx's "return to philosophy" in the 1850s.[19] But while Siegel is concerned with Marx's return to Hegel in the late 1850s in the *Grundrisse*, my concern is with the way Marx's astonishment and dismay at the course of events in the *early* 1850s have the effect of transforming his notion of philosophy. In the early years of the decade, Marx recognizes that for the moment he cannot change the world; the best he can do is try to understand it. His appropriation of the image of the "old mole" is the most obvious symptom of a more profound shift in both his philosophy of history and his relation to Hegel.

During the 1840s Marx repeatedly upbraided the Germans for their excessive interest in philosophy, which he believed placed them unwittingly in the service of the most reactionary elements. This is of course the basis of all of his attacks on "the German ideology." In the 1843 essay on Hegel's *Philosophy of Right,* he describes the dangerous asymmetry in Germany between philosophical and historical development: "Just as the ancient peoples lived their previous history in imagination, in *mythology*, so we Germans have lived our future history in thought, in *philosophy*. We are the *philosophical* contemporaries of the present without being its *historical* contemporaries."[20] Germany has in a sense mortgaged its future to philosophy. It is this insight that persuades Louis Althusser that Marx broke with speculative philosophy in 1843–44, and indeed he did break with the sort of speculative philosophy that showed no interest in the immediacy of historical experience. But it would be to misunderstand both Marx and Althusser to conclude that Marx broke with philosophy *tout court*. I want to suggest that Marx's initial break with philosophy still left him within an explicitly metaphysical, teleological system of thought, that not until after 1848–51 did Marx, by virtue of his astonishment and dismay at the course of events, lose faith in the materialist teleology that had sustained him since the mid 1840s. I am suggesting that we shift

18. Karl Marx, *The Revolutions of 1848*, ed. David Fernbach (New York: Vintage Books, 1974), 72.

19. See Jerrold Siegel, *Marx's Fate: The Shape of a Life* (Princeton, N.J.: Princeton University Press, 1978), ch. 10, 294ff.

20. Marx, *Early Writings*, 249.

Althusser's notion of the break from the 1840s to the post-1848 peri-od, which signals the truly crucial change in Marx's thinking. The so-called "epistemological break" from the humanist Marx to the scien-tific Marx left his philosophy of history just as teleologically oriented and just as Hegelian as it had ever been. Marx's prerevolutionary confidence in the scientificity of his categories of thought and the certainty with which he expressed his philosophy of history were no less overtly metaphysical than Hegel's determinations. Only after 1851 did Marx break with all essentializing philosophy, idealist and mate-rialist. Not before such texts as *The Cologne Communist Trial* and *The Eighteenth Brumaire of Louis Bonaparte* did philosophy in this new postphilosophical sense make its first appearance across the spectrum of Marx's thinking. While there is a "return to philosophy" and a "return to Hegel" in the 1850s, they must be understood in terms of a new notion of philosophy itself.

Althusser writes of Marx in 1843–44; "Therefore it was necessary to retreat *from* this ideological flight forwards in order to reach the things themselves, to touch real history and at last come face to face with the beings that haunted the mists of German consciousness."[21] I am suggesting that this first break is only an inversion or reversal of the German ideology rather than an escape from it. Althusser henceforth italicizes this *"retreat"* in his own text in order to mark its importance. But this retreat becomes genuinely important only after Bonaparte's coup. Marx's initial reversal of the Hegelian dialectic, his determina-tion to rise from the abstract to the concrete, left unchanged the philos-opher's fundamental prerogative to discover truths and essences. The expression "to touch real history" indicates, perhaps more than Al-thusser suspects, the extent to which the Marx of the 1840s remains bound to a Hegelian teleology: not only does Marx fail to overcome philosophy, but quite to the contrary, he takes philosophy more se-riously as a world-historical force than perhaps anyone ever had. It is still Marx the philosopher who believes that his new scientific philoso-phy can change the world.

After 1848 he has very few of these illusions left. After 1848 Marx's philosophy of history becomes a truly mature and tragic vision in which he recognizes that history is more incorrigible and more re-

21. Louis Althusser, "On the Young Marx: Theoretical Questions," in *For Marx*, trans. Ben Brewster (New York: Vintage Books, 1970), 76.

sistant to both his politics and his philosophy than he had previously suspected. Only after 1848 does his technique of dialectical materialism come into conjunction with his philosophy of history. After 1848 philosophy is no longer a programmatic prescription for the future but rather a means of recognizing the detours and deferrals that must always be analyzed in retrospect, never in advance. Philosophy thus conceived becomes a byword for caution and restraint, an expression of the intellectual's perpetual astonishment at history's refusal to be reduced to method. It would be rash on my part to suggest that during the 1850s Marx overcomes metaphysics. I will say, however, that he comes closer to overcoming metaphysics then than at any other stage in his career. Marx cannot do without metaphysics; the revolution cannot do without metaphysics. Marx must repeatedly lapse into the prophetic mode; he must repeatedly claim to be able to see into the future. There would be no such thing as Marxism had Marx not claimed to be the one who is supposed to know, the one who knows that everything is tending toward the proletarian revolution. All of that is obvious. What I am suggesting is that it is during the 1850s that Marx is most suspicious of philosophy's prophetic mode. I am suggesting that Marx in *retreat from* metaphysics during the 1850s—*retreating forwards,* as Althusser says, toward a notion of philosophy for which he did not have a name—I am saying that this Marx is an acutely modern figure. This Marx is still our contemporary. All of Marxism's notorious failings, like the prophecy that the revolution would come in the industrial rather than the agrarian societies, are uniformly attributable to a certain Hegelianism that Marx perennially struggled to throw off. Althusser's notion of the retreat in Marx's thinking is the most important discovery about Marx in modern times, but it must be refined in the terms I have outlined if its true force is to be realized. By standing the Hegelian dialectic right-side-up, Marx made philosophy synonymous with the power of political intervention to transform the world. One could speak here of Marx's *Aufhebung* of philosophy. After 1848, however, he discovered how much of his philosophy was still left behind, incapable of being transmuted into political form.

At the end of the *New Introductory Lectures on Psychoanalysis* (1937), Freud remarks of the new Marxist *Weltanschauung* that "although practical Marxism mercilessly cleared away all idealistic systems and illusions, it has itself developed illusions which are no less

questionable and unprovable than the earlier ones."[22] During the
1850s Marx is as free of such illusions as it is perhaps possible to be.
Prior to 1848 and after, say, 1864, Marx is a Marxist. In the interim,
however, he is simply Karl Marx; he once remarked to his son-in-law,
Paul Lafargue, "*Je ne suis pas marxiste.*" Prior to 1848, Marx is what
Althusser has called (though not with reference to Marx) "a Hegelian
politician": "The fact that there is no knowing the future prevents
there being any science of politics, any knowing that deals with the
future effects of present phenomena. That is why no Hegelian politics
is possible strictly speaking, and in fact there has never been a Hegelian
politician."[23] For such a politician the dialectic would play the role of
the oracle at Delphi. Marx's retreat from that illusion does not begin in
earnest until his English exile. Marx is never a vulgar soothsayer, but
he remains perilously close to the Hegelian politician. In the 1850s he
is less concerned with looking ahead than with looking back, particularly at the patterns of historical repetition between the First and Second Empires, and at the ensemble of economic and ideological forces
that he had been unable to calculate during the 1840s. While the
Hegelian politician leaves nothing to chance, Marx after 1848 becomes
the philosopher of the incalculable.

Let us pursue for a moment Althusser's notion of the retreat, and in
particular the way Althusser phrases it. In stepping back, as Althusser
says, Marx is actually stepping forward. The image is a suggestive one,
for while Marx, like his contemporaries, still has his back to the Real,
he has managed to step backward toward it; the others continue to
move increasingly further away. His step back is actually a step forward; for the others the delusory step forward only moves them further from the Real. The terms of Marx's decisive step back become
clearer, I believe, if we turn for elucidation not to Althusser but to
Heidegger. This will also enable us to pursue more directly the question of just what Marx's (re)turn to philosophy in the 1850s involved.

In August 1955, Heidegger presented his lecture *What Is Philosophy?* at Cerisy-La-Salle near Paris. Whether or not Althusser was in
attendance, his emphasis on the notion of the retreat in the 1961 essay
we have been discussing seems to echo the leitmotif of Heidegger's

22. Sigmund Freud, *New Introductory Lectures on Psychoanalysis,* trans. James
Strachey (New York: Norton, 1965), 180.
23. Louis Althusser and Etienne Balibar, *Reading Capital,* trans. Ben Brewster (London: NLB, 1977), 95.

lecture. Elaborating a passage from Aristotle's *Metaphysics*, Heidegger argues that "astonishment, as *pathos,* is the *archê* of philosophy," and develops Aristotle's contention that to be astonished is the fundamental condition of the philosopher. Astonishment is not simply something that initiates philosophical inquiry and is then left behind; rather it is something that "carries and pervades philosophy." What is above all important to Heidegger is that we understand *pathos* in a nonpsychological sense. In this passage, which has influenced so much of modern French philosophy, he suggests a translation that would recover the most primordial sense of the word:

> Astonishment is *pathos.* We usually translate *pathos* with passion, ebullition of emotion. But *pathos* is connected with *paschein,* to suffer, endure, undergo, to be borne along by, to be determined by. It is risky, as it always is in such cases, if we translate pathos with tuning [*Stimmung*], by which we mean dis-position [*Ge-stimmtheit*] and determination [*Be-stimmtheit*]. But we must risk this translation because it alone protects us from conceiving *pathos* in a very modern psychological sense. Only if we understand pathos as being attuned to [*Stimmung*] (dis-position), can we also characterize *thaumazein,* astonishment, more exactly. In astonishment we restrain ourselves (*être en arrêt*). We step back, as it were, from being, from the fact that it is as it is and not otherwise. And astonishment is not used up in this retreating from the Being of being, but, as this retreating and self-restraining, it is at the same time forcibly drawn to and, as it were, held fast by that from which it retreats.[24]

Heidegger chooses *Stimmung* to translate pathos because *Stimmung* derives from *Stimme,* which means *voice.* Astonishment is thus a tuning in the sense of pitch or tone, and to step back is to be restrained or held by a certain tone. The retreat is a way of taking up a position, a dis-position, in relation to the voice of Being. Heidegger is right to warn that this is a risky translation, for it is precisely the sort of gesture that has elicited accusations, above all by Derrida, that Heidegger is a philosopher of presence and proximity. What Heidegger means to say is that astonishment is a relation that involves not a logocentric listening but rather what in "The Origin of the Work of Art" he calls the "silent call" of Being. What he is talking about is an inaudible process,

24. Martin Heidegger, *What Is Philosophy?* (German/English edition), trans. Jean Wilde and William Kluback (New Haven, Conn.: College and University Press, n.d.), 81, 82–83. *Stimmung* marks the retreat from ontological difference.

the taking up of a position from which we *cannot* hear. It is precisely our stepping back out of range, our recoil at "the fact that [being] is as it is and not otherwise," that he means to suggest here. Thinking begins, in other words, with a retreat from the voice—that is, with a retreat from what-is, and that what-is becomes the object of thinking only at the moment of our astonished recognition that it is concealed from us and that we are in withdrawal from it. It is to miss Heidegger's point entirely to reduce his argument to yet another logocentric meditation on the presence of Being. "*Dis-posé*," writes Heidegger, "here means literally set-apart [*auseinander-gesetzt*], cleared, and thereby placed in relationship with what is." It is important to note that this relationship begins in concealment rather than in unconcealment. The primal event for Heidegger is always the unconcealment of concealment. Astonishment and *pathos* begin not with the presence of the voice, not with a sensory hearing, "not music of accidentally emerging feelings," and not with a memory of lost presence, but simply as an awareness that language is always moving back from Being without ever having been proximate or present to Being. "Attunement" is not an affective state at all but the recognition "that every precision of language [*jede Präzision des Sagens*] is grounded in a disposition of correspondence":25 that is, that language is always already in retreat from what is, "forcibly drawn to" and "held fast by" the drift of *différance*.

"And how about Marx and Nietzsche?" asks Heidegger. "Do they already step out of the course of modern philosophy? If not, how can we determine their place?" A new attunement (*Gestimmtheit*) means a new understanding of the relation of language to thinking. Modern philosophy after Hegel is coming, argues Heidegger, to the recognition not that language is in the service of thought but that "thinking, as co-respondence [*Ent-sprechen*], is in the service of language."26 Heideg-

---

25. Heidegger, *What Is Philosophy?* 77, 79. The importance of the terms *Stimmung* and *Gestimmtheit* in Heidegger's thinking cannot be overemphasized. As early as *Being and Time*, he posited "our mood, our Being-attuned" (*die Stimmung, das Gestimmtsein*) as the site where the Being of beings could be determined (*Sein und Zeit* [Tübingen: Max Niemayer Verlag, 1979], 134ff.). Seven years later the term *Grundstimmung* ("fundamental attunement") became the leitmotif of Heidegger's 1934 lectures on Hölderlin's "Germania" (cf. *Hölderlins "Germanien" und "Der Rhein,"* vol. 39 of Heidegger's *Gesamtausgabe* [Frankfurt-am-Main: Vittorio Klostermann, 1980], 78ff.). It is through the notion of "attunement" that Heidegger turned from the voice of *Dasein* to the aphonic, voiceless essence of language.

26. Heidegger, *What Is Philosophy?* 89, 93.

ger does not answer the question he poses regarding Marx and Nietzsche. It seems to me not unlikely that Althusser's essay "On the Young Marx" is an attempt at an answer. But it is not, I insist, until after 1848 that Marx is astonished in precisely Heidegger's sense of the *être en arrêt*—halted suddenly, restrained, and thus placed in a new position from which one no longer believes that philosophy can grasp what is, held fast by a new notion of philosophy. In stepping back from the notion of philosophy as the unconcealment of what is, Marx after 1848 moved toward a notion of philosophy as the unconcealment of the concealment that is language. Marx's retreat from politics and a certain notion of philosophy was also a retreat forward into a new notion of language and, in the case of *The Cologne Communist Trial,* a retreat forward into the language of a Balzacian novel.

In his account of the Prussian political reaction after 1848, Rodney Livingstone observes that the new coalition between the old ruling classes and the liberal bourgeoisie laid the foundation for the modern Bismarckian state.[27] Though the Revolution was short-lived, the government of Friedrich Wilhelm IV took steps to ensure that such an uprising would never happen again. His police force initiated an investigation of the Communist League in order to demonstrate to the working classes that political radicalism would not be tolerated. The trial in which the investigation culminated fulfilled the Prussians' wildest expectations, for it became a truly European spectacle. This effort coincided, writes Livingstone, with "the establishment for the first time of a modern centralised police system."[28] The eradication of the Communist League was the constitutive act of Prussia's new hegemonic police power.

Had Marx had his way, the Prussians would have lacked the raw material of conspiracy that they needed. While Marx and Engels argued that the League's function was purely ideological, devoted to propaganda and consciousness-raising, the faction under the leadership of Willich and Schapper insisted on active subversion of the

27. Rodney Livingstone, Introduction to Karl Marx, *The Cologne Communist Trial,* trans. Rodney Livingstone (New York: International Publishers, 1971), 10. Also see Allan Gilbert, *Marx's Politics: Communists and Citizens* (New Brunswick, N.J.: Rutgers University Press, 1981), and David Felix, *Marx as Politician* (Carbondale: Southern Illionois University Press, 1983).
28. Livingstone, "Introduction," 20.

Prussian state. Marx's faction ostensibly won the day by vote of the
Central Committee of the League. The opposition remained adamant,
however, and the League foundered amidst increasingly acrimonious
dissension. It was against this backdrop that the Prussians hatched
their plot.

In May 1851 a League member was arrested with various documents, including the *Communist Manifesto,* but this and subsequent
arrests failed to produce any hard evidence of a plot against the Prussian government. The Prussians wanted to do two things: discover
evidence of an actual Communist conspiracy, and link the conspiracy
to Marx and the exile party in London. Though the police were perfectly aware of the split in the League, it suited their purpose to lay
everything at Marx's door. He was, after all, the most famous of the
exiles and the most articulate, and thus the most desirable target. After
several months of futile searches, during which the defendants languished in prison, the Prussians finally resorted to forging the documents they needed. In particular, they forged a copy of the minutes of
the London League's Central Committee. But what finally clinched the
case and gave them confidence enough to bring it to trial was their
success in entrapping members of the Willich/Schapper faction who
had set out upon a series of preposterous conspiracies in Paris. This
Franco-German leg of the plot was discovered in September 1851,
several months after the original arrests were made. In *The Cologne
Communist Trial,* Marx repeatedly draws attention to the prosecution's habit of making arrests and charges, and then taking months
either to perpetrate or to manufacture evidence to justify the arrests.
The Prussians finally succeeded, however, in convicting seven of the
eleven defendants to sentences of between three and six years.

Needless to say, Marx points to "the political nature of the trial."
Forced to delay court proceedings for a year and a half because they
needed the time to complete their case, the Prussians, writes Marx,
capitalized on their dilemma by making the trial into a *"procès monstre"*: "The eyes of the European press were upon it and the curiosity
and suspicions of the public were fully aroused."[29] Marx is astonished,
in Heidegger's sense of the term, at the prosecution's habit of treating

---

29. Karl Marx, *Revelations Concerning the Communist Trial in Cologne,* in
Marx/Engels, *Collected Works,* 11:401. This is a revision of Livingstone's 1971
edition.

effects as causes. The tolerance of the judge and jury for these transparent illegalities brings Marx to a stunning denunciation of Prussia at the conclusion of his account, to which we will turn shortly. Most important, it is Marx's astonishment at the depravity of a modern industrial state that makes him aware of the insidious pattern of historical repetition at work in Cologne. The conduct of the Prussian government in this trial opened his eyes to things he could never have guessed at before.

Marx became involved in the case as soon as the first arrests were made in the spring of 1851. His seven-page letter to a member of the Cologne League concerning the defense of their colleagues was intercepted in the mail and used as a pretext on which to arrest the addressee. "His arrest," Marx writes, "denoted the proclamation of a new crime, that of corresponding with Marx." The point he goes on to make reveals with wonderful succinctness that the prophet of revolution has become the philosopher of chance:

> But how did Marx's letter fall into the hands of the Prussian government? Very simply. The Prussian government regularly opens the letters entrusted to its postal service and during the trial in Cologne it did this with particular assiduity. In Aachen and Frankfurt am Main they could tell you some pretty stories about it. It was pure chance whether a letter would slip through or not [*Es ist ein reiner Zufall, was entshlüpft oder er wischt wird*].[30]

To be sure, the success or failure of a revolution depends on larger forces than those normally associated with the postal services. Marx had come to recognize, however, that the postal service can have a very direct bearing on the operation and destiny of those larger forces. His retreat from a Hegelian notion of politics and philosophy amounts to a recognition of the constitutive incalculability that divides and conceals the very essence of both the political and the philosophical. It was the "pure chance" that a letter might not arrive at its destination that replaced in Marx's thinking the economic determinism he had inherited from his inversion of the idealist Hegelian teleology. Marx recognized that the possibility of the letter's interception is foundational. Astonished by the virulence of the Prussian reaction, he abandoned any teleology whatsoever during the 1850s. He recognized that the origin

---

30. Marx, *Revelations Concerning the Communist Trial in Cologne*, 11:424.

and the end, the *archê* and the *telos*, were always already internally divided by an incalculability that effectively concealed them from any mode of intervention, political or intellectual. It would be nonsense to say that Marx always believed that. The genius of the Marxist dialectic is its capacity to adjust to the immediacy and the specificity of the historical present and its refusal to project those findings into universal axioms. "Pure chance" was the truth of the 1850s. With the epoch of high capitalist expansion came the predominance of the incalculable. At that time and in that place, the "real conditions" of economic production and historical change were blocked by a fundamental concealment.

The Cologne Communist Trial enables us to grasp the principle that Althusser first formulated when he wrote of Marx's relation to Hegel: "Take away the teleology, there remains the philosophical category that Marx inherited: the category of a *process without a subject*."[31] This category marks the preontological structure of Marx's thinking during the 1850s as well as in the major economic writings that followed. Marx's finest work pushes up against the ontological difference between beings and Being, and between dialectical materialism and the Real. During the 1850s this subjectless process indeed appeared as a "*procès monstre*."

Finally, the Franco-German leg of the plot brings us back to the Bonapartist specter that for Marx haunted the European nineteenth century. The Prussians were careful throughout the case and throughout the trial to blur as much as possible the difference between Marx and the Willich/Schapper group. These efforts culminated in their forgery of a document called the "Red Catechism," which was entirely expressive of Willich's imagination but carefully written out in a perfect imitation of Marx's handwriting: "In Cologne or in Berlin qu'importe? they had the text copied in Marx's handwriting. For what purpose? 'So as to increase the value of their commodity.'"[32] The whole of the bourgeois relations of production can be glimpsed in the Prussian politics of conspiracy. Value in a bourgeois economy is a conspiratorial forgery, a reinscription within the commodity of a value that is not properly its own; however, this does not mean that its "proper"

31. Louis Althusser, *Montesquieu, Rousseau, Marx: Politics and History*, trans. Ben Brewster (London: Verso/NLB, 1982), 184–85.
32. Marx, *Revelations Concerning the Communist Trial in Cologne*, 11:445.

value can ever be determined as such but only that the reinscription is marked in the process of exchange. By acknowledging the fundamental concealment of value in capitalism, Marxism itself is already deconstructive and does not need to be reminded of the groundlessness of its fundamental notions. With reference to the Franco-German leg of the plot, Marx's decisive point is that the Prussians themselves were the victims of a certain forgery by their counterparts in the Bonapartist secret police.

The key figure among Willich's confederates in Paris was a certain Cherval, an *agent provocateur* who had escaped from an Aachen prison where he was serving a sentence for the forgery of banknotes. Cherval was precisely the sort of criminal conspirator Marx feared would come to prominence in the Willich group. At Cherval's urging, the Paris cell planned a variety of break-ins, embezzlements, and conspiracies, including floating a loan in order to finance the revolution. Marx's account of their activities is a veritable tour de force that calls immediately to mind Balzac's account of the sordid adventures of Jacques Collin, alias Vautrin, and his motley band of cutthroats in *Splendeurs et misères des courtisanes;* in that novel, Collin is both the greatest criminal in France and the chief of police. When the Prussians caught up with Cherval, the arch-conspirator became a willing police informer, and Marx writes of the "veritable *entente cordiale . . .* between conspirators and police agents."[33] But just when the Prussians believed they had exactly the witness they need in order to link the Communist League's activities to the Marx party in London, the French police entered the scene. Cherval was arrested in October 1851. Bonaparte's coup took place December 2, 1851. The Prussians, in other words, were trying to extradite a valuable police informer to testify at the Cologne trial at just the moment when the French police were in need of all the agents they could get.

The Prussians tried to bluff Cherval into believing that only by cooperating with them could he get out of a French prison and be cleared of the outstanding charges of forgery and escape. Marx's imaginative description of a visit paid to Cherval in prison by "a Prussian *faquin* [scoundrel] dressed in a black tail-coat and cuffs, with a bristling black moustache, and sparse grey hair cut short, in a word, a very pretty fellow," is unmistakably Balzacian, as we shall see shortly in

33. Marx, *Revelations Concerning the Communist Trial in Cologne*, 11:409.

Balzac's description of Corentin, the most notorious secret agent in *La Comédie humaine*. Cherval, however, was not fooled by this Prussian charade. He knew he didn't need the Prussians any longer, for he had already struck a deal with the French. When the Prussians came to take custody of him, the French told them he had mysteriously escaped. Marx is of course delighted at this Bonapartist twist in the plot:

> The Prussian government suffered its customary fate of being duped. The French government had allowed it to pull the chestnuts of the Franco-German plot out of the fire but not to eat them. Cherval had managed to gain the sympathy of the French government and a few days after the Paris Assizes it let him . . . flee to London. The Prussian government had hoped that in Cherval it would have a tool for the trial in Cologne, whereas in fact it only provided the French government with yet another agent. . . . The Minister of Police thought it great fun to deceive the dear Prussians.[34]

Cherval's "escape" was the beginning of a long series of incidents throughout the 1850s in which the French outwitted the Prussians. For Marx, the significance of the Cologne trial lies precisely in its having opened the way for Bonapartist co-optation. The Prussians finally did not need Cherval to win their trial, but more important for Marx, they had learned how to play the sordid Bonapartist game.

The rhetorical figure that Marx uses to characterize the logic/illogic of the trial in general and the Cherval plot in particular is the *hysteron proteron*, and indeed the informing principle of the prosecution's case is that of putting first (*proteron*) what should come last (*hysteron*). Speaking of Stieber, one of the Prussians closely involved with Cherval, Marx writes, "Only a Stieber can allow himself such a *hysteron proteron*."[35] But this rhetorical figure has significance beyond the prosecutor's characteristic reversal of cause and effect; for Marx it is finally a figure for the structure of nineteenth-century European history. What had come first has strangely reappeared in the place of what has come last. *Hysteron proteron* is the principle of historical repetition that for Marx is synonymous with Bonapartism.

In *The Eighteenth Brumaire* Marx wrote: "Hegel remarks somewhere that all the great events and characters of world history occur,

---

34. Marx, *Revelations Concerning the Communist Trial in Cologne*, 11:417–18.
35. Marx, *Revelations Concerning the Communist Trial in Cologne*, 11:416.

so to speak, twice. He forgot to add: the first time as tragedy, the second as farce."[36] Marx inscribes his own originality under the rubric of Hegel's forgetfulness, for as David Fernbach notes in his translation of *The Eighteenth Brumaire,* Hegel never made such a remark as far as anyone has been able to tell. Marx's point is that he has something to say that Hegel forgot to say altogether. This notion of historical repetition is specific to Marx; it is the unique vision brought on by the course of events after 1848. Instead of the Hegelian *Aufhebung* from the lower to the higher and from first to last, Marx sees a reverse *Aufhebung,* a reversal of first and last, tragedy devolving to farce instead of the progression from comedy to tragedy. Just as Napoleon's tragic betrayal of the French Revolution in the Eighteenth Brumaire of 1799 reappears as the execrable farce of his nephew's coup of 1851, so too in the Cologne trial Napoleon's tragic conquest of Prussia at the battle of Jena in 1806 reappears as the farce of Louis Bonaparte's indirect and perhaps even more insidious subversion of Prussia in 1852. The Prussians had vanquished themselves through this grotesque miscarriage of justice, but in so doing they followed the French example. They betrayed their country just as the French had betrayed theirs only ten months earlier. In the closing paragraphs of *The Cologne Communist Trial,* Marx excoriates both France and Germany under the rubric of a generalized Bonapartism:

> With this verdict of *Guilty* the Rhenish nobility and the Rhenish bourgeoisie joined in the cry uttered by the French bourgeoisie after December 2: "Property can be saved only by theft, religion only by perjury, the family only by bastardy, order only by disorder!"
> In France the whole political edifice has prostituted itself. And yet no institution prostituted itself so deeply as French courts of law and French juries. Let us surpass the French judges and jurymen, the judge and jury exclaimed in Cologne. . . .
> Jena! . . . That is the final outcome of a government that requires such methods in order to survive and of a society that needs such a government for its protection. The word that should stand at the end of the Communist trial in Cologne is . . . *Jena!*[37]

---

36. Marx, *The Eighteenth Brumaire of Louis Bonaparte,* 146, 146 n.7. Paul-Laurent Aussoun argues that Marx's idea comes not from Hegel but from Heine, who wrote in *Germany,* "After tragedy comes farce" (*Marx et la répétition historique* [Paris: Presses Universitaires de France, 1978]).

37. Marx, *Revelations Concerning the Communist Trial in Cologne,* 11:457.

With Bonaparte's coup and the conviction of the members of the Communist League, the political reaction to 1848 had reached its apogee. The prosecution's case was so illegal and illogical, writes Marx, that the jurymen found themselves in a position where they "must either find the defendants guilty—or the government." There was always a chance that a letter might slip through, but in this case it didn't. From the teleology of revolution Marx found himself perilously close, after 1848, to an inverted teleology of reaction. He had always to remind himself that within this uncanny pattern of repetition and reversal there was still a chance that a letter might slip through.

The many Bonapartist intrigues that followed the new Jena are recounted in *Herr Vogt* (1860), Marx's acerbic and sometimes hysterical response to the slanderous attacks upon himself by a Bonapartist agent who masqueraded as a German patriot. In responding to Carl Vogt's ludicrous attacks, Marx took the occasion to warn " 'all true republicans,' Italians, Hungarians, and even Germans, to beware of allowing themselves to be used as a cat's-paw by the Imperial Quasimodo."[38] From the Italian liberation movement to English commercial interests, Louis Bonaparte, like his uncle, could not resist trying to make every European interest into an unwitting proxy of French imperial power.

With this reference to the battle of Jena, our reading of Marx is complete. All the pieces are now in place for us to reconstruct the intertextual primal scene of *The Cologne Communist Trial* in Balzac's great political novel, *Une Ténébreuse Affaire* (1841). We are in a position to see that in his mourning for the fate of the revolution, Marx had incorporated the letter of Balzac's novel; and in that incorporated, intercepted letter lay the secret of Marx's uncanny approximation of the Real.

Balzac and the Counterrevolution

Marx's admiration of Balzac is well known, and there are allusions to characters and incidents from *La Comédie humaine* throughout Marx's oeuvre. A remark by Paul Lafargue will give some idea of the extent of Marx's admiration:

38. Marx, *Herr Vogt*, 17:221.

He admired Balzac so much that he wished to write a review of his great work *La Comédie Humaine* as soon as he had finished his book on economics. He considered Balzac not only as the historian of his time, but as the prophetic creator of characters which were still in the embryo in the days of Louis Philippe and did not fully develop until after his death, under Napoleon III.

Had Marx only completed *Capital,* we might have his book on Balzac. The notion of the prophetic nature of *La Comédie humaine* is shared by Engels as well, whose letter to Margaret Harkness of April 1888 has become the basis for the Marxist reading of Balzac:

> That Balzac was compelled to go against his own class sympathies and political prejudices, that he *saw* the necessity of the downfall of his favorite nobles, and described them as people deserving no better fate; and that he *saw* the real men of the future where, for the time being, they alone were to be found—that I consider one of the greatest triumphs of Realism, and one of the grandest features of old Balzac.[39]

It was Georg Lukács who fulfilled the promise of the scattered remarks on Balzac by Marx and Engels. It is above all in his reading of Balzac's late novel *The Peasants* that Lukács succeeds most brilliantly in delineating the "discrepancy between intention and performance, between Balzac the political thinker and Balzac the author of *La Comédie Humaine.*"[40] Balzac's attention to real economic conditions invariably gains the upper hand over his political prepossessions—which accounts, as both Engels and Lukács emphasize, for the predominantly "elegaic form" of Balzac's novels and for the deepening "melancholy" that results from his recognition of the historical destiny to which his political interests were doomed. *La Comédie humaine* thus becomes the chronicle not only of the rise of French capitalism but also of Balzac's own disillusionment.

In the notebooks that have come to be known as *The Passage Work,* Walter Benjamin cites a fascinating remark by Balzac: "Memory has value only as foresight. It is thus that history belongs to the sciences,

39. *Marx and Engels on Literature and Art,* ed. Lee Baxandall and Stefan Morawski (St. Louis: Telos Press, 1973), 150, 116.

40. Georg Lukács, *Studies in European Realism* (New York: Grosset & Dunlap, 1964), 21. The best general account is Fredric Jameson, "The Case for Georg Lukács," in *Marxism and Form* (Princeton, N.J.: Princeton University Press, 1971), esp. 191–205. Also see Pierre Macherey's elaboration of Lukács' reading of *Les Paysans* in *Pour une théorie de la production littéraire* (Paris: Maspero, 1966), 287–327.

and its usefulness consists in its application at every moment."[41] This remark suggests at a glance how deeply interested Balzac was in the possibility of what Althusser calls "a Hegelian politician." Recollection for Balzac no less than for Hegel is the way into the future. Though Balzac was twenty-nine years younger, his political thinking and particularly his estimation of the French Revolution and Napoleon are in some interesting respects comparable to Hegel's. For both Hegel and Balzac, Napoleon's signal importance was to have reversed the democratic tendencies of the French Revolution and to have introduced hierarchical restraints against an anarchic republicanism. For Hegel, the fall of Napoleon was a catastrophe that called into question the very possibility of the sort of constitutional monarchy that he believed only Napoleon could bring about on the Continent. In a letter of October 13, 1806, to his friend Niethammer on the occasion of Napoleon's victorious entrance into Jena, Hegel admiringly refers to him as "this soul of the world" (*diese Weltseele*). On August 29, 1807, he expresses the hope that Napoleon, as the embodiment of the World-Spirit, will bring to Prussia the sort of liberal monarchy of which Hegel thought the Prussians themselves incapable. And years later, on October 8, 1822, Hegel writes to his wife from Waterloo, where he had just stood in the exact place from which Napoleon had surveyed the battle: "I particularly noted the wood-covered height from which one can see for miles all around."[42]

Hegel sought nothing less than to walk in Napoleon's footsteps, or as Derrida phrases it in *Glas,* it is "only before the Napoleonic eagle that speculative idealism kneels."[43] In comparison, Balzac is much more cautious in his estimation of Napoleon. Emphasizing always his antirepublicanism, Balzac celebrates Napoleon's reinvention of hierarchy and a centralized authority but sees such efforts, however valuable they may be, as only a way station to the restoration of the legitimist monarchy. Balzac's attitude toward the fall of Napoleon and

41. Walter Benjamin, *Das Passagen-Werk,* ed. Rolf Tiedemann, 2 vols. (Frankfurt: Suhrkamp, 1982), 2:910. Benjamin cites many authors who, during the Second Empire, emphasized Balzac's prophetic powers. This is of course a commonplace in Balzac criticism in which his realism and his visionary imagination are fused. On this and other matters, see David Bellos's fine study, *Balzac Criticism in France, 1850–1900* (Oxford: Clarendon Press, 1976).

42. G. W. F. Hegel, *Briefe,* ed. Johannes Hoffmeister, 3 vols. (Hamburg: Felix Meiner, 1969), 1:120, 185; 2:357–58.

43. Jacques Derrida, *Glas* (Paris: Galilée, 1974), 206–7 (left-hand column).

the Bourbon Restoration under Louis XVIII is divided, however, for despite the return of the monarchy Balzac mourns the loss of the authority of Bonapartism. After Napoleon, he sees a process of devolution at work in France, leading to the July Revolution and then the, to him, altogether loathsome reign of Louis-Philippe. For Balzac the Revolution of July 1830 was an abomination and a return to 1789. Realizing that Louis-Philippe's government was incapable of handling the challenges to its power, which culminated in the uprisings of the spring of 1848, Balzac foresaw that only a return to a Bonapartist regime could bring order to the growing chaos. He died in 1850, too early to see his suspicions confirmed.[44] It was, in other words, the historical memory of Bonapartism that gave Balzac a certain foresight into the Second Empire that he did not live to see.

Balzac's conservatism enabled him to foresee the forces of historical reaction that Marx spent the 1850s trying to understand. While for Balzac, Napoleon was not altogether the tragic, heroic figure he was for Hegel, he nevertheless represented the only force, in practical historical terms, that seemed capable of bringing the heterogeneous interests of French society into some sort of union. I don't believe anyone has ever noted how the First and Second Empires seem to frame Balzac's career. Born in 1799, he was too young to experience the First Empire as an adult, and he died on the eve of the Second. Though Bonapartism fell short of Balzac's legitimist ideals, it was nevertheless the best thing history had to offer. The irony is that Bonapartism never represented a viable political alternative for Balzac himself, caught as he was between a weak monarchy and the government of Louis-Philippe.

Balzac was himself a would-be politician. In the early 1830s he had, without success, sought election as a deputy, and in 1835 he purchased and directed a legitimist newspaper, *La Chronique,* through which he unfortunately supported the ill-fated cabinet of Auguste Thiers that was formed in February 1836 and dissolved in September. With the Thiers cabinet went the last of Balzac's political hopes. Ironically, Theirs went on to lead one of the most extraordinary political careers of the whole nineteenth century, and it is he whom Marx vilifies in *The Civil War in France* for having ordered the merciless slaughter of the

44. On all these questions the indispensable source is Bernard Guyon, *La Pensée politique et sociale de Balzac* (Paris: Armand Colin, 1967). For a more recent study, see Ronnie Butler's excellent *Balzac and the French Revolution* (Totowa, N.J.: Barnes & Noble, 1983).

Communards in 1870. Balzac's political failure, however, marked the beginning of what some might regard as the period of his greatest work—beginning in 1837, significantly, with the story of Lucien de Rubempré's disastrous failure as a political writer in *Illusions perdues*.

In the remarkable story "Z. Marcas" (1840), Balzac offers a more succinct and direct glimpse of his own political despair. "Z. Marcas" is about a political journalist whose erratic career follows the fortunes of the various factions he supports, culminating finally in irreversible failure and obscurity. The existential despair of the story is reminiscent in my opinion of nothing so much as Herman Melville's bizarre parable of the writer's fate in "Bartleby the Scrivener." The "Z" in "Z. Marcas" is the mark of Balzac's own signature. "From a Balzacian viewpoint," Roland Barthes observes in *S/Z*, "this Z (which appears in Balzac's name) is the letter of deviation"[45]; that is, it marks the deviation that Balzac believed always characterized his destiny, particularly his political destiny. His destiny was always to miss his destiny, to fail to reach his destination, to miss his proper place. The "Z" is thus the mark of the incalculability of Balzac's political fortunes: "The Z preceding Marcas, which was seen on the address of his letters, and which he never forgot in his signature, this letter brought to mind something of fatality [*je ne sais quoi de fatal*]."[46] Balzac's meditation on the mystic significance of the name is in fact a meditation on his own destiny as a phantom politician: "Do you not see a troubling aspect in the construction of the Z? Does it not figure the wayward and phantastic zigzag of a tormented life?" Z. Marcas's complaint at "the impossibility of entering and living in the milieu where he belonged" is Balzac's complaint as well.

While Balzac saw Z. Marcas as a figure of his own political despair in the late 1830s, there is every reason to suspect that Karl Marx, another phantom politician from the opposite side of the political fence, would also have seen the uncanny resemblance of not only his political fate but even his name to those of Z. Marcas. Here the power of names seems cabalistic indeed. Though they stand for opposite po-

45. Roland Barthes, *S/Z*, trans. Richard Miller (New York: Hill & Wang, 1974), 106.
46. Honoré de Balzac, "Z. Marcas," in *La Comédie humaine*, ed. Pierre Castex, 12 vols. (Paris: Gallimard/La Pléiade, 1976–81), 8:829. All references in the text are to volume and page numbers of this edition. Anne-Marie Meininger's preface to "Z. Marcas" is the source of much valuable information on Balzac's political career (8:817–28).

litical objectives, Marx during the 1850s and Balzac during the late 1830s are both coerced by history into playing phantom politics. Surely so astute a student of Balzac as Marx could not have failed to note the uncanny pattern: *Balzac/Marcas/Marx*. Z. Marcas, Balzac's archetypal political victim, tells a youthful narrator who has political ambitions himself that a "profound politician" is "a man with a marvelous aptitude for grasping the remote connections between the facts of the present and the future" (8:833). But Marcas no longer believes in the possibility of such a politician, because even though "one can see the causes of an impending event . . . one cannot see the event itself" (8:849). Like Marx, Balzac experienced the impossibility of a Hegelian politics as a kind of catastrophe. And to compound the irony, for both Marx and Balzac it was only after their deaths that the kinds of politics they envisioned became reality.

It is within this context that we must read Balzac's great political novel *Une Ténébreuse Affaire* (1841), which has been translated under the titles *A Murky Business* and *The Gondreville Mystery*. Though we cannot prove that Marx read it, common sense in conjunction with a profound intertextual correlation between this book and Marx's *The Cologne Communist Trial* make a compelling circumstantial case. Unfortunately, the novel has generated very little interest even among Balzacians. When read within the pattern of historical repetition I have outlined, however, and in relation to the problem of the historical genesis of Bonapartism, the novel's historical and analytical significance may lead readers to discover one of Balzac's major, if not one of his very greatest, novels.

Une Ténébreuse Affaire is set in the years 1803–6, and it concerns the counterrevolutionary effort by a group of aristocratic émigrés in the province of Champagne to regain their confiscated property by force. The problem of the redistribution during Napoleon's Empire of the property confiscated from aristocrats who fled France is one in which Balzac has an intense interest, for he is deeply suspicious of the émigrés and at the same time fundamentally sympathetic to Napoleon. The question of the reappropriation of *les biens nationaux* is thus one in which Balzac can explore the most important conflicting economic and political forces of the early nineteenth century. On the one hand the returning émigrés elicit his aristocratic sympathies, while on the other hand the larger interests of France demand that he place those sympathies in perspective. Balzac finds himself finally in a position where he must oppose the forces of the aristocratic counterrevolution on behalf of France herself, and thus also on behalf of Napoleon. The failure of the counterrevolution is brought about, however, not by Napoleon himself but by an extraordinary conspiracy initiated by one of his counselors, a certain Fouché, who later becomes his Minister of the Imperial Police. Napoleon is unaware of Fouché's Machiavellian plot, though he greatly benefits from its results. We see Napoleon at the beginning and the end of the novel, and its fundamental theme is the ascendancy of Bonapartism, of which Fouché and his henchmen are the ambivalent but indispensable instruments.

Fouché, we discover, has been playing both ends against the middle. He appears to be Napoleon's loyal servant at a time when Napoleon has just established the Empire and is about to proclaim himself Emperor; as insurance against the possibility that Napoleon's imperial schemes will fail to generate the necessary support, however, he secretly enters into negotiations with the exiled Bourbons. When it appears certain that Napoleon will succeed, Fouché realizes he must destroy the documents that could now wreck his own career. His negotiations with the Bourbons have been conducted through a double agent named Malin, who, as a senator in the Empire, has just been awarded the estate of Gondreville in Champagne—precisely the confiscated property that the returning émigrés are seeking to recover. Fouché wants to show his loyalty to Napoleon by taking care of the problem of the émigrés, and he also wants to destroy the documents in Malin's possession. Napoleon, eager for a peaceful settlement with the émigrés, is willing to sell their property back to them but will not tolerate its seizure by force. Balzac sets up these opposing forces. On the one hand, Fouché wants to create a diversion that will enable him to recover the documents and at the same time emphasize his loyalty to the Empire. On the other hand, Napoleon wants a peaceful reconciliation. Balzac is saying that it is not Napoleon who is malevolent but the men around him.

Fouché relies entirely upon a police spy named Corentin, whom Balzac had introduced in his early work *Les Chouans* (1829), the only other political novel in *La Comédie humaine* and also a story of the failure of the counterrevolution. Corentin is indeed the evil genius of *Une Ténébreuse Affaire*. It is he who hatches the brilliantly successful plot to create a diversion by kidnapping Malin and blaming it on the émigrés who want the estate. Everything proceeds perfectly: the documents are recovered, and Malin is neutralized under Fouché's power; the aristocrats and the loyal peasant who assists them are arrested, tried for a crime they never committed, and sentenced—the aristocrats to prison, the peasant to death. But Corentin's genius is most fully manifested in the way he forges the evidence necessary to convict the defendants, including a letter in the handwirting of one of them. The trial itself becomes a spectacle in which the power of the newly found-ed Empire is asserted in all its might. The interests of Napoleon have been served, as have Fouché's. The novel ends in 1806 on the bat-tlefields of Jena where, amidst the firing of cannon, Laurence de Cinq-Cygne—the heroine and an aristocratic supporter of the émigrés—pleads with Napoleon for a commutation of their sentences. A police conspiracy, a spectacular trial with forged evidence, and a concluding scene on the battlefields of Jena—can there be any doubt about the primal scene of *The Cologne Communist Trial*?

Like the Prussian agent who visited Cherval in prison, Corentin is a haunting, spectral presence: "His pallid face seemed to be bloodless, his fine, short nose gave him the sardonic expression of a death's-head, and his green eyes were inscrutable. . . . he had neither passions nor vices. He was a spy, but at the diplomatic level, and he worked at it with the devotion of a purist [*et travaillait pour l'art pur*]" (8:514). Like a debased Hamlet, Corentin in his long, dark coat is not simply, like the Prussian, a *faquin* (scoundrel) but a "perfect *muscadin*" (dan-dy), which is italicized in Balzac's text just as *faquin* is in Marx's. These are indeed, as Marx says, "pretty fellows." Of Corentin's dress, Balzac writes that "in those times certain styles lasted longer than political parties: a symptom of the anarchy that 1830 has once again brought before us." It is not simply Corentin's clothing but Corentin himself who is a symptom that has lasted from the First Empire to the July Revolution. And Marx reminds us that he survives and indeed flour-ishes in the Second Empire. From a narrative set in 1803, Balzac leaps to the aftermath of the July Revolution. Corentin is the very spirit of a certain Bonapartist element that Balzac cannot bear to identify with Bonapartism. Here again we can see how Balzac's realism gets the better of his political prepossessions: his novel lets us see Bonapartism for what it is even though he himself refuses to look. Corentin makes his last appearance in *La Comédie humaine* three years later—in *Splendeurs et misères des courtisanes* (1844), which is set in the last decadent years of the Restoration—as a debauched villain and blackmailer who no longer knows any allegiance. In *Une Ténébreuse Affaire*, though he is already an artist in crime, he at least officially works for the state; in *Splendeurs et misères* he is an ambient force of malevolence and destruction. Marx enables us to see that in Corentin, Balzac—as he is wont to do—has prophetically, and in contradiction with his own political beliefs, depicted a man of the Second Empire.

What is perhaps most interesting, however, is that Corentin is the *agent provocateur* without whom Napoleon's will would not be implemented. This is the motive force of the plot and precisely that aspect of the novel's inner mechanisms that Balzac is most reluctant to face. One would suspect Balzac to identify his interests with the proud Antigone-like aristocratic resistance of Laurence de Cinq-Cygne and the ill-fated Simeuse brothers, who are both in love with Laurence and who both perish in battle after Napoleon pardons them at Laurence's entreaty. But Balzac argues not on behalf of the idealistic aristocrats but on behalf of Napoleon's effort at peaceful reconciliation with the émigrés. By identifying his interests with the reasonable but purely theoretical side of Bonapartism, Balzac enables himself to look the other way when it comes to Corentin's relation to Bonapartism. Ronnie Butler makes exactly the right points concerning Balzac's politics in *Une Ténébreuse Affaire:*

> Balzac's unqualified opposition to counter-revolution and his praise of Napoleon for successfully combatting it is clearly expressed when he contrasts the inflexibility of Laurence de Cinq-Cygne and the young émigrés with the realism of M. d'Hautserre and the Marquis de Charge-boeuf in their attitude to Napoleon. Malin, himself a Bourbon double-agent, pays tribute to the effectiveness of Napoleon's policy. Its success, he believes, is based not simply on the repression of royalist conspiracies, but is equally explained by his calculated political measures, notably his overtures to the émigrés and concessions to the clergy, which are designed to preempt the Bourbons and to forestall the counter-revolution.[47]

Malin's analysis reflects the voice of Balzac's conscience. The fact remains, however, that in practice it is the repression of royalist conspiracies that keeps Bonaparte afloat. By showing Napoleon at Jena magnanimously pardoning the aristocrats who had staged an armed rebellion against him, Balzac clearly underlines his opinion of the Em-

47. Ronnie Butler, *Balzac and the French Revolution*, 61.

peror's political wisdom. But Balzac wants to have it both ways. He wants to take the moral high ground with respect to Corentin; at the same time he makes Corentin's criminal genius the key to achieving Napoleon's political objectives. And because Napoleon is clearly pro-aristocrat, creating as he did a whole new aristocracy to replace the one that fled, he has Balzac's undying admiration.

Significantly, Napoleon does not pardon Michu, a peasant who had been an ardent Republican during the Revolution, as well as a devoted friend of Laurence and the Simeuses. Michu is executed, and we cannot help feeling that Balzac, as well as Napoleon, takes a certain delight in letting the blade fall on the neck of this proud revolutionary who fights tyranny wherever he finds it. Likewise, I cannot help believing that Marx must have noted with deep interest that it is Michu's handwriting that Corentin forges, using the forged letter to lure Michu's wife to the secret hiding place where he is holding Malin. Michu's wife is completely fooled, and Malin, who has no idea who his captors are, is certain that Michu is responsible when his wife appears on the scene. This is precisely what Corentin had intended, but his forgery works even better than he had planned. Fearing that the forged letter might be discovered, Corentin had concluded the missive by instructing Michu's wife to burn the letter. She does so, but at the last second she snatches a fragment from the fire and sews it into the hem of her dress. Far from compromising Corentin's scheme, the preservation of the forged letter clinches the case for the prosecution. The fragment is discovered when Michu's wife is interrogated, and its revelation during the trial has a stunning effect: it "burst like a thunderbolt on the accused and their attorneys." When shown the charred fragment, Michu, recognizing at a glance what has happened, says "My handwriting has been forged." To which the prosecutor replies, as would the prosecutors in Cologne, "Denial is your only recourse!" (8:668).

It is not Balzac's political position with respect to Bonapartism that must have interested Marx but the extraordinary thoroughness of his presentation of Bonapartism's inner workings. Balzac's attitude toward Napoleon reveals the extent to which the novelist himself is implicated in a surreptitious Bonapartism. Balzac wants at all costs to prevent the reader from blaming Napoleon for Michu's death, even though Napoleon could easily have saved him when he pardoned the others at Jena. To exculpate Napoleon and himself as well, Balzac must resort, as he often does, to a mystical physiognomy. Of Michu's face he writes: "The laws of physiognomy are exact not only in their application to character, but also in relation to the fatality of life. Some faces are prophetic. . . . Yes, Fate puts its mark on the face of those who are destined to die a violent death" (8:502–3).

Physiognomy is Balzac's compensation for his political failure. The Hegelian politician returns under the guise of the prophetic physiognomist. Marx has taught us, however, that *la Fatalité* is only another name for the power of the state to hatch conspiracies and forge documents. And since that is always the case, there is always a chance that a letter might slip through.

8 Dialectical Images: Benjamin/Dickens/Freud

> There takes place in every origin-phemonenon a determination of the figure in which an idea will constantly confront the historical world until it is revealed in the totality of its history. Origin does not, therefore, arise from the examination of actual conditions, but instead concerns their previous history and their subsequent development.
>
> WALTER BENJAMIN, *Origin of German Tragic Drama*

> *L'autre est la race des rêveurs, des songes-creux,*
> *Et de ceux qui, nés sous le signe de Saturne,*
> *Ont un lever d'étoile en leur coeur taciturne!*
>
> ALBERT GIRAUD, *Pierrot Narcisse*

> One system eats another up . . .
> Much as old Saturn ate his progeny.
>
> GEORGE GORDON, LORD BYRON, *Don Juan*

> *Qu'est ce qui ne se laisse pas transfomer en auto-affection orale, tenant l'os pour telos?*
>
> JACQUES DERRIDA, "Economimesis"

In this final chapter I use the ideas of Walter Benjamin in order to focus a new light on the entire Dickens canon. Through the preceding seven chapters we have situated the notion of the primal scene in the interval between memory and imagination, between historical knowledge and metaphorical construction, between philosophical truth and the free-play of interpretation. As an interpretive strategy, this notion of the primal scene has the important advantage of allowing us to play on both sides at once, to be attentive to the internal constraints that the text imposes upon us and at the same time remain open to the polysemic character of interpretation. Using the work of Freud and Heidegger in a synthesis that is itself an interpretive construction, I have staged a variety of primal scenes, working both within a single text and between texts. Whether the resulting intertext was internal to the text in question or the effect of intertextual transposition, my focus throughout has been on both the indispensability of such intertextual constructions and on the preontological undecidability that they enable us to unfold. Though we have considered works from a wide range of historical periods, the implicit suggestion has been that this interpretive strategy is a twentieth-century product. What we will see in Dickens, however, is the possibility that the *nineteenth*-century author may have evolved, although in a very primitive form, a novelistic strategy that has deep affinities with what I call the primal scene. From Benjamin's experience of the streets of Berlin and Paris, I will proceed to a reading of Dickens' experience of the streets of London that suggests strongly that Dickens staged and restaged a memory/construction of his childhood experience in each of his works. I will depict a Dickens for whom the art of novel-writing is analogous in every respect to a psychoanalyst engaged in a lifelong self-analysis.

The conclusion to be drawn from such a rereading of the Dickens canon, which enables us to illuminate a great number of important passages to which the criticism has never turned, is that Dickens' relentless urge to reconstruct and elaborate his primal scene makes his work the primal scene of psychoanalysis itself. A brief final section on Freud's "Dickensian style" will suggest that Freud's reading of Dickens can be marshalled in evidence of such a claim. The objective of this chapter is, therefore, to situate the prehistory of psychoanalysis in the Dickensian text—to construct, in other words, a Dickensian intertext that forces us to regard Dickens' relation to the history of psychoanalysis in an altogether new light. In thus unfolding the primal scene of literature-psychoanalysis, we will see that Freud's "memory" of Dickens—like Marx's memory of Balzac—is fundamental to his interpretive project.

Passages

"Passages" was Walter Benjamin's favorite expression for describing the historian's effort to uncover the relation between past and present.

To construct an interpretive "passage" was for Benjamin to reveal the relation of past to present in such a way as to transform the present—which is to say that for him the interpretive act was invariably a mode of political intervention. The recovery of historical origins was thus simultaneously the revelation of some heretofore concealed element of the present, because origin for Benjamin was whatever of the past inheres in the present. That is why he always experienced any form of technological transformation or renovation with such pathos, because what was in jeopardy in the act of physical destruction was the survival or retrieval of the experience of individuals, groups, and perhaps even entire classes of men and women from the past.

From his 1925 study of the baroque *Trauerspiel* to the abortive *Passagen-Werk*, a project he left incomplete at the time of his suicide in 1940, Benjamin's focus was unrelentingly on the role of language in the effort of retrieving the originary, the primordial, and the pre-historical. What links the various stages of his brief fifteen-year career, what links the theological Benjamin and the Marxist Benjamin, is his concern with the ability of language to uncover fundamental historical concealments. What was always in question for Benjamin was the ability of the language of philosophy and literary criticism to give voice to the dead and the oppressed, whose experience has always been elided from traditional historical understanding.[1]

Benjamin is not, however, a naive or deluded historian-interpreter who believes that he can retrieve either what was or what is. The lightning flashes (*Aufblitzen*) that occasionally illuminate the historical horizon are like flares bursting over an otherwise darkened battlefield. Benjamin's emphasis is always on the fleeting insubstantiality of the insights that alone may redeem the historical past. Benjamin's melancholy is the inevitable response to the dilemma of recognizing that such redemption is both the task of interpretation and that which can never

---

1. The scholarship on Benjamin is immense, but there is still no consensus on the shape or trajectory of his work. The publication of the *Passage Work* in 1982 has, I believe, rendered much of the work prior to that date inadequate. Susan Buck-Morss's article, "Benjamin's *Passagen-Werk*: Redeeming Mass Culture for the Revolution," *New German Critique* 29 (1983): 211–40, is not only sound but also points the way to the best earlier Benjamin criticism. Rainer Rochlitz's article "Walter Benjamin: Une Dialectique de l'image," *Critique* 431 (April 1983): 287–319, gives a brilliant résumé of Benjamin's ideas. Also see *Philosophical Forum* 15 (1983–84), a special issue entitled "Walter Benjamin: Philosophy, History, Aesthetics"; and Julian Roberts' fine study, *Walter Benjamin* (Atlantic Highlands, N.J.: Humanities Press, 1983).

be finally or fully accomplished. The mystical aura of Benjamin's figures of speech should not mislead us into believing that he is ever unmindful of the concealments that block language's access to the ontological ground of the *Jetzzeit* or "now time." For him, language is the key to the preontological dilemma, for it is language that blocks access to the Real in the very act of pointing the way to it; it is in and through language that one glimpses both the lightning flashes of truth and the circumambient darkness. The difficulty of reading Benjamin is the difficulty of balancing the preontological limitations of historical understanding against the promise of ontology. There is a mystical charge to the moment of unconcealment in Benjamin that must always be placed in tandem with the subsequent revelation that what has been unconcealed is the insurmountable concealment that is language itself.

Because I am using Benjamin as a means of opening a "passage" into the Dickensian text, and more particularly into Dickens' reconstructions of his childhood experiences, I am interested above all in *A Berlin Chronicle,* the posthumously published autobiographical fragment that Benjamin wrote in Ibiza in 1932. His theme is that of retracing the Ariadne's thread that would lead him back to the origins of his peripatetic fascination with the labyrinthine streets of Berlin and Paris. Within the context of Benjamin's own work, *A Berlin Chronicle* has the advantage of presenting all the fundamental ideas of his Baudelaire essays and the *Passage Work* project. His obsession with the Paris of the Second Empire is the logical extension of the ideas in *A Berlin Chronicle,* just as his Parisian *flânerie* of the 1920s and 1930s was an extension of his childhood *flânerie* in his native Berlin: "I should scarcely be able to abandon myself to the shifting currents of these memories of my earliest city life, had not Paris set before me, strictly circumscribed, the two forms in which alone this can legitimately—that is, with a guarantee of permanence—be done."[2]

Proustian reminiscence is the first form, especially the discovery in Proust that the greatest interpretive power can be found in the smallest image or detail. The second mnemonic form that Benjamin owes to Paris is "this art of straying; it fulfilled a dream that had shown its first traces in the labyrinths on the blotting pages of my school exercise books" (R, 9). Benjamin's "endless *flâneries*" in Paris, both above-

2. Walter Benjamin, *Reflections,* trans. Edmund Jephcott (New York: Harcourt Brace Jovanovich, 1978), 5. This edition is hereafter cited in the text as *R*.

ground and in "the underworld of the Métro and the North-South line," led him back, "and not entirely without an Ariadne's thread," to what Derrida would call the *archi-écriture* of his Berlin childhood, back to the prehistoric writing before writing, back to the language that language conceals. In the labyrinths of the streets and subway tunnels of Paris, Benjamin discovered once again the archaic world of his childhood. Straying into the byways of Auteuil or Neuilly, or finding his way to a brothel on rue de la Harpe, Benjamin was able to pursue the Proustian cult of childhood remembrance. In surpassing his "graphic fantasies," Paris led him to a buried series of inscriptions, to a kind of inscription that, even though he anticipated it, came as a revelation.

It is the modernity of Paris that Benjamin thanks for this unhoped-for discovery of the lost time of his childhood. Nowhere in his oeuvre is the linkage between the modern and the archaic more accessible or explicit than in *A Berlin Chronicle*. Benjamin found in society's most modern creations, in its most future-oriented products, the repository of the child's "archaic symbol-world" (*der archaischen Symbolwelt*). Looking into the future became synonymous with looking into the past; remembrance became a mode of foresight and prophecy. It was in those images that he could decipher the sort of conjunction he called "dialectical images" (*dialektische Bilder*). In the *Passage Work* he hoped to construct a panoramic ensemble of the dialectical images of the Second Empire, images that originated from every conceivable social and cultural direction, images in which a society's most primordial memories had become the site of its utopian dreams of the future.

The dialectical image is for Benjamin "the ur-phenomenon of history," and it is to be found in language, not simply in alphabetic script but in any kind of social hieroglyphic that the historian-interpreter can locate repeatedly enough to make the terms of its readability apparent.[3] It was, therefore, only by assembling a great deal of material that Benjamin could hope to enable the linguistic character of the social hieroglyphic to manifest itself. The thousand pages of citations collected the *Passage Work* indicate the scale on which he conceived his project, and it is precisely the purpose of his avoidance of commentary that the reader should make the innumerable transpositions through

3. Walter Benjamin, *Das Passagen-Werk*, ed. Rolf Tiedemann, 2 vols. (Frankfurt: Suhrkamp, 1982), 1:592. Hereafter cited in the text as *PW*.

which the language of the dialectical image could define itself. Such images do not reveal historical reality in an empirical sense; rather they are the delusory, phantasmagoric dream images through which a society unconsciously communicates its fears and desires. Dialectical images reveal the Second Empire's concealment of itself from itself. Dialectical images reveal the nature of the concealments under which the society of the past labored. "They are the residues of a dream world," Benjamin writes in his 1935 outline of the *Passage Work* (R, 162). In them, utopian phantasies "appear wedded to elements from prehistory" (*Urgeschichte*; R, 148); that is, in dreaming of its future, society, like the individual, uses the material from its primordial past. In constructing the Second Empire's "dialectical fairyland" (*dialektische Féerie*), which was one of the subtitles to the *Passage Work,* Benjamin sought to bring readers as close as possible to the reality of the lived experience of Parisian life of 1851–70.

In *A Berlin Chronicle* it is the experience of strong emotion that triggers the work of remembrance. It is the visit to the brothel, or being lost alone at night in the byways of a distant neighborhood that unleashes a long buried memory of the past. Remembrance intervenes in order to lessen the burden of anxiety in a moment of crisis. This is the role Benjamin envisions for the historian in the context of the society at large; he is the one who will bring to consciousness that which it has forgotten but must remember if it is to continue. At moments of historical crisis the historian's work of remembrance can, ideally, enable a society to overcome its most destructive repressions.

The dialectical image is Benjamin's version of the primal scene. Just as the psychoanalyst seeks to release the analysand from the repetition of symptomatic behavior by constructing the primal scene, so Benjamin's objective is to bring society at large to a kind of "awakening" (*Erwachen*), to a state of "mindfulness" (*Eingedenken*), in which, in gaining possession of its past, it wins control over its future. These images are "constellations" because they are formed from the interrelations within an aggregate of images and because the historian places them high above the horizon of the past, high enough perhaps to shed some light over a darkened present and future. They are, however, artificial constellations, constructions made in an unspoken language. Benjamin's dialectical images are situated in the unverifiable preontological zone between memory and imagination. Their authenticity can never be established because the dreaming collective that produced them no longer exists and could not confirm them if it did exist. They are the tentative responses to a politico-interpretive dilemma where knowledge of the origin is at once necessary and necessarily flawed. In the dialectical image the strategies of the avant-garde supplement the limitations of historical understanding.

In "The Author as Producer" (1934), Benjamin calls for a kind of image-writing that seeks to overcome "the barrier between writing and image" (*R*, 230); the dialectical image is the answer to that call. His term "literary montage" describes an associative method of composition in which the pieces of the puzzle are assembled on the basis of linguistic analogies and patterns of repetition. As in Freud's construction of the primal scene in the Wolf-Man case history, a visual scene emerges through linguistic associations; from fragmentary verbal relations a narrative or figure begins to take shape. The montage technique is the result of the determination to follow Ariadne's thread. The ultimate objective, of course, is to erase the author function itself and to let the story or figure emerge after the reader's own fashion. In the *Passage Work*, Benjamin is like an analyst who, after having offered an abundance of material, allows the patient a great deal of freedom in assembling his or her own primal scene. As in Derrida's *Glas* or Norman O. Brown's *Closing-Time*, where the lightning flashes of interpretation take place in the space between, respectively, the columns on Genet and Hegel, and on Vico and Joyce, the experience of reading the *Passage Work* is the experience of reading between the lines. The shuttling back and forth from one citation to another vividly recalls Freud's notion of an infinite analysis in *Die endliche und die unendliche Analyse*. Like Atropos in the myth of the Three Fates, only history itself can determine how the fabric of the text will finally be cut.

These ideas are nowhere more clearly announced than in *A Berlin Chronicle*, where the work of remembrance is synonymous with the discovery of the topography and underground of cities. From childhood, Benjamin's shortsightedness, his awkwardness, and his "very poor sense of direction" contributed to making his experience of the streets a focal point of both his anticipation and his anxiety: "It was thirty years before the distinction between left and right had become visceral to me, and before I had acquired the art of reading a street map" (*R*, 4). The work of remembrance and the construction of "passages" follow along these very same lines: the groping, molelike experience of the *flâneur* lost in a labyrinthine byway becomes a figure of the search for the dialectical images buried deep within the language of an epoch. The following citation from *A Berlin Chronicle* clearly points to the preontological function of the notion of the "passageway" in his thinking. The covered arcades of the Palais-Royal, which figure prominently in the *Passage Work,* are finally only an incidental historical example of what is for Benjamin the structure of historical understanding itself. It is not the physical edifices of the Paris of the 1820s that form the basis of Benjamin's notion of the "passage." The earliest arcade in the Palais-Royal and the dozens that followed during the Second Empire simply enabled him to give historiographic expression to a process that is fundamentally interpretive and autobiographical. In recovering the ancient city concealed behind the modern city, in resurrecting edifices, neighborhoods, and whole populations that were lost to human memory, the historian is all the while moving closer to the dialectical images that lie en route to his own origins:

> Language shows clearly that memory [*Gedächtnis*] is not an instrument for exploring the past but its theater. It is the medium of past experience, as the ground is the medium in which dead cities lie interred. He who seeks to approach his own buried past must conduct himself like a man digging. This confers the tone and bearing of genuine reminiscences [*Erinnerungen*]. He must not be afraid to return again and again to the same matter; to scatter it as one scatters earth, to turn it over as one turns over soil. For the matter itself is only a deposit, a stratum, which yields only to the most meticulous examination what constitutes the real treasure hidden within the earth: the images, severed from all earlier associations, that stand—like precious fragments or torsos in a collector's gallery—in the prosaic rooms of our later understanding. True, for successful excavations a plan is needed. Yet no less indispensable is the cautious probing of the spade in the dark loam, and it is to cheat oneself of the richest prize to preserve as a record merely the inventory of one's discoveries, and not this dark joy of the place of the finding itself. Fruitless searching is as much a part of this as succeeding, and consequently remembrance [*Erinnerung*] must not proceed in the manner of a narrative or still less that of a report, but must, in the strictest epic and rhapsodic manner, assay its spade in ever-new places, and in the old ones delve to ever-deeper layers. [R, 25–26]

This is the technique of "literary montage," where the connection between the images is never made explicit, where the narrative line must be retrieved by the reader. There are clearly resemblances here to what in Chapter 6 we discussed under the rubric of "paratactic style." Parataxis enables one to capture the process of discovery free of the connectives that would reduce it to a mere retrospective narrative line. The montage technique is an effort to preserve the "dark joy" of discovery and to prevent the retrieved images from being reduced to the status of mere objects. The analogy between memories and mere collectibles is a recurrent one in Benjamin. In *Central Park,* the aphoristic résumé of the *Passage Work* that he prepared in 1939, Benjamin writes that while "the key figure" of baroque allegory was the corpse, in the nineteenth century it is "memory" (*Andenken*) that registers "the transformation of the commodity into a collectible object" (*Objekt des Sammlers*). Memory during the Second Empire becomes "a secular relic."[4] In the alienated existence of the high capitalist epoch, the recovery of lost time becomes a secular religion. The historian preserves his memories after the architectural model of Renaissance mnemonics, "in the prosaic rooms of our later understanding."[5] It is precisely this mode of commodified recollection that Benjamin wants to overcome. Rather than arranging his memories, like a latter-day Camillo, in an orderly Vitruvian theater, he constructs a labyrinthine theater of language. For him, the stage on which the historian makes his discoveries is always situated in a darkened passageway deep within the underground of language.

There is also a sexual dimension to Benjamin's penchant for dark passageways. The "dark joy" of burrowing through the subterranean depths of memory and into the archaic underworld of the modern metropolis echoes his similarly profound Oedipal fascination with the penetration of the maternal, chthonian mysteries of the ancient earth. His childhood walks with his mother and his nurse are the foundation of *A Berlin Chronicle.* In the *Trauerspiel* book and the contemporary essay on Goethe's *Elective Affinities,* his emphasis is consistently on the deeply melancholy attraction that the historian feels for these dark, maternal sites of discovery, which alone seem to hold out the promise of meaning. In the *Trauerspiel* book we can see in the saturnine gaze of

4. Walter Benjamin, *Illuminationen: Ausgewählte Schriften,* ed. Siegfried Unseld (Frankfurt: Suhrkamp, 1980), 248, 245.
5. Cf. Frances Yates, *The Art of Memory* (Chicago: University of Chicago Press, 1966).

the baroque tragedian a prefiguration of the molelike preoccupations of the historian of the Second Empire:

> Everything saturnine points down into the depths of the earth; and so the nature of the ancient god of agriculture is preserved. According to Agrippa of Nettlesheim "the seed of the depths and . . . the treasures of the earth" are the gifts of Saturn. Here the downward gaze is characteristic of the saturnine man, who bores into the ground with his eyes. Tscherning shares this view: "Whosoever knows me not will recognize me from my attitude. I turn my eyes ever to the ground, because I once sprung from the earth, and so I now look only on my mother."[6]

For Benjamin, the principle of historical understanding is synonymous with a lifting of the Oedipal interdiction. The dialectical historian burrows his way back to his pre-Oedipal origins. The "dark joy" is accessible only if one is willing to cross the Oedipal threshold and dare to look upon the image of the maternal body.

In *A Berlin Chronicle*, Benjamin links his experience of the streets to his obsession with prostitutes. Throughout his childhood and adolescence he was always lost on the streets, reduced to a kind of aimless wandering, and learned his way around only as a result of his eagerness to find the quickest route to the brothel. It is always to the image of the threshold (*die Schwelle*) that Benjamin turns in connection with the prostitute because she marks for him the liminal zone of the preontological, the point where the experience of the city becomes indistinguishable from the experience of Being itself:

> At the beginning, however, this was a crossing of frontiers not only social but topographical, in the sense that whole networks of streets were opened up under the auspices of prostitution. But is it really a crossing, is it not, rather, an obstinate and voluptuous hovering on the brink, a hesitation that has its most cogent motive in the circumstance that beyond this frontier lies nothingness? But the places are countless in great cities where one stands on the edge of the void, and the whores in the doorways of tenement blocks and on the less sonorous asphalt of railway platforms are like the household goddesses of this cult of nothingness. [R, 11]

The prostitute is the site of an uncanny fusion of the modern cult of nothingness and the archaic cult of the hearth. At the center of the dark

6. Walter Benjamin, *The Origin of German Tragic Drama*, trans. John Osborne (London: NLB, 1978), 152–53.

labyrinth, in "the Minotaur's chamber," as Benjamin calls it, lies the prostitute, the secret key to the mystery of the streets. She is the "apotheosis" of the dialectical image for Benjamin: "The love of a prostitute is the apotheosis of the empathy of the commodity" (*PW*, 1:637). With her the dialectic comes to a standstill (*Dialektik im Still-stand*): "This standstill is utopia and the dialectic image therefore a dream image. . . . Such an image is the prostitute, who is saleswoman and wares in one" (*R*, 157). She is the emblematic expression of the prohibited Oedipal mystery at the heart of the city. The "dark joy" is the result of one's recognition of the insurmountably liminal quality of that mystery. At such moments we come into possession, writes Benjamin, of "our deeper self" (*R*, 57). At such moments we become mindful of the genuine experience (*Erfahrung*) that lies concealed behind our everyday existence (*Erlebnis*). It is this experience of the liminal, this "obstinate and voluptuous hovering on the brink" that constitutes for Benjamin the zone of the preontological.

One additional episode from *A Berlin Chronicle* will complete my outline of Benjamin's primal scene in the streets of the modern city. This episode again involves the problem of language and the question of "graphic fantasies." It concerns a drawing Benjamin made one afternoon while sitting in the Café des Deux Magots at St. Germain-des-Prés: "Suddenly, and with compelling force, I was struck by the idea of drawing a diagram of my life, and knew at the same moment exactly how it was to be done" (*R*, 30). A year or two later he lost the diagram and was never able to reproduce it. It resembled, he tells us, "a series of family trees," or more exactly "a labyrinth":

> I am not concerned here with what is installed in the chamber at its enigmatic center, ego or fate, but all the more with the many entrances leading into the interior. These entrances I call primal acquaintances [*Urbekanntschaften*]; each of them is a graphic symbol of my acquaintance with a person whom I met, not through other people, but through neighborhood, family relationships, school comradeship, mistaken identity, companionship on travels, or other such—hardly numerous—situations. So many primal relationships, so many entrances to the maze. [*R*, 31]

This cabalistic figure was Benjamin's cipher of the "hidden laws" that governed his life. It held the key to the "paths that lead us again and again to the people who have one and the same function for us: passageways [*Gänge*] that always, in the most diverse periods of life, guide us to the friend, the betrayer, the beloved, the pupils, or the master. This is what the sketch of my life revealed to me as it took shape before me on that Paris afternoon. Against the background of the city, the people who had surrounded me closed together to form a figure [*Figur*]" (*R*, 31–32). These "primal relationships" are the goal of the cult of remembrance as well as of historical understanding. One grasps them in a lightning flash of revelation only to lose them just as mysteriously. The "graphic symbols" of such relationships are the dialectical images that point the way to the truth of one's origins, at the same time forming a threshold beyond which it is impossible to pass.

Recollecting a visit to his maternal grandmother when he was a boy, Benjamin is struck by the many long-uninhabited rooms that nevertheless seemed so full of the haunting memories of the past. He writes that he spent some of "childhood's happiest hours" there. This makes it all the more uncanny that when he thinks of the house, "I am met on its threshold by a nightmare." Thinking back to the staircase through which one entered the house, he discovers that "in my memory it remains today the scene of a haunting dream that I once had in just those happy years. In this dream the stairway seemed under the power of a ghost that awaited me as I mounted, though without barring my way, making its presence felt when I had only a few more stairs to climb. On these last stairs it held me spellbound" (*R*, 42). And from there he could proceed no further. Here in brief is the structure of historical understanding in Benjamin. One is drawn onward by the dialectical image only to discover that one can proceed just so far along the passageway of remembrance before one is held spellbound, medusized by the chthonian forces whose mystery one feels strangely compelled to penetrate. It is because of this fundamental concealment, this insurmountable spell, that the structure of historical understanding for Benjamin is always allegorical: that is, fragmentary, deferred. Meaning and truth are always elsewhere; the act of interpretation is always suspended by an otherness it can never account for. On that staircase in his grandmother's house, he pushed up against the threshold of ontology.

In Benjamin's montage-allegory, romantic historiography reaches its apotheosis. From Michelet's poetic redefinition of history as the commemoration of the dead, and from Bachofen's quiet celebration of the chthonian mysteries of an ancient matriarchy of his own construction, it is not far to Benjamin's dialectical image-writing where the ghostly figure of the woman on the threshold lies at the dark center of historical understanding, and where the historian's creative reconstruction of the past is conceived of as a necessary and perhaps even heroic act of political intervention. From his experience of the streets, Benjamin was led back to the primal scene of both his personal identity and that of a society which, like himself, was doomed to extinction. His achievement was to have succeeded, under the pressure of that knowledge, in commemorating both his past and that of the world that perished with him. "Where there is experience [*Erfahrung*] in the strict sense of the word, certain moments of the individual past come into conjunction, in memory [*Gedächtnis*], with the material of the collective past."[7] In Benjamin the remembrance or interiorization (*Erinnerung*) of the individual's primal scene sometimes merges into the deeper reaches of the remembrance (*Gedächtnis*) of a collective primal scene. It is then that the differences between individual and collective experience and between voluntary and involuntary memory "lose their mutual exclusiveness." Such moments bring us to the intertextual space of the primal scene. Benjamin's romantic historiography leads us to the deep structures linking literature, philosophy, and psychoanalysis. He leads us into the passageways that connect these disciplines at their most fundamental level.

The Dickensian "No Thoroughfare"

> [Dickens] knew all about the back streets behind Holborn, the courts and alleys of the Borough, the shabby sidling streets of the remoter suburbs, the crooked little alleys of the City, the dark and oozy whays of the waterside.
>
> GEORGE AUGUSTUS SALA, *Charles Dickens: An Essay*

> *Le vrai Paris est naturellement une cité noire, boueuse, maleolens, étriquée dans ses rues étroites . . . fourmillant d'impasses, de culs-de-sac, d'allées mystérieuses, de labyrinthes qui vous mènent chez le diable.*
>
> PAUL-ERNST DE RATTIER, *Paris n'existe pas*

> Walking for walking's sake may be as highly laudable and exemplary a thing as it is held to be by those who practise it. My objection is that it stops the brain.
>
> MAX BEERBOHM, "Going Out for a Walk"

---

7. Walter Benjamin, "Some Motifs in Baudelaire," in *Illuminations*, trans. Harry Zohn (New York: Schocken Books, 1976), 159. Hereafter cited in the text as *I*.

If I couldn't walk fast and far, I should explode and perish.
CHARLES DICKENS TO JOHN FORSTER

Before entering the Dickens world, I want to add another Benjamin-ian theme to our itinerary. It concerns the connection between political mystification and literary form that we examined with respect to Bal-zac in Chapter 7, where we saw that Balzac's artistic strategies were predicated on the same impulse toward concealment and obfuscation that motivated Napoleon's secret police. The form of Balzac's novel thus became itself a kind of conspiratorial concealment. We saw fur-ther, thanks to Marx, that these strategies reached their apotheosis under the Second Empire. Benjamin turns to the question of Marx's exposé of political conspiracy during the 1850s in his 1938 essay "The Paris of the Second Empire in Baudelaire." As a result of Adorno's editorial interference, this essay was not published during Benjamin's lifetime. A much reduced version entitled "On Some Motifs in Baude-laire" appeared in 1939, but all the references to the Marx of the 1850s had been cut to satisfy Adorno's entirely unreasonable demands.[8] Ben-jamin used Marx to demonstrate that Baudelaire's literary strategies were themselves unwitting modes of political confusion and conspir-atorial misunderstanding. By returning to Benjamin's fundamental the-sis in the 1938 essay, we will be able to define the element of political confusion common to Dickens' novelistic strategy and to Baudelaire's poetic technique. We will see that Dickens' experience of the streets is inseparable from the political confusion and mystification that inten-sified throughout his career. His experience of the labyrinthine streets becomes a figure for a larger political impasse.

Like Marx, Benjamin's interest is in the link between Napoleon III's conspiratorial habit of mind and that of professional conspirators who misunderstood the goals of the revolution. If "mystery-mongering, sudden sallies, and impenetrable irony were part of the *raison d'état* of the Second Empire,"[9] the same can be said of those who unsuccessfully

---

8. Cf. *Aesthetics and Politics: Debates between Bloch, Lukács, Brecht, Benjamin, Adorno* (London: NLB, 1977), 100–141. Adorno believed that he was playing Marx to Benjamin's Blanqui (see below), and that Benjamin's method was anarchic because he failed to mediate his images "through the *total social process*."

9. Walter Benjamin, "The Paris of the Second Empire in Baudelaire," in *Charles Baudelaire: A Lyric Poet in the Era of High Capitalism*, trans. Harry Zohn (London: NLB, 1973), 12. Hereafter cited in the text as *CB*.

tried to oppose the regime. Benjamin cites a passage from one of Marx's articles during the 1850s that expresses precisely the same ideas on the dangers of deluded revolutionaries that we considered in Chapter 7:

> The only condition for revolution is for them the adequate organization of their conspiracy. . . . They embrace inventions which are supposed to perform revolutionary miracles: fire bombs, destructive machines with magical effects, riots which are to be the more miraculous and surprising the less rational their foundation is. Occupying themselves with such projects, they have no other aim but the immediate one of overthrowing the existing government, and they profoundly despise the more theoretical enlightenment of the workers as to their class interests. [Cited in *CB*, 13]

Benjamin's thesis is that the thinking of these "alchemists of the revolution," as Marx calls them, is not fundamentally different from that of Baudelaire himself: "This almost automatically results in Baudelaire's image: the enigmatic stuff [*Rätselkram*] of allegory in one, the mystery-mongering [*Geheimniskrämerei*] of the conspirator in the other" (*CB,* 17).

   In his effort to demonstrate a correspondence between the mysticism of the poets and that of the conspirators, Benjamin turns to one conspirator in particular, the ill-fated Auguste Blanqui, who developed a philosophy of eternal recurrence during the course of a long imprisonment. While Baudelaire proclaims, *"Tout devient allégorie pour moi,"* Blanqui envisions, in a work entitled *L'Eternité par les astres,* a mystical cosmology of despair that Benjamin found every bit as pathetic as Nietzsche's exactly contemporary notions. While Blanqui responded to his experience as a failed insurrectionist by retreating into a philosophy of eternal repetition, Baudelaire responded to the failure of 1848, in which he had taken part, by retreating into the mythical, archaic Paris of his imagination. Baudelaire watched the burgeoning modernity of Paris in panic and terror. He saw that with the destruction of the old Paris all the memories associated with those sites were threatened as well. In "Le Cygne," Baudelaire recognizes that in the transformation of Paris beneath the "scaffolding" and the "block and tackle" of renovation, his memories are becoming increasingly inaccessible: *"Et mes chers souvenirs sont plus lourds que des rocs."* Modernity has transformed the work of remembrance into a thing of agony, and his response is to flee into the magical world of his own making. For Benjamin, Baudelaire's importance is that he was the first to perceive this transformation in the work of remembrance. He was the first to hear the call to memory, though Proust would be the first truly to answer it.

That Baudelaire fled the call does not make him any less valuable a source of the Second Empire's dialectical imagery. If he is Benjamin's antihero, then Proust, were heroes possible, would be Benjamin's hero. For Benjamin, Proust's "enormous effort" to raise his catch of memories from the sea of *temps perdu* was a heroic act (*I*, 214). Proust succeeded in making the effort at recollection that so terrified Baudelaire that he fled into a phantastic world of Swedenborgian *correspondences*. In Benjamin's version of modernism, however, there is simply no room for heroes: "Modernism turns out to be his doom. The hero was not provided for in it; it has no use for his type" (*CB*, 95–96). Both Blanqui and Baudelaire are heroic types in an age that no longer either needs or tolerates them. While Blanqui languished in prison, Baudelaire sank into ennui. In "The Image of Proust" (1929), Benjamin argues that even Proust's hard-won recollections finally consumed rather than rejuvenated him.

The lightning-flash suddenness of Baudelairean allegory, the shocking *coup de main* in which he unexpectedly appropriates the least likely word or image for allegory, "betrays Baudelaire's hand. His technique is the technique of the *putsch*" (*CB*, 100). Common to both the ill-fated conspirator and the *poète maudit*, writes Benjamin, were "the obstinacy and the impatience, the power of their indignation and their hatred, as well as the impotence which was the lot of both of them. . . . Blanqui's action was the sister of Baudelaire's dream. The two are intertwined. They are the intertwined hands on a stone under which Napoleon III buried the hopes of the June fighters" (*CB*, 101). Baudelaire and Blanqui were tragic heroes condemned to live in an epoch that reduced them to figures of farce and pathos. It is against this horizon that I am going to project the world of Dickens' novels.

Benjamin's interest in Dickens seems to have extended no further than a reading of G. K. Chesterton's classic study, *Charles Dickens* (1906). He cites it in both "The Paris of the Second Empire in Baudelaire" and in the *Passage Work*. He is particularly interested in what Chesterton calls Dickens' "realistic principle—the principle that the most fantastic thing of all is often the precise fact." Dickens' power to endow inanimate objects with life creates what Chesterton calls an "elvish kind of realism," "the unbearable realism of a dream." Chesterton's next sentence must have particularly struck Benjamin: "And this kind of realism can only be gained by walking dreamily in a place; it cannot be gained by walking observantly."[10]

Benjamin is not interested in Chesterton's larger thesis regarding Dickens' experience in the streets, but it is important for us to turn to that thesis, for it contains in outline the essential features of my reading of Dickens. The difficult years of Dickens' childhood, writes Chesterton, "may have given him many moral and mental wounds, from which he never recovered. But they gave him the key of the street" (*CD*, 49).

Dickens' childhood suffering has, of course, become legendary in the annals of literary biography.[11] The victim of a demanding mother and a weak, spendthrift father, Dickens found himself at the age of twelve ignominiously employed at Warren's Blacking Warehouse, where, much to the amusement of passersby and much to his own everlasting shame, he was forced to use blacking to waterproof buckets in the warehouse window, a task at which he eventually became quite proficient.[12] Left to his own devices at so early an age, the young Dickens took to the streets. The origin of what Chesterton calls his "eerie realism," the power to "vitalize some dark or dull corner of London," is surely to be found here in the uncanny alienation he must have felt as a young boy wandering to and from the infernal warehouse, alienated to the point where the streets became a kind of home—a frightful place, to be sure, but a reprieve from both the agony of work and the despair of life with his family. Early on he came to know very well what his disciple, George Sala, calls "the crooked little alleys of the City, the dark and oozy whays of the water-side." This was indeed the neighborhood through which he had to pass to and from the site of his

10. G. K. Chesterton, *Charles Dickens* (New York: Schocken Books, 1965), 47–48. Hereafter cited in the text as *CD*.

11. Cf. Albert Hutter, "Psychoanalysis and Biography: Dickens' Experience at Warren's Blacking," *Hartford Studies in Literature* 8 (1976): 23–37.

12. Steven Marcus was the first to argue for something like a primal scene in Dickens. In his essay "Who Is Fagin?" he demonstrates with reference to *Oliver Twist* that the recurrent experience of that novel, where Oliver is captured by the gaze of the other, may be related to what he calls Dickens' "primal fantasy or recollection" of being watched in the window of Warren's Blacking (*Dickens: From Pickwick to Dombey* [New York: Simon and Schuster, 1968], 358–78).

shame. It was in this underworld, Chesterton suggests (in a passage cited by Benjamin), that Dickens discovered a kind of utopia: "The street at night is a great house locked up. But Dickens had, if ever man had, the key of the street. . . . He could open the inmost door of his house—the door that leads onto the secret passage which is lined with houses and roofed with stars" (CD, 45).

It is curious that since the phrase "the key of the street" is Chesterton's leitmotif, he does not acknowledge that it is also the title of the first article George Sala published in Dickens' magazine, Household Words, in 1851. It was Sala's keen observation of the streets that first attracted Dickens to him; Dickens must have recognized how well Sala understood his own work to that point. From "The Key of the Street" to Charles Dickens: An Essay (1870), Sala was doubtless the first to intuit the key to the master's world, and this insight makes him perhaps the most interesting of the "Dickens men." Like Sala, Chesterton recognized the streets as the "key" that opens the "secret passage" into the Dickens world. Like the arcades of the Palais-Royal, which were demolished in 1828 but which announced the phantasmagoric lifestyle of the Second Empire, the streets of London that Dickens experienced during the 1820s (he was born in 1812) announced the phantasmagoric London that he would construct throughout his novelistic career.

The primary sources of our understanding of Dickens' childhood experiences are David Copperfield (1850) and the autobiographical fragment that the author gave to John Forster in 1847 and that Forster published in the first chapter of his Life of Dickens (1872–74): "That I suffered in secret, and that I suffered exquisitely, no one ever knew but I. How much I suffered, it is, as I have said already, utterly beyond my power to tell. No man's imagination can overstep the reality." At the age of thirty-five, twenty-three years after the fact, Dickens makes an extraordinary admission: "I often forget in my dreams that I have a dear wife and children; even that I am a man; and wander desolately back to that time of my life."[13] He confesses that until his first child could speak, he could not bring himself to return to the neighborhood around Warren's. Since that child, Charlie, was born in January 1837, it was not

13. John Forster, The Life of Dickens, ed. A. J. Hoppé, 2 vols. (London: J. M. Dent, 1966), 1:25, 23. Forster was the first to reveal the truth about Dickens' childhood, of which Sala had no suspicion. See Elliot Engel, "Dickens's Obscure Childhood in Pre-Forster Biography," Dickensian 72 (1976): 3–12.

until perhaps 1839 or 1840 that Dickens was able to return to the back streets along the Strand near Hungerford Market. And then, in a statment Benjamin enables us to understand fully, Dickens writes that it was not until "the very nature of the ground had changed" that he "had the courage to go back to the place where my servitude began." Only after the neighborhood itself had been renovated could Dickens bring himself to tread such haunted ground. Roughly, then, it must have been during the period between the completion of *Nicholas Nickleby* and the beginning of the abortive *Master Humphrey's Clock* that Dickens began to wander the back streets at night. Interestingly, the renovation of the dilapidated wharfside neighborhood coincides not only with Dickens' return to the streets but also with a new maturity and complexity in his writing. The 1847 fragment continues: "In my walks at night I have walked there often, since then, and by degrees I have come to write this. It does not seem a tithe of what I might have written, or of what I meant to write."[14]

It is once again Benjamin who helps us grasp the relation between these compulsive walks and the problem of artistic creativity. It is precisely in conjunction with the problem of "the overtaxing of the productive person in the name of a principle, the principle of 'creativity,'" that Benjamin links Baudelaire and Dickens: "This overtaxing is all the more dangerous because as it fetters the self-esteem of the productive person, it effectively guards the interests of the social order that is hostile to him" (*CB*, 100). Benjamin regards Dickens' "steady peregrinations" and Baudelaire's effort "to capture the streets" as inhibiting or repressive activities, compulsions that overburden the artist, at once deflect and deplete his energies, and thus prevent him from directing those energies toward a concentrated probing of the social order. It is as though the artist is exiled into the streets by a demand for creativity that paradoxically, but very effectively, succeeds only in thwarting his true creative potential.

Benjamin's point seems to ring particularly true with regard to Dickens. Coerced as a child into an anxiety-producing cycle of overproduction, Dickens the adult, once again compelled to please the crowd, once again returns to the streets that he has always identified with such feelings of crisis. He is certain of only two things, that he must write and that he must walk. Dickens' primal scene was thus

14. Forster, *Life of Dickens*, 2:33.

perhaps reinforced by his artistic dilemma. The demand for something new becomes so overwhelming that his only recourse is to flee the study and rush into the street. But for Dickens the experience of the street is not simply an escape from creativity but rather the scene of his most difficult memories. For Dickens it seems that there was little occasion to escape either the burden of overproduction or the anxiety of his own childhood. He was indeed caught in a vicious circle, consumed by the obsessive pattern that indissolubly joined his nightwalks and his artistic production. In the public readings, which became his obsession in the 1860s and which finally killed him, one can see a kind of synthesis of these two deadly activities: he not only creates directly before his audience but must also run frantically from one lecture hall to another. It is as though in deciding against all advice and common sense to throw himself madly into his public readings, Dickens was simply trying to bring to an end as speedily as possible an insidious process that had begun as early as 1824 and that had been fully articulated by 1839–40. The streets are, therefore, the site both of Dickens' mystification as the place where his energies are at once generated and contained, and of his destruction as the place where he is consumed, devoured, eaten alive.

Benjamin links Baudelaire to Poe as well as to Dickens in his compulsion to walk the streets all night long. Benjamin does not suspect, however, that in this respect Poe is more closely linked to Dickens than to Baudelaire. Of Poe's "The Man of the Crowd" (1840), Benjamin writes that "the crowd is not only the newest asylum of outlaws; it is also the latest narcotic for those abandoned" (CB, 55). In Poe's story we follow a mysterious old man, whom Poe calls "the type and genius of deep crime," as he rushes madly through the city. After having followed him throughout the night, the narrator abandons his effort to understand the mystery that the old man seems to incarnate: the narrator's epigraph for the old man is: "*Er lasst sich nicht lesen*" (He does not permit himself to be read). Benjamin does not consider the possibility that Poe's confrontation with the mysterious unreadability of the night-walker may itself be a figure of Poe's confrontation with the text of Dickens. As Poe was writing this story, he was reading installments of *Master Humphrey's Clock* and *The Old Curiosity Shop*; he published reviews of these works as he had of Dickens' earlier *Sketches by Boz*. The old man in "The Man of the Crowd" combines elements from each of these texts: the sordidness of "The Drunkard's Tale" in

Boz and the obsessive nocturnal peregrinations of both Master Humphrey and Little Nell's grandfather. Poe was also doubtlessly influenced by the madman's tale in *Pickwick Papers*.

The Poe-Dickens relationship has yet to be fully analyzed.[15] When it is, we may discover that Poe, like Sala and Chesterton but before either of them, saw into the very essence of the Dickens world. Dickens met Poe in Philadelphia in 1842 and tried, unsuccessfully, to find an English publisher for his two-volume *Tales of the Grotesque and Arabesque*. Poe's untimely death in 1849 may have seemed to Dickens in retrospect a more horribly compressed version of his own fate as an overburdened artist. Poe was, in any case, in Dickens' thoughts in 1868 when, in the course of the American reading tour that contributed decisively to his death two years later, he paid a visit to Poe's aunt, Mrs. Clemm, in Richmond and gave her a hundred dollars. Dickens must have known that "The Man of the Crowd" had proved strangely prophetic of his own fate throughout the 1850s and 1860s, and that he too would never "pass from out of the turmoil of that street."

Benjamin describes the arcades of the Palais-Royal, whose most famous literary representation is in Balzac's *Illusions perdues* (1837), as being at once arcadia and inferno, utopia and the underworld, a fairyland for those who could enjoy the goods sold there, a nightmare for those who could not. Those wooden arcades were the forerunners of the glass and iron arcades or *passages* that sprang up all over Paris in the mid- and later nineteenth century. Inspired by Louis Aragon's surrealist meditation, *Le Paysan de Paris* (1926), in which Aragon discusses how his experience of the *Passage de l'Opéra* was heightened when he learned that this landmark would soon be demolished, Benjamin saw in the image of the *passage* the crystallization of all his thinking. "For it is only now that the pickaxe threatens them," writes Aragon, "that they have become the sanctuaries of a cult of the ephemeral, the ghostly landscape of forbidden pleasures and professions, incomprehensible yesterday and gone tomorrow."[16] In these glass-covered palaces of consumerism, these "human aquariums," as Aragon calls them, Benjamin saw a surreptitious return to the subterranean, submarine Paris, the ancient, chthonian Paris that was still

15. Cf. Gerald Grubb, "The Personal and Literary Relationships of Dickens and Poe," *Nineteenth-Century Fiction* 5 (1950): 1–22, 101–20, 209–22.

16. Louis Aragon, *Le Paysan de Paris* (Paris: Gallimard, 1926), 21.

lodged in the swamp of the Seine valley. What Aragon regarded as the "abysmal, unfathomable" effect of the greenish hue created by the tinted glass, which he suggestively compares to the "glimmer of a leg beneath a suddenly raised skirt," becomes in Benjamin the abyss of prehistory itself, the repository of all the experiences that conventional history invariably omits. For Benjamin the *passages* become the place where modernity disappears in the abyss of prehistory. The *Passage de l'Opéra* was also, as Aragon notes, Blanqui's Paris address.

Dickens recalls in the 1847 fragment that Warren's Blacking was not far from the Lowther Arcade in the Strand. Inspired by Benjamin's *Passage Work,* Johann Geist has catalogued all the nineteenth-century arcades. He cites a history of London toy shops that describes the Lowther Arcade, which was demolished in 1902, as "an Aladdin fairy palace crowded with all the glories and wonders a child's fancy can conceive."[17] Between Warren's Blacking and the Lowther Arcade, the twelve-year-old Dickens must have suffered exquisitely indeed. The "secret passage" of Dickens' primal scene runs from the workhouse to a child's fairyland. The task of reading Dickens is the task of locating that "secret passage" in each of his texts, and of rewriting the history that history always forgets.

Baudelaire's term for the artist's resistance to remembrance, and for the negativity that remembrance entails, is *spleen.* Of Baudelaire's opposition, *spleen et idéal,* Benjamin writes: "The *idéal* supplies the power of remembrance; the *spleen* musters the multitude of the seconds against it" (*CB,* 142). In blocking the restorative work of remembrance, spleen locks one into the repetition compulsion. Baudelaire cannot continue the work of remembrance within the context of his own experience of history and must therefore seek redemption in an otherworldly version of prehistory. Proust, however, fares better: "The fact that Proust's restorative will remains within the limits of earthly existence, whereas Baudelaire's transcends it, may be regarded as symptomatic of the incomparably more elemental and powerful counterforces that Baudelaire faced" (*CB,* 141). For Benjamin, Baudelaire's experience of spleen registers the burden of historical alienation, a burden so onerous that Baudelaire is finally driven out of history altogether, though not without leaving behind some "scattered

17. Johann Geist, *Arcades: The History of a Building Type* (Cambridge, Mass.: MIT Press, 1983), 328.

fragments of genuine historical experience" (*CB*, 144). In Baudelaire's experience the work of remembrance is inseparable from the cutting edge of Time, *le Temps*, whose devouring energies, in the form of spleen, consume every effort by the poet to remain in history, to seek a literal truth. The poet is finally devoured by Time, cut off from history, swallowed by the allegorical figurations that sweep away all his efforts to remember and to constitute a moment of "genuine historical experience." Of the Baudelairean image, Barbara Johnson writes: "In order to work, the figure must forget, kill, erase, the literal meaning it is supposed to derive from."[18] Following a logic very similar to Benjamin's, Johnson's deconstructive reading of Baudelaire retraces the path of Baudelaire's flight from history into allegory. It is ultimately Time itself that figures the consuming, irresistible power of allegory. It is, paradoxically, the figure of Time that negates the possibility of historical experience or literal meaning. And it is to the figure of devouring Time, set loose on the dark streets of mid-nineteenth-century London, that we turn now in our reading of Dickens.

Dickens announces at the beginning of *Master Humphrey's Clock* that he hopes "to beguile time from the heart of time itself." While Humphrey appears to be making only a clever allusion to his habit of offering up a new tale every week from "the piles of dusty papers" that he keeps in the case of his grandfather clock, the 1847 fragment suggests how much more was at stake in Dickens' relation to time in 1839–40.[19] Dickens originally planned to have Humphrey narrate the so-called *Giant Chronicles*. "Nothing," writes Chesterton, "could have been nearer the heart of Dickens than his great Gargantuan conception of Gog and Magog telling London legends to each other all through the night."[20] The two fourteen-foot statues of the giants in the Guildhall were to come to life at night and tell stories of events they had witnessed in centuries past. Though this plan was soon abandoned, Dickens' account of his novelistic objectives is revealing: he wants "to cheat [the hours] of their heaviness," "to scatter a few slight

18. Barbara Johnson, *Défigurations du langage poétique: La Seconde Revolution baudelairienne* (Paris: Flammarion, 1979), 86.

19. Charles Dickens, *Master Humphrey's Clock*, in *Works*, ed. Charles Dickens, Jr., et al., 25 vols. (New York: Collier, 1911), 17/2:7.

20. G. K. Chesterton, *Appreciations and Criticisms of the Works of Charles Dickens* (Port Washington, N.Y.: Kennikat Press, 1966), 237. Here Dickens adapts the dialogue between the two chimneys at the opening of Le Sage's *Le Diable boiteux*.

flowers in the Old Mower's path," and to slow "the tread of Time."
This passage, read against the horizon of the 1847 fragment, shows
that it is clearly Time itself that Dickens hopes somehow to mediate,
avoid, or deflect. *Master Humphrey's Clock* is Dickens' first, and un-
derstandably abortive, effort to master the memory of what he calls
"the slow agony" of his youth. It is no wonder that he had to abandon
the project. The wonder is that he had the courage to confront it so
directly in the first place. In the future he would be more cautious.

Dickens met Carlyle in 1840. The question of this relationship is a
complex one that has not been reduced by the numerous studies on the
subject.[21] My impression, however, is that Dickens' fascination with
Carlyle is responsible for much of what Marx would call Dickens'
political "mystery-mongering." The formative influence of Carlyle's
reactionary politics upon a generation of British liberals is one of the
most intriguing subjects in the history of Victorian ideology. Dickens'
radical political posturing during the early 1840s is unquestionably the
upshot of his misreading of Carlyle. Carlyle's coolness to Dickens,
which Dickens never understood, is itself a good indication of his
suspicion of the younger man's effort to translate his right-wing revolution into a watered-down blend of utopian socialism and pater-
nalistic liberalism.

I will return to some of these questions in the context of Carlyle's
response to *Dombey and Son*. Here, however, my interest in Dickens'
relationship with Carlyle is limited to a solitary passage from the latter's masterpiece *Sartor Resartus* (1833), for it is from this passage that
Dickens, who claimed to know Carlyle's work better than anyone else,
probably derived the figure of Saturn-Chronos, or Time, a figure that
would play such a prominent role in many of his novels. "It continues
ever true," proclaims Carlyle's Teufelsdröckh, "that Saturn, or Chronos, or what we call *Time*, devours all his children. . . . Me, however,
as a son of Time, unhappier than some others, was Time threatening to
eat quite prematurely."[22] In the devouring jaws of Saturn, Dickens
found the perfect figure for his post-1839 experience of remembrance.
For from then on, he too felt that he was about to be devoured by his
past. Moreover, as we will soon see, he uses the figure of Saturn to

21. Cf. Michael Goldberg, *Carlyle and Dickens* (Athens: University of Georgia Press,
1972).
22. Thomas Carlyle, *Sartor Resartus*, ed. C. F. Harrold (New York: Odyssey Press,
1937), 127.

describe his experience of the streets, to endow the inanimate streets with an uncanny, monstrous life. For Dickens, the "Agenbite of In-wit," the gnawing memories of his shameful victimage as a child are figured in this most archaic of images. In his novels Saturn becomes a dialectical image in which the crisis of alienation in the modern city is mixed with elements of prehistory. The melancholy image of Saturn, which had fascinated Benjamin in his *Trauerspiel* book, becomes in Dickens an image of the prehistory of the nineteenth century.

Let us take a step back to *Nicholas Nickleby* (1839). The prime mover of the plot is the moneylender, Ralph Nickleby, whose Carlyean motto is "Time *is* money." How literally Dickens means this is most obvious in the vision that Ralph's secretary has of his master swallowing "one of every English coin."[23] It is Ralph's rapacity that drives his nephew Nicholas and his impoverished family into the streets. As a kind of latter-day Saturn, Ralph's throat is of the utmost interest to Dickens. When Ralph hesitates as he hypocritically blesses the niece whom he is at the same time trying to prostitute to one of his de-bauched clients, Dickens writes: "The blessing seemed to stick in the throat, as if it were not used to the thoroughfare, and didn't know the way out" (*NN*, 301). Not knowing one's way out is indeed the basic problem of *Nicholas Nickleby,* and one that applies as much to Dickens' plot construction as to his imagery. Having carefully constructed a labyrinth from which Nicholas and his sister have absolutely no possibility of escaping, Dickens introduces the utopian *deus ex machina* of the Cheeryble brothers, which gives the novel's conclusion an entirely supplementary and fortuitous character. The dark center of the labyrinth and the true conclusion to the novel are reached when, following the villainous Sir Mulberry Hawk's murder (in a duel) of his newly reformed protégé, thus ending any hope that the Nicklebys might escape Hawk's grasp, Nicholas wends his way through London's sorriest neighborhoods. We should note that this occurs in chapter 53, which was published in the seventeenth installment in August 1839— that is, on the cusp of the author's *crise de conscience* of 1839–40. With Hawk still a menace, and with all hope apparently gone of ever possessing his beloved Madeline, Nicholas, after a sleepless night, "paced the streets and listlessly looked round on the gradually increas-

---

23. Charles Dickens, *Nicholas Nickleby*, ed. Michael Slater (Harmondsworth: Penguin, 1978), 708. Herafter cited in the text as *NN*.

ing bustle and preparation for the day" (*NN*, 790). It is then that he sees those who "died in soul, and had no chance of life," those who are led toward terrible ends "by circumstances darkly curtaining their very cradles' heads." It is here amidst the byways of the poor and the wretched that we can glimpse the primal scene of *Nicholas Nickleby*. "But youth is not prone to contemplate the darkest side of a picture it can shift at will" (*NN*, 791). Soon all obstacles to the family's happiness are overcome.

There is another moment in the text that serves as a counterblast to the utopian conclusion. The dialectical image in *Nicholas Nickleby* is to be found in the description of Manchester Buildings, the apartment house where Nicholas goes for an unsuccessful job interview with a Member of Parliament. Dickens transforms this building into the phantasmagorical figure of an insatiable Saturn. The remarkable edifice lies in "the ancient city of Westminster," in "a narrow and dirty region." The most curious feature of this lodging house for parliamentarians is that its architecture strangely causes every sound to reverberate as it makes its way to the solitary entrance of the building. Whenever there is "a gust of wind sweeping across the water which washes the Buildings' feet," it blows every sound, be it the continual "rattling of latch-keys" or an M.P. "practising the morrow's speech," toward the structure's "awkward mouth." One might imagine that as a parliamentary reporter Dickens himself had had occasion to call upon an MP in such a building. Nothing that goes into the Manchester Buildings can get out by advancing but only by retreating. The edifice constitutes a figure of the ontological impasse that characterizes the novel in general. The Manchester Buildings, like *Nicholas Nickleby,* is a "no thoroughfare" that "leads to nothing beyond itself." Like all of Dickens' saturnine imagery, the Manchester Buildings is a figure for the infinite figurality of the Dickens world:

> All the livelong day there is a grinding of organs and clashing and clanging of little boxes of music, for Manchester Buildings is an eel-pot, which has no outlet but its awkward mouth—a case-bottle which has no thoroughfare, and a short and narrow neck—and in this respect it may be typical of the fate of some few among its more adventurous residents, who, after wriggling themselves into Parliament by violent efforts and contortions, find that it too is a no thoroughfare for them; that, like Manchester Buildings, it leads to nothing beyond itself; and that they are fain at last to back out, no wiser, no richer, not one whit more famous, than they went in. [*NN*, 258–59]

It is interesting that this first fully articulated image of Saturn as a topographical site should be concerned primarily with the fate of politicians. It is they who are being devoured by Manchester Buildings. Given such a dolorous state of affairs, there can be no hope of ever addressing one's grievances to the House of Commons. Dickens' refusal to run as the Liberal candidate for Reading, when he was asked to do so two years later, was already a foregone conclusion for readers of this page of *Nicholas Nickleby*. Politics would always be for Dickens synonymous with the most grievous corruption and depravity. Here he depicts the MPs as being trapped in the belly of the beast. Politics like every other potential avenue of escape is a "no thoroughfare." The "no thoroughfare" structure is "typical of the fate" of all true denizens of the Dickens world.

The last installment of *Nicholas Nickleby* was published in October 1839. *The Old Curiosity Shop* began to appear in late April 1840. In the interim Dickens had begun to walk in earnest. "Night is generally my time for walking"[24]—so begins *The Old Curiosity Shop*. The narrator goes on to tell us of his fascination with "that never-ending restlessness, that incessant tread of feet wearing the rough stones smooth and glossy." Poe saw that beneath the calm veneer of this narrator's speech lay the mad obsession of the old man in "The Man of the Crowd." When Dickens realized that the tale he had begun as one of Master Humphrey's stories would soon outgrow the first-person narrative, he shifted to third person, but not without incurring certain problems. At the end of the novel he reveals that the first-person narrator was actually the younger brother of Nell's grandfather. This is contradicted, however, by the younger brother himself, whose remarks elsewhere make it clear that he was not in London at the time he claims to have met Nell and her grandfather in the course of one of his night walks. A remark by one of the puppeteers whom Nell meets in the countryside could well serve as the novel's epigraph: "Can't you think of anything more suitable to present circumstances than saying things and then contradicting 'em?" (*OCS*, 199). This contradiction is important insofar as it seems to be related to the novel's larger concern with the themes of mystery and impenetrability. The problem is that of determining just who is walking so late at night and why. Is it Humphrey, or the younger brother, or Dickens himself? It would ap-

24. Charles Dickens, *The Old Curiosity Shop*, ed. Angus Easson (Harmondsworth: Penguin, 1972), 43. Herafter cited in the text as *OCS*.

pear, therefore, that Dickens feels a certain uneasiness about identifying with these troubled night walkers. When the mysterious first-person narrator remarks that Nell's grandfather's nocturnal wandering
"only became the more impenetrable, in proportion as I sought to
solve it" (OCS, 55), he is defining the fundamental concealment of the
novel as a whole. Here we seem to hear Dickens' own reflection on the
mysterious compulsion that sends him into the streets. The revelation
that the old man is actually en route to the gambling tables does
nothing to clear up the abiding mystery. For the fact is that the narrator himself, whoever he is, is similarly compelled to walk, and his
unnamed obsession has nothing to do with gambling, nor can we
believe that it is due simply to his love of the sound of footsteps.

It is well known that in depicting the death of Little Nell, Dickens
experienced a repetition of the traumatic grief he felt at the death of his
sister-in-law, Mary Hogarth, in May of 1837. "The old wounds" that,
as he told Forster, "bleed afresh" as he writes the death scene[25] cannot
be separated from those "many and mortal wounds" of which Chesterton spoke in connection with Dickens' childhood. The writing of
Nell's death scene simply underlines the already obvious point that for
Dickens the work of remembrance was not restorative; quite to the
contrary, it was traumatic. Every effort to master the compulsive memories of loss and abandonment seems only to have increased the intensity of the compulsion. Nell, says the first-person narrator, "seemed to
exist in a kind of allegory," which he would have missed entirely had it
not been "for the heaps of fantastic things I had seen huddled together
in the curiosity-dealer's warehouse. These, crowding upon my mind, in
connection with the child, and gathering round her, as it were, brought
her condition palpably before me" (OCS, 56). The allegory is of course
that of the Christ-Child in the manger at the Adoration, and Little
Nell's pilgrimage, suffering, and death present a transparent version of
a secular Calvary. Dickens' most interesting twist in the presentation of
Little Nell lies in her very name, for her fate is already inscribed in the
pun Little *Knell*. Like the curiosities that surround her, Nell herself has
a clearly defined destiny. Dickens was doing much more than simply
playing on the Christian piety of his audience; he was also defining his
vocation as an artist as the commemoration of the dead. Like an

25. *The Letters of Charles Dickens*, ed. Madeline House and Graham Storey, 5 vols.
(Oxford: Clarendon Press, 1965–), 2:181–82.

analyst ministering to himself, Dickens in *The Old Curiosity Shop* reconstructs the primal scene of his own deepest anguish. In the act of sounding the knell that only he could hear, he confronted the most impenetrable mystery in his existence.

The figure of Time makes its appearance late in the novel, in the scene where the old sexton leads Nell to a subterranean well in the church crypt, "in a dim and murky spot" that stands at the mysterious center of the novel. The well is a veritable abyss that both Nell and the sexton agree "looks like a grave itself." "I have often had the fancy" observes the sexton, "that it might have been dug at first to make the old place more gloomy, and the monks more religious. It's to be closed up, and built over" (*OCS*, 511). Like a "no thoroughfare" in a London back street, this fanciful *memento mori* is about to be covered over, concealed, renovated, rebuilt. Like Nell's, its knell is about to be rung. The allegory is plain enough: Nell is looking into the abyss of death under the watchful eye of Old Time himself. Here it is the grave rather than Chronos that will do the swallowing. Daniel Maclise's well-known illustration of the scene helps to make even more apparent the connection between the sexton's dangerous abyss, into which he is fearful Nell might fall ("lest you should stumble and fall in"), and the figure of Saturn-Chronos. Alexander Welsh remarks of the drawing, "The sexton . . . suggests, with his crutch, the figure of Time."[26] And Jane Cohen reminds us in her excellent study of Dickens' illustrators that Maclise's drawing appears in the first edition of the novel immediately after the words, "The child complied and gazed down into the pit" and is followed on the page by the words, "It looks a grave itself"; thus Dickens' text literally becomes a legend to the emblem of Old Time. Cohen also notes that Dickens suggested including an hourglass in the drawing, but Maclise protested that that would be overdoing it, and Dickens pressed him no further.[27]

Dickens himself is quite explicit about the pun on Nell's name, and as might be expected, he allows the novel's trickster, Dick Swiveller, to make the point for him. Twice, in connection with Swiveller, Dickens cites a line from *The Merchant of Venice:* "Let us all ring fancy's knell" (3.2.70). The first occasion is early in the novel when Swiveller

26. Alexander Welsh, *The City of Dickens* (Oxford: Clarendon Press, 1971), 206.

27. Jane R. Cohen, *Charles Dickens and His Original Illustrators* (Columbus: Ohio State University Press, 1980), 165.

vists the shop hoping to woo Nell, who he believes will be a rich
heiress. But Nell and her grandfather have already left on their fateful
pilgrimage, and Swiveller disappointedly quips, "Let us go ring fancy's
knell" (*OCS*, 224). The second occasion is right after the funereal
scene in the church crypt. We are once again back in London. Dickens
writes that the ringing of a doorbell sounded peculiar just then in
Swiveller's ears; it sounded like, "if we may adopt the sound to his
then humour, a knell" (*OCS*, 514). It would seem that like Oscar
Wilde, Dickens himself could not read *The Old Curiosity Shop* without laughing. Despite his genuine melancholy, he could nevertheless
laugh at the curiously morbid turn of his fancy. He clearly recognized
how crucial these feelings of remorse and the uncanny were to his
creativity. His linguistic exuberance with regard to Nell's name plainly
reveals the delight he also takes in elaborating the impenetrable mystery that the work of remembrance had become for him. What Dickens
says of the old bachelor who comes to Nell's aid late in the novel is true
of himself: "He was not one of those rough spirits who would strip fair
Truth of every little shadowy vestment in which time and teeming
fancies love to array her" (*OCS*, 496). The truth of one's relation to the
otherness of one's incorporated memories can only ever appear
through the figure of concealment. In *The Old Curiosity Shop*, Dickens
recognized the disfiguration that is inherent in every figure, and the
concealment that characterizes every revelation.

  In *Barnaby Rudge* (1841), part of which was composed contempo-
raneously with *The Old Curiosity Shop*, Dickens rings not fancy's but
"the murderer's knell."[28] The "remorseless toll" on the village bell for
Little Nell (*OCS*, 657) becomes in *Barnaby Rudge* the tocsin or alarm
bell rung in London during the Gordon Riots of 1780. The death knell
becomes the tocsin. Dickens believed that *Barnaby Rudge* signaled the
emergence of his radical politics. "By Jove how radical I am getting,"
he wrote to Forster in August 1841. "I wax stronger and stronger in
the true principles every day."[29] But if Dickens believed he was demonstrating his solidarity with the Chartists, whose agitations dominated
the political scene in 1841, he certainly had an odd way of showing it,
for he depicts the Gordon Riots and the Bastille-like raid on Newgate

  28. Charles Dickens, *Barnaby Rudge*, ed. Gordon Spence (Harmondsworth: Penguin, 1973), 589. Herafter cited in the text as *BR*.
  29. Cited in Norman Mackenzie and Jeanne Mackenzie, *Dickens: A Life* (New
York: Oxford University Press, 1979), 104.

Prison as the work of a collective and motiveless madness. More precisely, Dickens links Rudge's private madness and guilt at the murder of his master, years before, to the public madness of the rioters. Though Dickens may have thought he was furthering radical principles, his text is an unabashedly reactionary tract. As Gordon Spence remarks in the introduction to his edition of the novel, Dickens' "imaginative sympathy, necessary for artistic creation, is combined with a recoil in horror from 'the rabble's unappeasable and maniac rage,' and this combination of opposing emotions gives a peculiar tension to Dickens's description of the riots" (*BR*, 29).

What is radical in *Barnaby Rudge* is not its politics but the way it reduces the logic of revolution to the etiology of an individual neurosis. It is through the tolling of the tocsin that Dickens stages this reduction. The primal scene of the novel is Rudge's murder of his master, Reuben Haredale, who is slain just as he grasps the bell rope and has begun to sound the alarm. The significance of this primal scene becomes particularly evident when we recall that it takes place in Haredale's estate, which is called the *Warren*. Dickens' covert allusion here to his primal scene at Warren's Blacking underlines the structural role that the murder will play in the novel as the principle of repetition. The murder at the Warren haunts Rudge just as Warren's haunts Dickens. The return of the repressed occurs when Rudge hears the tocsin during the riots and falls into a "visionary" state. To him the bell speaks "the language of the dead"; "the Bell tolled on and on and seemed to follow him" (*BR*, 504). Rushing madly through the riot-torn streets, through byways and thoroughfares, Rudge finds that for him there is no escape from the memories of his tortured conscience: "What hunt of spectres could surpass that dread pursuit and flight! Had there been a legion of them on his track, he would have better borne it. There would have been a beginning and an end, but here all space was full. The one pursuing voice was everywhere." Dickens has discovered the creative uses to which his own agonizing experience of remembrance could be put. The "remorseless toll" of *The Old Curiosity Shop* has become "the remorseless crying of that awful voice" of the tocsin in *Barnaby Rudge,* and Dickens could doubtless hear in both the remorseless voice of his own memories.[30] Rudge continues to hear the toll even after it has ceased because "the

30. With respect to the influence that Poe and Dickens had on each other, no text is more revealing than *Barnaby Rudge*. Poe wrote two reviews of the novel; in the first, he successfully guessed the novel's denouement on the basis of only three installments. Poe

knell was at his heart." Dickens' ambivalence in *The Old Curiosity Shop* about identifying with the nerve-racked night walkers has here become a full-scale identification: though Dickens is a victim and Rudge a criminal, *Barnaby Rudge* signals Dickens' recognition that in their suffering they are alike. This recognition will be one of the most important leitmotifs in his subsequent novels. It is this profound identification with the conscience of the criminal that constitutes the true radicality of *Barnaby Rudge*.

In *Martin Chuzzlewit* (1844), Dickens intensifies his focus on the tortures of conscience. Jonas Chuzzlewit's crime is not simply murder but parricide. Instead of the tocsin or death knell, Dickens here pursues the figure of the "veil" in order to describe the way memories enclose and wrap around the recollecting self. The schizophrenic Sairey Gamp is the vehicle of Dickens' verbal wit in *Chuzzlewit*. Through her inimitable discourse Dickens transforms London itself into a kind of monstrous Leviathan; the streets become part of the digestive apparatus of a gigantic saturnine figure that is very much like a whale. In Sairey's imaginary alter ego, whom she calls Mrs. Harris, Dickens takes the notion of an incorporated other to its obvious extreme. The resulting doubleness of Sairey's discourse is expressed above all in her penchant for the phrase "What a blessed thing is this vale of a life," which in her

---

particularly objected to Dickens' "error of *exaggerating anticipation*," by which he meant the failure to keep the reader guessing about the murder. Poe singled out Barnaby's pet raven as a means by which Dickens might have avoided being too obvious: "The raven . . . might have been made, more than we now see it, a portion of the conception of the fantastic Barnaby. Its croakings might have been *prophetically* heard in the course of the drama. Its character might have performed, in regard to that of the idiot [Barnaby], much the same part as does, in music, the accompaniment in respect to the air." It was three years later in his own famous poem that Poe reinvented the Dickensian raven by "making him emblematical of *Mournful and Never-ending Remembrance.*" See Edgar Allan Poe, *Essays and Reviews*, ed. G. R. Thompson (New York: Library of America, 1984), 239, 243, 25. The final quotation is from "The Philosophy of Composition" (1846), in which Poe describes how he wrote "The Raven"—without, however, mentioning Dickens. Dickens doubtless recognized that Poe had grasped the essence of Dickens' own world or, more precisely, that their two worlds intersected on the question of "*Mournful and Never-ending Remembrance.*" In 1850, Dickens had David Copperfield reflect upon his fateful parting from his friend Steerforth with the familiar refrain from "The Raven": "Never more, oh God forgive you, Steerforth! to touch that passive hand in love and friendship. Never, never, more!" (*David Copperfield*, ed. Trevor Blount [Harmondsworth: Penguin, 1966], 498). We might also note that these words, which conclude ch. 29, were written in early 1850 and appeared in the February installment of the novel. Since Poe died in October 1849, we might regard David's farewell to Steerforth as Dickens' tribute to Poe.

Cockney accent becomes this "wale of a life."[31] This mispronuncia-
tion in turn causes her to have an understandable fondness for the
parable of Jonah and the whale. In Sairey's speech the words "vale,"
"veil," "wale," and "whale" become not only homonyms but syn-
onyms. Dickens uses the slippage of the signifier in Sairey's speech to
link conscience or recollection casting a deadly *veil* over consciousness
with the parable of Jonah being swallowed by the *whale*. The work of
remembrance has here become both an enclosing veil and a devouring
whale.

As she watches the evil Jonas board a vessel in an effort to flee
England and a host of troubles, Sairey says that she hopes the ship ends
up in "Jonadge's belly," obviously confounding, as Dickens notes,
"the prophet with the whale in this miraculous aspiration." Though
Jonas's flight is thwarted, Sairey's wish is fulfilled on the figurative
level of the devouring conscience. Describing Jonas as he is about to
commit yet another murder, this time to silence a blackmailer, Dickens
writes: "It may be (as it *has* been) that a shadowy veil was dropping
round him, closing out all his thoughts but the presentiment and vague
fore-knowledge of impending doom" (*MC*, 800). The veil/whale has
been closing around him since the novel's beginning. And of course the
setting for the final moment of irreversible enclosure is (how could it be
otherwise?) the streets. Making his way to his murderous rendezvous
by way of "a narrow covered passage or blind alley . . . not much in
use as a thoroughfare at any hour," and passing through "great
crowds . . . rushing down an interminable perspective" (*MC*, 795,
798), Jonas is simultaneously devoured by conscience and the streets.
Having murdered the blackmailer, Jonas "became in a manner his own
ghost and phantom, and was at once the haunting spirit and the haunted man" (*MC*, 804). Dickens has learned to make the night walker's
phantasies the central focus of his fiction.

As Manchester Buildings was the consummate image of *Nicholas
Nickleby*, Todgers' lodging house stands at the center of the labyrinth
that is *Martin Chuzzlewit*: "Todgers's was in a labyrinth, whereof the
mystery was known but to a chosen few." Near the river and not far
from Monument Yard, one enters, in the neighborhood around
Todgers', a mysterious archaic world. To walk near Todgers' is to

31. Charles Dickens, *Martin Chuzzlewit*, ed. P. N. Furbank (Harmondsworth: Penguin, 1968), 480, 699, 828. Hereafter cited in the text as *MC*.

experience the "no thoroughfare" structure in its purest form. Here one is devoured not by conscience but by its most phantasmagoric expression, the city itself; "A kind of resigned distraction came over the stranger as he trod these devious mazes, and, giving himself up for lost, went in and out and round about and quietly turned back again when he came to a dead wall or was stopped by an iron railing, and felt that the means of escape might possibly present themselves in their own good time, but that to anticipate them was hopeless." In the following passage, which brings the preceding remarks to their conclusion, Dickens transforms the inanimate back streets of London into a living, breathing prehistoric monster:

> Among the narrow thoroughfares at hand, there lingered, here and there, an ancient doorway of carved oak, from which, of old, the sounds of revelry and feasting often came; but now these mansions, only used for storehouses, were dark and dull, and being filled with wool, and cotton, and the like—such heavy merchandise as stifles sound and stops the throat of echo—had an air of palpable deadness about them which, added to their silence and desertion, made them very grim. . . . In the throats and maws of dark no-thoroughfares near Todgers's, individual wine-merchants and wholesale dealers in grocery-ware had perfect little towns of their own; and, deep among the foundations of these buildings, the ground was undermined and burrowed out into stables, where cart-horses, troubled by rats, might be heard on a quiet Sunday rattling their halters, as disturbed spirits in tales of haunted houses are said to clank their chains. [MC, 186–87]

Just as Manchester Buildings was concerned with politics, Todgers' is concerned with the London commodity trade. It is the transformation of the old neighborhood into warehouses for the storage of various commodities that has turned the ground around Todgers' into a beast that stifles sound and seems to have devoured life itself. Here is Dickens' bitterest indictment to date of the warehouses in the neighborhood of Warren's Blacking. It is a far more radical political gesture than he may have realized, for what Dickens does here is link the "no thoroughfare" structure to the power of capital itself. The killing, devouring force of Saturn and Old Time is here identified with the accumulation and distribution of commodities. Dickens is attacking the very principle of a capitalist economy. The "throats and maws of the dark no-thoroughfares near Todgers's" constitute one of the most striking dialectical images in the entire Dickens canon because here the very principle of capital formation is figured in terms of the most barbaric prehistoric force.

Between *Martin Chuzzlewit* and *Dombey and Son* (1848), Dickens' experience of the streets seems to have become increasingly more obsessive and anxiety-producing. It was during these years that he began to turn to mesmerism, doubtless in an effort to understand and perhaps rid himself of the memories that oppressed him.[32] Vacationing in Italy after the completion of *Chuzzlewit,* he performed mesmeric cures on his sister-in-law Georgina Hogarth and on Madame de la Rue. One can imagine that Dickens had a special insight into the uncanny dominance that the hypnotist is able to wield over his subject. His experience of his own incorporated other enabled him to appeal with a particular efficacy to the unconscious desires of his "patients." In the hypnotic session he was able to exert over them the same sort of power to which he himself submitted with regard to his own agonizing memories. Knowing the susceptibilities of the conscious self, he knew how to circumvent its watchfulness and place it under his spell. In his mesmeric experiments, as in his writing, he was able to work upon others the same suggestive art of persuasion and domination that had been practiced on him by that "remorseless voice" within. In the difficult years following the crisis of 1839–40, he had come to realize that every effort to flee the voice led to yet another "no thoroughfare."

In *Pictures from Italy* (1847), which collects the essays he wrote on his European sojourn, Dickens remarks that the byways of Lyons in summer were a veritable inferno: "All the little side streets whose name is Legion, were scorching, blistering, and sweltering." In Rome he was struck by a "narrow little throat of street . . . dressed out with flaring lamps."[33] The newly installed gaslamps of Rome remind him of nothing so much as the pathway to hell. This transposition of modernity into prehistory, of modern Rome into the ancient underworld, is of a piece with Dickens' overall effort during the mid-1840s to exorcize the demons of modernity. He wanted to drive out the demons from himself, from his "patients," and from the modern world at large. His frequent use during this period of the phrase "whose name is Legion" is telling in this regard. Its source is the story of a man possessed by

32. Cf. Fred Kaplan, *Dickens and Mesmerism* (Princeton, N.J.: Princeton University Press, 1975).

33. Charles Dickens, *Pictures from Italy,* in *Works,* 16/2:11, 140.

devils (Mark 5:9) who, when Christ asks him his name, responds, "My name is Legion, for there are so many of us." No biblical image speaks more directly to Dickens' dilemma. Like Christ, Dickens wanted to cast out the demons. During the mid 1840s his inability to do so made him increasingly desperate.

Since the word "dickens" is a euphemism for the "devil," one might say that Dickens was trying to escape from the truly proper name that was ready-made within his signature. Writing to Forster from Lausanne in 1846, in a letter that Benjamin cites in "The Paris of the Second Empire in Baudelaire," Dickens complains that he, like his fictional characters, needs the crowd if he is not to become stagnate and unproductive. "I cannot express," he wrote of the streets of London, "how much I want these" (CB, 49).

Forster relates another incident that reveals in much starker terms the extent of Dickens' desperation. In Paris on the night of February 12, 1847, Forster writes, "he seemed troubled with a phantasmagorical belief that all Paris had gathered around us that night on the Rue St. Honoré, and urged him on with frantic shouts."[34] At the time of this incident, Dickens had published only four installments of Dombey and Son. It was in 1847, we should recall, that Dickens wrote and gave to Forster the autobiographical fragment. In Dombey and Son we will see both the persistence of that "remorseless voice" and Dickens' first effort to translate his mesmeric experiments into fictional form.

In Dombey and Son the oral sadism that characterized the saturnine streets of the earlier novels is extended across the entire social spectrum. Dickens here appropriates the image of Saturn-Chronos to depict what Raymond Williams calls "an unprecedented—crowding and rushing—human and social organization."[35] Dickens' response to the capitalist expansion of the late 1840s, which laid the foundation for the prosperity of the 1850s, was to project the image of Time the devourer into the new sign of the times. Dombey and Son was written in the period of the overproduction crisis that culminated in the recession of 1847, which was followed by an extraordinary economic recovery. In his saturnine imagery Dickens registers the complex transformation that England experienced during this period.

34. Forster, *Life of Dickens*, 1:452, n. 1.
35. Raymond Williams, Introduction to Charles Dickens, *Dombey and Son*, ed. Peter Fairclough (Harmondsworth: Penguin, 1970), 29. This novel is cited in the text as *DS*.

The novel opens with a personification of the "remorseless twins," "Time and his brother Care." These two are at work preparing the sorry fate of Dombey's newborn son Paul, whose infant creases are already being smoothed out "with the flat part of [Time's] scythe, as a preparation of the surface for his deeper operations" (*DS*, 49). Swallowing and consuming are the prerogatives of both the father and his trading firm, Dombey and Son. He himself is a kind of Chronos sporting a "very loud ticking" pocket watch. As a result of the expansion in trade and shipbuilding, "all other trades were swallowed up" (*DS*, 179). The expanding railway system is likewise a kind of Saturn that has "swallowed up" the landmarks of a former age (*DS*, 289). London itself, the hub of this unprecedented technological and economic revolution, is figured as a monster who has "swallowed up" countless lives (*DS*, 562).

The devouring zeal that characterizes the collective experience of the age is no less true of personal relationships. Here it will suffice to deal with only the most egregious example of the predatory capitalist. The figuration of *Dombey and Son* reaches its apotheosis in the character of Carker, Dombey's business manager, who not only runs off with Dombey's wife but is responsible for bringing the firm to bankruptcy. Dickens himself reminds us that the name Carker comes from the Middle English "cark"—which means "to worry" or "to care"— when he alludes to the "carking anxieties" (*DS*, 208) that afflict the denizens of the Dombey world. Dickens told Forster that he wrote *Dombey* in a time "full of disquietude and anxiety."[36] In the character of Carker this "disquietude" is translated into a nightmarish distortion of humanity. More precisely, it is through the figure of Carker's mouth and teeth that the menacing anxieties of the age come most sharply into focus. They are figures for the hypnotic and destructive power of capital over individuals and over society at large. The consummate image of *Dombey and Son* is that of Carker as he rushes, "with his gleaming teeth, through the dark rooms like a mouth" (*DS*, 852). When Carker parts his lips, which are as elastic as "India rubber," what he reveals are "two unbroken rows of glistening teeth, whose regularity and whiteness were quite distressing" (*DS*, 239). They are the fetish object par excellence. They embody the secret mystery of both his sexual and his economic power. More interestingly still, they

36. Forster, *Life of Dickens*, 1:423.

literally have a hypnotic effect upon the others. They are the key to his apparent managerial skill, and they enable him to weave a spell over certain susceptible individuals such as Rob the Grinder, who, in a kind of magnetic stupor, does Carker's bidding.

But it is their effect upon Dombey's wife, Edith, that is most interesting of all. Edith is strangely the one most alert and most vulnerable to the mesmeric power of Carker's orality: "She raised her eyes no higher than his mouth, but she saw the means of mischief vaunted in every tooth it contained" (DS, 610). Her everlastingly heaving "milk white" bosom seems from the novel's beginning to be the inevitable destination of Carker's "worrying" teeth. Though Dickens teases us into anticipating that Carker's oral sadism will eventually regress to its most primordial object, he never lets Carker go all the way. We are finally less interested in whether or not Edith will go to bed with him, which she does not, than whether or not he will bite her always conveniently available breasts. In his essay on the "Oral Dickens," Ian Watt also notes the sublimated violence of this aspect of the text. Moreover, he points out that "it was only because of Lord Jeffrey's objection that Dickens did not . . . allow Carker to sink his ever-bared teeth into Edith's white breasts."[37] One wishes Lord Jeffrey had stayed out of it. Like Poe and his Egaeus, who is obsessed with Berenice's "excessively white [teeth], with the pale lips writhing about them, as in the very moment of their first terrible development,"[38] Dickens, with more than a little humor and spite, projects his anxieties upon Carker's phantasmagoric mouth.

Dickens stages the overcoming of these anxieties in the scene where Carker is annihilated by a speeding locomotive, "whirled away upon a jagged mill, that spun him round and round, and struck him limb from limb, and licked his stream of life up with its fiery heat, and cast his mutilated fragments in the air" (DS, 875). Such a histrionic fate belies the gravity of Carker's menace. Dickens is here rewriting Teufelsdröckh's dystopian vision of the universe as "one huge, dead, immeasurable steam-engine, rolling on, in its dead indifference, to grind me limb from limb. O, the vast, gloomy, solitary Golgotha and Mill of

---

37. Ian Watt, "Oral Dickens," *Dickens Studies Annual*, vol. 3, ed. Robert B. Partlow, Jr. (Carbondale: Southern Illinois University Press, 1974), 178.

38. Edgar Allan Poe, *Collected Works*, ed. Thomas Mabbot, 3 vols. (Cambridge, Mass.: Belknap/Harvard University Press, 1978), 2:215.

Death."[39] Carlyle's "Mill of Death," with its possibly ungenerous allusion to J. S. Mill's utilitarianism, becomes Dickens' "jagged mill," which, like the blade Jupiter used to castrate his devouring father Saturn, here cuts down the oppressive force of capital. Or so Dickens would have us believe, for the question is whether it is the economic system that must be changed or merely the villains into whose hands that system has unfortunately fallen. On reading the recently published *Dombey and Son* and *Vanity Fair*, Carlyle was disappointed: "Not *reapers* they, either of them. In fact, the business of rope-dancing goes to a great height."[40] Carlyle must have recognized that *Dombey*'s conclusion is only a sentimental evasion of the problems the text presents. The dismantling and reconstruction of the Dombey family, which is the fundamental task of the narrative, simply enables a new group of capitalists to enter the field after the larger-than-life figures of an earlier epoch have been disposed of. The economic and political system is left untouched, and this despite all of Dickens' rumblings about the rapacity of unrestrained capitalist expansion. Completed in April 1848, while the Continent was rocked by revolution, *Dombey and Son* clearly reveals why the forces of counterrevolution were able to win in England without a fight, for the radicals themselves, like Dickens, did not focus upon concrete economic and political changes. In *Dombey and Son*, Dickens managed both to rail against social injustice and to defend the status quo. Here too perhaps lies part of the secret of his great success with his audience.

Raymond Williams notes that it is not until "after 1850, when most of the society became more settled, more confident, more optimistic of reasonable change, [that] Dickens became harsher, more disturbed and questioning, more uncertain of any foreseeable outcome" (*DS*, 30). As we have seen, however, the "no thoroughfare" structure was already there; it had been hidden at the dark center of the Dickens world since 1839. It is more precisely the case that it is not until after 1848–50 that the impasse, which had been so effectively concealed, is finally brought to the surface. What Dickens reveals then is the fundamental concealment that has been the motive force of his work for a decade.

Dickens' post-1848 dilemma is well described by Monroe Engel:

39. Carlyle, *Sartor Resartus*, 164.
40. Cited in Charles Richard Saunders, *Carlyle's Friendships and Other Studies* (Durham, N.C.: Duke University Press, 1977), 242.

"This is the dejection of a man who sees life bound in the rigor mortis of an old dead system, yet cannot reconcile himself to any violent breaking free."[41] Though he was antagonistic to the political structure, to the class structure and the economic oppression on which it depended, Dickens was unwilling to commit himself to any program of reform. Unlike Marx, who bided his time during the 1850s and waited for the right time to act—which came in 1864 with the founding of the International Workingmen's Association—Dickens had from the beginning placed himself not on the margins of politics, but completely above politics. The dust heaps in *Our Mutual Friend* (1865) are Dickens' figure for the Houses of Parliament and the refuse they produce. In a letter of July 3, 1850, on the subject of the death of Sir Robert Peel, Dickens wrote: "He was a man of merit who could ill be spared from the Great Dust Heap down at Westminster."[42] For Dickens all politics were tainted. He approved of Peel's laissez-faire policies because they at least approximated his own apolitical thinking. In seeking, like Carlyle, not political or economic remedies but personal conversions, revolutions of the head and heart rather than of the marketplace or the assembly hall, Dickens became vulnerable to all sorts of idealizing political mystagogues. As a bridge to my reading of *David Copperfield* (1850) and the later Dickens, I am going to turn to an exemplary incident that demonstrates the price Dickens paid for his political naiveté. This incident has the additional advantage of enabling us to link Dickens directly to the Marx of the 1850s.

In November 1850, just as the last installment of *David Copperfield* appeared, Dickens wrote an article for *Household Words* about a certain Dr. Gottfried Kinkel, who in 1848 had been a professor of theology at the University of Bonn but who now languished in a Prussian prison under a life sentence for his participation in the uprising of the spring of 1848. Dickens' purpose is to win sympathy for the much-maligned Professor Kinkel, who was clearly the victim of the hysterical atmosphere of the Prussian reaction to the events of 1848. Dickens hopes that his article will persuade men of good conscience to inter-

41. Monroe Engel, *The Maturity of Dickens* (Cambridge, Mass.: Harvard University Press, 1959), 42. Also see George Orwell's classic remarks on Dickens' political prepossessions in "Charles Dickens" (1940) in his *Collected Essays, Journalism and Letters,* ed. Sonia Orwell and Ian Angus, 4 vols. (New York: Harcourt, Brace & World, 1968), 1:413–60.

42. *Letters of Charles Dickens*, ed. Walter Dexter, 3 vols. (Bloomsbury: Nonesuch Press, 1938), 2:220–21.

vene on Kinkel's behalf and petition the Prussian government to allow Kinkel "permission to emigrate to England or America."[43]

There is certainly nothing objectionable about Dickens' humanitarian concern in the case; as he observes, the Prussian government had plainly decided to make Kinkel an example to other middle-class intellectuals. What is objectionable is Dickens' uncritical celebration of Kinkel as the very spirit of the liberal conscience. He was not alone in falling under the professor's spell; many radicals regarded Kinkel as the incarnation of the spirit of the revolution. It was in order to dispel such delusions that Marx and Engels wrote a book entitled *The Great Men of the Exile,* the first third of which is given over to a scathing indictment of Kinkel and everything he represents. This work was written in 1852 but was not published until the twentieth century. What Marx found most objectionable about the widespread sympathy for Kinkel was that it created a romantic and highly sentimental misconception of the revolution. It is in this respect that Dickens' article is particularly culpable. He presents us with a vision of Kinkel "in sackcloth, with shaven head, and attenuated frame . . . spinning his last threads." Dickens seems to have seen in Kinkel an image of the selfless patriot he himself would like to have been:

> He sides with the Left, or democratic party; he advocates the cause of the oppressed people and the poor; he argues manfully and perseveringly the real interests of all governments, in granting a rational amount of liberty, showing that in the present stage of the moral world, it is the only thing to prevent violence, and to secure good order. His speeches breathe a prophetic spirit.[44]

One would never guess from Dickens' account that Kinkel was a supposed revolutionary. Dickens makes him out to be something very close to a conservative Englishman, rather like himself beneath all his radical prattle. I do not know whether Dickens read Kinkel's speeches, but Marx did, and he quotes from them extensively. Far from the "prophetic spirit" Dickens appears to have heard there, Marx reveals a ridiculous poseur whose writing was filled with theological bombast and political nonsense. Dickens goes on to assure his readers that

43. Charles Dickens, "Gottfried Kinkel: A Life in Three Pictures," in Karl Marx, *The Cologne Communist Trial,* ed. Rodney Livingstone (New York: International Publishers, 1971), 285.

44. Dickens, "Gottfried Kinkel," 282.

Kinkel had nothing to do with "red republicanism" and that he had joined the revolution only in order to secure for Prussia "a constitutional monarchy, like ours in England," adding enigmatically, "with such improvements as ours manifestly needs."

A few weeks after the appearance of Dickens' article, Kinkel escaped from prison and fled to England, where he visited Dickens. His escape sent a shock wave through the Prussian government. In his introduction to Marx's *Cologne Communist Trial*, Rodney Livingstone demonstrates that the escape of the celebrated Kinkel was a key factor in the government's decision to launch its conspiracy against the Communist League.[45] The Prussians needed another scapegoat, and with Kinkel safe in England, the Communists would have to do. Livingstone cites a letter from King Frederick Wilhelm IV to his prime minister, expressing his fears for the survival of the government now that Kinkel was once again on the loose. It is indeed preposterous that the harmless professor should have sent fear and trembling into the hearts of the Prussian ruling class. It was in order to demystify the similarly hysterical atmosphere that Kinkel inspired among many of the revolutionaries themselves that Marx satirized him in *The Great Men of the Exile*.

In Marx's close stylistic analysis of his speeches, Kinkel emerges as a politico-theological pundit whose rhetorical technique is that of the blustering "*rodomontade*." Marx writes that Kinkel's method was to inspire his students to righteousness by endowing "every little occurrence in his theologico-lyrical past" with prophetic significance.[46] Marx points to passages where Kinkel alternately imagines that he is Noah, Elijah, even Christ. Marx on Kinkel resembles nothing so much as Swift's *Tale of a Tub*, where the rhetoric of enthusiasm is unmasked as the hideously self-indulgent farce it is. Kinkel's pietistic posturing helped to send the revolution in the wrong direction, and it is a sign of Dickens' political naiveté that he was so easily fooled. More alarming still, Kinkel's fundamentally apolitical brand of messianic Christianity was perhaps the alternative Dickens seriously preferred to politics of any sort, radical or otherwise. Like Kinkel, Dickens was more concerned with professions of Christian sympathy for the poor than he

45. Rodney Livingstone, Introduction, to Marx, *The Cologne Communist Trial*, 18–19.

46. Karl Marx and Frederick Engels, *The Great Men of the Exile*, in Marx/Engels, *Collected Works*, 20 vols. (New York: International Publishers, 1975–), 11:231 n. 1.

was with concrete strategies. That Dickens should have turned to Gottfried Kinkel indicates that he was in search not of a political strategy but of a messianic revelation. In his later works Dickens depicts a world so depraved, so fallen, so far beyond the pale of political remedies that only a redeemer could save it. He constructs a muddle so dark and unreadable, a labyrinth so inescapable and defeating that it could be illuminated only by the sudden flashes of what Benjamin calls "chips of Messianic time" (*I*, 263). Dickens' admiration of Kinkel's "prophetic spirit" is finally an indication of the depth of his own political despair. In the later Dickens the personal experience of the "no thoroughfare" has become the structure of historical experience in the modern world.

Mr. Micawber anticipates the task of the *Passage Work* when he offers to assist young Copperfield in "penetrating the arcana of the modern Babylon" that was London in the 1820s.[47] Copperfield's penetration into the dark heart of the city culminates late in the novel when, in an effort to find Emily, David and Peggotty follow her friend, the prostitute Martha Endell, into a neighborhood that was "as oppressive, sad, and solitary by night, as any about London" (*DC*, 747). David calls this chapter his "night-picture," and it is indeed a Dantean vision: amidst the corruption of "strange objects, accumulated by some speculator," the riverside has been transformed into a "melancholy waste," where everything has "gradually decomposed into that nightmare condition, out of the overflowings of the polluted stream" (*DC*, 748). This is where Martha has come to end her life. Like Benjamin, David is led by the prostitute into a virtually undiscovered part of the city. It is only after having reached this dark center of urban indifference that the novel's work of reparation can begin. Martha is saved, and Emily is recovered soon afterward. Here in the ebb tide where the Thames has become the River Styx, David learns that despair is the inability to forget. In the blighted stream that "creeps through the dismal streets, defiled and miserable," Martha sees an image of herself: "I know it's like me." "I have never," writes David, "known what despair was, except in the tone of those words." What Martha says of the river, "I can't forget it. It haunts me day and night," is what David feels about his ignominious past at Murdstone and

---

47. Dickens, *David Copperfield*, 211. References in the text to *DC* are to page numbers of the edition cited in n. 30.

Grinby's, and it is what Dickens had written of Warren's in the 1847 fragment.

The inability to forget is the great theme of *David Copperfield*. It is what compelled Dickens to restage what I am calling his primal scene in each of his novels after 1839. It is what compelled him to write the 1847 fragment, which in turn he elaborated into *David Copperfield*. We have already considered Martha Endell; besides David himself, I will also want to look closely at the character of Rosa Dartle. In each of them Dickens examines a different response to the pain of memory.

David's experience of the work of remembrance can be best presented in an early scene where he visits Micawber, who has been imprisoned for debt. Micawber is trying to be something of a politician in this scene, for he has organized the debtors to sign a petition "for an alteration in the law of imprisonment for debt." The futility of the gesture is what David finds most affecting. As he describes the prisoners filing past to sign the petition, David stops to wonder whether in the act of recollecting and writing the scene he has not sentimentalized the strange and sordid pathos it actually represents:

> I set down this remembrance here, because it is an instance to myself of the manner in which I fitted my old books to my altered life, and made stories for myself out of the streets, and out of men and women; and how some main points in the character I shall unconsciously develop, I suppose, in writing my life, were gradually forming all this while. . . . When my thoughts go back now to the slow agony of my youth, I wonder how much of the histories I invented for such people hangs like a mist of fancy over well-remembered facts! When I tread the old ground, I do not wonder that I seem to see and pity, going on before me, an innocent romantic boy, making his imaginative world out of such strange experiences and sordid things. [*DC*, 224–25]

Dickens discovers in this extraordinary passage what Freud discovered in the 1890s when he noticed that the patient's ability to see him- or herself in the recollected scene called into question the legitimacy of the scene and offered an opportunity for the analyst to uncover other displacements and repressions. Dickens discovers further that no recollection can proceed beyond the "mist of fancy" that hangs over the ostensibly "well-remembered facts." For David, the work of remembrance is never pure; it is always derivative, already woven into the fabric of the books he has read, in this case the prison scenes in the novels of Defoe, Fielding, and Smollett. In recognizing that in the very act of writing, something is always developing "unconsciously," David recognizes and reveals the fundamental concealment, the insurmountable unreadability, at work in the act of writing and remembering.

There is another element in this passage that we have not touched on before. It is related to the growing suspicion in the later Dickens that writing itself is tainted, that a life of writing, like a political life, is a charade, a ghastly pretense without meaning or truth. David's recognition here that his memories are unreliable, and that something is always at work that makes the determination of the literal truth difficult if not impossible, is the first step in a process that will continue to intensify throughout the last twenty years of Dickens' life and will culminate in Boffin's preposterous charade as a miser in *Our Mutual Friend* and in the enigmas of *The Mystery of Edwin Drood*. David's recognition here marks an inevitably reflexive extension of the "no thoroughfare" structure to the act of composition itself. Dickens, who had long identified with the criminal, will soon see his own work as essentially criminal, for like the criminal the writer steals, misrepresents, and hoards; even worse, like an insane criminal he often perpetrates these crimes unconsciously, without even knowing what he is doing. Like those of the prisoners filing by to sign Micawber's petition, the writer's signature no longer has any legitimacy whatsoever.

Rosa Dartle is another who cannot forget the "slow agony" of her shame, the shame of having been manipulated and betrayed by Steerforth. Rosa is Dickens' most brilliant sketch of a woman scorned. The scar on her upper lip is the external mark of what David calls "some wasting fire within her." She is disfigured in a way that David finds troubling and impossible to interpret. "She brings everything to a grindstone," Steerforth says of her, "and sharpens it, as she has sharpened her own face and figure these years past. She is all edge" (*DC*, 352). Her pride and her inability to accept disappointment have worn her down. She has in effect put herself to the grindstone of her own conscience. For Rosa, remembrance is destructive and disfiguring. It is through the imagery of the grindstone that we will be able to link Rosa's agonizing experience of recollection to David's.

David's stepfather is named Murdstone, and the firm he owns in London is called Mur*dstone* and *Grin*by's, which contains an anagram of Grindstone. Thinking back to the experience at Warren's Blacking is for Dickens like putting himself to the grindstone. Even Murdstone's eye, like that of several Dickensian villains, is "disfigured . . . by a cast" (DC, 71), which is to say that he possesses the hypnotic power of the evil eye. His effect on David is to disfigure the boy's experience of memory for ever. He takes it upon himself to dull the edge of David's character. Bantering with a friend about his plan to marry David's mother, Murdstone warns his friend to be careful lest David, who is with them, should catch their drift:

> "Quinion," said Mr. Murdstone, "take care, if you please. Some-body's sharp."
> "Who is?" asked the gentleman, laughing.
> "Only Brooks of Sheffield." said Mr. Murdstone. [DC, 72]

Sheffield is the center of the English cutlery industry. Unlike Rosa, however, David does not allow the disfiguring experiences of his past to gnaw away at his very being. The truth for Dickens was somewhere between the two. There is a great deal of Charles Dickens in Rosa Dartle. He would have preferred, no doubt, to have more David Copperfield in him than there actually was.

Chesterton, who understands so well the role of wounding in Dickens, cites a description by Mrs. Carlyle that helps me to make this link between Rosa and her creator. Mrs. Carlyle remarked that Dickens "has a face made of steel":

> This was probably felt in a flash when she saw, in some social crowd, the clear, eager face of Dickens cutting through those near him like a knife. Any people who had met him from year to year would each year have found a man weakly troubled about his worldly decline; and each year they would have found him higher up in the world. His was a character very hard for any man of slow and placable temperament to understand; he was the character whom anybody can hurt and nobody can kill. [CD, 59]

Like Rosa, it seems that Dickens himself was "all edge."

The leitmotif of David's relationship with his stepfather is disfiguration. David's first traumatic experience occurs even before his arrival in London, when, on the occasion of being beaten by Murdstone for no reason whatsoever, David in desperation bites his torturer's hand. Murdstone is temporarily disfigured by the experience, but David is permanently so: "It was only a moment that I stopped him, for he cut me heavily an instant afterwards, and in the same instant I caught the hand with which he held me in my mouth, between my teeth, and bit it through. It sets my teeth on edge to think of it" (*DC,* 108). We will examine the relation between this passage and a very similar scene in Freud's case history of the Rat-Man in the final section of this chapter. Here, however, it is important to note that this scene is David's primal or originary trauma. The content is certainly consistent with Dickens' interest in oral aggression, but more important than the scene itself is David's response to it. What Dickens is describing here, I believe, is the catastrophic effect of painful memories upon the mind of the child. "The fathers have eaten sour grapes, and the children's teeth are set on edge" (Ezekiel 18:2). This is the line that Dickens and his readers would have heard in reading David's account. What Dickens is saying is that the disfiguring effect of painful memories is an experience no less catastrophic than hereditary sin would be. The linkage of these two ideas is itself important, and we will pursue it momentarily in connection with *Little Dorrit.* In *David Copperfield,* the biting scene is the primal scene because it is this incident that disfigures David's experience of memory and his relation to his own past.

The effect of the experience on David is so disruptive that henceforth he cannot "recall how I had felt, and what sort of boy I used to be, before I bit Mr. Murdstone: which I couldn't satisfy myself about by any means, I seemed to have bitten him in such a remote antiquity" (*DC,* 121). David remembers the scene; the Rat-Man cannot. But for both of them the biting scene marks the limits of remembrance and the threshold of prehistory. It is the thought of this humiliating incident that David finds so unbearable that it sends him out of the house: "What walks I took alone, down muddy lanes, in the bad wintry weather, carrying that parlour, and Mr. and Miss Murdstone in it, everywhere: a monstrous load that I was obliged to bear, a daymare that there was no possibility of breaking in, a weight that brooded on my wits, and blunted them" (*DC,* 174). "There's something in his soul," as Claudius says of Hamlet, "O'er which his melancholy sits on brood" (3.1.166–67). The pain of David's memories has "blunted" his purpose. He will never be able to escape his "daymare." But by writing, he will at least be able to sharpen his blunted wits. Like Mr. Dick—whose way of dealing with the memory of a "great disturbance and agitation," "his allegorical way of expressing it" (*DC,* 261), is to write what he calls his King Charles Memorial—David also turns to writing as a way of managing or containing the destructive work of remembrance. Mr. Dick writes about a certain Charles who lost his head; Dickens must write repeatedly about the primal scene in which his experience of life was inalterably disfigured.

George Gissing called *Bleak House* (1853) "a brilliant, admirable, and most righteous satire upon the monstrous iniquity of old Father Antic the Law."[48] Gissing's point is well taken; old Father Antic the Law is the latest guise in which Dickens presents Old Father Time. Dickens told Forster that the motto of the novel should be *Tempus edax rerum*, "Time, devourer of things," because both Chancery and Krook's shop consume everyone and everything they come in contact with:

> *Edax rerum*, the motto of both, but with a difference. Out of the lumber of the shop emerges slowly some fragments of evidence by which the chief actors in the story are sensibly affected, and to which Chancery itself might have succumbed if its devouring capacities had been less complete. But by the time there is found among the lumber the will which puts all to rights in the Jarndyce suit, it is found to be too late to put anything to rights. The costs have swallowed up the estate, and there is an end to the matter.[49]

From Chancery and Krook's to the vampiric lawyer Vholes, who in effect "had swallowed the last morsel of his client,"[50] Richard Carstone, *Bleak House* unveils a world in the process of cannibalizing itself.

Bleak House continues *Copperfield*'s examination of the notion of disfigurement. Here in fact it becomes the organizing principle linking the novel's two narratives, for both Esther Summerson's first-person narrative and the Jeremiad-like third-person narrative are concerned with, respectively, private and public disfigurement. While Esther is literally disfigured after a bout of small pox, the omniscient narrator focuses our attention relentlessly on the disfigurements of the London landscape. What Esther calls "my disfigurement, and my inheritance of shame" (*BH*, 667) refers simply to her bastardy and the ravages that the disease has wrought on her face—ravages that render literal the figurative scars of her illegitimacy. She had caught the contagion from Jo, who brought it from out of the unspeakable world of Tom-all-

48. George Gissing, *The Immortal Dickens* (London: Cecil Palmer, 1925), 225–26.
49. Forster, *Life of Dickens*, 2:115.
50. Charles Dickens, *Bleak House*, ed. Norman Page (Harmondsworth: Penguin, 1971), 924. Hereafter cited in the text as *BH*.

Alone's, where her ill-fated father had spent his last ignominious days. The omniscient narrator surveys the disfigurements of London as he poetically traces a "stream" of moonlight through the "wilderness" of the city. Like David in his "night-picture," he follows the "stream" by houses and bridges "where wharves and shipping make it black and awful, where it winds from those disfigurements through marshes whose grim beacons stand like skeletons washed ashore" (*BH*, 719). Even the moonlight is disfigured in *Bleak House*. The two narratives, despite their radical difference in tone, are finally like the city crowd that rushes by the pathetic Jo "in two streams—everything moving on to some purpose and to one end." And that "one end" is to be consumed in the deadly cycle of voracious possession. Jo's fate is emblematic of that of the *Bleak House* world in general: "At last the fugitive, hard-pressed, takes to a narrow passage, and a court which has no thoroughfare" (*BH*, 687). Like the court in which Jo perishes, Chancery Court is a "no thoroughfare."

During the early and mid-1850s Dickens' experience took on an increasingly somber and morbid cast. These were the years of his father's death and of his divorce. But the forces at work upon Dickens cannot be contained by the notion of the family. During this period his night walks took on a more frantic character than ever before, and he became dangerously obsessed with death and corpses, as evidenced by his regular pilgrimages to the Paris Morgue.[51] The culmination of Dickens' most melancholy, most insomniac years to that date was of course *Little Dorrit* (1857). "There is no denying," writes Chesterton, "that this is Dickens' dark moment. . . . He did what all really happy men have done: he descended into Hell."[52] *Little Dorrit,* argues Chesterton, is about the terrible similarity between "ancient Calvinism and modern Evolutionism," for both deny the possibility of human freedom. It is to this awful thought that Chesterton believes Dickens succumbed in *Little Dorrit,* and he is right. In Arthur Clennam, Dickens pursued once more a narrative of a man who suffers for the fault of another. In the shadow that Mrs. Clennam casts on her hus-

51. Cf. Robert Newsome, *Dickens and the Romantic Side of Familiar Things: Bleak House and the Novel Tradition* (New York: Columbia University Press, 1977); and Albert D. Hutter, "The Novelist as Resurrectionist: Dickens and the Dilemma of Death," *Dickens Studies Annual: Essays on Victorian Fiction,* ed. Michael Timko et al. (New York: AMS Press, 1983).
52. Chesterton, *Appreciations and Criticisms,* 187.

band's illegitimate son, Dickens projected yet one more version of the destructive work of remembrance. Mrs. Clennam is Rosa Dartle grown old and sadistic. So injured is she by her husband's infidelity that she makes his bastard feel as though his life is under an incomprehensible shadow. In Mrs. Clennam the work of remembrance has become destructive as never before in Dickens. The past is twisted into unrecognizability. She misreads and distorts the past so radically that there is no longer any way to retrace origins or even approximate the legitimacy of memory. Moreover, in Arthur she has raised an individual who is so perfectly conditioned by her Calvinist teaching that he never questions the impenetrable mysteries that surround him but accepts them as being quite natural, no matter how painful. Arthur's misreading of his dilemma, like Mrs. Clennam's misreading of her husband's reminder to share his estate with his mistress's family, is finally of a piece with the infinite deferrals and delays of the Circumlocution Office. In *Little Dorrit,* absolutely everything has become an allegory; there is no way out of the destructive figures of twisted memory into the literal truth of history. Dickens' lesson in *Little Dorrit* is that when memory has been undermined utterly and irreversibly, there is no longer any freedom.

After *David Copperfield,* Dickens began to lose hope of ever overcoming the destructive effects of remembrance and even of the ability of writing to contain those effects. He began, in other words, to lose faith in the legitimacy of the constructions he had made of the world and of his experience. In *Bleak House* and *Little Dorrit* the process of deterioration became rampant. By the time of *Little Dorrit,* Dickens felt as though he had completely slipped out of history into allegory. His feeling was precisely what Benjamin describes with regard to Baudelaire's experience of urban *spleen,* the experience of losing the capacity for experience:

> The big-city dweller knows this feeling on Sundays; Baudelaire has it *avant la lettre* in one of his *Spleen* poems:
>> Suddenly bells leap forth with fury,
>> Hurling a hideous howling to the sky,
>> Like wandering and homeless spirits
>> Who break into stubborn wailing.
> The bells, which once were part of holidays, have been dropped from the calendar, like human beings. They are like the poor souls that wander restlessly, but outside of history. [I, 184–85]

Baudelaire's experience of a Parisian Sunday in 1857 is echoed by Dickens' account of Arthur's experience of a contemporaneous London Sunday: "In every thoroughfare, up almost every alley, and down almost every turning, some doleful bell was throbbing, jerking, tolling, as if the Plague were in the city and the dead-carts were going round."[53] As always in Dickens, the resulting anxiety is registered in a vista of the streets: "Nothing to see but streets, streets, streets. Nothing to breathe but streets, streets, streets." Into the city dweller's experience of the tolling of bells on a Sunday, Dickens projects the experience of his night walks, the experience he has projected at least since *Barnaby Rudge:* "There was a Legion of Sundays, all days of unserviceable bitterness and mortification, slowly passing before him" (*LD*, 69). In *Little Dorrit* the experience of the modern city gives way to the archaic sensation of the "eternal return."

Little Dorrit is full of "no thoroughfares," both literal and figurative, from Mrs. Gowan's parlour at Hampton Court to Casby's London residence (e.g., *LD*, 70, 185, 359). In this novel the clanking machinery of the plot is louder than ever, which is the clearest indication of the lengths to which Dickens must go in order to stage the denouement. Through his reliance on the preposterous codicil to Gilbert Clennam's will, Dickens makes appallingly apparent just how desperate he is in the "no thoroughfare" that is *Little Dorrit*. His terrible recognition here is that the novel has become an extension of the world it vilifies, that like the bureaucrats of the Circumlocution Office, he too has become accustomed to a life lived in the "howling labyrinths of sentences" (*LD*, 458).

The "clicking" sound of a clock or of a trap closing is the key to Dickens' analysis of the work of remembrance in *Great Expectations* (1861). "Something clicked in his throat," writes Pip of Magwitch, "as if he had works in him like a clock, and was going to strike."[54] The "click" is Saturn's signature in *Great Expectations*. When Magwitch comes to visit him in London years later, Pip writes, "The click came in his throat which I well remembered" (*GE*, 338). The "click" registers the shock effect one feels at finding oneself caught in the trap of repetition. Wemm*ick*, whose name and "post-office of a mouth" are

---

53. Charles Dickens, *Little Dorrit*, ed. John Holloway (Harmondsworth: Penguin, 1967), 68. Hereafter cited in the text as *LD*.
54. Charles Dickens, *Great Expectations*, ed. Angus Calder (Harmondsworth: Penguin, 1965), 50. Hereafter cited in the text as *GE*.

implicated here, describes Jagger's courtroom technique: "Always seems to me as if he had set a mantrap and was watching it. Suddenly—click—you're caught" (*GE*, 321). In the "click" one hears the sound of involuntary memory, of compulsive and traumatic remembrance. As an admirer of Browning, Dickens may well be citing from "Childe Roland to the Dark Tower Came" (1855):

> When, in the very nick
> Of giving up, one time more, came a click
> As when a trap shuts—you're inside the den.

Dickens' rewriting helps us to see that Browning's man-eating giant is a figure of the destructive work of memory. When Miss Havisham tells Pip that though the mice have gnawed her wedding feast, "even sharper teeth than teeth of mice have gnawed at me" (*GE*, 116), we recognize that both of them are caught in the trap of memory.

The "man of *ressentiment*," writes Nietzsche, is a devious man who never forgets and who loves "hiding places, secret paths and back doors."[55] Dickens' experience of memory gave him an extraordinary insight into the kind of fawning, obsequious villain he most despised. The resulting identification with such figures is responsible for some of the most ambivalent and disturbing moments in his work. Dickens' horrified recognition in *Our Mutual Friend* is that the future of England is in the hands of such men and very little can be done to change it. No well-meaning alliance between the déclassé aristocrats and the proletariat can alter the historical inevitability toward which the whole novel tends.[56] The only alternative Dickens is able to imagine at this point is the otherworldly utopian one expressed in Jenny Wren's haunting refrain, "Come back and be dead." "Only those who are Lazarus back from the dead," writes Hillis Miller of *Our Mutual Friend*, "can be reconciled to their inescapable enclosure in society."[57] In the world of *Our Mutual Friend*, only those who have died can live; only those who have undergone a mythic rebirth can tolerate the labyrinthine corruption of modern life. Dickens' flight from politics and

55. Friedrich Nietzsche, *On the Genealogy of Morals/Ecce Homo*, trans. Walter Kaufmann and R. J. Hollingdale (New York: Vintage Books, 1969), 38.

56. For a contrary view, see Edmund Wilson, "Dickens: The Two Scrooges," in *The Wound and the Bow* (London: Methuen, 1961), 72.

57. J. Hillis Miller, *Charles Dickens: The World of His Novels* (Bloomington: Indiana University Press, 1971), 325.

memory has led him to a phantasmagoric myth of redemption on the rooftops above "the people who are alive, crying, and working and calling to one another in the close dark streets."[58] Such a myth indicates how desperate Dickens was to forget, to say, along with Riah, Jenny, and Eugene Wrayburn, that one's "life down in the dark was over" (*OMF*, 334).

Eugene's sadistic torture of Bradley Headstone provides a more accurate gauge of Dickens' dilemma in *Our Mutual Friend*. Eugene's construction of what he calls "abstruse No Thoroughfares" provides an insight into Dickens' estimation of his own art as a novelist. Eugene's relation to his victim becomes a figure, in the following passage, of Dickens' relation to his reader. The most egregious example of his manipulation of the reader in *Our Mutual Friend* is of course the good-hearted Boffin's charade as a miser. But the problem is larger than that. In the gratuitous complications of John Harmon's disappearance and in his reliance once again on a ridiculous search for a missing will, Dickens openly abuses his readers, as Henry James was perhaps the first to realize in his scathing review of the novel. We would be wrong, however, to regard these faults as the result of Dickens' dotage. No, quite to the contrary, they are instrumental to his effort to stage the autodestruction of art, to reveal, like Mr. Venus, all the normally concealed "articulations" of the novel's bone structure. In *Our Mutual Friend*, Dickens sought nothing less than to sound the death knell of the novel as a vehicle of truth and meaning. In Eugene's description of taunting Bradley, Dickens gives us an allegorical account of his assault on novel reading and writing:

I study and get up abstruse No Thoroughfares in the course of the day. With Venetian mystery I seek those No Thoroughfares at night, glide into them by means of dark courts, tempt the schoolmaster [Bradley] to follow, turn suddenly, and catch him before he can retreat. Then we face one another, and I pass him as unaware of his existence, and he undergoes grinding torments. Similarly, I walk at a great pace down a short street, rapidly turn the corner, and, getting out of his view, as rapidly turn back. I catch him coming on post, again pass him as unaware of his existence, and again he undergoes grinding torments. Night after night his disappointment is acute, but hope springs eternal in the scholastic breast, and he follows me again to-morrow. Thus I

58. Charles Dickens, *Our Mutual Friend*, ed. Stephen Gill (Harmondsworth: Penguin, 1971), 334. Hereafter cited in the text as *OMF*.

enjoy the pleasures of the chase, and derive great benefit from the healthful exercise. [*OMF*, 606]

"Reading in its critical use," to borrow Eugene's own phrase, must be alert to the artist's clandestine allegories and to his love of conceal-ment, mystery, and ruses of all sorts. Dickens can undo the mimetic expectations of his readers only by acknowledging, with horror, his complicity as an artist with the "man of *ressentiment*."

At the time of the Staplehurst railway accident on June 9, 1865, Dickens was nearly finished with *Our Mutual Friend* and in fact had the next installment on board with him. As is well known, the effect of the accident on his already weakened condition was catastrophic. It reopened, one might say, all the deep psychological scars of the past. For the next five years he suffered a traumatic fear of any sort of swift movement, and died on the fifth anniversary of the accident, June 9, 1870. "I have sudden vague rushes of terror," he wrote to a friend more than three years after the crash, "even while riding in a hansom cab, which are perfectly unreasonable but quite insurmountable."[59] The accident placed an unbearable strain upon Dickens' prediposition to involuntary reactions and compulsive memories. In conjunction with these difficulties, he also suffered from a circulatory disorder as a result of the gout and, after 1865, a number of apoplectic symptoms, including occasional paralysis of the left side. Like Baudelaire's poet in *Le Soleil,* Dickens now walked with a "jerky gait" (*pas saccadé*), and like Freud at the close of *Beyond the Pleasure Principle,* he could hope it was no sin to limp. It was under these dolorous conditions that he wrote *No Thoroughfare* (1867) and the unfinished *Mystery of Edwin Drood* (1870).

Like Dickens himself during this period, the supercilious Obenreizer in *No Thoroughfare* and the demonic Jasper in *Drood* experience uncontrollable traumatic seizures. The two texts are closely related; in many respects *No Thoroughfare* is a dress rehearsal for *Drood*. In the character of John Jasper, Dickens' exploration of the problems of memory and forgetfulness reaches the logical end toward which it had been tending. Dickens had always been concerned with the inability to forget, and now in Jasper he constructs a criminally insane split per-

---

59. Cited in Edgar Johnson, *Charles Dickens: His Tragedy and Triumph,* 2 vols. (New York: Simon & Schuster, 1952), 2:1021.

sonality whose normal self cannot recollect the acts committed by its psychotic double. Jasper kills his nephew Edwin Drood in an insane and, as it happens, unnecessary rage of sexual jealousy. In the completed portion of the novel, there is no doubt that he is the guilty one. The problems begin when we try to figure out how Dickens planned to bring him to justice, and how and whether Jasper would become aware of his crime. In the most well-reasoned and convincing account of the *Drood* problem to date, Charles Forsyte maintains that Dickens planned to have Jasper hang himself in prison when he suddenly breaks through the barrier separating his divided personality and remembers what he has done.[60] This means that in his very last work Dickens finally discovered a situation in which remembrance seemed to have been blocked formally and finally, in which forgetfulness was possible—but no, even in the depths of Jasper's psychotic mind, memory slowly and inexorably makes its way to the surface. Here at the very end of his career, Dickens reminds himself and his readers that there is "no thoroughfare," no way to escape from the insidious work of remembrance.

In Cloisterham, where *Drood* is set, almost all the streets and byways are "no thoroughfare."[61] This is a place where there are all sorts of obstacles to communication and where one makes one's way only with difficulty. As Mr. Grewgious, through whose eyes we first recognize Jasper's villainy, looks into the Cloisterham cathedral where Jasper is leading the choir, he exclaims, "'Dear me . . . it's like looking down the throat of Old Time.' Old Time heaved a mouldy sigh from tomb and arch and vault; and gloomy shadows began to deepen in corners" (*ED*, 117). Old Time's uncanny sigh passes almost unnoticeably into the "one feeble voice" of the choirmaster.

In *No Thoroughfare*'s opening paragraph, we are presented with a phantasmagoric image in which the sonorous tolling of the "heavy bell" of St. Paul's sweeps over the sound of all the other London church bells just "as if the winged father who devours his children, had made a sounding sweep with his gigantic scythe in flying over the city."[62] As Dickens' experience of memory literally became crippling, and as he felt more than ever haunted by "the pen-and-ink-ubus of

60. Charles Forsyte, *The Decoding of Edwin Drood* (New York: Scribner, 1980).
61. Charles Dickens, *The Mystery of Edwin Drood*, ed. Arthur J. Cox (Harmondsworth: Penguin, 1974), 51. Hereafter cited in the text as *ED*.
62. Charles Dickens, *No Thoroughfare*, in *Works*, 22/2:1.

writing" (*ED*, 117)—which was one of his very favorite expressions—
it was the image of the devouring Saturn that seemed to tighten its grip
over his imagination. "Always seems to me as if he had a mantrap and
was watching it. Suddenly—click—you're caught."

Freud's "*Dickens'scher Styl*"

Like most nineteenth-century readers of Dickens, Freud's favorite
novel was *David Copperfield*. Like so many others, he identified with its
hero; more interestingly, he regarded his father as a kind of Mr.
Micawber, a weak and ineffective but well-meaning man. Freud's use of
Dickens as a marker for his own biographical experience is not, however, what I mean to suggest under the rubric Freud's "*Dickens'scher
Styl*." I want to talk about Freud's unconscious use of Dickens and
about Dickens' influence upon the most fundamental aspects of Freud's
thinking. In other words, I want to distinguish my understanding of
Freud's Dickensian style from what Ernest Jones means when, after
citing a particularly mawkish and sentimental love letter from Freud to
Martha, he remarks, "Isn't that the style of Dickens?"[63] Freud's
Dickensian style has nothing to do with the anecdotal or the sentimental. It has a great deal to do, however, with the problem of memory and
with the necessity, indeed the compulsion, to construct alternative scenes
in those instances where memory has become unreliable or somehow
suspicious.

The primal scene is a circumstantial construction that is predicated
when there is a need to interpret but at the same time a fundamental
concealment or absence of the sort of evidence that could definitively
substantiate a particular interpretation. Throughout this book I have
shifted the primal scene away from its narrow psychoanalytic meaning
as the child's observation of sexual intercourse, which subsequently
takes on a traumatic character in the course of the child's own sexual
development. I have shifted the notion of the primal scene into a much
larger frame of reference, in which the repetitive and ambivalent character of a recollected scene figures more prominently than its sexual
content. The primal scene is the figure of an interpretive dilemma,

63. Ernest Jones, *The Life and Work of Sigmund Freud*, 3 vols. (New York: Basic
Books, 1953–57), 1:126.

which is to say, it is the figure of the dilemma of interpretation. As an interpretive strategy, it has the virtue of enabling us to respond to what, rigorously speaking, is an unreadable and unanalyzable situation.

The notion of Freud's Dickensian style is a way of responding to this dilemma. In the two brief incidents in the Freudian text with which I shall conclude this chapter, Freud (although there is no corroborating evidence) seems to be thinking of the Dickensian text. The text of Dickens seems to have become lodged somewhere between Freud's conscious recollection and unconscious forgetfulness, somewhere between concealment and unconcealment where two voices seem to be speaking at once, but not in an Oedipal struggle for priority; two voices, but neither demanding to be heard at the expense of the other.

In Chapter 3 I discussed the Rat-Man case history, *A Case of Obsessional Neurosis* (1909), in connection with the question of Freud's commitment to the truth of his constructions. Though Freud had already realized by this stage in his career the necessity of being flexible with regard to the legitimacy of the analyst's constructions, he was very insistent about the reality of one in particular. Freud's predicament began when he "ventured to put forward a construction to the effect that when [the Rat-Man] was a child of under six he had been guilty of some sexual misdemeanour connected with masturbation and had been soundly castigated for it by his father. This punishment, according to my hypothesis, had, it was true, put an end to his masturbating, but on the other hand it had left behind it an ineradicable grudge against his father and had established him for all time in his role of an interferer with the patient's sexual enjoyment."[64] What prevented Freud from elaborating this construction in cooperation with his patient was the unexpected corroboration it received from the patient's mother: "To my great astonishment the patient then informed me that his mother had repeatedly described to him an occurrence of this kind which dated from his earliest childhood and had evidently escaped being forgotten by her on account of its remarkable consequences." In response to Freud's deep interest in this incident, the patient questioned his mother about it, and she not only confirmed it

---

64. *The Standard Edition of the Complete Psychological Works of Sigmund Freud*, ed. James Strachey et al., 24 vols. (London: Hogarth Press and the Institute of Psycho-Analysis, 1953–74), 10:205. References in the text to *S.E.* are to volume and page numbers of this edition.

but added that "he had been given the punishment because he had *bitten* someone" (*S.E.,* 10:206). She could not recall who was bitten, though she believed it was his nurse, nor did she suggest that his misdeed was "of a sexual nature." Freud would have preferred, of course, to learn that the Rat-Man had bitten his father and that the misdeed had been masturbation. It is at this point that Freud turns to the patient, only to discover that "he himself, however, had no recollection of it whatever."

Though Freud has made this "childhood scene" (*Kindheitszene*) the key to the entire analysis, he has absolutely no success in his efforts to elaborate it with his patient. Freud's uneasiness in this dilemma is evident above all in his relegation of what by his own acknowledgment is the crux of the case to a long footnote before returning to the body of the text to recount the disruptive effect this disputed event had on the analysis. Freud confesses his disappointment ("I had expected it to have a greater effect") and regrets the patient's illogicality ("that capacity for being illogical which never fails to bewilder one in such highly intelligent people as obsessional neurotics"), but he never flinches for a moment from his certainty that his construction, now filled in with the help of the patient's mother, is the indisputable historical truth. It is Freud's steadfast conviction that begins to drive the patient to distraction: "Things soon reached a point at which, in his dreams, his waking phantasies, and his associations, he began heaping the grossest and filthiest abuse upon me and my family, though in his deliberate actions he never treated me with anything but the greatest respect" (*S.E.,* 10:209). Despite such intense resistance, Freud claims that "the path was clear to the solution of the rat idea" and that "the treatment had reached its turning-point."

The biting scene is crucial for Freud because it enables him to explain the patient's delirious phantasy of the rat punishment by linking it to his unfilial conduct as a child. The patient's obsessive fascination with the Oriental rat torture, his delirious fear that he will be tortured by rats biting his anus and sexual parts, becomes, according to Freud's logic, a phantasmatic effort both to make restitution to his father and to repeat the primal offense. By torturing himself with various permutations of the rat phantasy, he would be able to atone for having bitten his father so many years before. "The notion of a rat," writes Freud, "is inseparably bound up with the fact that it has sharp teeth with which it gnaws and bites" (*S.E.,* 10:215–16). The patient's *Rat-*

ten (rats) become *Raten* (installments) toward the paternal debt. The patient's neurosis had begun with the belief that he could enjoy sexual pleasure only at his father's expense. For the Rat-Man, lovemaking and the idea of his father's death were inseparable. Of the pleasures of sex, he thought, "One might murder one's father for this." Of his marriage plans, he thought, "If I marry the lady, some misfortune will befall my father." Freud's solution is to construct a primal scene, though he does not call it that, in which his father's intervention in his son's infantile sexual pleasure would have been traumatic enough to explain the ensuing neurotic symptoms.

Regardless of the patient's resistance, Freud is convinced that the explanatory power of the biting scene was what finally completed the cure: "When we reached the solution that has been described above, the patient's rat delirium disappeared" (*S.E.,* 10:220). Freud is making quite a controversial statement here, for he is arguing that the patient's recovery derived from a scene that he was never able to remember and against the acceptance of which he struggled violently. Nor does Freud hide from us the fact that the patient broke off the analysis abruptly, obviously unwilling to bear with Freud any further. How could the analyst be so certain of the patient's recovery if the patient prematurely terminated the analysis? Again, Freud has recourse to a footnote—"It was impossible to unravel this tissue of phantasy thread by thread; the therapeutic success of the treatment was precisely what stood in the way of this" (*S.E.,* 10:207 n.1)—indicating a very speedy and remarkable recovery. Freud insists that he is not to be "blamed for this gap in the analysis" and that it finally matters very little in a case like this where therapeutic success has been achieved. One cannot help noting how very convenient the patient's recovery is, since it enables Freud to avoid the whole question of the relation between the legitimacy of the construction and the patient's work of recollection. Freud leaves us up in the air: on what basis are we to believe that a patient could experience such a remarkable cure without ever either accepting the analyst's construction or verifying it through his own recollection?

Freud is saying in effect that it was the strength of the analyst's conviction in the truth of the biting scene that finally led the patient toward recovery. There is no reason whatsoever to doubt Freud's honesty in reporting the patient's recovery. The fact that he reports it in a footnote suggests not that he is lying but that something irregular is at work here. Freud must have sensed it himself, because in another footnote appended to the case history in 1923, he repeats his claim that "the patient's mental health was restored by the analysis which I have reported upon in these pages" before revealing that the Rat-Man "perished in the Great War." The Rat-Man was a deeply disturbed individual, obsessed by a wide range of morbid superstitions and beliefs among which the rat idea was simply the most pathological symptom. Is Freud trying to say that he succeeded in removing all of the Rat-Man's obsessions, which would seem to be the necessary prerequisite to "mental health," or only that most oppressive and recurrent phantasy, the rat idea? It is impossible to say. In the Rat-Man case history Freud provides us with a unified narrative of his own experience of discovery, one in which the biting scene enables him to achieve a sense of closure and interpretive satisfaction that would otherwise have been out of reach. Of the effect of all this upon the patient, there is no comparable sense of closure. Psychoanalysis in the Rat-Man case history seems closer to a poetics than to therapy.

It is with regard to this question of narrative closure and interpretive satisfaction that I pose the question of Freud's Dickensian style. Freud knew Dickens' novels well and alludes to several of them in his works and letters. No one would dispute his knowledge of the scene in *David Copperfield* where David bites Mr. Murdstone; nor is it unlikely that he would have appreciated Dickens' interrogation into the effect of the scene upon David's subsequent development. As we have seen, the biting scene is as crucial to David's effort to understand himself as it is to Freud's effort to understand the Rat-Man. We also know, however, that when Freud thinks of a literary or philosophical work in connection with a case history or a theoretical question, he invariably mentions it. In connection with the Rat-Man case, he cites two passages from Goethe's *Faust* (*S.E.*, 10:216 n.1). In the first, Mephistopheles conjures up a rat in order to gnaw through a magic threshold. The second reads:

> For in the bloated rat he sees
> A living likeness of himself.

Freud also notes in his daily record of the analysis, most of which is included in the Addendum to the case in the *Standard Edition*, that he gave the patient a copy of Zola's novel, *Joie de vivre*, because its hero vividly exhibits obsessional characteristics (*S.E.*, 10:306). Neither of these texts is as intimately linked to Freud's narrative in the Rat-Man case as the biting scene in *David Copperfield,* yet surely if he had thought of *David Copperfield* at any time during the analysis, he would have mentioned it. Why does Freud fail to think of the one text—which happens to be one of his favorites—that applies to the case at hand in such an uncannily precise way? We cannot dismiss this extraordinary lapse by attributing it to some widespread penchant on the part of nineteenth-century children for biting their fathers or step-fathers. No, we must deal with the facts at hand, and they are very simple. Freud is a great admirer of *David Copperfield,* and he has written a case history that follows the outlines of *Copperfield* to an extent that cannot be explained by mere coincidence.

I spoke earlier of using Dickens to understand the most fundamental aspects of Freud's thinking. What I mean by that is precisely Freud's desire for narrative closure and a holistic interpretation. These are of course a novelist's prerogatives, but Freud makes them his own. Had he not, there might never have been such a thing as psychoanalysis. It is Freud's Dickensian style, a style that is both Freudian and Dickensian, that makes him, *avant la lettre,* anticipate a childhood trauma. And his Dickensian style is responsible, when he learns of a biting scene, for his deep and abiding conviction that here he has come upon the truth. What he has come upon, of course, is his unconscious memory of *Copperfield.* Freud's conviction with respect to the biting scene is a marvelous indication of how brilliantly successful Dickens was in holding the nineteenth century under his spell. Freud's Dickensian style is an exemplary instance of what Benjamin calls *Eingedenken,* a kind of "mindfulness" or "holding in place of memory" in such a way that one is neither really conscious of nor oblivious to it, but rather permeated by it, and of what Heidegger calls *Andenken* or "commemoration."

"It was not until just before taking leave of the treatment," writes Freud of the Wolf-Man, "that he remembered having been told that he was born with a caul. He had for that reason always looked on himself as a special child of fortune whom no ill could befall" (*S.E.,* 17:99). The "caul" or *Glückshaube,* which literally means "lucky hood," is linked in the Wolf-Man's thinking to a complex of images including veils, shadows, butterflies, and, as Freud says, "other impalpable things." The Wolf-Man experienced threats to his narcissism not as a breaking of the caul but rather as a feeling of becoming even more separated from the world. In Freud's wonderful wording: "Thus the caul was the veil which hid him from the world and hid the world from him" (*Die Glückshaube ist also der Schleier, der ihn vor der Welt und ihm die Welt verhüllte*). For Freud, the patient's acceptance of the primal scene had become synonymous with the breaking of the veil. Opening his eyes to the truth of Freud's construction had, as Freud writes, "become transformed into the necessary condition for his recovery" (*S.E.*, 17:101). As we have seen in earlier chapters, however, it was impossible for the Wolf-Man ever to attain the sort of conviction Freud wanted; the caul or veil constituted a fundamental concealment that he would never surmount. Freud's extraordinary success was to have brought the Wolf-Man up against the very limits of that veil. It was Freud who helped him realize whatever good luck the caul had destined him for.

David Copperfield was also born with a caul (*DC,* 49), and as we have seen, he too learned to press up against the threshold that joins and separates remembrance and imagination. The Wolf-Man, while crossing the Channel on his way to England in 1938, and more hopeful than ever of seeing through the veil, experienced a Dickensian reverie: "On the ship crossing the Channel I had the feeling I had somehow or other come into a new world, and I even imagined I was surrounded by figures reminiscent of Dickens's novels. This was one of the first signs that I was beginning to observe and take notice of the world around me."[65]

In the culture of psychoanalysis, Dickens has always been the figure of both its prehistory and its future.

65. *The Wolf-Man by the Wolf-Man*, ed. Muriel Gardiner (New York: Basic Books, 1971), 128.

Postscript

The Lord whose oracle is in Delphi neither speaks nor conceals, but gives a sign.

HERACLITUS

A sign are we, without meaning,
Without pain are we and have nearly
Lost our language in foreign lands.

FRIEDRICH HÖLDERLIN, "Mnemosyne"

Like Benjamin's dialectical images, the primal scenes of literature, philosophy, and psychoanalysis that I have constructed in this book describe neither the contents of consciousness nor the reality of history. They constitute neither the deep structure of the human mind nor the organic structure of the past. They are neither categorical nor empirical. We can say of them what Adorno said of Benjamin's image constellations:

> The historical images, which do not constitute the meaning of being but dissolve and resolve its questions, are not simply self-given. They do not lie organically ready in history; neither showing nor intuition is required to become aware of them. They are not magically sent by the gods to be taken in and venerated. Rather, they must be produced by human beings and are legitimated in the last analysis only by the fact that reality crystallizes about them in striking conclusiveness.[1]

The *Urszene* as I have redefined it is not an *Urbild,* not an "archaic image" or the primordial content of consciousness, but an interpretive construction that is the result of history's resistance to language. What

---

1. Theodor Adorno, "The Actuality of Philosophy," *Telos* 31 (1977): 131 (translation modified). This was Adorno's inaugural lecture to the philosophy faculty of the University of Frankfurt in 1931. It was originally published in 1973 in the first volume of his *Gesammelte Schriften.*

is primordial can no longer be thought of in terms of either mind or the empirical. What is primordial is the sign and the necessity operating through it that binds interpretation to the zone of *différance* and to the interplay of memory and phantasy.

My notion of the primal scene is an effort to write a new chapter in the history of what Adorno calls "that old concept of philosophy which was formulated by Bacon and passionately contended around the time of Leibniz, a conception which idealism derided as a fad: that of the *ars inveniendi*." The *organon* of this "art of invention," Adorno goes on to say, is "fantasy": "An exact fantasy, fantasy which abides strictly within the material which the sciences present to it, and reaches beyond them only in the smallest aspects of their arrangement: aspects, granted, which fantasy itself must originally generate." Speaking as a psychoanalyst, François Roustang has likewise remarked: "There is no escape, the analyst is condemned to invent."[2] My intent has been both to recover the affirmative character of the necessity that binds us to an *ars inveniendi* and to ensure that we do not forget that the art of invention and interpretation must testify to the resistance to history and to the question of Being that is lodged within the essence of language itself.

My notion of the primal scene is an effort to balance rhetorically the irrepressible demands of both a formalist and a historical criticism, and to forge a new synthesis between the apparent contradictions of the deconstructive new "new criticism" and the Marxist new "new historicism." Rather than repressing these contradictions, the primal scene enables the project of the deconstruction of the subject to exist side by side with the historicist project of the reconstruction of the object. The primal scene ensures that the double operation of deconstituting the subject's relation to language and reconstituting language's relation to the object retains its necessary tension and complexity. My objective in this book has been to reveal that we never really have a choice between the imperatives "Always deconstruct" and "Always historicize," for we are bound to both by a necessity that is at once linguistic and historical.

2. François Roustang, *Dire Mastery: Discipleship from Freud to Lacan*, trans. Ned Lukacher (Baltimore, Md.: Johns Hopkins University Press, 1982), 71.

Index

Library of Congress Cataloging-in-Publication Data

LUKACHER, NED, 1950–
   Primal Scenes.

   Includes index.
      1. Hermeneutics.   2. History—Philosophy.
3. Memory.   I. Title.
BD241.L85   1986   190   85-25513
ISBN 0-8014-1886-0 (alk. paper)